S0-AZG-200

Michigan

Michigan

Jeff Counts

With photographs by the author

The Countryman Press ✴ Woodstock, Vermont

First Edition

ISBN 978-0-88150-737-9

Cover photo courtesy of Lake Shore Resort, Saugatuck, MI & Andrew Milauckas
Interior photos by the author unless otherwise specified
Book design by Bodenweber Design
Page composition by PerfecType, Nashville, TN
Maps by Mapping Specialists Ltd., © 2008 The Countryman Press

Published by The Countryman Press, P.O. Box 748, Woodstock, Vermont 05091

Distributed by W. W. Norton & Company, Inc., 500 Fifth Avenue, New York, NY 10110

Printed in the United States of America

10 9 8 7 6 5 4 3 2 1

DEDICATION

To all those who helped me on the road to writing this book.

EXPLORE WITH US!

Welcome to the first edition of the most comprehensive guide to Michigan. It's the perfect companion for exploring both the Upper and Lower Peninsulas and shorelines along Lakes Michigan, Huron, and Superior. I have tried to select the best places, but have included many lodging establishments and restaurants simply because they're your only options in some parts of the state. The selections are based on my personal experiences and on those of a cadre of friends and business associates—not on paid advertising. Like other *Explorer's Guides*, this book is a classic traveler's guide, with a clear, easy-to-use layout. Sidebars mark the author's personal favorites in each chapter—a subjective selection, but good guidance when you only have a day or so to spend in an area. (Please e-mail me at streamside@sbcglobal.net if you have any specific questions or comments about the information provided herein.)

WHAT'S WHERE

In the beginning of the book there is an alphabetical listing of local information and highlights of the state that you can quickly reference. You'll find advice on everything from Yooper culture to where the best beaches are.

LODGING

Please don't hold the publisher or the respective innkeepers responsible for the rates listed here. Changes are inevitable. Taxes on rooms vary throughout the state, with many communities imposing their own.

RESTAURANTS

In most sections, there is a distinction between *Dining Out* and *Eating Out*. Restaurants listed under *Eating Out* are generally inexpensive and more casual; reservations are often suggested for restaurants in *Dining Out*. A range of prices is included for each entry.

SMOKING

Michigan is all over the board when it comes to smoking in public places, restaurants, and bars. In Ann Arbor, smoking is allowed in only a handful of places, while in the Upper Peninsula, you're lucky to find a nonsmoking section in a tavern. It's best to call ahead to find out the smoking policy.

KEY TO SYMBOLS

- ✎ **Child friendly.** The crayon denotes a family-friendly place or event that welcomes young children. Most B&Bs prohibit children under 12.
- ♿ **Handicapped access.** The wheelchair icon denotes a place with full Americans with Disabilities Act (ADA) standard access, still distressingly rare in many remote areas.

☂ **Rainy day.** The umbrella icon points out places where you can entertain yourself, but stay dry in bad weather.

🐾 **Pets.** The dog's paw icon identifies lodgings that allow pets, still an exception to the rule. Accommodations that accept pets may charge an extra fee or restrict pets to certain areas, as well as require advance notice.

⚭ **Wedding friendly.** The wedding rings icon denotes places and establishments that are good venues for weddings.

🍸 **Liquor.** The martini glass icon denotes taverns, bars, and restaurants where alcohol is served.

▼ **Gay friendly.** The triangle icon indicates establishments that make an extra effort to welcome gay clientele.

CONTENTS

INTRODUCTION

This book will help you discover everything from uncrowded beaches along Michigan's 2,288 miles of coastline, remote Upper Peninsula inland lakes, and trout-fishing streams to upscale urban restaurants, backwoods taverns, and trendy art galleries.

The state has never been covered this extensively in a travel book, and during the year it took to research and write it I put many miles on my old Jeep while checking out a wide range of attractions and services. I hope the guide helps you explore a state too often known for its smokestacks rather than its stunning views of the Great Lakes and tremendous opportunities for fishing, backpacking, hiking, bird-watching, kayaking, and swimming. However, there is more to Michigan than outdoor pursuits; it has a thriving wine industry and the arts flourish. Even Michigan devotees will find something new in this book.

The guide is divided into generally accepted regions, with each section containing a brief description of the area, a short look at its history, and what there is to do. There are three distinct regions in the state, the southern portion, which is filled with cities; the north and the Lake Michigan coast, where people vacation; and the Upper Peninsula, which is almost a state unto itself. I have included many of the areas in those regions, but not all, as I've tried to stick with the areas that are of most interest to travelers.

The book takes you from the gentle, warm beaches of cottage country along the Lake Michigan shoreline to the dense backwoods of the Upper Peninsula where bear, moose, and wolf roam.

I critique upscale restaurants (*Dining Out*) and everyday options (*Eating Out*), plus North Woods taverns, bakeries, and even grocery stores in rustic areas where the eating options are limited. Except for along the Lake

THE NEW BUFFALO WELCOME CENTER WAS THE NATION'S FIRST SUCH ESTABLISHMENT.

Michigan coast, and in the urban areas of southern Michigan, you won't find many topnotch restaurants, but I have listed the best I found.

I describe many of the state's inns, B&Bs, and family-owned motels, and in some cases have broken with the *Explorer's Guide* tradition and listed chain hotels and motels because there are few other options in certain areas. I also included many housekeeping cabins and cottages sought after by anglers, hunters, bicyclists, and winter-sports enthusiasts.

In-state travel accounts for about 75 percent of the state's tourism, and heading to the family cottage or favorite campground is part of the Michigan lifestyle, which includes hunting for deer, bear, woodcock, and grouse during fall and

A SHORT HISTORY OF MICHIGAN

Native American tribes, most notably the Ojibwa, or Anishnabe, as they call themselves, had long lived in Michigan, fishing and trapping, before the French arrived in the late 17th century to trade with the tribes for beaver pelts. The lucrative business of swapping blankets and muskets for furs was centered in Sault Ste. Marie and at the Straits of Mackinac and Detroit.

The fur trade helped spark clashes between the British and French, and eventually the French left Canada in 1763 when they were defeated by the British, but not before the French left their mark on Michigan in the way of place-names, such as Detroit, Sault Ste. Marie, Grand Traverse Bay, the Au Sable River, and dozens of other places and streets.

The Revolutionary War broke out not long after the French flag came down in Michigan, and the Americans eventually took possession of the state. However, the British recaptured Mackinac Island and Detroit during the War of 1812, and it wasn't until several years later that the borders between Michigan and Canada were firmly established.

But even the end of hostilities in the state didn't exactly bring throngs of settlers here. In 1820, there were only 7,452 souls living in the entire state, many of them French Canadians. It wasn't until the opening of the Erie Canal in the 1820s that immigrants, mostly from New England and upstate New York, started to arrive, and the population went from about 28,000 in 1830 to more than 200,000 by 1840, which was enough to make Michigan a state by 1837. Most settled on southern Michigan farms, and the immigrants established small, New England–style towns.

The fur trade was still booming on Mackinac Island when John Jacob Astor established the headquarters of the American Fur Company there in 1822, and the trade helped him become the first American millionaire. However, by the 1850s the fur trade collapsed, partly because of the rise in popularity of silk hats.

snowmobiling and downhill and cross-country skiing in winter. Except for steel-head anglers, most folks stay home during the muddy months of March and April.

I put an emphasis on northern Michigan and the Upper Peninsula (U.P.), where a lot of travelers go, but I also included a section on the Detroit area, which receives many visitors, especially The Henry Ford, Museum and Green-field Village.

Getting around Michigan is fairly easy, unless you're looking for mass transit, of which there is little. Detroit is the Motor City, and people in this state drive. There are no toll roads, and there has been a focus on road building ever since the first Ford Model T rolled off the assembly line.

By then, Michigan was experiencing its second economic boom in the Upper Peninsula, where copper and iron were being mined. But that may not have occurred, in Michigan at least, if the state hadn't lost the so-called Toledo War. As statehood approached in 1835–1836, Michigan claimed a disputed strip of land along its border with Ohio, but Ohioans objected, and militias were raised to fight a battle over the issue. No shots were fired and President Andrew Jackson stepped in and a compromise was proposed, giving Michigan the entire U.P. if it dropped its claim on Toledo. In the end, Michigan came away the winner, and millions of dollars of copper and iron were mined, starting in the 1840s in the Keweenaw Peninsula and Marquette region.

However, much of the state remained unsettled until the 1860s when the logging boom started. Nearly knotless Michigan white pine was the miracle-building product of the day because it could easily be sawed, and much of it was needed to rebuild Chicago after The Great Fire in 1871. Port towns with sawmills sprang up along the Great Lakes to meet the demand, and loggers thought the supply was endless. It wasn't. By about 1910, much of the pine was gone, and forest fires burned from Lake Michigan to Lake Huron, fed by woody debris left in the forests by the loggers.

Lumber barons were looking to invest the millions of dollars they made just about the time Henry Ford and other early auto pioneers were starting factories in need of capital. The first Model T came off the assembly line at Ford Motor Co. in 1908, and Ford's system of producing cars cheaply put many Americans behind the wheel.

Also, as the logging boom was starting to come to an end the state's tourist economy started to thrive. The first resort hotels along the Lake Michigan coast started sprouting up in the 1870s, but it wasn't until railroad and steamship companies built the Grand Hotel on Mackinac Island (see Mackinac Island) in 1887 that tourism started to become an important industry. The hotel sought to encourage people to escape the heat of Chicago and other midwestern cities and travel north by either rail or steamship.

Apart from rush hours in Detroit and Grand Rapids, you're pretty much doing the speed limit all the time. "Up North" the distances may look long on the map, but there's little traffic between towns, and ground can be covered quickly while just doing the speed limit.

But don't let that keep you from getting off the freeways and seeing the small historic towns in southern Michigan, especially along US 12, or driving the unpaved county and logging roads to see the North Woods. Before taking a backcountry tour, make sure to have a good set of county maps, especially in the U.P., where the road atlas is often wrong, and make sure to have a full tank of gas, as stations are far apart.

I'll help you discover the beaches of Lake Michigan and the small resort towns of Petoskey, Charlevoix, and Glen Arbor, along with the well-visited Traverse City, but I'll also take you off the beaten path to Beaver Island in Lake Michigan and to small U.P. towns where the only eating establishment is a woodsy tavern lined with fish and animal mounts. I hope this book captures the diversity of the landscape: The pastel colors of the Pictured Rocks National Lakeshore; the wilderness of Isle Royale National Park, where you can hear wolves howl at night; and the stillness of millions of acres of undeveloped forestlands in the western U.P.

I've provided opinionated and detailed information about Michigan, which makes this guide different from others that dispatch legions of writers to gather facts about a place and present a synthesized version with little attitude. That's not the case with *Michigan: An Explorer's Guide.* The Countryman Press has a two-decade tradition of getting a real guide to write each book in the series.

THE LAKE SUPERIOR SHORELINE

Having spent years as a journalist and outdoorsman, I feel comfortable living up to the journalistic integrity for which this series is known. This guide doesn't accept advertising or free meals or lodging. You won't find chamber of commerce type stuff here, and you won't find Web site information that makes everything look pretty and glosses over the sore spots.

My first Michigan tour guide was Ernest Hemingway, whose early short stories painted a picture of the outdoor life in northern Michigan that started my 35-year love affair with the North Country. *The Big Two-Hearted River* started me fly-fishing the Fox River, the story's setting. I suspected Hemingway, like any good angler, didn't want to tell others of a good fishing spot. Years later when reading a book by Hemingway's son, Jack, *Misadventures of a Fly Fisherman,* I learned Hemingway simply liked the name and used it in his story. It fooled Hemingway's son, who along with several companions went to the Two-Hearted, only to get their car stuck in the sand. The same thing happened to me when I tried to fish the river. That's the type of information you'll find in an *Explorer's Guide.*

This guide is tailored to Michigan with the addition of a category called *Staying Connected,* which advises travelers on cell phone use, Internet access, and the locations of National Public Radio outlets. I've included markets in areas where there are few restaurants, and I also note where gas stations are rare.

While I've checked out much of what's in this guide, I've also included information gathered during decades of traveling the state and talking to travelers and outdoors people. That information came from sitting around campfires at night or from conversations with local anglers, hunters, and berry pickers at taverns throughout Michigan. One of my prime sources has been Michigan author Jim Harrison (*Legends of the Fall* and *True North*), who wrote many of his stories about Michigan from his secret U.P. hideaway. As Harrison once said: "Hemingway was a tourist in Michigan." With this guide, you won't be.

WHAT'S WHERE IN MICHIGAN

AREA CODES Starting in the Lower Peninsula, area codes are 313 (Detroit), 734 (western Wayne County and Ann Arbor), 810 (northern Oakland County), 269 (southwestern Michigan), 517 (central Michigan), 989 (northeastern Michigan, Saginaw Valley, and the Thumb), 231 (northwestern Michigan), and 906 (the entire Upper Peninsula).

AGRICULTURAL FACTS AND FAIRS Although Michigan is known for making cars, agriculture is also a top industry, with about 10 million of 36.3 million total acres in croplands. Much of that is devoted to corn, soybeans, beans, potatoes, and sugar beets on the state's 53,315 farms. Fruit growing and wineries along the Lake Michigan shoreline attract travelers for winery tours (see *Wineries, What's Where in Michigan*) and U-pick opportunities for apples, berries, and other fruits. The Traverse City area is the top producer of tart cherries in the nation and holds an annual Cherry Festival (see Traverse City). During late July and August, the roads of western Michigan are lined with farmers selling cherries and other produce. Maple syrup and honey are other productions you'll find at roadside stands.

The **Michigan State Fair** (313-369-8250; www.michigan.gov/mistatefair) is held annually in early September in Detroit, and despite its urban venue it still attracts many farmers who come to show off their cattle and produce. The **Upper Peninsula State Fair** (906-786-4011; www.michigan.gov /upsf/) is held in mid-August in Escanaba. Both are weeklong events. There are 83 counties in Michigan, and most have agricultural fairs starting in August. For a complete listing, go to www.michigan.org.

AIRPORTS AND AIRLINES There are seven major airports with regular commercial service. Metro Airport in Detroit is the major one and it's a hub for Northwest Airlines. Bishop Airport in Flint also serves the Detroit area. Gerald R. Ford Airport in Grand Rapids has regular service. Midland–Bay City Saginaw and Lansing Airports have major airline service too, but most are connector flights to Detroit, Chicago, or Cleveland. Marquette's K. I. Sawyer Airport has the most service to the Upper Peninsula.

AMTRAK **Amtrak** service (1-800-USA-RAIL; www.amtrak.com) between Detroit and Chicago has been fairly reliable, although there are often delays. There are stops in New Buffalo, Kalamazoo, Battle Creek, Jackson, and Ann Arbor. Additional trains run to Grand Rapids and Port Huron.

ANTIQUARIAN BOOKSELLERS The **Michigan Antiquarian Book & Paper Show** (www.curiousbooks .com) is in early April, usually in Lansing. It attracts dealers from across the Midwest.

ANTIQUING There are more than 500 antique shops scattered around the state on town main streets and along the highways. The towns with the biggest concentration of shops are Ann Arbor, Saugatuck, and the Traverse City region. The state maintains a list of the shops and shows at www .michigan.org.

APPLES Fall brings plenty of pick-your-own-fruit opportunities, and many orchards sell apples and cider. There are more than 255 farm markets, U-pick operations, and agricultural tourism locations across the state. For a guide, go to www.michigan .org, the state tourism Web site, or to the **Michigan Department of Agriculture** Web site at www.mda.state. mi.us/market/u-pick. The Lake Michigan coast is a vast fruit-growing area.

ARTS CAMPS **Blue Lake Fine Arts Camp** (1-800-221-3796; www.blue lake.org), Twin Lake, runs summer programs for young musicians. **Interlochen Center for the Arts** (231-276-5635; www.interlochen.org) near Traverse City has summer programs in the arts for young people and adults.

BED & BREAKFASTS See *Inns*.

BICYCLING Mountain biking is popular throughout the state, and many state parks have dedicated trails. Go to www.michigan.gov/dnr for listings of mountain bike trails. The **Michigan Mountain Biking Association** (www.mmba.org) can provide additional information. There are many dedicated bike-touring trails in the state, along with thousands of miles of paved county roads. The **League of Michigan Bicyclists** (517-334-9100; www.lmb.org) comprises 36 clubs and has information on rides and routes. The **Wheelway** between Petoskey and Harbor Springs is one of the more intriguing ones. It's a bike pathway that existed as far back as the 19th century (see Petoskey). Even the Detroit area has dedicated bike paths on Hines Drive in western Wayne County and in the 13 **Huron-Clinton Metroparks** (1-800-477-2757; www .metroparks.com). There are also numerous organized rides. Go to www.michgian.org for a listing. Some of the best bicycle touring is on Michigan's islands (see Grand, Mackinac, and Beaver Islands).

BIRDING The **Seney National Wildlife Refuge** (906-586-9851; www.fws.gov/Midwest/Seney/Contact) is one of the top destinations in the Upper Peninsula and attracts birdwatchers nationwide. The Kirtland's warbler nests in only a few counties in the Upper and Lower Peninsulas, Wisconsin, and Ontario, and birdwatchers come from across the nation for a chance to see one. They nest on the ground under the branches of 5- to 20-year-old jack pine. The U.S. Forest Service Mio Ranger District (989-826-3252; www.fs.fed.us) conducts tours.

BOATING There are hundreds of boat launches and public and private marinas in Michigan. Go to www.michigan.gov/dnr for a list of public launches and marinas. Also, www.michiganweb.com maintains a list of private marinas. Many public marinas and boat docks are listed in this book.

BOOKS One of the first books about Michigan was Henry Wadsworth Longfellow's *Song of Hiawatha*, his epic poem published in 1855. The only trouble with it was that the Maine poet had never been to Michigan and actually based it on the nonfiction works of Henry Rowe Schoolcraft, an early explorer and writer in Michigan who learned of many Native American legends from his wife, Jane Johnston, who was half Ojibwa and taught him the language. Some of the best stories about Michigan were written by Ernest Hemingway, who spent summers in northern Michigan, and appear in his collection of short stories, *In Our Time.* Many of his other early works include references to Michigan. John D. Voelker, an Ishpeming native, wrote a crime thriller in the 1950s that was turned into a popular Hollywood movie, *Anatomy of a Murder.* He also wrote lesser-known essays on fly-fishing and they are collected in *Trout Madness* and *Trout Magic.* Both define backwoods brook trout fishing in the Upper Peninsula. In more recent times, Tom McGuane and Jim Harrison, who attended Michigan State University together, have helped define Michigan. McGuane's *The Sporting Club*, published in 1969, chronicles the decline and ruin of an elite Michigan outdoor club. Most of Harrison's fiction centers on Michigan people, many of them Yoopers, Upper Penin-

sula natives, who face life in the backwoods with much humor. More recently, Jeffrey Eugenides produced *Middlesex,* which deals with the life of a hermaphrodite, and uses many details about life in the Detroit area and in northern Michigan. However, nobody writes more eloquently about the streets of Detroit than Elmore Leonard, whose first book was published in 1953 and his latest, *Up in Honey's Room,* in 2007. A *Michigan Atlas & Gazetteer* published by DeLorme is almost a necessity when traveling off the major roads, especially in the U.P. A note of caution: in some areas of the U.P., the maps aren't always correct. The *National Geographic Field Guide to Birds,* the Michigan edition, is helpful in that it only lists birds found in the state.

BREWERIES Just about every town in Michigan of any size has a brewpub, and many are listed in this book. The beer can be bought in large containers called "growlers" and taken home. However, several small brewers sell their beer in stores. **Bell's Brewery** (269-382-2338) in Kalamazoo was one of the first small brewers in the state and started in 1983 after restrictions were lifted on small brewing establishments. **Arcadia Brewing Company** (269-963-9690) of Battle Creek makes British-style ales. Both offer brewery tours.

BUS SERVICE **Greyhound** (1-800-231-2222; www.greyhound.com) serves many Michigan cities, but much of the service to small towns is limited. Because of its auto-making heritage, few people take mass transit in Michigan. A newer bus service, **Megabus** (1-877-GO2-MEGA; www.megabus.com) has been offering cheap rates on its nonstop route between Chicago and Detroit. It takes about five hours, but the downside is that it simply drops off passengers on the street because it doesn't have terminals.

CAMPING More than 3 million acres of federal and state forestlands are open to rustic, backwoods camping, which means you can set up camp on any piece of public land, unless prohibited. Before you do, check with federal or state forest officials. There are also thousands of sites in federal and state campgrounds, usually with water pumps, picnic tables, fire pits, and some form of rest rooms. State parks offer more amenities and services, especially for recreational vehicles. There are also hundreds of local municipal and private campgrounds. This book lists many campgrounds for both tents and recreational vehicles. (Also see *State Parks*, What's Where in Michigan.)

CANOEING There are about 45 rivers open for paddling in Michigan. These tend to be short, sandy, and relatively shallow. One of the most popular rivers to paddle is the Au Sable at Grayling. We'd like to direct you away from there to other rivers, and to the Au Sable at Mio, farther downstream where it is wider and deeper and the paddling actually better. The Au Sable at Grayling is narrow and difficult to maneuver in, and it also has many fly anglers who are at odds with paddlers. There has been much rude behavior on the part of canoeists. If you encounter fly anglers, ask them which way they would like you to pass. If you do that, chances are there won't be any problems. The state offers a listing of canoe liveries at

www.michigan.org. One of the best guides to paddling the state's rivers is *Canoeing Michigan Rivers: A Comprehensive Guide to 45 Rivers*, by Jerry Dennis and Craig Date.

CHILDREN Throughout this book, restaurants, lodgings, and attractions that are of special interest to families with children are indicated by the crayon icon (✐).

COTTAGE RENTALS Michigan has thousands of cottages and cabins for rent. The state park system has many such cabins, particularly at Wilderness State Park on Lake Michigan and at the Porcupine Mountains Wilderness State Park in the Upper Peninsula. Go to www.michigan.gov/dnr for listings. The state's major tourism Web site, www.michigan.org, also lists many cottage rentals. In this book various real-estate firms that handle rentals are listed. Also, many local chambers of commerce noted throughout have rentals listed on their Web sites.

DEER SEASON The rifle deer season starts in mid-November and runs through early December. It's nearly a state holiday in Michigan, which has

about 800,000 deer hunters. Some small businesses, particularly in rural communities close for a few days because they and their employees are off deer hunting. It's a festive season in many small towns. The bow season starts in early October. For information on hunting, go to www.michigan .gov/dnr.

CUSTOMS INFORMATION Michigan shares a water border with Canada, and since the 9/11 terrorist attacks, crossings are taking much longer due to security and there are significant waits at the three bridges and tunnel that connect the two countries. Compounding that is the free-trade agreement between the countries. And waits at the Ambassador Bridge in Detroit are often several hours, partly because the bridge handles 27 percent of the trade between the nations. Waits are shorter at the Detroit-Windsor Tunnel, which can be difficult to find (see Detroit). The other crossings are at the Blue Water Bridge in Port Huron and at the International Bridge in Sault Ste. Marie in the Upper Peninsula. A

passport will eventually be needed for travel to Canada, but that wasn't finalized when this book was written. There are also many restrictions on what can be taken across the border. For more information, contact **U.S. Customs and Border Protection** (www.cbp.gov), Ambassador Bridge (313-226-3141), Detroit-Windsor Tunnel (313-226-5716), Blue Water Bridge (810-794-3321), or International Bridge (906-632-2631).

EVENTS Outstanding annual events are listed within each chapter of this book.

FALL FOLIAGE The colors start to change anywhere from mid-September in the Upper Peninsula to early October in southern Michigan. The first week of October can be the best for northern Michigan and the Upper Peninsula. Most seasonal restaurants and lodging places are open through late October.

FIRE PERMITS Permits are not needed for cooking or recreational fires or anytime there's snow cover near the fire. Permits are issued by the state Department of Natural Resources (www.michigan.gov/dnr) for garden debris. Department of Natural Resources offices throughout the state post signs telling campers if fire danger is high or low. There are occasional forest fires in Michigan.

FISHING Michigan offers angling for most freshwater species, including salmon and steelhead, lake trout and various other trout species, walleye, perch, and bass. The state **Department of Natural Resources** maintains a list of places to fish and the species available (www.michigan.gov/

dnr). A good book for fly anglers is *Trout Streams of Michigan,* by Bob Linsenman and Steve Nevala. Linsenman is also the author of *Steelhead.* Both books were published by The Countryman Press. Fishing the Great Lakes for salmon, steelhead, and trout requires a good boat and knowledge. **The Michigan Charter Boat Association** (1-800-MCBA-971; www.mi charterboats.com) has about 300 members who fish the lakes.

FORTS Two of the best are at the Straits of Mackinac. Fort Michilimackinac on the mainland and Fort Mackinac on Mackinac Island were used in the 18th and 19th centuries when the straits were the center of fur trading in the Great Lakes. There are military reenactors at both during the summer months. Visit **Mackinac State Historic Parks** (231-436-4100; www.mackinacparks.com), 207 W. Sinclair St., Mackinaw City.

GAMBLING Detroit, where it's legal, has three casinos (see Detroit), and Native American tribes own casinos on tribal lands scattered throughout the state. Many are covered in this book. Click on www.michigan.org for a complete list.

GOLFING There are more than 850 golf courses in Michigan, and many, but not all, are included in this book. Apart from southeast Michigan, where the majority of Michigan residents live, you can find a concentration of courses in the **Grand Traverse Region** and near **Gaylord.** For a listing of all courses, click on www.michgian.org/travel/golf/.

HIKING **Isle Royale National Park** in Lake Superior is one of the least-visited parks in the system; one reason is access. It requires a 50-mile boat ride from the Keewanaw Peninsula. The island is 50 miles long, there are no vehicles on the island, and all access is either by boat or on foot. North Manitou Island in Lake Michigan, offshore from the Leelanau Peninsula, is part of the **Sleeping Bear National Lakeshore,** and offers an island intersected by trails, and no vehicles. The **North Country Trail** runs through the Lower Peninsula along the west side of the state and along the shoreline of Lake Superior. It's part of the system that runs from New York to North Dakota. A prime section of the trail is in the **Pictured Rocks National Lakeshore.** Click on www.northcountrytrail.com to contact the North Country Trail Association for information. There are hundreds of miles of shorter trails maintained by the **Michigan Department of Natural Resources** (www .michigan.gov/dnr).

HISTORY See sidebar above on Michigan history.

HUNTING Michigan has hunting seasons for deer, bear, and elk, along with upland birds (like grouse and woodcock) and waterfowl. There is also a turkey season. Licenses are required, and a special permit is needed for elk. Seasonal licenses can be obtained online from the **Michigan Department of Natural Resources** (www.michigan.gov/dnr).

INNS There are hundreds of B&Bs and inns in Michigan, and I've looked at many of them, and taken the word of others, before including them in this book. **Michigan Lake to Lake Bed & Breakfast Association** represents about 210 members and maintains a list at www.laketolake.com.

ISLANDS There are about 900 offshore islands in Michigan, most of which are uninhabited. We describe each of the islands that offer overnight lodging or camping—**Isle Royale National Park, Grand, Mackinac, Beaver,** and **Manitou.**

KAYAKING This is a fast-growing activity in Michigan, partly because of the easy access to lakes and rivers. Urban kayaking is even being done in the Detroit River. This book lists many access points.

LAKE LEVELS The Great Lakes are at record low levels, so before booking a resort check to see what effects there may be. In some areas along Lake Michigan, it means there is additional sandy beach area. However, some marinas and boat launches have been affected and boaters can face difficulty getting their craft in the water. Historically, the lakes go through cycles, but climate change has had an effect, with warmer winters and less snowpack. (The snowpack replenishes the lakes.) Also, when winters are warmer, the lakes don't freeze over, so more water evaporates.

LIGHTHOUSES There are 115 lighthouses on the four Great Lakes surrounding Michigan, and this book lists many of them, some of which have been turned into bed & breakfasts. Several are open to the public and have museums attached. For a full listing, go to (www.michigan.org), a tourist Web site hosted by the state. One of the best is the **Au Sable Light Station** near Grand Marais in the Upper Peninsula. It has been restored by the National Park Service, which gives daily tours from late May through early September.

MICHIGAN PUBLIC BROADCASTING There are a large number of National Public Radio stations in the Lower Peninsula, but they trail off in the Upper Peninsula. This book lists the stations available in the U.P., and Canada's version of public radio can be received in the eastern U.P. and in southeastern Michigan.

MAGAZINES *Traverse* (231-941-8174; www.traversemagazine.com) is a monthly that has lush color pages devoted to Traverse City and northern Michigan. They do a great job of writing about the Up North lifestyle, its people, and places. *Lake* (1-877-362-8592; lakemagazine.com) is another full-color publication; it comes out nine times annually and is devoted to the lifestyle of Harbor Country in southwestern Michigan and along the Lake Michigan shoreline in Indiana. *Porcupine Press* (906-439-5111; upmag.net), a monthly tabloid, is the alternative press of the Upper Peninsula and does a good job of humorously portraying the quirky, backwoods lifestyle of the region. While it's not really vulgar, you many not want to leave it on the backseat of the car for the kids to see.

MUSHROOM HUNTING Picking morel mushrooms is a popular activity during May in northern Michigan, but it's not for the uneducated. Every couple of years, somebody gets ill eating the wrong kind. These mushrooms are valued by chefs for their taste and end up in many Michigan restaurants. The **Michigan Department of Natural Resources** (www.michigan.gov/dnr)

conducts programs in the spring on how to identify a morel.

MUSIC **Interlochen Center for the Arts** (231-276-5635; www.inter lochen.org) near Traverse City brings jazz, blues, folk, classical, and blue-grass music to northern Michigan during summer months (see Grand Traverse Region).

MUSEUM VILLAGES **The Henry Ford, Museum and Village** (313-982-6001; www.thehenryford.org) in Dearborn attracts about 1.5 million visitors a year, who tour the collection of 19th and early 20th century historic homes and see the artifacts. The vil-lage is a bit eclectic and there's no central theme. Henry Ford, the founder of Ford Motor Co., simply bought what he wanted and had it shipped here. There's the Wright brothers' home and bicycle workshop, Daniel Webster's home, a rustic courthouse where Abraham Lincoln practiced law, slave quarters, 17th-

century New England homes, a Mary-land plantation home, a stone British cottage, a blacksmith shop, a 19th-century working farm, and many oth-ers. It would take several days just to see the village. The museum houses many vintage and antique cars and would take several more days to see.

NATIVE AMERICANS There's a strong Native American presence in the state. Most are Ojibwa/Chippewa and there are several reservations, along with various bands living on smaller parcels. They call themselves the Anishnabe. The French called them the Ojibwa and that name was angli-cized into Chippewa.

PARKS AND FORESTS Northern Michigan is home to **Isle Royale National Park**, an island in Lake Superior, **Pictured Rocks National Lakeshore** and the **Sleeping Bear Dunes National Lakeshore**. The Ottawa National Forest has more than 1 million acres in the western

INFORMATION (OFFICIAL) ABOUT MICHIGAN

The Michigan Economic Development Corporation handles tourism in the state and maintains a Web site (www.michigan.org) and a toll-free number (1-800-644-2489) so visitors can talk to a travel counselor Mon.–Fri., 9–5. The agency annually produces *Michigan Travel Ideas* and will mail it on request. They also accept e-mail requests at the Web site.

There are 13 welcome centers around the state staffed by travel coun-selors with good local knowledge. The centers are filled with information and brochures about attractions, lodging, dining, and places to see. They are: Clare, at the juncture of US 127 and US 10; Coldwater, I-69 at the 6-mile marker; Dundee, US 23, between Exits 5 and 9; Iron Mountain, US 2 and US 141, downtown Iron Mountain; Ironwood, US 2 at the Michigan/Wisconsin border; Mackinaw City, I-75, north, Exit 338; Marquette, MI 28, near MI 41 and MI 28 intersection; Menominee, US 41, downtown; Monroe, I-75, north-bound at the 10-mile marker; New Buffalo, eastbound I-94, Michigan/Indiana state line; Port Huron, westbound I-69, Exit 274; St. Ignace, northbound I-75 at the Mackinac Bridge and Sault Ste. Marie, I-75, Exit 394.

Upper Peninsula, most of it open to public use. The Hiawatha National Forest (906-786-4062; fs.fed.us.gov/Hiawatha) covers nearly 900,000 acres of the central Upper Peninsula, and the Huron-Manistee has slightly less than 1 million acres.

PUBLIC TRANSPORTATION Don't look for it in many towns. There is no reliable public transit in Detroit. There's a piecemeal bus system, but it's dysfunctional. And don't even think about hailing a taxicab. You don't see any in Detroit or in most other large cities. When calling for a cab, expect at least a 40-minute wait. Your best bet is to rent a car.

POPULATION 9.9 million.

SIZE Michigan encompasses 58,110 square miles and is the largest state east of the Mississippi. It also has 38,575 square miles of Great Lakes waters and 1,305 square miles of inland waters. Only Alaska has more territorial water.

SKIING, CROSS-COUNTRY With its gently rolling hills, Michigan is perfect for cross-country skiing, but in recent years there's been less and less snow, apparently due to climate change. Even the Detroit area was awash with cross-country skiers until the lack of snow forced them to travel farther north. Even northern Michigan has had unreliable snow for several years. Western and northwestern Michigan and the Upper Peninsula have been the best places to go in recent years. There are about 220 trail systems recognized by the state, and endless possibilities for backcountry skiing on two-track roads on state and federal forestlands. Click on www.michigan.org for conditions and a list of trails. This book also includes many of these. Scandinavian immigrants brought cross-country skiing and ski jumping to Michigan's Upper Peninsula in the 19th century, and the **U.S. National Ski Hall of Fame and Museum** (906-485-6323; www.skihall.com) in Ishpeming celebrates their accomplishments.

SKIING, DOWNHILL While Scandinavian immigrants to the Upper Peninsula brought their sport with them, and founded a ski club in Ishpeming in the 1880s, it wasn't until the 1950s that downhill skiing really got going in Michigan. Most Michigan hills aren't very high and the runs are fairly short, so the majority of skiers are from the Midwest and travel for weekend skiing. Most decent ski areas are found in northwest Michigan and the western Upper Peninsula. The larger hills in the Lower Peninsula are at **Boyne Highlands, Nub's Nob, Schuss Mountain, Shanty Creek,** and **Caberfae.** In the Upper Peninsula, the major areas are **Norway Mountain, Pine Mountain, Mount Bohemia, Ski Brule, Porcupine Mountains,** and **Indianhead.**

SKI JUMPING Ski jumping began in the 19th century when Scandinavian immigrants started gathering for weekend events in the western Upper Peninsula and teams traveled from town to town. These days the jumping is done at **Pine Mountain Ski Jump** in Iron Mountain and at **Copper Peak** in Ironwood. Various competitions are held each winter. Click on www.michigan.org for listings.

SNOWMOBILING Without snowmobiling, many northern Michigan and

Upper Peninsula towns wouldn't make it through the winter. Snowmobilers pump millions of dollars into the local economies each winter, and some towns in the U.P. are busier in winter than in summer. While much of central and northern Michigan was covered with snow during winter a decade ago, they aren't these days, and snowmobilers are being pushed farther north. There are 6,000 miles of trails groomed by the state **Department of Natural Resources** (www.michigan.gov/dnr), and these are open from early Dec. to late March, if there's snow. The **Michigan Snowmobile Association** (616-361-2285; msasnow.org) is a good source of information. For a listing of trails, click on www.michigan.org. Local chambers of commerce listed in this book often provide snowmobiling maps.

SNOWSHOEING Snowshoeing is experiencing a rebirth in Michigan and most cross-country ski outfitters and centers rent snowshoes.

SPIRITUAL CENTER **The Song of the Morning Yoga Resort and Retreat** (989-983-4107; goldenlotus .org), 9607 Sturgeon Valley Rd., Vanderbilt, is an 800-acre retreat in the Pigeon River State Forest of the Lower Peninsula. It offers yoga, meditation, and healing programs.

STATE PARKS There are about 60 state parks, most of which allow camping, and many of which are located on either the Great Lakes or inland lakes. Michigan's state parks are popular and well used. Most have improved facilities, such as flush toilets and showers, and are equipped to handle recreational vehicles that need

a power source. The state **Department of Natural Resources** (1-800-44-PARKS; www.michigan.gov/dnr) manages the facilities, and campsites can be reserved. The entrance fee is $20, and camping fees range from $10–$20 a night. There are about 50 state forest campgrounds, which are a good alternative to the often-crowded state parks. The campgrounds generally only offer rustic camping with outhouses, water pumps, fire pits, and picnic tables. This book lists many state parks in the various geographical sections. (Also see *Camping*, What's Where in Michigan.)

TIME ZONES Most of Michigan is on Eastern Standard Time, but four western U.P. counties along the Wisconsin border use Central Standard Time. Other western Upper Peninsula counties on Eastern Standard Time are farther west than Chicago, and during summer it's light until about 11 PM.

TRAFFIC AND HIGHWAY TRAVEL TIPS Except for rush hours in the Grand Rapids and Detroit areas and on holiday weekends, there is little traffic in Michigan, unless there's road construction. There are no toll roads. The only fee is $2.50 for crossing the Mackinac Bridge. Traffic pretty much moves along at the posted speed limits, which are 70 miles per hour on freeways, 65 on city expressways, and 55 on rural two-lane roads. On many days, Detroit area freeways resemble the Indianapolis 500. This is the Motor City after all, and a lot of the drivers are car guys from the Big Three. Don't expect drivers on the freeway to let you merge from the ramp, as in other cities. Watch out for the semi trucks in southern Michigan, they're big and heavy. In other states they may be carrying consumer goods, but in the Detroit area they're hauling a lot of steel.

WEATHER Every state likes to brag about its bad weather. Michigan doesn't have to. If you come, always bring fleece to wear, even in summer. Because you're surrounded by the Great Lakes, the weather can turn rainy quickly, and temperatures can plunge into the 50s, even in the summer.

WINERIES Old Mission Peninsula near Traverse City has five wineries that can be toured, **Bowers Harbor, Brays Estate Vineyard, Chateau Chantal, Chateau Grand Traverse,** and **Peninsula Cellars.** Go to **www .wineriesofoldmission.com** for a map and hours. The nearby Leelanau Peninsula has about a dozen more. Go to www.lpwines.com for listings, maps, and hours. This book has a listing of wineries that can be toured and hours (see Grand Traverse). Another handy wWeb site for winery tours is www.michiganwines.com.

YOOPERS This term is used to describe Upper Peninsula residents and their accent, which has been influenced by the large number of Finns, Swedes, and French Canadians who came in the 19th century to work in the copper and iron mines. It's a very distinct accent that is expressed best in a common bumper sticker: SAY YEAH TO DA U.P., EH. The Yooper culture is well portrayed in Jeff Daniels's movie *Escanaba in da Moonlight,* which is about a Yooper who hasn't killed his first deer.

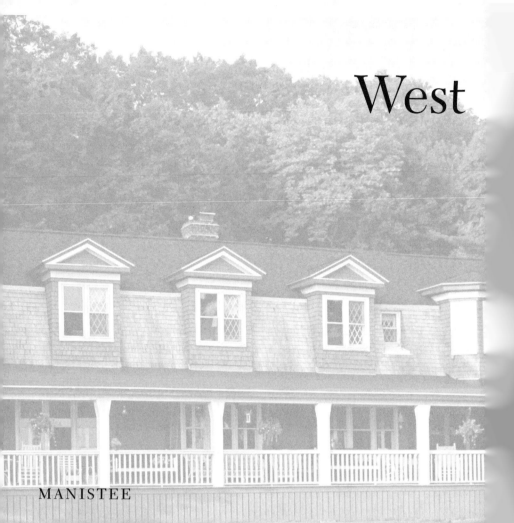

West

MANISTEE

LUDINGTON, INCLUDING THE
VILLAGE OF PENTWATER

MANISTEE

Manistee is a town of 6,585. It has the same sandy Lake Michigan beaches as the Grand Traverse region, but not its economy. It just isn't as trendy as Traverse City, which is its allure. The restaurants aren't as crowded and the prices are lower. Manistee is close to the Sleeping Bear Dunes and has plenty of attractions, including the Manistee River running through downtown.

There is a long history of Native Americans living in the area around the mouth of the Manistee River, and there's some speculation that Father Marquette visited the community, but no firm evidence. The first real commercial business was an American Fur Company store and office owned by John Jacob Astor.

A fire in 1871 destroyed much of the wooden structures, but like the Great Chicago Fire, it prompted residents to rebuild using brick and stone, and those buildings are still evident today.

Lumber barons eventually set up shop and constructed fancy Victorian homes near downtown, and during the lumbering era the town saw an economic boom. Victorian mansions abound, and the business district has numerous ornate commercial buildings from the late 19th and early 20th centuries. But the seemingly endless white pine forests were depleted by 1911 and the town slipped into decline.

One bright spot has been the restoration of the Ramsdell Theatre, which was built in 1903 and served as the town's opera house during its heyday.

The city is on the State and National Register of Historic Places and is an attraction for architecture buffs. A Victorian fountain has been built across from the City Marina, and a new river walk attracts strollers. The endless miles of undisturbed Lake Michigan shoreline includes sandy beaches, and you could spend weeks exploring them.

GUIDANCE Manistee Area Chamber of Commerce (1-800-288-2286; www .manisteecountychamber.com), 11 Cypress St., Manistee, MI 49660. Open daily, business hours. Information is available on the area.

GETTING THERE *By car:* Manistee is more difficult to get to than Traverse City, as the town and the surrounding communities are strung along US 31, a curvy road

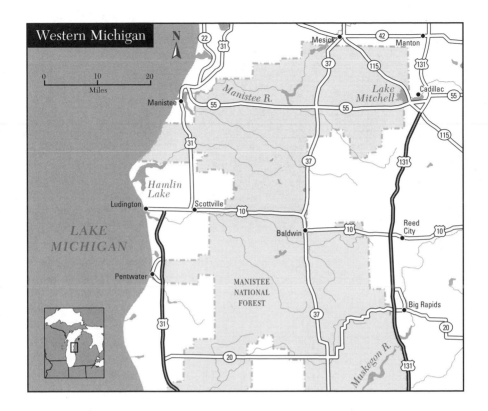

Western Michigan

N

that follows the Lake Michigan shoreline. The most direct route is to take US 131 to MI 55, and then continue west. From Traverse City, US 31 is the best route.

By air: See Cherry Capital Airport, Traverse City.

WHEN TO COME For summer tourism, the season is late May–early Sept., but there is much charter fishing activity in Lake Michigan for salmon and steelhead, which takes place in late summer and fall. The fall foliage season lasts through late October. Cross-country and downhill skiing attract winter visitors. As with all of Michigan, don't bother to come from winter breakup in mid-March through early May, unless you're a steelhead angler.

MEDICAL EMERGENCY **West Shore Medial Center** (231-398-1000), 1465 E. Parkdale Ave., Manistee. Dial 911.

✳ To See & Do

✎ **Historic Ramsdell Theatre** (231-723-9948; www.ramsdell-theater.org). The theater opened in 1903 during the height of the lumber boom in northern Michigan and was used for many years for productions. It was built by Thomas

RAMSDELL THEATRE

Jefferson Ramsdell, an attorney and early settler in Manistee. But by the 1990s, the building had decayed and was renovated as part of Manistee's efforts to emphasize its Victorian heritage. It is now used by a group of local players for productions, many of which take place during the summer months.

✒ ☯ *S.S. City of Milwaukee* (231-723-3587; www.carferry.com), 99 Arthur St. (US 31), Manistee, MI 49660. Open late May–early Sept. The vessel is the remnant of a fleet of ships that once carried railroad cars and passengers across Lake Michigan between Michigan and Milwaukee. Actually, at the time, residents of Manistee made regular shopping trips to Milwaukee. The ships operated from the 1890s through the late 1970s. The 360-foot vessel was saved from the scrap yard in 1983, and it is now a National Historic Landmark. Admission: $8, adults; seniors and children 6–17, $5; family rates, $25.

GAMBLING **Little River Casino** (1-888-568-2244; www.littlerivercasino.com), 2700 Orchard Hwy., Manistee. Open year-round. Run by the Little River Band of Ottawa Indians, the casino offers slot machines and game tables. The Indians also bring in big-name entertainers on occasion.

✳ Outdoor Activities

CHARTER BOAT FISHING Manistee is a center for charter boat fishing in Lake Michigan for salmon and trout. **Manistee Area Charter Boats** (231-398-9355; www.fishmanistee.com), corner of US 31 and First St.

FLY-FISHING Some of the best fly-fishing waters in Michigan are in the Manistee area. Trout, salmon, and steelhead are all taken on a fly. The prime streams are the Manistee, Pere Marquette, Little Manistee, and Pine rivers.

Schmidt Outfitters (231-848-4191; www.schmidtoutfitters.com), 918 Seaman Rd., Wellston, offers fly-fishing lessons, equipment, and guide services for most rivers. They also offer lodging.

The Pere Marquette Lodge (231-745-3972; www.pmlodge.com), 8841 S. MI 37, Baldwin, MI 49304. Frank Willets owns this Orvis-endorsed lodge, which offers a fly shop, guide service, and float trips on the Manistee and other area rivers. Fall salmon and steelheading trips produce a lot of action. There's also a motel and cabins.

✳ Lodging

The Ramsdell Inn (231-398-7901; www.ramsdellinn.net), River and Maple sts., Manistee. The 10-room boutique hotel is for Victorian buffs, with its ornate decorations in a stone building constructed in 1891. It was mostly an office building at the time, but was converted into a hotel, with some suites. The three-story building was renovated in 2003, and the stained-glass windows and carved woodwork have been preserved. The rooms give you the feeling that a

19th-century lumber baron is expected to drop in. The inn is a great example of finding new commercial uses for older structures. I've always loved the stone column in front of this place and have hoped for years that the building wouldn't be lost. It's in the downtown area, close to historic Victorian neighborhoods, shops, pubs, and restaurants. Rates are $119–$219.

MARINA/MOTELS Manistee Inn & Marina (231-723-4000 or 1-800-968-

MANISTEE RIVER

6277; www.manisteeinn.com), 378 River St., Manistee. Located along the Manistee River in the downtown area, the inn has 25 rooms. They're basic hotel rooms, nothing special, but if you're a boater coming in from several days on the lake, it would be a good place, and could be within walking distance of your craft. It's also close to restaurants and shopping and has wireless Internet. The inn has 15 slips on the Manistee River and can accommodate boats up to 25 feet. Water and electric hook-ups available. Rates are $90–$150.

Riverside Motel & Marina (231-723-3554; www.riversidemoteland marina.com), 520 Water, St., Manistee. Open year-round. Rooms in this 20-unit motel are simple and sparse, but clean. Many have a view of the Manistee River and doors leading to the water. The rooms have phones and satellite TV. There are boat docks available, as well as a fish-cleaning station. There are lawn chairs, grills, picnic tables, and an outdoor pool. Rates are $89–$139.

BED & BREAKFASTS **Lady Jane's Bed & Breakfast** (231-723-1171; www.ladyjanemanistee.com), 35 Second St., Manistee. The three-story Dutch colonial home was built in 1890. It has two suites, each on different levels, and is located near the Victorian section of downtown and less than a mile away from Lake Michigan beaches. The rooms have cable TV, small refrigerators, and air-conditioning. The suites are furnished with some antiques. The upstairs suite could accommodate two couples. Rates are $100–$125.

In Arcadia
Arcadia House (231-889-4394),

17304 Northwood Hwy. (MI 22), Arcadia. I liked the four inside rooms, but my favorite was the carriage house, a two-story unit located nearby, which has three bedrooms, a kitchen, and a sauna. It houses up to six people. The four rooms in the 1910 home are furnished in a country-cottage style, and are clean, neat, and not overdone. They are a little cramped for some people, but the action is outdoors on the porch or in taking walks to Lake Michigan. Rates are $109–$119.

In Onekama
The Canfield House (1-866-889-5756; www.thecanfieldhouse.com), 4138 Portage Point Dr., Onekama. This seven-room B&B has some nice diversity in its room styles, several of which are decorated in a romantic Victorian style. Others are more for sportsmen who visit the area to fish and hunt. The porch takes up much of the first floor and has comfortable outdoor seating. The inn has 200 feet of private beach on Portage Lake, and boaters could make good use of the location. The innkeepers are Paul and Jane Mueller. Rates are $105–$145.

MOTELS 🐾 **Lake Shore Motel** (231-723-2667), 101 S. Lakeshore Dr., Manistee. Located on the lake, this basic 21-room motel is a good location for beach activities. The rooms are nothing fancy, but they're just the thing if most of your activities are outside. Rates are $75.

RENTALS **Manistee Vacation and Cottage Rentals** (231-493-0368; www.greatrentals.com/manistee). A Web site with rentals in the Manistee area.

✳ Where to Eat

DINING OUT

In Onekama

Ⴟ **The Glenwood** (231-889-3734; www.glenwoodrestaurant.com), 4604 Main St., Onekama. Open daily for lunch and dinner. This delightful old inn overlooking Portage Lake has been a summer lodge, hotel, and restaurant since the early 1900s and is now a restaurant owned by Chris and Donna Short. They serve many regional favorites, including whitefish, perch, and salmon. There are also hearty steaks on the menu, along with chicken and pasta dishes. Reservations suggested. Entrees are $15–$26.

EATING OUT Ⴟ **Little River Casino** (1-888-568-2244; www.littleriver casino.com), 2700 Orchard Hwy., Manistee. This Native American–owned casino serves family-style dinners, and it's a good place for a breakfast buffet. Dinners include a prime rib and seafood buffet. Prices are $8–$20. There's a children's menu.

✳ Selective Shopping

Kaleidoscopic Art Market (231-723-5565), 279 First St., Manistee. Open Mon.–Sat., 10–6. Northern Michigan artists are featured in this small, but well-stocked gallery.

River Street Gallery (231-398-4001), 384 River St., Manistee. There are traditional and contemporary works by local and other artists, including paintings, sculpture, glass, pottery, and jewelry.

LUDINGTON, INCLUDING THE VILLAGE OF PENTWATER

The Lake Michigan shoreline city of Ludington has long been a favorite weekend destination for southern Michigan visitors because of its beaches and charter fishing. It's also the port of the *S.S. Badger,* a car ferry that makes regular runs across Lake Michigan to Wisconsin.

Many folks use the ferry to avoid the drive around the south end of Lake Michigan through Chicago, while others simply like to take the trip as an excursion. Because of the large number of travelers, there are more bed & breakfasts and lodging places available than in other lakefront towns along the coast.

Many Great Lakes anglers make this their home port, and numerous fishing craft are moored in the marinas. A large number of charter boats operate from here.

As with many Great Lakes communities, Father Jacques Marquette, a French missionary, was one of the first Europeans to visit. However, in this case, he died in Ludington and was buried here.

Ludington eventually became a lumber town with sawmills, and the shipping of lumber became its top industry. But by 1911, much of the white pine that drove the economy was gone, and the town started to decline. However, because of its location at the mouth of the Pere Marquette River, and its pristine, sandy Lake Michigan beaches, Ludington became the fifth most visited tourist destination in the state.

GUIDANCE Ludington Area Convention and Visitors Bureau (1-877-420-6618; www.ludingtoncvb.com), 5300 W. US 10, Ludington, MI 49431. The bureau produces a brochure with travel tips.

Pentwater Chamber of Commerce (231-869-4150; www.pentwater.org), 324 S. Hancock St., Pentwater, MI 49449. The chamber's Web site lists many cottages for rent.

MEDIA *Ludington Daily News* (231-845-5181; www.ludingtondailynews.com). A source of local information on a daily basis and a good place to look for vacation rentals.

STAYING CONNECTED Most cell phone plans work well here. Some lodging places have free wireless access, but not all. There are a large number of radio stations. The NPR outlet is 90.3 FM and it's from Blue Lake Fine Arts Camp.

TOWNS & VILLAGES Pentwater (population 958) was a Lake Michigan lumber boomtown in the 19th century, but it's now a tourist town with a large marina that attracts many boaters, especially from the Grand Rapids area. The village was founded in 1853 when a lumber mill and boardinghouse were erected. Lumber baron Charles Mears built a channel to Lake Michigan so lumber could

Father Marquette Shrine, South Lakeshore Drive, Ludington. When you start reading the historical markers in towns in the Upper Midwest, Father Jacques Marquette's name keeps coming up as one of the first European visitors to the area. His explorations are amazing. He and Louis Jolliet were the first non–Native Americans to see much of the Great Lakes region, along with the Mississippi River. Marquette's name graces a city, university, river, college halls, and buildings throughout the region, and it's a reminder of the French influence on the Great Lakes region and through the lower Midwest.

Marquette was born in Laon, France, and became a Jesuit priest at 17. He was eventually sent to Quebec in 1666 to minister to Native Americans and quickly became adept at their languages. He was then sent to the Great Lakes region, where he worked at a mission in Sault Ste. Marie and then at another near what is now Ashland, Wis. It was there that he first heard about the Mississippi River. However, warring Native American tribes kept him from making the journey and he eventually ended up at the Straits of Mackinac.

There, he was granted a leave, and he and Joliet left St. Ignace on May 17, 1673, headed for the Mississippi River. The pair, along with five voyageurs of mixed French and Indian ancestry, made what now seems an epic canoe trip. They followed Lake Michigan to the Green Bay area and traveled up the Fox River. They portaged to the Wisconsin River and floated downstream through the Mississippi basin to the river itself, and eventually followed it to the mouth of the Arkansas River. There they encountered Indians with items Marquette thought were European. Fearing a confrontation with the Spanish, they turned around and paddled back north to the mouth of the Illinois River, and followed it back to what is now Chicago. After spending the winter of 1674 there, in the spring he paddled west again to Native American villages to celebrate mass. While returning to St. Ignace, he fell victim to dysentery and died somewhere near Ludington.

be shipped from his mill to Chicago. There are a large number of B&Bs in the village, which mostly stretches along the harbor area.

✳ To See & Do

✍ ⊚ **Historic White Pine Village** (231-843-4808; www.historicwhitepine village.org), 1687 S. Lakeshore Dr., Ludington. Open daily, late May–early Sept. The research library and gift shop are open in the winter. The village has more than 25 buildings and sites that preserve the region's past. There is a self-guided tour.

Big Sable Point Lighthouse (231-845-7343; www.bigsablelighthouse.org), Ludington State Park. Open early May–late Oct. The lighthouse was built in 1867 to aid Great Lakes shipping, and is open to tours. The tower is 112 feet high, one of the largest in the region. The station was automated in 1968 and is on the National Register of Historic Places. There is a gift shop. Donations are $2 for adults, $1 children.

✍ **Ludington Mural Walk** (231-845-0324; www.ludingtonmurals.org). Downtown Ludington has eight murals on various buildings that depict scenes from the area's history.

✍ **S.S. Badger** (1-800-841-4243; www.ssbadger.com), Ludington. The car ferry makes trips between Ludington and Manitowoc, Wis., daily spring–fall. The 90-mile trip takes about three hours. Some folks take the ferry to avoid driving through Chicago on their way west, while others take it for an excursion. You can bring your vehicle or just be a passenger. It's one of the few ships that still ferries passengers on the Great Lakes, and the only remaining car ferry. Fares: $62 for an auto, SUV, van; $75 for pickup campers; and $4.95 per foot for motor homes. On top of that, there's a passenger charge of $59 for an adult (one way), and $26 for a child.

✳ Outdoor Activities

SAND DUNE RIDES **Mac Woods Dune Rides** (231-873-2817), 629 N. 18th Ave., Mears. Dune buggies take visitors on a tour of 1,800 acres of sand dunes.

HORSEBACK RIDING **Indian Ridge Stable** (231-757-4514), 1525 S. Poplar, Custer. Riding on 500 acres of hills.

BEACHES **Nordhouse Dunes Wilderness Area** (231-723-2211), Manistee Ranger Station, 412 Red Apple Rd., Manistee. The 3,450-acre area is located just north of Ludington State Park, along Lake Michigan between Manistee and Ludington. The area is accessible only by footpaths and is known for its 4 miles of undeveloped Lake Michigan beachfront. It's the only designated wilderness area on the Lake Michigan shoreline in the Lower Peninsula, and it includes dunes that are 3,500 to 4,000 years old and stand about 140 feet high. The dunes are interspersed with vegetation such as juniper, jack pine, and hemlock. Camping is available in the dunes area, but you must be 400 feet from the lake or 200 feet from Nordhouse Lake. Access is from Nurnberg Road off US 31.

Ludington State Park (231-843-2423; www.michigan.gov/dnr), 8800 W. MI 116, Ludington, 8 miles north of Ludington on Lakeshore Dr. and MI 116. The 5,300-acre park, located between Lake Michigan and Hamlin Lake, is known for its beaches and sand dunes. There are 355 campsites, including three mini-cabins for rent, and several miles of unspoiled beaches on both lakes. Hamlin Lake tends to be a little warmer and is a good place for kids. It is also a prime spot for canoeing and kayaking. There are sandy beaches around it to explore while paddling. Canoes and kayaks are available for rent from the state park store (231-843-2423). There are boat launches on both lakes.

Stearns Park (231-845-6237), N. Lakeshore Drive, Ludington. The park is a few blocks from downtown Ludington and is one of the largest city beaches in the state, offering miles of sandy shoreline. Picnic areas, grills, playground equipment, and concession stands are available in summer. Admission is free.

CANOEING & KAYAKING There are endless possibilities in Lake Michigan. Hamlin Lake is a good bet too; the inland lake is surrounded by dunes and public lands. Kayak rentals are available at Ludington State Park (see *Ludington State Park*).

BICYCLING County back roads provide many miles of cycling. There are also dedicated pathways: **Cartier Park Pathway**, a 1-mile paved loop at Bryant and Rath avenues; **Hart-Montague Bicycle Trail**, a 22.5 mile paved trail with access at John Gurney Park in Hart, east of US 31, runs south to Montague; **Ludington State Park Bike Trails** (see *Ludington State Park*); **North Lakeshore Drive** to MI 116, Ludington, along Lake Michigan.

✳ Lodging

All are open year-round unless otherwise noted.

BED & BREAKFASTS

In Ludington
Abbey Lynn Inn Bed & Breakfast (231-795-5421; www.abbeylynninn .com), 603 E. Ludington Ave., Ludington. The colonial style home was built in 1890 and has five rooms, all with private baths. Most are decorated in a country style, but one room is done in a colonial style and has a four-poster bed. There is a full breakfast. Rates are $75–$130.

☀ **Candlelite Inn** (231-845-8074 or 1-877-997-0099), 709 E. Ludington Ave., Ludington. The innkeepers of

this six-room B&B are Tony and Melanie Barnard. The rooms in the turn-of-the-century home near downtown Ludington are decorated in various styles, but with a country theme. Two rooms have private entrances and are pet friendly. There is a hot-tub room. The porch would be a great place to spend a morning with a cup of coffee. Murder mystery weekends are offered. Rates are $109–$149.

⊗ **Cartier Mansion Bed & Breakfast and Conference Center** (231-843-0101; www.cartiermansion.com), 409 E. Ludington Ave., Ludington. The neoclassical mansion was built by a lumber baron in 1903 and was featured in the grand homes of the Midwest and historic homes of America.

CARTIER MANSION BED & BREAKFAST

There are five fireplaces, a black walnut library, and a mahogany music room. The six rooms have high-speed Internet. This is truly an elegant place that reflects the wealth of Michigan lumber barons of the time. The Grand King Suite has a four-poster bed, sitting room, and large bath. Most of the rooms are larger than what many B&Bs have to offer in Michigan. Wedding friendly. Much of the original woodwork is intact, and various types of wood were used. Rates are $125–$225.

Inn at Ludington (231-845-7055 or 1-800-845-9170; www.inn-ludington .com), 701 E. Ludington Ave., Ludington, MI 49431. There are six rooms in this 1890 Victorian-style mansion. All have private baths. The innkeepers are Kathy and Ola Kvalvaag. While many B&Bs slavishly try making every room a replica of Victorian life, the inn has a different theme for each room, ranging from the classic Great Lakes Victorian Suite to the Scandinavian Room. A full breakfast is served, and there is Internet access. Rates are $90–$165.

Lamplighter Bed & Breakfast (231-843-9792 or 1-800-301-9792; www.ludington-michigan.com), 602 Ludington Ave., Ludington. There are five rooms in this 1894 home, all with private baths. Jane and Bill Carpenter are the innkeepers. These are larger rooms and they're furnished with many antiques and artworks. The owners favor Renoir. The honeymoon suite has a hot tub. No children. A full breakfast is served, and there is Internet service. Rates are $145–$170.

Ludington House Bed & Breakfast (231-845-7769; www.ludington house.com), 501 E. Ludington. This 1878 lumber baron's home has eight rooms, all with baths. It was built by Antoine Cartier, who came to the area from Quebec in the 1850s, with his wife and nine children. The rooms all have a Victorian feel, and are furnished with some antiques. There are family suites, and the place can hold up to 20 people for events such as reunions. The innkeepers are Bill and Kris Stumpf. Internet access provided. Rates are $68–$160.

In Scottville
Carrier Ridge Lodge (231-757-4848 or 1-866-315-6343; www.carrier ridge.com), 3222 N. US 31, Scottville. This three-room lodge is just what a sportsman or woman is looking for. Located about 8 miles east of Ludington, it's close to the Manistee National Forest and hunting and fishing opportunities. There are trails for cross-country skiing and hiking on the property. Each rustic room has a private bath, telephone, and queen-sized bed. No children. A full breakfast is served in the dining room. The porch has comfortable furniture and there are opportunities for wildlife viewing. Rates are $120–$140.

∞ **The Candlewyck House** (231-869-5967; www.candlewyckhouse .com), 438 E. Lowell St., Pentwater. Open May–Nov. 1. The six-room 1868 farmhouse is close to Lake Michigan and shopping and dining in Pentwater. The rooms have private baths, air-conditioning, TV, and access to a mini-kitchen. Two rooms have gas log fireplaces. There are free bicycles for guests, and kayak rentals are available. A full breakfast is served, and there's a patio dining area available during warmer months. Wedding friendly. Rates are $115–$155.

Hexagon House (231-869-4102; www.hexagonhouse.com), 760 6th St., Pentwater. Five rooms. The inn was built in 1870 by S. E. Russell as a boardinghouse for lumbermen visiting the area from Chicago and other Great Lakes towns. They would climb to the top and watch the ships arrive in the harbor. The structure was restored in 1996, and the current innkeepers are Dave Durham and Ed Farnham. The rooms are larger than a normal B&B, and they are fit for lumber barons. I liked the way they've kept to the spirit of the place, while accommodating modern travelers. The five rooms and public rooms have a more masculine feel than other B&Bs. There are queen-sized beds and TVs in the rooms and a large porch for sitting. Rates are $115–$215.

The Ida Jean (231-869-5407; www .idajean.com), 379 E. Lowell St., Pentwater. The four rooms each have a theme, including one done in Americana style. Some of the rooms may seem a bit cluttered for male tastes, but there's a diversity of rooms and a room to fit any taste. The home was built in 1873 and has been in the innkeeper's family for many generations. It has been updated over the years, and all rooms have baths. Rates are $70–$85.

The Pentwater Abbey (231-869-4094; www.pentwaterabbeybb.com), 85 W. 1st, Pentwater. The innkeeper is Karen Way. This place is pure Victorian and was built in 1868. There are many antiques, clawfoot tubs, and hand-carved fireplaces. A full breakfast is served. The three rooms are decorated in a simple style, and the home itself is not a grand lumber baron mansion. It is more representative of how middle class people actually lived in the 19th century. Rates are $85–$125.

Safe Harbor Inn (231-869-2168 or 1-866-407-2577; www.safeharborinn .com), 174 Rutledge, Pentwater. This four-room B&B was built in the 1870s and has a large porch for summer afternoons. The innkeepers are Richard and Suzanne Hutchings. I liked the solid feeling of this basic midwestern house. The rooms have a cottage feel, and the public rooms are done with simple country furniture. Charles Shultz, the creator of the Peanuts comic strip, was a family friend of the Van Plet family, which previously owned the home, and as the family stories are told, the Lucy character was modeled after a family member. I can't vouch for the story, but it is appealing. A full breakfast is served. Rates are $65–$95.

RESORTS In Mears **Dunes Waterfront Resort** (231-873-5500; www .duneswaterfrontresort.com), 5900 Water Rd., Mears. The resort is on Silver Lake and near Lake Michigan sand dunes. There is a pool and hot tub. The rooms are standard motel issue, but many have a balcony and a view of the lake. They have cable TV with premium movie channels and wireless Internet access is available. Rates are $87–$172.

MOTELS Channel Lane Inn (231-869-5766; www.channellaneinn.com), 10 Channel Lake, Pentwater. The inn

THE OLD HAMLIN RESTAURANT

is located on the water, next to Mears State Park and Lake Michigan. This is the place to stay if you want to wander along the beach from your room. The inn is family friendly, with kitchenettes in most of the motel-style rooms. There are some larger suites with two bedrooms. Grills and picnic tables are available. Daily rates are $120–$220; weekly, $700–$1,400.

✳ Where to Eat
EATING OUT ☿ PM Steamers (231-843-9555; www.pmsteamers), 502 Ludington Ave., Ludington. This dockside restaurant caters to the appetites of boaters, with a reliance on steak, seafood, whitefish, and perch. The dishes aren't fancy, but they're designed to please hungry boaters who have spent a day on the water. Entrees are $14–$24.

☿ **Old Hamlin Restaurant** (231-843-4251), 122 W. Ludington Ave., Ludington. This venerable place has been owned and operated by the same family for more than 60 years, and summer visitors and locals keep coming back for the buffet dinners and entrees. Breakfast is served all day, and there's a salad bar and a regular bar.

☿ **Luciano's Ristoranti** (231-843-2244; www.lucianosristoranti.com), 103 W. Ludington Ave., Ludington. This is the place to go for Italian food in Ludington. The food is topnotch, and it's served in an intimate, casual setting. There are pasta dishes, pizza, and Panini-style sandwiches. My favorite was the goat cheese and roasted peppers. There's a good selection of wines. Entrees are $10–$17.

☿ **Jamesport Brewing Co.** (231-845-2522; www.jamesportbrewing .com), 410 James St., Ludington. This brewpub has a menu that is a bit upscale from basic pub fare. There is a cherry bourbon–glazed sirloin, shepherd's pie, Thai peanut noodles, and beef tenderloin. There are burgers and such for lunch. Entrees are $8–$15.

House of Flavors (231-845-5785), 402 W. Ludington Ave., Ludington. This family-style restaurant is an updated version of an old diner and features plenty of comfort foods, including turkey dinners, bacon and egg breakfasts, burgers and fries, and 50 different kinds of ice cream. Prices are $6–$9.

In Pentwater

Y **Gull Landing** (231-869-4215), 412 S. Hancock St., Pentwater. Pub food is available inside and on an outside deck with a view of the marina. Prices are $8–$12.

Y **The Boat House Bar & Grille** (231-869-4588), 5164 W. Monroe. Open daily for lunch and dinner. There is pub food for the boating crowd overlooking Pentwater Lake, mostly pizza and burgers. Prices are $8–$12.

✳ Selective Shopping

GALLERIES **Majestic Art Gallery** (231-843-0369; www.majesticart gallery.com), 115 S. James St., Ludington. Local artist Sharon Mott sells her contemporary originals and limited-edition prints in the shop.

Fish, gardens, and nature are prime subjects.

Melting Sands Glass Studio (231-794-9101; www.meltingsandsglass .com), 5910 E. Ludington Ave., Ludington. Open Tues.–Sat., 10–6. Glass artist Jud Scott makes hand-blown glass art in a studio that's open to the public. There is a small gallery with his items.

The Red Door Gallery (231-392-4709; 310 W. Ludington Ave., Ludington. The gallery carries the works of more than 20 contemporary artists, many of them local and regional. The works are all original pieces, and there is studio space and a classroom.

SHOPS **The Mermaid's Perch** (231-843-6893; www.mermaidsperch.com), 416 S. James, Ludington. The name pretty much says it all—tons of mermaid-related items such as dolls, ornaments, soap, brushes, and numerous other items, including coffee.

ANTIQUES **Cole's Antiques** (231-845-7414; www.colesantiquesvilla .com), 322 W. Ludington Ave., Ludington. Open year-round, various hours. With 4,800 square feet, this place caters to many tastes. It would be the place to go to furnish an "Up North" hunting and fishing lodge. There are antique and collectable duck decoys and many Victorian items that reflect the area's heritage.

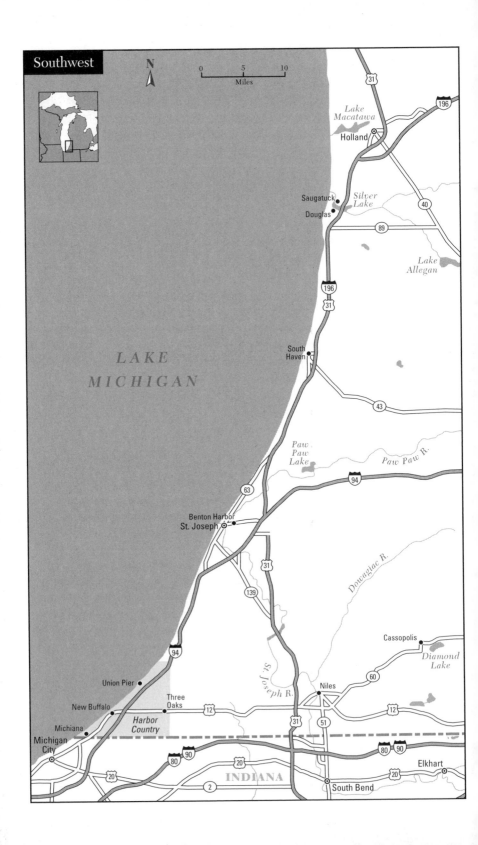

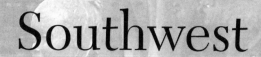

Southwest

SAUGATUCK & DOUGLAS

HOLLAND

HARBOR COUNTRY

SAUGATUCK & DOUGLAS

The Saugatuck/Douglas area is called "the Art Coast" because of its many galleries and sculptures, but there is more to do here than gaze at the works of contemporary artists. There's also Oval Beach, one of the top-rated beaches along the Lake Michigan shoreline, and miles of good bicycling.

It's located about three hours from Chicago and Detroit, making it a popular weekend getaway for urban residents. As with many Great Lakes shoreline communities, it had its historical roots in the lumber industry and later became a tourist town.

Saugatuck is closely aligned with Chicago. The Great Chicago Fire was a boon for the Michigan lumber industry, especially along the Lake Michigan shore. Thousands of board feet of white pine were shipped to Chicago from the Saugatuck area to rebuild the city.

As the lumber boom started to die down about 1910, Chicago artists discovered the area and an artist colony developed. That movement is still in evidence as you stroll down Butler Street in Saugatuck or through nearby Douglas. Some artists maintain studios/galleries where they work and sell their own art.

The town's character retains a Victorian flavor, with many 19th-century homes still standing, some of them serving as B&Bs. Many Michigan lumber towns were destroyed or severely damaged in the early 20th century by forest fires that hit the state at the end of the lumber era. Loggers of the day left the woods filled with debris that easily caught fire. The 1911 fire basically burned the width of the state from Lake Michigan to Lake Huron.

Also, the community has been able to stave off the onslaught of chain restaurants, hotels, and convenience stores. Most lodging is found in small inns and bed & breakfasts.

The city of Holland, 5 miles to the north, serves as the modern business district for the area and offers mall shopping and large grocery stores.

GUIDANCE **Saugatuck and Douglas Convention & Visitors Bureau** (269-857-1701; www.saugatuck.com, 2902 Blue Star Highway, Douglas). Open year-round Mon.–Fri., 9–5. A good walking tour map is available. Saugatuck and Douglas have been gay friendly for many years. There's even a Web site, www.gaysaugatuckdouglas.com.

GETTING THERE *By air:* **Gerald R. Ford International Airport,** Grand Rapids, is 44 miles east, or about 45 minutes. **Detroit Metro Airport** is 220 miles east, and Chicago's O'Hare Airport is 140 miles southwest. Rental cars are available at the airports.

By car: From Grand Rapids, Lansing, Detroit, via I-96, Exit 41. From Chicago, after St. Joseph, take I-96 north toward Holland, Exit 36.

By train: The **Pere Marquette** (1-800-USA-RAIL www.amtrak.com) runs from Chicago to Holland and Grand Rapids seven days a week. There is no direct train to Saugatuck. Car rentals are available in both cities.

WHEN TO COME Because of its proximity to Chicago and Grand Rapids, Saugatuck is a year-round town, but for an uncrowded time try September. By October, fall color travelers are again on the road. April and May can offer some good weather, but April can be cold.

GETTING AROUND In Saugatuck, most places you will want to go are close enough to walk. Bicycling is a great option. An **Interurban** bus service travels between Saugatuck, Douglas, and Saugatuck Township. It's a dial-a-ride service, and travelers must call 269-857-1418 for a ride 30 minutes prior to leaving.

PARKING Parking is a problem during summer months, especially on weekends, so finding a place to stay within walking or bicycling distance of the downtown shopping/dining district is an advantage. But once you find a spot, there are no time restrictions.

VILLAGES Fennville is a town of about 1,400, located 7 miles south of Saugatuck on MI 89. The small community is in the vineyard region of southwestern Michigan. It has wineries that can be toured and a large number of bed & breakfasts for such a small place.

✴ To See & Do

✐ **Saugatuck Center for the Arts** (269-857-2399; www.sc4a.org), 400 Culver St., Saugatuck. Open daily on weekdays. The center sponsors music and arts events during the summer, including a children's film festival.

✐ **Chain Ferry,** Kalamazoo River, Saugatuck. The Kalamazoo River separates Saugatuck, and the ferry is a holdover from the 19th century, carrying passengers back and forth during the warmer months. It is a boat guided by a chain.

✴ Outdoor Activities

SAND DUNES *✐* **Saugatuck Dune Rides** (269-857-2253; www.saugatuck dunerides.com), Saugatuck. Drivers take passengers on dune buggy rides.

CRUISES ⦚ **Saugatuck Boat Cruises** (269-857-4261; www.saugatuckboat cruises.com), 716 Water St., Saugatuck. Open May–Oct. Daily cruises on a paddlewheel boat on the Kalamazoo River. There is also a sunset cruise.

BEACHES **Oval Beach,** Oval Beach Rd., off Park. The Lake Michigan beach is rated one of the top ones in the region. It has white sand and is fairly shallow.

Saugatuck Dunes State Park (269-637-2788). Take Highway 196 to Exit 41, head west 0.25 mile to 64th Street, and then go west on 138 Avenue to the park entrance. The dunes park is for day-use only, and there's no camping. But there are 2.5 miles of shoreline (a picnic area on 300 acres) with a coastal dune system.

✳ Lodging

The Maplewood Hotel (269-857-1773; www.maplewoodhotel.com), 428 Butler St., Saugatuck. The 15 rooms have private baths, air-conditioning, TV sets, and phones, and some have fireplaces and hot tubs. There is a heated pool outside. A continental breakfast is available. Some parts of the structure date to the 1860s, but there have been extensive renovations over the years. Rates are $140–$250.

Landings of Saugatuck Inn & Marina (269-857-7612; www.landings ofsaugatuck.com), 726 Water St., Saugatuck. The inn offers boaters a place to tie up and spend a night in the units and two-bedroom suites, some of which have kitchens. The rooms are cozy and are done more in a B&B style than you'd expect. Rates are $135–$375.

Bayside Inn (269-857-1870; www .baysideinn.net), 618 Water St., Saugatuck. The inn's rooms and suites are decorated in a contemporary style, have a view of the Kalamazoo River, and have private baths, cable TV, and wireless Internet. You can walk to many downtown restaurants and shops. Rates are $80–$325.

Lake Shore Resort (269-857-7121; www.lakeshoreresortsaugatuck.com),

WICKWOOD INN

2885 Lake Shore Dr., Saugatuck. The 30-room resort is within walking distance of Lake Michigan and offers contemporary rooms to a mostly adult crowd. Children under 12 are not accepted. It's out of the hustle and bustle of downtown and is a good place to stay if you're looking to spend much of your time at the beach or bicycling. The rooms have air-conditioning, cable TV, and refrigerators. Rates are $80–$190.

BED & BREAKFASTS Wickwood Inn (269-857-1552; www.wickwoodinn .com), 510 Butler, Saugatuck. The 11 rooms are lushly decorated, each with its own theme, ranging from Adirondack to English cottage style and none have telephones or TV sets. Much time is spent in the living room, library, game room, and gazebo. There is also a restaurant (see *Dining Out*). Rates are $175–$365.

The Ivy Inn (269-857-4643; www .ivy-inn.com), 421 Water St. Saugatuck. The former boardinghouse, built in the 1890s for workmen of the day, is now a B&B with six rooms. It is located in the heart of the gallery district and is across the street from the Kalamazoo River. The innkeepers, Linda and Louie Brooks, are longtime Saugatuck residents. The rooms are comfortable but on the sparse side. My favorite room was one of the smaller ones with a balcony. The library is well-stocked and is pleasantly restored, but the real delight is an ivy-covered back porch that provides a cool, relaxing time on a hot summer afternoon. A garden patio offers a quiet spot. Rates are $110–$145.

Saugatuck's Victorian Inn (269-857-6043; www.vicinn-mi.com), 447

Butler St., Saugatuck. The inn is in the heart of downtown, and within walking distance of the Kalamazoo River. The Victorian home has been restored and all rooms have private baths and air-conditioning. The front porch is large and covered and is a nice place to spend an afternoon. Rates are $110–$225.

Beechwood Manor Inn (269-857-1587; www.beechwoodmanorinn .com), 736 Pleasant St., Saugatuck. The inn, a 19th-century home, offers three rooms and a cottage. The rooms are large and have private baths, cable TV, and wireless Internet. The cottage has three bedrooms and a modern contemporary kitchen. Rates are $150–$225.

The Belvedere Inn & Restaurant (269-857-7557; www.thebelvedere inn.com), 3656 63rd St., Saugatuck. There are 12 rooms and suites in the inn, which also has a restaurant (see *Dining Out*). Some rooms have fireplaces, and each is decorated in a different style. A full breakfast is served. The inn was a summer home, built in the 1920s by a wealthy Chicago family. It was renovated in 1995. The grounds were a fruit farm. The innkeepers are Shaun Glynn, who serves as the chef, and Pete Ta. Rates are $135–$200.

▼ **The Kirby House** (269-857-2904; www.kirbyhouse.com), 294 Center St., Saugatuck. The 1890 Queen Anne–style B&B is gay owned and straight friendly, as the owners say, and is a registered historic site. The home has oak woodwork, tall ceilings, a wraparound porch, and five fireplaces. The rooms have wireless Internet, and a pool and hot tub are outside. Rates are $100–$190.

✳ Where to Eat

DINING OUT ♈ **Marro's Italian Restaurant** (269-857-4248; www.marrosrestaurant.com), 147 Water St. Open daily for lunch and dinner. All you have to do to find this place is follow the crowd, which starts lining up at this woodsy-style restaurant late in the afternoon. It's a big place inside and has a menu to match. There are pasta and Italian dishes, along with steaks, seafood, and pizza. Entrees are $18–$34.

♈ **Belvedere Inn & Restaurant** (269-857-5777; www.thebelevedereinn.com), 3656 63rd St., Saugatuck. Open daily for breakfast, lunch, and dinner, May–Dec. Reservations are recommended. There aren't many places that offer four-course dinners these days, but this is one. The entrees range from châteaubriand for two to lamb, chicken, seafood, and a few pasta dishes. Dessert includes gelato, chocolate cheesecake, and a French-style apple pie. The inn also offers rooms (see *Lodging*). Prices are $40–$50.

♈ **The Dining Room at Clear-**

PUMPERNICKEL'S EATERY

brook (269-857-2000; www.clearbrookdining.com), 6494 Clearbrook Dr., Saugatuck. Open daily for dinner in summer and weekends in the off-season. Closed mid-Feb.–mid-April. This is white-linen, country-club dining at a golf course (see *Golfing*, What's Where in Michigan). The focus is on traditional meals and the menu is filled with solid offerings such as Angus beef, walleye, salmon, lamb, and chicken. The grillroom offers steaks, chicken, ribs, and fish dishes. Dining room entrees run $30–$45; grillroom entrees run $12–$18.

EATING OUT ♈ **Pumpernickel's Eatery** (269-857-1196; www.pumpernickelssaugatuck.com), 202 Butler St., Saugatuck. Open daily for breakfast, lunch, and dinner. From the outside, this looks more like a tavern than a dining establishment. There are burgers and sandwiches for lunch, but there's also a small, well-selected dinner menu that includes lake perch, salmon, chicken, veal, and pasta. Entrees are $11–$14.

♈ **The White House Bistro** (269-857-3240; www.whitehousebistro.com), 149 Griffith St., Saugatuck. Open daily for lunch and dinner. This place is a block off the main drag, but it's worth the effort to find it. The menu is eclectic, with a lot of Greek foods and lamb, but there is American food, too. The names for the dishes are amusing. There's the Jackie 'O' Greek, a salad and a Spiro Agnew gyro sandwich. For dinner there is perch, steak, pasta, and chicken, which is served with rice and minted peas. Entrees are $17–$35.

♈ **Restaurant Toulouse** (269-857-1561; www.restauranttoulouse.com), 248 Culver St., Saugatuck. Open daily. The menu is French, country style, and features pan-seared duck, scallops coquilles, pork, chicken, and salmon. The wine list is extensive for such a small place. There is a pleasant outside patio for dining. Entrees are $18–$22.

Ⓨ **Coral Gables Restaurant** (269-857-2162; www.coralgablessaugatuck .com), 220 Water St., Saugatuck. Open daily for lunch and dinner. Some places grow stale with age, and this is one of them. The entertainment complex has been around for a long time, and the décor and menu are in need of updating. The menu has some pretty basic items—Great Lakes fish, chicken, some pasta, pork chops, ribs, and steaks—but no innovative dishes. Entertainment is provided on many summer weekends, and there's a deck on the Kalamazoo River where you can dine. Entrees are $11–$20.

Ⓨ **Butler Restaurant** (269-857-3501; www.thebutlerrestaurant.com), 40 Butler St., Saugatuck. This place has been around since 1961 and for good reason: The large menu ranges from burgers to ribs and seafood and the restaurant is located right on the water. The building has been used as a restaurant since it opened in 1882. It was next to the rail terminal that brought visitors from Chicago. There is an outside patio bar during warmer months. Entrees are $10–$15.

Ⓨ **Chequers of Saugatuck** (269-857-1868; www.chequersofsaugatuck .com), 220 Culver St., Saugatuck. Open daily for lunch and dinner. This English-style pub has a good selection of beers and some pub food, including Welsh rarebit, fish and chips, and shepherd's pie. Prices are $8–$10.

✳ Selective Shopping

Saugatuck became an art colony for Chicago artists in the late 19th century, and there are still many studio galleries. Most galleries are open daily May–Sept. Call for winter hours.

Bruce Baughman Studio & Gallery (269-857-1299; www.bruce baughmangallery.com), 241 Butler St., Saugatuck. The artist is at work here many days, using his vivid colors in a lot of portrait work.

James Brandess Studios & Gallery (269-857-1937; www.jamesbrandess .com), 238 Butler St., Saugatuck. The artist paints many local landscapes and is at work in the studio many days. The works are easily recognizable.

Luoma Art Gallery (269-857-7428; www.rtbyluoma.com), 48 Center St., Douglas. Contemporary artwork with a focus on nature is on display, done by Scott Luoma and his mother, Joan.

Marcia Perry's Ark Gallery & Sculpture Studio (269-857-4210; www.marciaperry-ark.com), 6248 Blue Star Hwy., Saugatuck. Marcia Perry displays contemporary wood sculptures and other works.

Thimgan Hayden Studio & Gallery (269-857-8494; www .thimganhayden.com), 36 Center St., Douglas. The classical painter does portraits, figures, landscape, and still life, and works in oils.

In Fennville
Blue Coast Artists (269-236-9260; www.bluecoastartists.com), 6691 120th Ave., Fennville. The gallery houses the works of six local artists who work in various mediums, including pottery, painting, wood, and glass.

SPECIALTY SHOPS **Fenn Valley Winery** (269-857-5170; fenn valley.com), 310 Butler St., Saugatuck. Stop by and try some of the local wine in this tasting and retail shop.

Tabor Hill Wine Port (269-857-4859; taborhill.com), 214 Butler St., Saugatuck. Local Tabor Hill wines can be tasted here, and there are cases of wine for sale.

International Home (269-857-2805; www.internationalhomesaugatuck .com), 360 Water St., Saugatuck. This home shop has quirky glassware and other eclectic house wares.

✳ Special Events

Mid-June **Annual Waterfront Film Festival.** Free outdoor screenings and a street festival.

Late June **Saugatuck Venetian Festival** (www.venetianfestival.com). Two days of events along the Kalamazoo River, where decorated boats sail by. There is an arts fair, food, and fireworks.

HOLLAND

This city of about 35,000 was founded by Dutch Calvinist separatists in 1847 under the leadership of Dr. Albertus van Raalte, and it still holds onto its Dutch heritage, with a spring tulip festival that attracts thousands, a small parochial college (Hope), and many churches—170 at last count. The community has been visited on several occasions by members of the royal family of the Netherlands, the last time in 1982.

GUIDANCE **Holland Area Chamber of Commerce** (616-392-2389; holland chamber.org), 272 E. 8th St., Holland. Open daily on weekdays.

TO SEE & DO *See Saugatuck & Douglas.*

✴ Lodging

Most lodging in Holland is in chain hotels/motels. Saugatuck is 7 miles south of Holland and has other options (see Saugatuck).

BED & BREAKFASTS **Dutch Colonial Inn** (616-396-3664; www.dutch colonialinn.com), 560 Central Ave., Holland. The home, built in 1928, has five guest rooms and suites, some with fireplaces and hot tubs. Breakfast features Dutch cooking, such as pig-in-the-blanket, and fresh baked goods. Rates are $109–$169.

✴ Where to Eat

DINING OUT The Saugatuck & Douglas area, 7 miles south of Holland, offers more fine-dining establishments than Holland (see Saugatuck).

EATING OUT ⵟ **Beechwood Inn** (616-396-2355; www.bwoodinn.com), 380 Douglas Ave., Holland. This outdoorsy place is a bit up from a tavern, and offers whitefish, steak, ribs, and chicken, as well as the normal pub fare for lunch. Entrees are $10–$17.

ⵟ **New Holland Brewing Company** (616-355-6422; www.newhollandbrew .com), 66 E. 8th St., Holland. The brewpub brews up a storm of different beers and offers pub food in its tavern. Prices are around $9. There is a children's menu.

ⵟ **Boatwerks Waterfront Restaurant** (616-396-0600; www.boatwerks restaurant.com), 216 Van Raalte Ave., Holland. Open daily for lunch and dinner. There's pub food for lunch and entrees for dinner in this casual dining establishment with a view of the lake. The menu runs from lake perch to salmon, chicken, and steak. Entrees are $14–$20.

✳ Special Events

Early May **Holland Tulip Festival**

(616-396-4221; www.tuliptime.com). The local Dutch Americans show up in their wooden shoes to scrub the streets for the week-long event, which attracts thousands who come to see the tulips bloom. The event includes parades, entertainment, klompen dancing, and concerts.

HARBOR COUNTRY

The eight communities along Lake Michigan south of Benton Harbor/St. Joseph are collectively called Harbor Country. They are about a two-hour drive from Chicago, making it weekend country for Windy City residents.

Harbor Country has long been tied to Chicago; its fledgling tourist industry started in the 1890s when a local businessman built a resort hotel for people traveling to the 1893 Chicago Exposition. Not long after, Chicagoans starting coming by train and later by car on US 12 to rent small cabins and cottages near the lakeshore. Even during the Great Depression, people kept coming to the generally rural communities. One of those was Chicago poet Carl Sandberg, who had a small goat farm in the region.

These days second-home construction is booming. The Harbor Country communities of Michiana, New Buffalo, Lakeside, Sawyer, Grand Beach, Three Oaks, Union Pier, and Harbert are now a second home to many Chicagoland families, and there are many bed & breakfasts and older inns catering to those folks.

New Buffalo, with about 2,700 residents, is the largest of the eight communities, and it has more established services available.

GUIDANCE **Harbor Country Chamber of Commerce** (269-469-5409; www .harborcountry.org), 530 S. Whittaker St., New Buffalo. Open Mon.–Fri. 9–5 and Sat.–Sun. 10–3. The chamber is a good source of area maps, lodging ideas, and restaurant information. It also provides a free guide to the area.

GETTING THERE *By car:* The Harbor Country communities start at the Indiana state line and are accessible from various exits off I-94. A good alternative route is to get off the freeway at New Buffalo and follow the Red Arrow Highway, which was the first artery to take travelers from Chicago to the area in the 1920s. It goes through the heart of the towns.

By air: It's closer to Chicago than it is to most Michigan airports. Try **O'Hare** or **Midway.**

By train: There is daily **Amtrak** (1-800-USA-RAIL; www.Amtrak.com) service from Chicago to St. Joseph, 410½ Vine, via the **Pere Marquette,** which runs to Grand Rapids.

MEDICAL EMERGENCIES Call 911.

MEDIA *Lake Magazine* (1-877-362-8582; www.lakemagazine.com), 701 State St., LaPorte, IN 46350. The slick, lush, color publication defines the lifestyle of Harbor Country and gives you a peak inside the better homes in the region.

✳ To See & Do

BEACHES Warren Dunes State Park (269-426-4013; www.michigan.gov/dnr), 12032 Red Arrow Hwy., Sawyer. Open year-round. The prime attraction in the 1,952-acre park is the sand dunes on Lake Michigan. There are 3 miles of shoreline. Camping is available in 182 modern campsites and 36 rustic ones. Six miles of hiking trails are used for cross-country skiing in winter.

Grand Mere State Park (269-426-4013; www.michigan.gov/dnr), Thornton Dr., Stevensville. The 1,000-acre park has more than 1 mile of Lake Michigan beach, along with sand dunes to climb and hiking trails. There are also inland lakes open to fishing.

New Buffalo Park (269-469-1522), Whittaker St., New Buffalo. The beach is within walking distance of downtown, and there are rest rooms and a recreation area for children.

GREEN SPACE Harbert Road Nature Preserve (269-469-1676), Harbert Rd., Harbert. The 90-acre preserve offers hiking, walking, bicycling, and cross-country skiing. There are opportunities for wildlife-watching and plant study.

U-PICK FARMS Harbor Country is part of Michigan's fruit-growing region, and there are numerous opportunities to pick berries and vegetables in-season. There are about 25 farms. For a good list, click on www.harborcountry.org/upick/.

A LAKE MICHIGAN BEACH

.com), 1 Oak St., Three Oaks. Open most days 9–5; call ahead in winter. Serious
cyclists and others should stop here to see the antique bicycles and get information on many routes before they ride in the area. The museum is in an old train
depot; the Three Oaks Spokes Club is centered here and is active in the region.
The Apple Cider Century, a cycling event, is based out of the museum and held
in late Sept. Admission is free.

BOATING **New Buffalo Public Boat Launch** (269-469-1522), North Whittaker
St., New Buffalo. Eight ramps provide access to the Galien River and Lake
Michigan.

Oselka's Snug Harbor (269-469-2600), 514 Oselka Dr., New Buffalo. The private marina offers dockage and fuel.

FISHING Lake Michigan is a hotbed for salmon fishing, and there are many
charter boat operations, mostly out of St. Joseph. The **Michigan Charter Boat
Association** (1-800-MCBA-971; www.micharterboats.com) maintains a listing of
captains who work out of the area. Click on their Web site for a complete listing.

GOLFING **Grand Beach Golf Course** (269-469-4888; www.grandbeach.org),
48200 Perkins Blvd., New Buffalo. A 9-hole course with a 66.2 rating.

Whittaker Woods Golf Community (269-469-3400; www.golfwhittaker.com),
12578 Wilson Rd., New Buffalo. An 18-hole, par-72 course between Grand
Beach and Union Pier.

✳ Lodging

⊗ **Sans Souci Euro Inn & Cottages** (269-756-3141; www.sans
-souci.com), 19265 S. Lakeside Rd.,
New Buffalo. There are suites, cottages, and vacation homes on 50 acres
near Lake Michigan. Some have up to
four bedrooms. There is Internet
access and a nature trail. Rates are
$225–$500.

Whitechapel Inn (269-586-2301;
www.whitechapelin.com), 18 W. Mer-
chant St., New Buffalo. The 10-room
inn is located near downtown New
Buffalo, close to shopping. Many of
the rooms have different color
themes, and they are clean, almost
sparse. Rates are $118–$275.

Inn at Union Pier B&B (269-469-
4700; www.lanierbb.com), 9708

Berrien St., Union Pier. The inn has
13 rooms and a guest cottage, all with
private bathrooms and furnished with
many antiques. Some have private
balconies and Swedish fireplaces. It's a
short distance to Lake Michigan.
Rates are $185–$210.

**Pine Garth Inn Villa & Guest Hous-
es** (269-469-1641; www.pinegarth.com),
15790 Lakeshore Rd., Union Pier. The
restored summer estate overlooks Lake
Michigan and has seven rooms, many
with lake views. There are also five cottages that sleep four to six and have
fireplaces and hot tubs. There's a private beach. Rates are $175–$250; cottages mostly rent by the week.

Pumpernickel Inn (269-469-1200;
www.pumpernickelinn.com), 16090

Red Arrow Hwy., Union Pier. The European B&B has five rooms and suites. Two rooms don't have baths. Each room has a different color, and there's a refreshing Euro feel to them, instead of the traditional Victorian look. An attached small café serves breakfast, lunch, and dinner. Rates are $40–$95.

Sandpiper Inn (269-469-1146; www .sandpiper.inn.net), 16136 Lakeview Ave., Union Pier. The Georgian-style, nine-room inn overlooks Lake Michigan, and the rooms have private baths, hot tubs, TV, phones, and private decks. A hot breakfast is served. The porches on the first and second levels are great gathering places. Rates are $175–$275.

Warren Woods Inn (1-800-358-4754; www.warrenwoodsinn.com), 15506 Red Arrow Highway, Union Pier. The inn was built in 1863 and has been extensively restored, and the nine rooms have private baths, hot tubs, and fireplaces. There's also a three-bedroom cottage. Lake Michigan is nearby.

✳ Where to Eat

DINING OUT All establishments are open daily unless otherwise noted.

Y **Hannah's Restaurant** (269-469-1440; www.hannahsrestaurant.com), 115 S. Whittaker St., New Buffalo. Open for lunch and dinner. The old house is a perfect place for this almost Chicago-style restaurant, which serves a lot of thick steaks, prime ribs, pork chops, Wiener schnitzel, seafood, and ribs. Entrees are $15–$20.

Y **Timothy's Restaurant** (269-469-0900), 16220 Lake Shore Rd., Union Pier. The coconut/macadamia nut–crusted grouper here is a dish not often found in Michigan. They also have some interesting takes on whitefish, steak, lamb, and duck. The building is a 1920s inn near Lake Michigan. The wine choices are lim-

HANNAH'S RESTAURANT IN NEW BUFFALO

A HOME ON LAKE MICHIGAN

ited, but intelligent. Entrees are
$23–$30.

Ⓨ **Bistro on the Boulevard** (269-
883-6600; www.theboulevardinn
.com), 521 Lake Blvd., St. Joseph.
Open for breakfast, lunch, and dinner.
They have done some interesting
things with walleye and whitefish, and
also have tweaked up some comfort
foods such as meat loaf and chicken.
There is a large wine list and various
types of martinis. A pub menu is
available. Entrees are $17–$26.

EATING OUT Ⓨ **Beachwood Restaurant** (269-469-5300), 197347 W. US
12, New Buffalo. Open for dinner.
The offerings are ribs, steak, liver,
pork cops, lamb, chicken, and pasta in
this upscale tavern near the lake.
Entrees are $15–$25.

Ⓨ **Redamak's Restaurant** (269-469-
4522), 616 E. Buffalo St., New Buffalo. Open for lunch and dinner. The
burgers have been bringing folks back
here for more than 30 years. There
are also soups and dinners in a basket,
including fried fish, clams, and
shrimp. Prices are $6–$8.

Pumpernickel Inn (269-469-1200;
www.pumpernickelinn.com), 16090

Red Arrow Hwy., Union Pier. The
B&B (see *Lodging*) has a small café
serving lunch and dinner. Pastas,
chicken, meat loaf, and ribs are on
this limited, but well-thought-out
menu. Entrees are $8–$18.

Rosie's (269-469-4382), 128 N. Whittaker St., New Buffalo. This is the
place to go for sausage gravy and other
American breakfast standards. It's
where the locals eat. Prices are $6–$8.

✳ Selective Shopping

The shops are open year-round and
daily unless otherwise noted.

Courtyard Gallery (269-469-4110),
813 E. Buffalo St., New Buffalo. Call
first on Sunday. The gallery features
original contemporary art, sculpture,
ceramics, and glass, much of it done
by regional artists.

Judith Racht Gallery (269-469-
1080), 13707 Prairie Rd., Harbert.
Contemporary art, with special shows
for various artists. There are also special shows for folk art, furniture, and
quilts.

Center of the World Woodshop
(269-469-5687; www.centerofthe
world.net), 13400 Red Arrow Hwy.,

Harbert. The wooden furniture is locally made. Pieces are for sale, and they also take custom orders.

Michigan Thyme Shops & Café (269-469-3470), 107 N. Whittaker St., New Buffalo. You'll fine women's boutique clothing, beauty aids, and specialty food items. There is also jewelry and some men's clothing.

WINE TASTING St. Julian Wine Tasting Room (269-469-3150), 9145 Union Pier Rd., Union Pier. Open daily, 10–6. The winery, located in Paw Paw, is Michigan's oldest and is family owned.

ANTIQUES STORES Most of the shops are open daily spring through fall. Call for winter hours.

Dunes Antique Center (269-426-4043), 12825 Red Arrow Hwy., Sawyer. You could spend a lot of time looking here. There is original artwork, prints, furniture, pottery, lighting, and other items.

Lakeside Antiques (269-469-4467), 14876 Red Arrow Hwy., Lakeside. There are three buildings with furniture, accessories, and artworks. You could lose a whole day in this place, just looking.

Jenny's Shop (269-756-7219), 9 N. Elm St., Three Oaks. There are antiques and collectibles, along with some furniture.

✳ Special Events

Mid-August **Annual Lakefront Arts Festival** (www.lubeznikcenter .org), Lubeznik Center for the Arts, Michigan City, Ind.

Early September **SawyerFest** (www.harborcountry.org). Arts and crafts and sidewalk sales.

Northwest

GRAND TRAVERSE REGION

LITTLE TRAVERSE BAY REGION

NORTHWEST

S tretching from the Lake Michigan coastline to Lake Huron is an area generally called "Up North" by most state residents. It is summer-cottage country
for many southern Michigan residents, who make the trek on weekends to their
second homes on the Great Lakes, smaller inland lakes, and rivers and streams.

Most of the communities were once lumber-mill towns and ports from which
white pine was shipped around the Great Lakes, much of it to rebuild Chicago
after its fire of 1871. Many have elegant Victorian homes constructed by lumber
barons, now converted to bed & breakfasts.

Weekenders are attracted to the beaches, while outdoors people fish the
waters of Lakes Huron and Michigan for steelhead, salmon, and trout. The interior, much of it public forestland, attracts anglers, campers, and hunters.

The Grand Traverse and Little Traverse Bay regions in the northwest portion
of the Lower Peninsula attract the most visitors, and they have trendy restaurants, shops, and some large resorts. In the winter, downhill skiing brings many
to those regions. You'll find better restaurants and accommodations in the Traverse City and Petoskey regions, while in the interiors you'll find basic mom-
and-pop motels and North Woods taverns.

Gaylord in the central highlands is a golfing center, and it has a good number
of resorts. Meanwhile, Grayling, just south of Gaylord, is the hot spot for fly
anglers who are attracted to the Manistee and Au Sable rivers.

While streams of vacationers head for the Grand Traverse region, northeastern Michigan is relatively quiet and receives fewer visitors. That side of the state,
along Lake Huron, bills itself as the "Sunrise Side," and it's a good value for
budget-conscious travelers and those seeking more solitude.

GRAND TRAVERSE REGION
TRAVERSE CITY; LEELANAU PENINSULA;
GLEN ARBOR & EMPIRE; FRANKFORT

TRAVERSE CITY

Traverse City is the unofficial capital of northern Michigan, providing shopping, entertainment, dining, and professional services to the region. But while it is a bustling commercial hub, it's also a prime tourist destination that manages to blend an urban environment with outdoor recreation in the city limits. Trendy shops, art galleries, coffee houses, restaurants, antiques shops, and brewpubs line the streets downtown, which is a short walk from the Grand Traverse Bay shoreline's parks and public beaches. This blend of upscale amenities with a view of the bay and time on the beach make Traverse City a perfect spot for a vacation, weekend getaway, or a retirement home.

Lodging is diverse. Several lakefront resorts provide high-end rooms and suites, and mom-and-pop motels provide basic accommodations, many across from the beach. There's also Traverse City State Park, which offers space for RV or tent camping. Restaurants range from family style to high end, and most are a stone's throw from the water.

The city's location makes it a great home base from which to explore Old Mission Peninsula, north on MI 37, which is home to wineries and some of the most expensive lakefront property on the Great Lakes; Leelanau County, where the three lovely resort towns of Suttons Bay, Leland, and Northport are located; and the Sleeping Bear Dunes National Lakeshore.

The downtown thrives on its Victorian roots, with commercial buildings and older homes receiving extensive renovations. City planners have helped preserve the original architecture on Main Street and have blended in new brick buildings that don't look out of place.

Within 30 minutes of town you can play golf at The Bear, designed by Jack Nicholas; wander 35 miles of Lake Michigan beach at the Sleeping Bear Dunes; take a bike tour through the wine country and cherry orchards of Old Mission Peninsula; trout fish on the Boardman River; wander through the shops of Suttons Bay; or just have a day at the beach in Traverse City.

At night you can stay at the Park Place Hotel, with a view of the bay, and have dinner in a fine restaurant. And if there's time, you can catch an evening concert

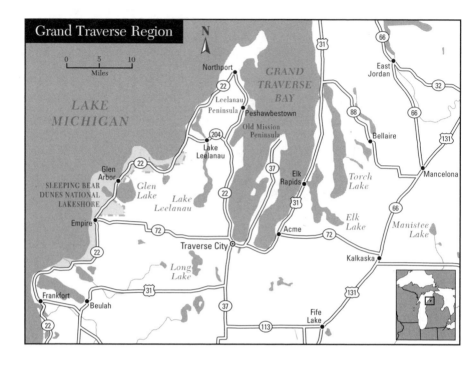

at the Interlochen Center for the Arts, about 30 minutes south of Traverse City. The next day may find you on a sailing trip around Traverse Bay on one of the schooners or taking one of the wine tours in Leelanau or Old Mission Peninsula.

This mixture of urban amenities and outdoor activities didn't come about by accident. Traverse City has been attuned to tourism for more than 100 years. Like most northern Michigan lakeside communities, Traverse City was first a fur-trading outpost in the 1700s. But by the 1850s, the beaver hat had lost its allure and the white pine and hardwood forests attracted logging operations, which made use of Traverse City's port to ship lumber. Commercial fishing was also a big industry in the 19th century, but that has dwindled, although there is at least one boat still in operation, Leland—Carlson Fisheries.

By 1910, most of the forests were cut and the lakes overfished. Agriculture overtook logging, with cherries taking center stage because of the climate. The region now produces more than half of the tart cherries grown in the U.S. Wine-making came to the region in the 1960s.

But something else had happened during the 19th century. Tourists from Chicago started coming via steamships and on railroads during the summer months to stay at resort hotels, and Traverse City residents were among the first in the Great Lakes to see the opportunity. Many of those visiting Traverse City in the 1870s stayed at the Campbell House, which evolved into the Park Place, which still caters to travelers.

GUIDANCE **Traverse City Chamber of Commerce** (231-947-5075; www .tcchamber.org), 202 East Grandview Parkway, Traverse City. Open Mon.–Fri.,

9–5. The chamber publishes an online newsletter about the Grand Traverse Region at www.yourplacegrandtraverse.org. The chamber has basic information about the community, but for travel information contact the **Traverse City Convention & Visitors Bureau** (1-800-940-1120 or 231-947-1120, visitor information 1-800-872-8377; www.mytraversecity.com), 101 W. Grandview Parkway, Traverse City. Open 9–5 weekdays and 10–2 weekends. They offer good information on the entire region, including wine tours of local vineyards.

MEDIA *Traverse City Record Eagle* (231-946-2000; www.record-eagle.com), published daily for news about events in Traverse City and the region. *Traverse Magazine* (231-941-8174; www.traversemagazine.com) is a lush, color monthly publication that lists plenty of events in the Grand Traverse region. The lifestyle coverage gives you a glimpse inside the luxury homes along the Michigan shoreline and a taste of the best dining in the region.

GETTING THERE *By car:* There are no freeways in the Grand Traverse area. The best access from southern Michigan is via I-75 to Grayling, and MI 72 to Traverse City. US 131 is the other major route, running south of Grand Rapids. US 31 roughly follows the Lake Michigan coast and is a pleasant drive if you're not in a hurry. Traverse City is about 4½ hours from Detroit and about 3½ hours from Grand Rapids.

By air: **Cherry Capital Airport** (231- 947-2250; www.tvcairport.com), 727 Fly Don't Drive, Traverse City. This is the prime northern Michigan airport, with regular service to Minneapolis, Chicago, and Detroit. There is seasonal service from Cincinnati, Atlanta, and New York. The carriers are: Northwest Airlines, Northwest Airlink, American Eagle, United Express, and Delta. Rental cars are available at the airport.

THE BOARDMAN RIVER IN TRAVERSE CITY

GETTING AROUND The city is bike friendly, with numerous racks and designated cycling lanes. There is a decent pathway along Grand Traverse Bay.

PARKING There are several parking structures in downtown Traverse City, along with metered street parking. July–Aug. are difficult months, but there are few problems at other times of year.

MEDICAL EMERGENCY Munson Medical Center (231-935-5000), 550 Munson Ave., Traverse City. A full-service emergency room and hospital serving much of northern Michigan. Call 911.

✳ To See & Do

✇ **Grand Traverse Bay.** Much of the lakeshore along the bay is parkland and public beach. It is the main attraction in downtown Traverse City.

✇ **Interlochen Center for the Arts** (231-276-7200; www.interlochen.org), Interlochen, 15 miles from Traverse City. The center is a fine-arts boarding high school that in the summer runs camps and holds concerts and other fine-arts events on its 1,200-acre campus. School alumni include TV newsman Mike Wallace. Recent performers during summer were The Wailin' Jennys, Peter Frampton, Lyle Lovett, and K. D. Lang. There are also summer arts camps for students and arts instruction for adults.

✇ **Tall Ship *Manitou*** (231-941-2000; www.tallshipsailing.com), 13390 SW Bay Shore Dr., Traverse City. There are daily windjammer cruises on Grand Traverse Bay. In the evening, the ship is used as a bed & breakfast. Cruise rates are $20–$40; B&B rates are $200 per couple.

✇ **The Maritime Heritage Alliance** (231-946-2647; www.mhatc.net), 322 Sixth St., Traverse City. Open May–Oct; call for hours. The group owns two replicas of Great Lakes sailing vessels, which were constructed by volunteers using traditional boat-building methods. The 92-foot schooner *Madeline* is a replica of a schooner that served as Traverse City's first school. The *Welcome* is a 55-foot replica of a British armed sloop. Volunteers conduct tours when the vessels are in port.

City Opera House (231-941-8082; www.cityoperahouse.org), 106 E. Front St., Traverse City. The opera house was built in 1891 and used for performances until 1920. It has been restored and is used for performances again, along with meetings, dances, and other events.

✇ **Music House Museum** (231-938-9300), 7377 US 31, Acme. Open daily May–Dec. The museum has an extensive collection of rare automatic musical instruments, and there are demonstrations of how they work. Admission is $10 for adults and $3 for children.

CLASSES ✇ **Inland Seas Association** (231-271-3077; www.greatlakeseducation .org), P.O. Box 218, Suttons Bay. Open June–Aug. The association offers floating classes on the two-masted schooner, *Inland Seas,* and the sloop, *Liberty.* The vessels sail Grand Traverse Bay with adults and children for the ecology and science classes.

BEACHES Most of the Grand Traverse Bay lakefront downtown is a free public beach. Parking is in lots along US 31; some have meters (see *Traverse City State Park*).

LAKE FISHING Grand Traverse Bay offers fishing for salmon and trout. There are about a dozen charter-fishing boat services. Go to www.mytraversecity .com/fishing/ for more information.

BICYCLING Traverse City is a bicycle-friendly town, with marked lanes. There is a pathway along the lakefront. Better cycling can be found on county roads and in Leelanau County (see Leelanau County). MI 37 in Old Mission Peninsula is another destination. There is little traffic and the roads take a rider through the cherry orchards and grape vineyards.

FLY-FISHING The Boardman and Manistee rivers near Traverse City offer top trout fishing possibilities. A good resource is *Trout Streams of Michigan,* by Bob Linsenman and Steve Nevala (The Countryman Press).

The Northern Angler (231-933-4730; www.thenorthernangler.com), 312 S. Union, Traverse City. The shop has all the gear and flies you need to fish the local rivers. Kirk Novak, the owner, can also turn you on to local conditions, fishing spots, and local guides.

Streamside Orvis (231-933-9300; www.streamsideorvis.com), 223 E. Front St., Traverse City. Dave Leonhard is one of the best fly-casting teachers in Michigan, and he offers fly-fishing schools. The Orvis shop has fly-fishing gear, along with clothing.

GOLFING There are 19 golf courses in the Traverse City area. Here is a sampling. (A complete listing of courses can be found at www.mytraversecity.com.)

The Bear at Grand Traverse Resort and Spa (231-938-2100; www.grand traverseresort.com), Acme. The 18-hole course is one of the most well known in northern Michigan. It hosts the Michigan Open.

The Leelanau Club at Bahle Farms (231-271-2020; www.leelanauclub.com), Otto Rd., Suttons Bay. The 18-hole course has views of Suttons Bay.

Champion Hill (231-882-9200; www.championhill.com), 510 Marshall Rd., Beulah. An 18-hole course with views of Lake Michigan.

Elmbrook Golf Course (231-946-9180; www.elmbrookgolf.com), 1750 Townline Rd., Traverse City. An 18-hole course, the oldest in Traverse City.

CANOEING & KAYAKING Grand Traverse Bay is sheltered enough to offer good paddling. You might try the leeward side of the Leelanau Peninsula, although much of the shoreline is private property.

Alvian's Canoe and Boat Livery (231-276-9514), 6470 Betsie River Rd., Interlochen. Float trips on the Betsie River take one to four hours, beginner to intermediate.

Chippewa Landing Canoe Livery (231-824-3627), Manton. Manistee River float trips, two hours to 10 days.

Ranch Rudolf (231-325-5622), 6481 Brownbridge Rd., Traverse City. (See *Ranch Rudolf, Lodging.*) Short trips on the Boardman River.

GRAND TRAVERSE WINE TOURS

Michigan isn't Napa Valley, but the state's wines have gained respect since the late 1960s when European-style grapes were first introduced to the region. There are 20 wineries in the Grand Traverse area and most offer tours and tasting. The wine is also sold at the respective vineyards.

There are seven wineries on the Old Mission Peninsula, which juts into Lake Michigan from Traverse City. All have wine-tasting rooms, and a tour makes a good afternoon trip. Most are open year-round, Mon.–Sat., but call ahead during colder months. All are on or near MI 37, the only major road on the peninsula: **Black Star Farms** (231-271-4970; www.blackstarfarms .com), 360 McKinley Rd.; **Bowers Harbor Vineyards** (231-223-7615; www.bowersharbor.com), 2896 Bowers Harbor Rd.; **Brys Estate Vineyard and Winery** (231-223-9303; www.brysestate.com), 3309 Blue Water Rd.; **Chateau Chantal** (231-223-4110; www.chateauchantal.com), 15900 Rue de Vi; **Chateau Grand Traverse** (231-223-7355; www.cgtwines.com), 12239 Center Rd.; **Left Foot Charley** (1-800-515-1081; www.leftfootcharley.com), 806 Red Dr.; **Peninsula Cellars** (231-933-9787; www.peninsulacellars.com), 11480 Center Rd.

The Leelanau Peninsula has 13 wineries that can be toured. Most are open year-round, Mon.–Sat., but call ahead in winter. For a wine trail map to the Leelanau, click on www.lpwines.com. They are: **Bel Lago** (231-228-4800; www.bellago.com), 6530 S. Lake Shore Dr., Cedar; **Black Star Farms** (231-944-1270; www.blackstarfarms.com), 10844 E. Revold Rd., Suttons Bay; **Chateau De Leelanau** (231-271-8888; www.chateaudeleelanau.com), 5028 SW Bayshore Dr., Suttons Bay; **Chateau Fontaine** (231-256-0000; www.chateaufontaine.com), 2290 S. French Rd., Lake Leelanau; **Cherry Republic** (231-334-3150), 6026 S. Lake St., Glenn Arbor; **Ciccone** (231-271-5553; www.cicconevineyards.com), 10343 E. Hilltop Rd., Suttons Bay; **Gill's Pier** (231-256-7003; www.gillspier.com), 5620 N. Manitou Trail, Northport; **Good Harbor Vineyard** (231-256-7165; www.goodharbor.com), 34 S. Manitou Trail, Lake Leelanau; **L. Mawby** (231-271-3522; www.lmawby.com), 4519 S. Elm Valley Rd., Suttons Bay; **Leelanau Cellars** (231-386-5201; www.leelanaucellars.com), 5019 NW Bay Shore Dr., MI 22, Omena; **Longview Winery** (231-2282880; www.longviewwinery.com), 8697 Good Harbor Trail, Cedar; **Shady Lane Cellars** (231-947-8865; www.shadylane-cellars.com), 9580 Shady Lane, Suttons Bay; **Willow Vineyard** (231-271-4810; www.traversebiz.com), 10702 E. Hilltop Rd., Suttons Bay.

CROSS-COUNTRY SKIING **Sand Lakes Quiet Area.** There are numerous loops in the area, and the trails are ungroomed. In summer, there are hiking trails closed to motorized vehicles. The trailhead is at Broomhead Road, 4 miles south of MI 72 between Acme and Kalkaska.

Lost Lake Ski Trail. Three loops offer 6.5 miles of trails through the natural area. Access is 1 mile north of US 31 on Gonder Road, just west of Interlochen.

Vasa Trail. There are groomed trails in the Pere Marquette State Forest. The trailhead is on Bartlett Road in Acme and has a large parking lot and indoor rest rooms.

✳ Lodging

There are a large number of resort hotels along US 31 and MI 72 with access to Grand Traverse Bay. Also along this artery are a number of smaller mom-and-pop motels that offer cheaper rates.

HOTELS **Park Place Hotel** (231-946-5000 or 1-800-748-0133; www.park -place-hotel.com), 300 E. State St., Traverse City. The hotel was opened in 1873 during the first tourism boom in northern Michigan, and it was responsible for attracting many people from Chicago and other midwestern cities. Through the years it has evolved into a modern, topnotch hotel, with a 10-story tower built in 1930. It overlooks Grand Traverse Bay and is within walking distance of downtown and the waterfront. Like many historic hotels, the rooms can show their age at times, but the owners have done their best to keep the 140 rooms updated. There are suites on the ninth floor, and some offer balconies and bay windows. Rates are $100–$200. (also see *Dining Out.*)

RESORTS ✐ **Park Shore Resort** (1-877-349-8898; www.parkshoreresort .com), 1401 US 31 North, Traverse City. This four-story resort on Grand Traverse Bay offers one-stop shopping for a family. The kids can spend the day at the beach, while parents work out in the gym, kayak, or hang out in the cocktail lounge. The 80 rooms are large and modern, and some have whirlpools, fireplaces, and private balconies. Apart from the beach, there is a heated indoor pool and spa. There is also a cocktail lounge and casual dining. A laundry room is available, along with free wireless Internet. Winter rates run $49–$79 and summer rates $100–$300.

✐ **The Great Wolf Lodge** (231-941-3600; www.greatwolflodge.com), 3575 US 31 North, Traverse City. This is a family place with lots of kids, drawn there by a water park and a 52,000-square-foot indoor entertainment area. There are indoor and outdoor pools, restaurants, and arcades. The giant North Woods–style building has 281 rooms with TV, microwave, and refrigerator. Rates are $239–$415.

Pinestead Reef Resort (231-947-4010; www.pinestead.com), 1265 US 31 North, Traverse City. Timeshare condos can be rented, and there are studios and one- to two-bedroom suites available. The location on Grand Traverse Bay is the drawing card, and there's a private beach. The rooms are furnished in basic hotel style and are not fancy, but are serviceable. This place would be good for a small family. Free Internet service is offered. Rates are $69–$149.

Pointes North (1-800-968-3422; www.pointesnorth.com), 2211 US 31 North, Traverse City. This resort/condo/hotel is a newer type of development springing up along the Lake Michigan coast. The attraction is the 300-foot sandy beach. The rooms are elegant and all have a view of the bay. This place has the look and feel of a country club, so it wouldn't be my top choice for a family vacation. It's an adult's only place. Rates are $199–$219.

✿ **Cherry Tree Condo Hotel** (231-855-1122 or 1-800-439-3093; www.cherrytreecondohotel.com), 2345 US 31 North, Traverse City. This beachfront resort is for a family. There's a game room for kids and an outdoor playground, along with an indoor pool and spa. The rooms are smoke free, clean, and have a contemporary feel. Some rooms have kitchenettes and fireplaces. High-speed Internet is

available. Rates are $64–$289.

BED & BREAKFASTS Grey Hare Inn Vineyard Bed & Breakfast (231-947-2214; www.greyhareinn.com), West Rue de Carroll Rd., Old Mission Peninsula. The B&B is located on a working farm and vineyard and offers stays and wine tasting. There are three rooms, with a French farmhouse feel. One room has a hot tub. Rates are $135–$250.

Wind in the Pines (231-932-8608; www.windinthepinesbb.com), 13573 S. Gallagher Rd., Traverse City. Located on 6 acres just west of downtown Traverse City, this three-room B&B is a real find in an urban environment. The rooms have an Up North feel, with natural-log paneling. They are sparsely furnished and clean, just the type of room you want to stay in after a day outdoors. A full breakfast is served daily in the dining room, which features a fireplace. The lower-level guest rooms have access to

OLD MISSION INN

a separate ground-floor entrance. Rates are $100–$125.

Neahtawanta Inn (1-800-220-1415; www.neahtawantainn.com), 1308 Neahtawanta Rd., Traverse City. Located on the Old Mission Peninsula in an 1885 cottage that has served as a summer hotel since 1906, the inn is an alternative place to stay to get away from Traverse City. Old Mission is much quieter than the city, and it's only a few minutes from restaurants and other downtown activities. There are four rooms, plus a two-bedroom suit that has a small kitchen and a living room. The inn is located on Traverse Bay, and it offers a great place to watch a sunset. The Victorian-style porch is just the place for long, lazy summer afternoons. Innkeepers Sally Van Vleck and Bob Russell are longtime environmental and peace activists who run the inn based on a philosophy of conservation and respect for the earth. Sally is a yoga teacher and offers classes in the morning. Breakfasts are vegetarian. Rates are $105–$260.

MOTELS **Traverse Bay Lodge** (231-947-5436; www.traversebaylodge .com), 460 Munson Ave., Traverse City. This place is a step up from a normal motel, and it's comfortable and close to downtown Traverse City. The rooms are nothing special, but they are clean and serviceable. There is an indoor pool and spa and an exercise room. Rates are 59–$209.

Ranch Rudolf (231-947-9529; www .ranchrudolf.com), 6841 Brownbridge Rd., Traverse City. Open year-round. The ranch offers 16 rooms and 25 campsites and is on the banks of the Boardman River, a trout stream. The resort offers horseback riding, canoe-

ing/tubing, a restaurant, and cross-country skiing. Rates are $78–$185.

RENTALS **Up North Vacation Rentals** (1-800-901-8922; www .visitupnorth.com), 441 East Front, Traverse City. The property management company offers rentals that range in price from $1,000–$2,000 a week in the Traverse City area and the region.

✳ Outdoor Activities

CAMPING **Traverse City State Park** (231-922-5270; www.michigan.gov/ dnr), US 31, on Grand Traverse Bay, 2 miles from downtown. The 47-acre urban park is mostly devoted to camping, and it fills up quickly in the summer. You can make reservations by calling the park. There are 343 campsites, all very close together.

Interlochen State Park (231-276-9511; www.michigan.gov/dnr), MI 37, Interlochen. The park is 15 miles southwest of Traverse City and is less crowded than the Traverse City Park. It has 200 sites between Green and Duck lakes, which are known for fishing and swimming. The Interlochen Center for the Arts is adjacent to the park.

✳ Where to Eat

DINING OUT ♈ **Bowers Harbor Inn** (231-223-4222; www.bowersharbor inn.net), 13512 Peninsula Dr., Traverse City. Open daily for dinner. The menu is small, but the choices are excellent in this inn, which was built by a lumber baron. The rack of lamb is done with a pistachio crust, bread pudding, and mint paint. There are similar treatments to rainbow trout, beef, pork shoulder, and chicken. Try the cheesecake tart for dessert. Entrees are $22–$34.

Ⓨ **Minervas** (231-946-5093; www .park-place-hotel.com), 300 E. State St., inside the Park Place Hotel, Traverse City. Open daily for breakfast, lunch, and dinner. Steaks, seafood, local lake fish, and chicken make up the heart of the menu. There is a large wine list with many local wines. The Beacon Lounge is in the restaurant. Entrees are $22.

Ⓨ **Freshwater Lodge Restaurant** (231-932-4694; www.michiganmenu .com), 13890 S. West Bayshore Dr., Traverse City. Open for lunch and dinner. When it comes to offering a diversified menu, this is the place. Many northern Michigan restaurants have a standard menu with a focus on steaks and whitefish, but the lodge offers much more, and has a few surprises. The steaks are large, and they do have a different twist on the whitefish—a parmesan whitefish. Ribs and chicken are also on the menu. The décor is classic Up North, with a woodsy lodge feeling. The service is excellent. Entrees are $14–$20.

Ⓨ **The Boathouse Restaurant** (231-223-4030; www.boathouseonwestbay

MACKINAW BREWING COMPANY

.com), 14039 Peninsula Dr., Traverse City, on Old Mission Peninsula. Open daily for dinner and serving a Sunday brunch. Great Lakes fish take top billing, including Canadian walleye and whitefish. There are also seafood dishes, pork, steak, and lamb. You'll find fine china and white tablecloths here and a view of Grand Traverse Bay. Entrees are $25–$34.

Ⓨ **The Bowery** (231-223-4333; www .boweryrestaurant.com), 13512 Peninsula Dr., Traverse City, on Old Mission Peninsula. Open for dinner. When you ask local residents for a good place to eat, they'll tell you about the Bowery. The menu is filled with local favorites: steak, cedar plank salmon, pork shoulder, whitefish, perch, and ribs. Entrees are $13–$20.

EATING OUT Ⓨ **Mackinaw Brewing Company** (231-933-1100), 161 East Front St., Traverse City. Open for lunch and dinner. This brewpub in the heart of downtown serves up everything from burgers to fine dinners in a historic building. You'll find a lot of locals eating here, and for good reason. The herb-crusted whitefish is a good spin on a traditional northern Michigan dish. A pan-fried walleye with cherries is another favorite. And the burgers are big. The pub brews up its own beers and ales, all of which are worth trying. Entrees are $11–$17.

Ⓨ **North Peak Brewing Company** (231-941-7325), 400 W. Front St., Traverse City. The handcrafted beer flows in this restored candy factory. It is a crowded, noisy place that's more of a pub than a restaurant, but there is pizza, steaks, pasta, and sandwiches. Prices are $5–$9.

Ÿ **Mode's Bum Steer** (231-947-9832), 129 E. State St., Traverse City. Open Mon.–Sat. This venerable place is an old-style steakhouse that also serves seafood and ribs. No children after 5. Prices are $6–$23.

Blue Tractor (231-922-9515; www .bluetractorcookshop.com), 423 S. Union, Traverse City. Located in a roadhouse-inspired building, the Tractor offers five kinds of burgers and other American foods. Prices are $5–$14.

Mabel's Restaurant (231-947-0252), US 131, Traverse City. Open daily. This is where the locals go for breakfast. It offers homemade family-style comfort food, and there are daily specials. Prices are $5–$15.

In Interlochen

Ÿ **Hofgrau** (231-276-6979), 2784 MI 137, Interlochen. Open daily. The rustic family tavern offers seafood, steaks, ribs, chicken, and sandwiches. Prices are $7–$20.

✳ Selective Shopping

Most Traverse City shops are open Mon.–Sat., unless otherwise noted.

Old Mission General Store (231-223-4310), 18250 Mission Rd., Old Mission Peninsula. Open daily, 8–9. The 163-year-old store has an old post office, antiques, penny candy, and a few sandwiches. It was the first general store between Fort Wayne and Mackinaw.

The Candle Factory (231-946-2280; www.candles.net), 301 Grandview Parkway, Traverse City. You can't image how many different kinds of candles there are until you come into this place, which has been around since 1971. This isn't your normal candle and gift shop, and it

A VINEYARD ON OLD MISSION PENINSULA

features candles from around the nation.

ANTIQUES STORES **Rolling Hills Antiques** (231-947-1063; www .rollinghillsantiques.com), 5085 Barney Rd., Traverse City. Open daily, 11–6, except Tues. Housed in an 1870s dairy barn, the shop is run by Glen and Diane Lundin, who specialize in furniture and accessories from the late 1700s to the early 1900s. This includes early American, country primitive, and Victorian.

ART GALLERIES Most galleries are open year-round, Mon.–Sat. Call for winter hours.

Suttons Bay Galleries (231-271-4444), 102 Jefferson St., Suttons Bay. Open daily; call first. The gallery has fine art from the 15th to 20th century and features antiquarian prints, illuminated manuscripts, maps, rare books, and original Russell Chatham lithographs and paintings.

Belstone Gallery (231-946-0610), 321 E. Front St., Traverse City. Contemporary American arts and crafts are the center of this gallery, which features fine art, glass, jewelry, pottery, and wood artwork.

Gallery Fifty (231-932-0775; www .galleryfifty.com), 830 Cottageview Dr., Traverse City. Original paintings and mixed media items are the mainstay of this shop, with metal, pottery, glass, and jewelry. Many northern Michigan artists are featured.

BOOKSTORES Horizon Books (231-946-7290; www.horizonbooks.com), 243 E. Front St., Traverse City. Open daily. The small chain bookstore has many offerings of local history and nature-related materials, along with most of the best sellers and beach books.

※ **Special Events**
Early July **National Cherry**

Festival (www.cherryfestival.org). The nearly week-long event in downtown Traverse City features everything you'd want to know about cherries, which are the region's largest agricultural crop. There's a queen, musical entertainment, rides, and the U.S. Navy's Blue Angels usually perform.

Late July **Traverse City Film Festival** (www.traversecityfilmfest.org). Documentary filmmaker Michael Moore, who spends his summers in the area, helped get this going, and he has shown some of his films here. The festival centers on independent, foreign, and documentary films shown in the State Theatre, City Opera House, and the Old Town Playhouse.

LEELANAU PENINSULA

Leelanau County is Traverse City's upscale suburb, with million-dollar lakefront homes, several trendy villages, and two celebrities who have summer homes, chef Mario Batali and filmmaker Michael Moore.

Life centers around the villages of Suttons Bay, Lake Leelanau, Leland, and Northport, where most restaurants and shopping are found. But just because there are a couple of celebrities around, don't expect a lot of glitz. Northport has a lovely beach and a view of Grand Traverse Bay, but it doesn't have a sewer system, so restaurants don't thrive here. Leland has several good ones, but don't expect fine dining.

Lodging is difficult to find on the peninsula, so most visitors opt to stay in Traverse City or find rental homes, which go for up to $3,000 a week.

Being outdoors is the lifestyle, and there are many beaches to wander during the day. Bicycling the lightly traveled country roads is popular, along with tours of area wineries. Leelanau State Park at the tip of the peninsula offers camping and miles of unspoiled beaches.

There's a large Native American presence, with the Grand Traverse Band Indian Reservation located off MI 22 near Omena, where the tribe operates a gambling casino.

The peninsula has its roots in farming, fishing, cherry orchards, and now grape growing and wineries, of which there are more than a dozen. However, the real economy is the building and maintenance of cottages and second homes in the area, an industry that employs many in this county of about 21,000.

GUIDANCE **Leelanau Peninsula Chamber of Commerce** (231-271-9895; www.leelanauchamber.com), 5046 S. West Bayshore Dr., Suttons Bay. Open daily on weekdays. The chamber has maps and material on touring the more than 12 wineries on the peninsula.

GETTING THERE *By car:* From Traverse City or Empire, MI 22 is the only route. This road circles the peninsula.
By air: See Traverse City.

WHEN TO COME The high season is from late May–Oct.; however, there are enough downhill ski areas to keep most lodging places, restaurants, and shops open during winter. Don't come late March–April, as there is nothing but mud in Michigan.

STAYING CONNECTED **The Cyber Express Coffee Bar,** Harbor Square off MI 22, Leland. Open March–Dec., 7 AM–7 PM. Internet connections are available for $5 an hour. It is the only place in Leland with Internet and public fax service.

MEDICAL EMERGENCY **Munson Medical Center** (231-935-5000), 550 Munson Ave., Traverse City. A full-service emergency room and hospital that serves much of northern Michigan. Call 911.

✳ To See & Do

In Northport
Leelanau State Park (231-386-5422; www.michigan.gov/dnr), 15310 N. Lighthouse Pt. Rd., Northport. Located at the tip of the peninsula, the park has 1,300

DOWNTOWN SUTTONS BAY

acres, much of it white sandy beach. Camping is available, and there are several rustic cabins for rent.

Grand Traverse Lighthouse (231-386-7195; www.grandtraverselighthouse .com), Leelanau State Park, Northport. (See *Leelanau State Park.*) Open daily late May–Sept., 10–6. The 1858 lighthouse was in operation until 1972. A climb to the top gives you a good view of Lake Michigan and Grand Traverse Bay. Admission is $4 for adults and $2 for children.

In Leland

✍ **Manitou Island Transit** (213-256-9061), in Fishtown. Open May–Oct., with daily boat trips to South and North Manitou islands in Lake Michigan. There are also sunset cruises. Island round-trip fares are $29 for adults and $15 for children 12 and under. The islands are part of the **Sleeping Bear Dunes National Lakeshore** (231-326-5134; www.nps.gov), 9922 Front St., Empire. The two islands in Lake Michigan are part of the extensive park, and South Manitou offers backpacking and camping opportunities. The islands were once inhabited by farm families and there are extensive road systems that are easily hiked. Permits are required for backpacking and are available on the island. Access is via boat from Leland.

✍ **Historic Fishtown** (www.preservingfishtown.org). Located near the marina in downtown Leland is the historic area that once was a center for commercial fishing. By the 1980s it was revived as a collection of shops. The Carlson family keeps the commercial fishing scene alive, and it has a store in Fishtown that sells Lake Michigan whitefish. The old fishing shanties that line the banks of the Leland River are one of the most photographed places in Michigan.

✍ ⛪ **Leelanau Historical Museum** (231-256-7475; www.leelanauhistory.org), 203 E. Cedar St., Leland. Open late May–early Sept., Tues.–Sat., 10–4. The riverside museum has exhibits and archives on the development of the region and displays of Native American arts and crafts. During summer there are arts-related events.

SCENIC DRIVES Follow MI 22 around the peninsula. It follows Grand Traverse Bay and Lake Michigan and takes you through the villages of Suttons Bay, Omena, Northport, and Leland, and then south to Glen Arbor, Empire, and Frankfort. A short drive through the Sleeping Bear Dunes National Lakeshore off MI 22 is also worthwhile (see *Sleeping Bear Dunes*).

BEACHES

In Leland

Tucked away on Lake Drive is a public beach that can be accessed via Reynolds Road from MI 22 (Manitou Rd.). The beaches are sandy, warm, and shallow for kids.

In Northport

The beach is in a city park downtown, and because it's on the leeward side of the peninsula, it's shallow and the wave action is light, making it good for kids. There is play equipment, picnic tables, and rest rooms.

Leelanau State Park offers some of the best beaches in the area (see *To See &* 75
Do).

GRAND TRAVERSE REGION

BICYCLING There is little truck traffic, and cycling can be done on most main roads. However, there are plenty of county roads with little or no traffic. Michigan 22 has wide shoulders and many cyclists.

✳ Lodging

See Traverse City for more accommodations.

Falling Waters Lodge (231-256-7611 in season, 231-256-9832 year-round; www.fallingwaterslodge.com), 200 W. Cedar, Leland. Open April–mid-Nov. The location at Leland's historic Fishtown, on the water, makes this a good place to stay for those who want to wander the shops and sit next to the waterfalls that drain Lake Leelanau into Lake Michigan. Many of the rooms have a balcony overlooking the falls, Fishtown, and Lake Michigan. This is a place where you can leave your car parked and walk to the beach or to shopping or just to take a stroll. The rooms are clean and sparse, and not fancy. There is cable TV. Rates are $129–$239.

Whaleback Inn (1-800-942-5322; www.whalebackinn.com), MI 22, Leland. The inn offers rooms and cottages for rent, many with a view of Grand Traverse Bay. Most have an Up North feel, with rustic furniture and natural wood. The cottages have full kitchens. Other rooms have wood-burning fireplaces and hot tubs. The inn has access to the bay. Scott and Tammie Koehler are the innkeepers. Room rates are $119–$189 and cottages run $270.

Leland Lodge (231-256-9848; www.lelandlodgeresort.com), 565 E. Pearl St., Leland. The lodge is next to the

Leland Country Club and offers golf packages. There are 18 rooms and five cottages, all with coffee makers, refrigerators, microwaves, cable TV, and phones. Room rates are $79–$199 and cottages/efficiency apartments run about $1,500 per week.

The Riverside Inn (231-256-9971; www.theriverside-inn.com), 302 River St., Leland. The inn has six rooms with private baths, and also a restaurant (see *Dining Out,* Leland). There are two suites. The 1902 building is next to the Leland River. Rates are $70–$170.

BED & BREAKFASTS Snowbird Inn (231-256-9773; www.snowbirdinn .com), 473 Manitou Trail, Leland. The small B&B is on 18 acres near Leland in an old farmhouse and offers a large breakfast. There is a library and a porch for sitting. Rates are $150–$160.

Aspen House (1-800-762-7736; www.aspenhouseleland.com), 1353 Manitou Trail, Leland. The restored 1880s farmhouse offers three rooms, mostly done in a Victorian style. The rooms are a bit cramped, but the countryside is open. Rates are $130–$165.

Near Lake Leelanau
Jolli-Lodge (1-888-256-9291), 29 N. Manitou Trail, Lake Leelanau. The lodge is on Lake Michigan's Good Harbor Bay and offers six rooms, two

apartments, and cottages with full kitchens and one to three bedrooms. There are grills and picnic tables on the grounds. Rates are $85 per night; weekly cottages run about $1,000.

Traditions B&B (231-271-2716; www.traditionsbnb.com), 1800 N. Eagle Hwy., Lake Leelanau. The three-room inn is near a cherry orchard. Each room in the Cape Cod–style home has a private bath. There are no TV sets, computers, or hot tubs. Rates are $95–$135.

In Suttons Bay
Korner Kottage (231-271-2711; www.kornerkottage.com), 503 N. St. Josephs Ave., Suttons Bay. The four rooms have private baths, air-conditioning, cable TV, refrigerators, and wireless Internet. No credit cards. The yard is filled with metal sculptures. Rates are $133–$169.

The Vineyard Inn on Suttons Bay (231-941-7060; www.vininn.com), 1338 N. Pebble Beach, Suttons Bay. There are 12 waterfront suites, which have been redecorated in a European style. The rooms overlook Suttons Bay, and many have a patio or balcony. The inn offers tours of nearby wineries. Rates are $100–$250.

LEELANAU CELLARS WINE TASTING ROOM

Leelanau Cellars Tasting Room

In Northport
Days Gone By (231-386-5114; www.daysgonebybnb.com), 201 N. High St., Northport. The five-room B&B is in an 1868 home. The innkeepers are Jane and Jack Poniatowski. The rooms have different themes and private baths. It's a well-landscaped place and close to downtown Northport. Rates are $129–$150.

MOTELS **Sunrise Landing** (231-386-5010; www.sunriselanding.com), 6530 N. West Bay Shore Dr., Northport. The 11-room motel has access to Grand Traverse Bay and has been remodeled. The units have air-conditioning, refrigerators, microwaves, satellite TV, and wireless Internet. Some rooms have kitchenettes, and there are rental houses that sleep up to 12. Rates are $100–$135.

✳ Where to Eat

DINING OUT

In Leland
℣ **The Cove** (231-256-9834; www.thecoveland.com), 111 River St., Leland. Open daily for lunch and dinner. This place has been a mainstay for years. It is located near Fishtown and has a bar on a deck overlooking Lake Michigan and the Leland River. Great Lakes fish are on the top of the menu, and they do a campfire whitefish. Perch, walleye, and salmon are offered as well, along with steaks, chicken, and pasta. Entrees are $19–$26.

℣ **Leland Lodge** (231-256-9848; www.lelandlodgeresort.com), 565 E. Pearl St., Leland. The menu includes rainbow trout, roast duck, whitefish, pasta, and steak. There is an indoor dining room and a deck for the warmer months. The lodge is rustic, with plenty of natural wood. Rooms are available (see *Lodging*). Entrees are $15–$21.

Ŷ ∲ Bluebird Restaurant (231-256-9081), 102 E. River St., Leland. Open daily for lunch and dinner. This place has been operated since 1923 by the Telgard family, and its North Woods bar has long been the local hangout. There are some different choices here, such as the smoked cherry wood pork loin and bourbon chicken with andouille sausage. There are also Great Lakes fish and steaks. Entrees are $15–$20.

Ŷ ∞ The Riverside Inn (231-256-9971; www.theriverside-inn.com). Open daily for dinner. The colonial-style inn offers formal and casual dining. The menu includes seafood, whitefish, lamb, duck, and ostrich. There is a decent wine list, including many local products. Entrees are $20–$32.

Early Bird (231-256-9656), 101 S. Main, Leland. Open daily, 7–2. This is where the locals congregate for breakfast and lunch. No credit cards.

Village Cheese Shanty (231-256-9141), located in Fishtown, Leland. Open daily, May–Oct. Fresh sandwiches made daily. The capicolla ham, mozzarella cheese, tomato, and red onion were the perfect lunch. There is a good selection of cheeses, sausage, and locally made wine.

In Suttons Bay
Ŷ Samuel's (231-271-6222; www .samuelssuttonbay.com), 111 St. Joseph Ave., Suttons Bay. Open for breakfast, lunch, and dinner. The menu has been updated, but still centers on walleye, whitefish, chicken, and steak. There is a whitefish smoth-

ered with crawfish etouffee. The wine list includes local products. Prices are $10–$15.

Ŷ Village Inn (231-271-3300), 201 St. Joseph Ave., Suttons Bay. Open daily for lunch and dinner. This friendly little tavern offers good burgers and other fare in the bar and small dining rooms. Entrees are $10–$15.

In Lake Leelanau
Ŷ Dick's Pour House (231-256-9912), 103 Phillip, Lake Leelanau. Open daily for lunch and dinner. This venerable town tavern has been in operation since 1935 and is now run by a third generation of the Plamondon family. This is where the locals hang out. The menu runs from burgers to a Friday fish fry and prime rib. Prices are $8–$15.

✳ Selective Shopping
Rivers & Main (231-256-8858), 102 N. Main St., Leland. Open May–Dec., 9–9. Located in the town's main intersection, this is a good place to get a cup of coffee and sit outside on the rustic furniture, which is for sale. They offer copper home wares and other decorative items. They also have fine candies and local wines.

Benjamin Maier Ceramics (231-590-1084), 102 N. Main St., Leland. Open daily in summer. Maier's ceramic pottery challenges the imagination with its earthy colors and swirling shapes. Such high art items aren't often found in northern Michigan.

Haystacks (231-256-9675), 103 N. Main St., Leland. Open daily, 9–5; shorter winter hours. Women looking for madras and other unusual clothing will find it here. Not the usual resort town sweatshirt shop.

Tampico (231-256-7747), 112 N.

Main St., Leland. Owners Kathy and Cris Telgrd have brought a bit of the Southwest to northern Michigan with their silver jewelry, Mexican folk art, and Navajo craft items. There is a good selection of rustic furniture and yard art, such as metal sun faces.

Bahle's of Suttons Bay (231-271-3841), 210 Suttons Bay. Open daily on weekdays. The Bahle family has been in business for four generations, and in this day of big box store shopping, having an upscale clothing store in the same spot where the family general store has been since 1876 is a pleasure. The men's ware department sells everything from suits and sport coats to hunting and fishing jackets. Karl Bahle is there to wait on you.

ART GALLERIES **Brenda J. Clark Gallery** (231-256-0026; www.brenda jaclark.com), Harbor Square, off Lake St., Leland. Open daily May–Oct., 10–5. Clark's impressionistic, colorful works are a standout in this town. Her gallery offers only her works, many of which are of the rolling landscapes of Leelanau County. She and her husband, Johnston, run the gallery.

Mimi Nieman Gallery, Harbor Square, Leland. Open June–Aug., Wed.–Sun. The artist's gallery features her own works in oil and watercolors, and many of the subjects involve the local Leelanau landscape.

In Omena
Tamarack Gallery (231-386-5529; www.tamarackgallery.com), MI 22, Omena. Open daily. The gallery, owned by Sally Viskochil, has been a fixture in northern Michigan for more than 30 years, with its mix of contemporary art and artistically done rustic furniture and home wares. It's hard to miss. There are only three buildings

A PERFECT DAY IN LELAND

8 AM.	Breakfast at the Early Bird Restaurant on Main St., where the locals tend to start their day.
8:30 AM.	Bicycle ride through the neighborhoods of Leland and along MI 22.
10 AM.	Stroll through the shops in Fishtown and watch the yachts come and go at the Leland Marina. Get sandwiches to go from the Cheese Shop in Fishtown.
11 AM.	Head to the beach for the day. The best one is at the end of Reynolds Road off MI 22.
3 PM.	Stroll through downtown Leland, stopping at the various galleries and shops. Get some fudge at Murdock's Fudge Shop.
5 PM.	Cocktails at The Cove, an outside tavern on the banks of the Leland River, next to the falls.
6 PM.	A Lake Michigan whitefish dinner at the Bluebird Restaurant on River Street.
7:30 PM.	A drive through town to look at the older homes.
8:30–10 PM.	Watch the sunset on Lake Michigan.

in Omena on the west side of MI 22—the general store, the post office, and the gallery. The shop is a destination shopping stop for many fans.

BOOKSTORES **Leelanau Books** (231-256-7111; www.leelanaubooks .com), 109 N. Main St., Leland. Open daily, 10–5. This locally owned shop has a good selection of books related to Lake Michigan, local history, and the region. There are some nice maps of the Grand Traverse region that would make framed pieces for a cottage or lodge. There are also beach books and a decent children's section.

In Northport
Dog Ears Books (231-386-7209; www.dogearsbooks.net), 106 Waukazoo St. (MI 22), Northport, MI 49670. Open daily. I found some real, old, classics in the shop, which has a good number of antique and vintage books. There are also the required best sellers, paperback beach books, and local history books.

GLEN ARBOR & EMPIRE

Although the two communities are now filled with summer people, trendy restaurants, and shops, they were once lumbering and fruit-growing centers. The warm breezes from Lake Michigan helped foster the fruit industry and now vineyards are taking the place of apple and cherry trees.

The communities are at either end of the Sleeping Bear Dunes National Lakeshore, which was created by Congress in 1970. Thousands of visitors come to the dunes during summer months to hike, camp, and swim.

Both towns are pretty much May–September places, catering to visitors. Most businesses are closed in the colder months, but there are some exceptions. Each community has year-round residents. While the dunes are public property, Glen Lake is surrounded by second homes.

GUIDANCE **Glen Lake Chamber of Commerce** (231-334-3238; www.visit glenarbor.com), Glen Arbor. Open Mon.–Fri., year-round. Their Web site has good links to local rental houses.

CANOEING, KAYAKING & RENTALS The Crystal River offers paddling opportunities near Glen Arbor.

Crystal River Outfitters (231-334-4420; www.crystalriveroutfitters.com), 6249 W. River Rd., Glen Arbor. Open daily 9–6:30, late May–early Sept. The outfitter offers float trips, boat rentals, and bike rentals.

✳ Lodging

BED & BREAKFAST **Glen Arbor Bed & Breakfast** (231-334-6789; www.glenarborbnb.com), 6548 Western Ave., Glen Arbor. The six-room B&B is within walking distance of shopping and restaurants in Glen Arbor. The rooms are tastefully decorated in a country, Victorian style, and have air-conditioning and cable TV. There is a nice porch. It was built in 1873 and has been a boardinghouse for loggers, a restaurant, and a private

TO SEE & DO

Sleeping Bear Dunes National Lakeshore (231-326-5134; www.nps.gov), 9922 Front St., Empire. The dunes offer 35 miles of Lake Michigan shoreline access, scenic drives, a dune-climbing area, historical exhibits, camping, and backpacking.

The best place to start is at the **Philip A. Hart Visitor Center** (231-326-5134, ext. 328), MI 72, Empire. There are maps and guides to the dunes and information on camping in the various sites.

To get a good idea of where you are, take the Pierce Stocking Scenic Drive off MI 72. Open daily late April–mid-Nov., 9–sunset. The 7.4-mile, self-guided trip provides a good view of the dunes and the park's vegetation.

The dune climb off MI 22 north of Empire can entertain kids for hours, as they endlessly climb up and then roll down the dunes. A parking lot, rest rooms, and picnic tables are available. You can walk to the Lake Michigan shoreline from here, but it's a good hike. Make sure to take water.

Grand Haven, on MI 22, offers a look back at the area's rural past. There is a general store, blacksmith shop, and the Cannery Boat Museum. Nearby is the Sleeping Bear Point Coast Guard Station Maritime Museum, open daily mid-May–Oct. At 3 o'clock there's a reenactment of a rescue drill once practiced by the Coast Guard. There are life-saving boats on display, along with other equipment.

The campsites are at the D. H. Day and Platte River Campgrounds. Both offer services for RVs and tents. Backcountry camping is allowed on a permit system.

home. There are also two guest cottages for rent. Room rates are $89–$185 and cottages run $795–$1,095 per week.

RESORT The Homestead (231-334-5100; www.thehomesteadresort.com), Wood Ridge Rd., Glen Arbor. The Homestead is an older-style lodge that has gone upscale. It has become a near village and has various types of lodging available, ranging from hotel rooms to condos and homes for rent. There is a private beach and a restaurant and a children's center. Rates are $100 and up.

RENTALS The state of Michigan has a good Web site with plenty of cabin and cottage rentals listed: www.michigan.org/travel/lodging/.

✳ Where to Eat

DINING OUT

In Empire

Ψ **The Manor on Glen Lake** (231-334-0150; www.themanoronglenlake.com), 7345 W. Glenmere Rd., Empire. Open daily during summer for lunch, dinner, and Sunday brunch. Call for winter hours. The menu ranges from beef to seafood, Great

Lakes fish, chicken, duck, and lamb, and it rotates on a daily basis. The view from the 100-year-old restored inn is of the Sleeping Bear Dunes. There is a decent wine list. Entrees are $20–$35.

In Glen Arbor

Y **LeBear Windows** (231-334-2530; www.dineatwindows.com), 5705 Lake St., Glen Arbor. Open daily for lunch and dinner. Steak, seafood, chicken, Great Lakes fish, duck, and lamb are available in a contemporary restaurant. Prices are $20–$30.

EATING OUT

In Glen Arbor

Y **Good Harbor Grill** (231-334-3555), 6584 Western Ave., Glen Arbor. Open daily May–Oct. for breakfast, lunch, and dinner. Seafood is on the top of the menu, along with steaks, chicken, and ribs. There are also vegetarian entrees. Prices are $5–$20.

Y **Art's Tavern** (231-334-3754; www.artsglenarbor.com), 6487 Western Ave., Glen Arbor. Open daily for breakfast, lunch, and dinner. The fried smelt were a real find. They have been dropped from the menu of many Up North taverns because of their scarcity. The classic "old school" tavern menu pushes up a bit from the usual burgers to charbroiled steaks and fish. Prices are $10–$18.

Y **Boone Dock's** (231-334-6444), 5858 Manitou (US 22), Glen Arbor. Open daily for lunch and dinner. The log lodge has one of the largest decks I've seen at a tavern, and it's usually filled with diners. There are burgers, shrimp, and steaks at this sprawling place. Prices are $10–$15.

✳ Selective Shopping

In Glen Arbor

✎ **Cherry Republic** (231-334-3150; www.cherryrepublic.com), 6026 S. Lake St., Glen Arbor. Open daily,

GLEN ARBOR LAKESHORE INN

year-round. These folks have figured out everything you can possibly do with cherries, and they're all on display here. There are more than 150 food products made from the region's biggest agricultural crops, including soda pop, candy, dried cherries, salsa, wine, chili, and ice cream.

Glen Arbor Botanicals (231-334-3405), 6590 Western Ave., Glen Arbor. Open daily, May–Oct. The small shop offers framed pages from antique books with illustrations of plant life from around the globe.

In Empire
Ripple Effect Studio and Gallery (231-326-2047; www.jeffripple.com), 10085 W. Front St., Empire. Open daily, May–Oct. Jeff Ripple uses vintage large-format cameras to capture nature scenes, particularly of the Great Lakes. He also is a painter.

BOOKSTORES Cottage Book Shop (231-334-4223; www.cottagebooks .com), 5989 S. Lake, Glen Arbor. Open 10–5, year-round. The small, independently-owned shop focuses on local and regional authors and stocks books on local history and the natural features of the region. There are some summer beach books, but also books by writers with ties to Michigan. Readings and book signings by local authors are common.

FRANKFORT

This town of about 1,500 is the commercial center for several towns around Crystal Lake, including Elberta, Benzonia, Beulah, and Honor. Like most western Michigan port towns, Frankfort was a lumber town, with mills dependent on the vast white pine forests. These days, tourism is the prime industry.

Charter boat fishing for salmon and trout in Lake Michigan is another thriving industry, and much of the area is a destination for anglers. Visitors to the nearby Sleeping Bear Dunes find lodging, restaurants, and shopping in the Benzie County towns.

The attractions are the beaches along Lake Michigan and on Crystal Lake, canoeing and kayaking in the Betsie and Platte rivers, and bicycling the back roads. Traverse City, the shopping capital of northern Michigan, is only about 45 minutes away (see Traverse City).

The mix makes the area popular in the summer, and a large number of lodging and camping options are available. There are a good number of bed & breakfasts, motels, and inns. In the winter, downhill and cross-country skiing and snowmobiling keep the area active. Downhill skiing once boomed in the area, but climate change has put a dent in the amount of snow the area receives.

The Platte and Betsie rivers are top destinations for trout anglers, and the inland lakes are good for bass and other species.

GUIDANCE Frankfort-Elberta Chamber of Commerce (231-352-7251; www.frankfort-elberta.com) 400 Main St., Frankfort. Open daily, weekdays.
Benzie County Chamber of Commerce (231-882-5901; www.benzie.org), 826 Michigan Ave., Benzonia (US 31/MI 115). Open daily, weekdays.

✴ To See & Do

Point Betsie Lighthouse (231-352-4915; www.pointbetsie.org), on Point Betsie, off MI 22, north of Frankfort. Open late May–mid-Oct. on weekends only. The lighthouse has been undergoing a complete renovation. It was built in 1858 and marks the entrance to the Manitou Passage, which ships use as a route on Lake Michigan. Tours are available. Admission is $2 for adults and $1 for children.

✴ Outdoor Activities

CANOEING & KAYAKING Lake Michigan, Crystal Lake, and the Platte River near Honor offer paddling opportunities.

Crystal Lake Adventure Sports (231-882-2527), 214 S. Benzie Blvd., Beulah. Offers kayak and bike rentals.

Riverside Canoe Trips (231-325-5622), 5042 Scenic Hwy., Honor. Paddle trips on the Platte River and Sleeping Bear Dunes National Lakeshore.

SURFING Michigan isn't California, but they do surf on Lake Michigan when the conditions are right. **Sleeping Bear Surf & Kayak** (231-326-9283), Empire.

BEACHES The city beach at the end of Main Street features a sandy, shallow Lake Michigan beach, with playground equipment. It's free.

BICYCLING It's pretty much limitless here. There's a 9-mile paved dedicated trail from Frankfort to Beulah, which follows Crystal Lake much of the way. Access is in downtown Frankfort near the beach, off Main Street. Michigan 22 is lightly traveled and a rider could easily tour the Sleeping Bear Dunes National Lakeshore.

FRANKFORT MARINA

SALMON AND STEELHEAD FISHING There are more than a dozen charter boats operating out of Frankfort. **The Michigan Charter Boat Association** has a good list at www.micharterboats.com.

✳ Lodging

Betsie Bay Inn (231-352-8090; www.betsiebayinn.com), 231 Main St., Frankfort. The Victorian-style inn has 17 rooms. The diversity of room style is refreshing, and you can select from a Victorian motif or more modern natural wood. Some rooms have hot tubs, saunas, and log stoves. There are queen- and king-sized beds. A restaurant and bar are available (see *Dining Out*). Rates are $105–$255.

In Beulah

Brookside Inn Rustic (231-882-9688; www.brooksideinn.com), 115 N. Michigan Ave. (US 31), Beulah. The 20-room inn has some of the most eccentric rooms I've ever seen. There is a mix of Up North knotty pine with

antiques. The rooms come with a private spa, log stove, and sauna. The prices include dinner and breakfast for two. Rates are $235–$290.

RESORTS

In Onekama

Portage Point Historic Inn and Lakefront Resort (231-889-4222; www.portagepointinn.com), 8513 S. Portage Pointe Dr., Onekama. The inn, located between Lake Michigan and Portage Lake, has been a vacation spot since about 1903. The lodging is in one- to four-bedroom cottages, a hotel, and condominium rentals. There are dunes on the big lake, and warmwater beaches on Portage Lake.

BETSIE BAY INN

A marina is capable of handling most yachts and has services for boaters. There is a restaurant (see *Dining Out*). Hotel rates are $159–$306 and condos and cottages rent by the week during summer for $1,000–$3,000.

BED & BREAKFASTS Stonewall Inn (231-352-9299) 428 Leelanau Ave., Frankfort. This Victorian Italianate home is the oldest in the area, built in 1860, and was for a while the Frankfort Land Co. It's on the National Register of Historic Places. There are four rooms decorated with antiques and Civil War memorabilia. I liked the feel of the place, with the Civil War sabers and uniforms. The Lincoln room has a 6-foot, walnut headboard. Dave and Sandy Jackson are the innkeepers. Rates are $110–$125.

MOTELS Bay Port Lodging (231-352-4442; www.bayportlodging.com), 905 Forrest Ave., Frankfort. There's a selection of lodging here, including a cabin with a kitchen, cottage rooms, and double suites for rent by the day or week. The rooms have refrigerators and cable TV. There is a large freezer available for anglers and parking for boats, trailers, and snowmobiles. Daily rates are $75–$115; weekly rates run $470–$650.

COTTAGES & CABINS Weekly cottage and cabin rentals are big in this region. Families often spend the same week each summer in a favorite rental unit.
The Farm House Cottage (231-632-0833), 2574 Herring Rd., Arcadia. Located on Upper Herring Lake, the place is an old farmhouse that sleeps 12. There are kayaks and a pontoon boat. Rates are $225 per night and $1,500–$2,800 per week.

The Beach House on Upper Herring Lake (231-632-0833; www.the beachhousemi.tripod.com), 5484 Indian Trail, Frankfort. The 2,000-square-foot house with four bedrooms and two baths has 80 feet of frontage on Upper Herring Lake. The home is modern and furnished. Rates are $225 per night and $1,500–$3,000 weekly.

Up North Vacation Rentals (1-877-334-3345, Glen Arbor, or 1-800-901-8922, Traverse City; www.visitupnorth.com). The real-estate firm has many homes for rent in northern Michigan.

✳ Where to Eat

DINING OUT ℣ Bunty & JoJo's Casual Restaurant and Tantelle Fine Dining (231-352-7251; www.betsiebayinn.com), 231 Main St., Frankfort. The inn has most of the bases covered when it comes to eating out. They offer casual dining, fine dining, a wine cellar, and a pub all in one building. We'd pick the casual dining, with its reasonable prices yet interesting menu. The salmon cutlet with chorizo sausage, roasted corn, and red pepper sauce is an interesting take on a regional favorite. The whitefish with the roasted red pepper remoulade is another innovative dish. The appetizers in the upscale dining room are items not often found Up North: sautéed potato gnocchi and gratin of wild mushrooms. The Hotspur Pub is decorated like a classic British pub and invites you to spend the evening at one of its round tables. The Thisle Brae Wine Cellar is an intimate place to share a glass of wine with a friend. Entrees are $14–$25.

EATING OUT ℣ Portage Point Historic Inn and Lakefront Resort

(231-889-4222; www.portagepoint inn.com), 8513 S. Portage Pointe Dr., Onekama. Open daily, year-round. This is the place to take a family after a day at the beach. The historic inn (see *Lodging*) is open to the general public and has steaks, seafood, whitefish, and pub fare. There are nightly specials during the high season. Prices are $8–$15.

℘ **Funistrada** (231-334-3900; www .trattoriafunistrada.com), 4566 MacFarlane, Burdickville. Open for dinner Tues.–Sun. You'd have to travel a long way to find Italian dishes like the ones offered here—chicken saltimbocca, lemon artichoke veal, and New York strip steak coated in cracked pepper and pan-seared in a balsamic reduction. This place isn't ideal for small children. Reservations recommended. Entrees are $20–$30.

℘ **Dinghy's Restaurant & Bar** (231-352-4702), 417 Main St., Frankfort. This family pub offers pizza, burgers, and other pub fare. There are a few entrees like steak, ribs, chicken, and shrimp. Entrees are $13–$19.

Crescent Bakery (231-352-4611), 404 Main St., Frankfort. Open daily. There is fresh baked bread and more at this bakery, which is a version of an updated, small town café. Breakfast is served all day, including a Mediterranean morning panini, which has scrambled eggs, tomatoes, and goat cheese. Lunches include homemade soups, East Coast–style pizza, and deli sandwiches. There are pastries and coffee in the morning. Prices are $4–$7.

LITTLE TRAVERSE BAY REGION

PETOSKEY; HARBOR SPRINGS; BOYNE CITY; EAST JORDAN; CHARLEVOIX; BEAVER ISLAND

PETOSKEY

The first visitors to the Little Traverse Bay region arrived via steamship in the 1870s, many of them from Chicago. They came to beat the city's summer heat and stayed in hotels, but later returned and built ornate Victorian cottages on and near the Lake Michigan shoreline.

I was reminded of those days before air-conditioning recently when driving to Petoskey. The air-conditioning in the car had gone out, and I'd spent a hot July day on the road. As I descended the small hills and caught a glimpse of Little Traverse Bay, I could feel the temperature drop about 10 degrees. It was a relief and it's probably what the tourists felt in the 19th century.

Among the Chicago families drawn to the region by the climate were the Hemingways and their oldest son, Ernest. In 1899, Dr. Clarence Hemingway had a cottage constructed on Walloon Lake, just south of Petoskey, and little did he know at the time that the lakes and surrounding countryside would become the settings for some of Ernest Hemingway's best short stories.

It was on the rivers and lakes that Ernest whet his appetite for fishing, and in the woods where he learned how to hunt. His boyhood summer home is now on the National Register of Historic Places, although the house isn't open to visitors. The area is a delight for Hemingway buffs who want to find landmarks from his short stories. One such place is the Horton Bay General Store, which now houses a gourmet deli.

But there's more to Petoskey than the Hemingway factor. The historic business district offers excellent shopping that ranges from fine art to antiques and small gift shops. It's worth spending an afternoon strolling the Gaslight District, which has a view of the bay.

The town's centerpiece is the Perry Hotel, and yep, Hemingway slept here. But he wasn't the only tourist passing through town to stay here. The Perry was one of the first tourist hotels in northern Michigan, and it catered to the well-to-do of the Victorian era. Those folks, many from Chicago and other midwestern cities, fled the heat of summer and found a refuge on the shores of Lake Michigan.

With a population of 6,080 people, Petoskey is the largest town in the region,

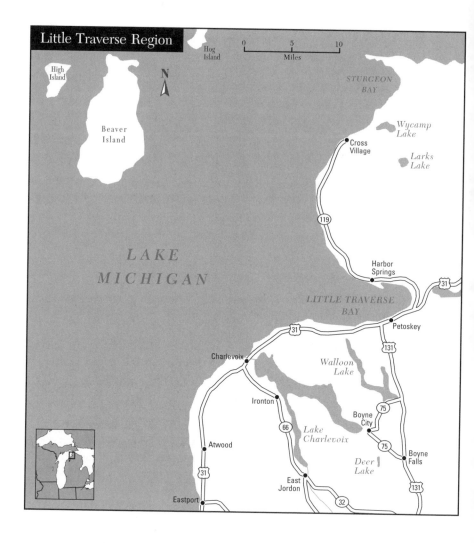

Little Traverse Region

Hog Island

High Island

N

STURGEON BAY

0   5   10
Miles

Beaver Island

Wycamp Lake

Cross Village

Larks Lake

119

LAKE MICHIGAN

Harbor Springs

31

LITTLE TRAVERSE BAY

31

Petoskey

131

Charlevoix

Walloon Lake

Ironton

75

Boyne City

66

Lake Charlevoix

75

Atwood

Boyne Falls

Deer Lake

31

East Jordon

131

Eastport

32

and it serves as a regional hub to the surrounding resort communities of Charlevoix, Harbor Springs, East Jordan, and Boyne Country. Traffic is very light in the area, and most towns are within a half-hour drive.

The prime activities in town are bicycling, walking, shopping in the downtown area, and golfing. There are 25 courses in the Little Traverse Bay region. There are no prime sandy beaches in town. Those are located farther north and south on the Lake Michigan shoreline. But there are pleasant walks to take along the bay in the downtown area.

GUIDANCE **Petoskey Chamber of Commerce** (231-347-4150; www.petoskey .com), 401 E. Mitchell St., Petoskey, MI 49770. Open 9–5. Pick up a walking tour map of downtown historic buildings or vacation planning guides for the region.

GETTING THERE *By car:* US 131 is the major artery through the area; US 31 follows the Lake Michigan shoreline and is a more scenic ride, but it's longer. It is 347 miles from Chicago and 243 from Detroit.

By air: **Cherry Capital Airport** (231- 947-2250; www.tvcairport.com) 727 Fly Don't Drive, Traverse City. This is the prime northern Michigan airport, with regular service to Minneapolis, Chicago, and Detroit. There is seasonal service from Cincinnati, Atlanta, and New York. The following carriers service the airport: Northwest Airlines, Northwest Airlink, American Eagle, United Express, and Delta. Rental cars are available at the airport.

Pellston Regional Airport (231-539-8423; www.pellstonairport.com), on US 31, just north of Pellston. Northwest Airlines runs linking flights from Detroit Metro to this small airport. Rental cars are available.

STAYING CONNECTED Many larger hotels/ have wireless Internet access, and there are a few Internet cafés. Most cell phones work well in this area. NPR radio listeners are lucky in this area: 100.9 FM from East Jordan serves the Little Traverse Bay area.

✍ **Petoskey Public Library** (231-758-3100; www.petoskeylibrary.org), 500 E. Mitchell. Open Mon.–Sat., 9–5. A good place to check on your e-mails.

PARKING Petoskey's Gaslight District can get crowded during summer afternoons, but if you look, you can find metered street parking and lots spread through downtown. There is a good lot near the Perry Hotel. To beat the crowds, there is also free parking in Waterfront Park next to the bay. An underground walkway under US 131 connects with downtown.

GETTING AROUND A bicycle is a good way to see the sights in Petoskey. There are numerous bike racks throughout downtown. A 29-mile bike path runs through Waterfront Park and connects Petoskey to Harbor Springs and Charlevoix.

WHEN TO COME The high summer season is from late May–September. Downhill skiing is a winter attraction.

MEDICAL EMERGENCY **Northern Michigan Hospital** (1-800-248-6777; www.northernhealth.org), 416 Connable Ave., Petoskey. Call 911.

THE HORTON BAY GENERAL STORE

DOWNTOWN PETOSKEY

✳ To See & Do

✄ ⚲ Little Traverse History Museum (231-347-2620; www.petoskey musuem.org), 100 Depot Court, Petoskey. Open May–Dec. The building was once the Chicago and West Michigan Railroad depot, which was built in 1892 to handle the large number of summer visitors. Ernest Hemingway, who was one of the summer people, is a major focus of exhibits and there are photos of the author and other items. There are also railroad-related displays.

Bay View (www.bayviewassoc.com). Located just north of Petoskey, off US 31, the enclave started as a Methodist summer retreat in 1875 and now has 440 Victorian-era "cottages" in the community. The best way to see the community is on a bicycle or on foot. Park in Waterfront Park in Petoskey and follow the bike trail north to Bay View. During summer months the Bay View Association hosts various musical events, classes, and seminars with a strong Christian content. For information, call 231-348-9551.

Petoskey Gaslight District walking tour. Pick up a walking tour map at the Petoskey Chamber of Commerce (see *Guidance*). The historic district has maintained its late-19th-century appearance. (See *Lodging, Dining Out,* and *Selective Shopping* for hotels, restaurants, and stores on the tour.) Make sure to see the Perry Hotel, which was built in 1899; the City Park Grill, where Hemingway ate, probably drank, and played pool; the First Presbyterian Church, built in 1888; the Carnegie Building, a former library built in 1909; Mitchell Street Frameworks, East Mitchell Street, next to J. C. Penny's, built in 1895.

✄ Waterfront Park. Access is off US 31 near the Gaslight District. The best way to see the park is by bicycle. Park near the old depot, the Little Traverse History Museum, and cycle on a path along Little Traverse Bay. There are a few beach access points, but not many. The shoreline is fairly rocky here and not suitable for swimming. There are various public rest rooms in the park.

✄ SEE-North Exploration Center (231-348-9700; www.seenorth.org), 220 Park Ave., Petoskey. The center features 16 interactive learning stations about plants, animals, and habitats of northern Michigan. There is also a gallery spotlighting the work of nature photographers. The center presents a series of "Nature at Noon" programs on Thursdays during summer in Pennsylvania Park.

✄ Historic Trolley Tours (231-347-4000), Petoskey. Tours start at Stafford's Perry Hotel and take about 90 minutes. They are offered twice weekly.

GAMBLING Odawa Casino Resort (1-877-4-GAMING; www.victories-casino .com), US 131, Petoskey. A Native American gambling casino with slot machines and game tables. Restaurants and bars are located in the complex.

CLASSES **Crooked Tree Arts Center** (231-347-4337; www.crookedtree.org), 461 E. Mitchell St. Open daily; call ahead in winter. This community arts group hosts summer music and arts instruction at it 114-year-old downtown building. It also hosts home tours, concerts, and other arts-related events. There are two art galleries, with works by local artists.

GREEN SPACE **Little Traverse Conservancy Nature Preserves** (231-347-0991; www.landtrust.org), 3264 Powell Rd., Harbor Springs. The conservancy has more than 25,000 acres of protected property that can be accessed by the public. This includes sandy beaches and forestlands. The preserves are: The Charles A. Ransom, Thorne Swift, Allan and Virginia McCune, and Round Lake.

✳ Outdoor Activities

BICYCLING AND RENTALS The region is a haven for bicyclists. The county road systems offer endless possibilities. But first try the 29-mile bike pathway between Harbor Springs and Charlevoix, which has recently been completed. A good access point is in Waterfront Park, where there is plenty of parking. The portion between Petoskey and Petoskey State Park closely follows the route of the original Little Traverse Wheelway, which went from Petoskey to Harbor Springs in the 1880s and 1890s. A gate over the trail at the east end of Waterfront Park is similar to the one making the "wheelway," during that era. **Bahnhof Sport** (231-347-2112; www.bahnhof.com), 1300 Bay View Rd., Petoskey, and **High Gear Sports** (231-347-6118; www.highgearsports.com), 1187 US 31, offer rentals and repairs.

BEACHES **Petoskey State Park** (231-347-2311; www.michigan.gov/dnr), 2475 MI 119, 1.5 miles north on MI 119 from US 31. This was the old city of

LITTLE TRAVERSE HISTORICAL MUSEUM

Petoskey swimming beach, and it still offers a sandy beach on Little Traverse Bay for swimming. The 303-acre park also has two campgrounds with 98 sites. The Old Baldy Trail leads to Old Baldy, a stable sand dune that can be climbed. Portage Trail goes through the woods. There are cross-country ski trails in the winter. It's a good place to access the Petoskey–Harbor Springs bike path.

BOATING The state **Department of Natural Resources Marina** (231-0348-0350; www.michigan.gov/dnr), Waterfront Park, Petoskey. The state runs a 100-boat marina, with 50 seasonal slips and 50 transient ones. Wireless Internet is available.

GOLFING *Also see Harbor Springs, Charlevoix, Boyne Falls for more courses.*

Bay Harbor Golf Club (231-439-4028 or 1-800-462-6963; www.bayharbor.com), 3600 Village Harbor Dr., Bay Harbor. The club offers 27 holes, including the Links, Quarry, and Preserve, which stretch along 2.5 miles of Lake Michigan shoreline.

Crooked Tree Golf Club (231-439-4030), 600 Crooked Tree Dr., Petoskey. An 18-hole, par-71 course.

✷ Lodging

All are open year-round, unless otherwise noted. (Also, see Harbor Springs.)

Stafford's Perry Hotel (231-347-4000 or 1-800-737-1899; www.staffords.com), 100 Lewis St., Petoskey. The hotel, built in 1899, is the last Victorian-age hotel in town. Now owned by the Staffords, who also own the landmark Bay View Inn nearby, the hotel offers first-class accommodations and meals. The front porch is just the place to spend a summer afternoon after shopping. The rooms have all been updated, and they have private baths. There are three restaurant venues (see *Dining Out*). Rates are $85–$269.

Bay View Inn (231-347-2771 or 1-800-258-1886), US 31, Petoskey. The 31-room Victorian inn was built in 1886 and passed through a variety of owners until Stafford C. Smith eventually bought it in the early 1960s. The place has aged well. The rooms have been updated, and have a Victorian feel that's not too overwhelming. Each room has a private bath, air-conditioning, and wireless Internet. There are televisions and phones in the inn's common areas. It's the oldest summer hotel north of Grand Rapids. There is a dining room. Rates are $90–$245.

Terrace Inn (1-800-530-9898; www.theterraceinn.com), 1549 Glendale, Bay View. Open June–Nov. The inn was built in 1911 and it has the feel of an older, aging inn. I liked the Arts & Crafts lobby. However, the outside is in need of a paint job and some cleanup work. The inn has 40 rooms, all with private baths. Some rooms have air-conditioning, telephones, and TV with cable. Many don't. There is wireless Internet, a few whirlpool rooms, and a dining room. Rates are $79–$169.

BED & BREAKFASTS 🍸 **Walloon Lake Inn** (231-535-2999; www

.walloonlakeinn.com), Winsor St., Walloon Lake Village, one block off MI 75 (Springvale Rd.). The inn has been renovated and each of the five rooms has a private bath. There is a continental breakfast served at the water's edge, and a restaurant (see *Dining Out*). Rates are $65–$90.

RESORTS ⅋ ∞ **Hidden River Golf & Casting Club** (1-800-325-4653; www.hiddenriver.com), 7688 Maple River Rd., Brutus. This place covers two passions, fly-fishing and golf. Located on the Maple River just north of Petoskey, the resort offers a golf course with a trout stream running through it. There are cabins that accommodate up to six people and a restaurant. Fly-fishing lessons are offered on the 1.5 miles of trout stream, and guides are available. Wedding friendly. The Rainbow

Room Restaurant serves lunch and dinner (see *Dining Out*).

✳ Where to Eat

DINING OUT The restaurants are open year-round, unless otherwise noted.

⅋ **The City Park Grill** (231-347-0101; www.cityparkgrill.com), 432 E. Lake St., Petoskey. Open daily for lunch and dinner. The historic building has been a restaurant since it opened in 1910. While the décor has remained Victorian, the menu has been well updated. Most of the food is cooked from scratch, and you'll find some unique dishes here and daily specials. The portions are large, and some of the appetizers could pass for a dinner. The creole gumbo was enough for a dinner. The menu is diverse for northern Michigan and

RESORTS

Bay Harbor (1-800-462-6963; www.innatbayharbor.com), 3600 Village Harbor Dr., Bay Harbor. Located off US 31, the 1,200-acre resort/residential complex is so big that it has its own town name. It's actually on the edge of Petoskey, and was the site of a cement-mining operation for more than 100 years until 1994 when developers erased the mining scars and built the sprawling complex, which includes a resort hotel, golf courses, marinas, a horse-riding course, condos, and luxury homes.

When constructed, it was seen as an environmental victory because it turned former industrial property into a thriving resort, and restored 5 miles of Lake Michigan shoreline. Since then, Bay Harbor has developed into a village, with its own shops and restaurants.

Inn at Bay Harbor (1-800-462-6963). The inn has 152 rooms and suites, an outdoor pool area, and sandy beaches on Lake Michigan. The rooms are large and contemporary and many have a view of Little Traverse Bay. The suites are bigger than some homes, with 720 to 3,000 square feet, and some have fully equipped kitchens, appliances, fireplaces, and hot tubs. Rates are $119–$881.

DINING

Sagamores (231-439-4059; www.innatbayharbor.com), 3600 Village Harbor Drive, Bay Harbor. Open for breakfast, lunch, and dinner. All the tables have a view of Little Traverse Bay. It is resort casual upscale dining here, with a full menu that has some surprises. There is traditional Midwest pot roast alongside Cajun fried perch, a nice twist on this regional dish. Salmon picatta is another nice twist. They also have an extensive wine list. Entrees are $18–$35.

The Inn Café offers casual dining for young families, with deli sandwiches, fresh bread, and the inn's own ice cream.

South American is a tavern in the inn that offers dinner. The name isn't a way of trying to be exotic in Michigan; it's actually named for a cruise ship that once sailed the Great Lakes. The menu is a bit upscale for a tavern and includes blackened breast of duck, fish, and roast beef. Entrees are $25–$43.

you'll find Italian dishes and some New Orleans–style food. Occasional entertainment. Entrees are $10–$16.

Ÿ **Stafford's Perry Hotel** (231-347-4000 or 1-800-737-1899; www.staffords.com), 100 Lewis St., Petoskey, MI 49770. Open for lunch and dinner. The hotel offers three eating venues: the upscale, elegant H. O. Rose Dining Room; the Rose Garden Veranda; and the Noggin Room Pub. The chefs have put new twists on northern Michigan favorites such as walleye, salmon, and planked whitefish. The whitefish is baked on an oak plank, giving it an almost smoked taste. The perch is a local favorite. Entrees are $17–$29.

Ÿ **Chandler's** (231-347-2981), 215 Howard St., Petoskey. Open daily for breakfast, lunch, and dinner. This is a newer place that is bringing some upscale meals to the area. Steak, seafood, chicken, and veal are on the menu. The veal is sautéed and served with tomato and goat cheese. For

lunch, there is a half-pound burger. Entrees are $33–$43.

Ÿ **Whitecaps** (231-348-7092; www.whitecapsrestaurant.com), 215 E. Lake St., Petoskey. Open for lunch and dinner. This is a contemporary place, with a menu to match. I liked their take on local Lake Michigan whitefish, which they sauté in olive oil with white wine, lemon, and butter. The cedar-planked salmon with a maple syrup glaze is a good use of local food products. There is also steak and lamb. Entrees are $21–$31.

Walloon Lake Inn (231-535-2999; www.walloonlakeinn.com), P.O. Box 459, Walloon Lake Village. Open daily. The bed & breakfast (see *Bed & Breakfasts*) tucked in by Walloon Lake's south side is a delight. Owner/chef David Beier has created an ambitious menu for this hidden-away spot. There is Rainbow Trout Hemingway, which is served with mushrooms, shallots, fresh lemon, and—in a tip of the hat to Ernest—a bit of cognac. Try the filet mignon with morel mushrooms. Morels are a Michigan mushroom, with legions of local fans. Entrees are $20–$30.

Y **The Rainbow Room Restaurant** (1-800-325-4653; www.hiddenriver com), located in the Hidden River Golf & Casting Club (see *Resorts*), 7688 Maple River Rd., Brutus. Steaks, fish, and seafood are the heart of the menu, which is a bit limited, but caters to folks who want hearty meals after a day on the links or in the stream fishing. Entrees are $17–$20.

EATING OUT Open year-round, unless otherwise noted.

Y **Mitchell Street Pub** (231-347-1801; www.mitchellstreetpub.com), 426 Mitchell St., Petoskey. Open Mon.–Sun. This is a favorite of locals who come for the burgers and beer. The walls are packed with vintage items and memorabilia, including moose heads and nautical equipment. While it's pretty much pub food, you can get a salad and a few entrees, which run around $13.

Mim's Mediterranean Grill (231-348-9994), 1823 US 31 North, Petoskey. Open Mon.–Sat. Mim's brings Greek food to northern Michigan. There is calamari, spanakopita, gyro, and other such staples. Prices are $5–$8.

Jesperson's Restaurant (231-347-3601), 312 Howard St., Petoskey. Open daily for breakfast, lunch, and dinner. Jesperson's has been here since 1906, and it's a basic American small town café. Locals congregate here for breakfast, which is midwestern fare, bacon and eggs. Prices are $6–$10.

Grand Traverse Pie Company (231-348-4060; www.gtpie.com), 316 E. Mitchell St., Petoskey. Open for breakfast, lunch, and dinner. This is a good place to start the day with fresh-brewed coffee and rolls. The centerpieces are the pies, especially traditional Michigan cherry, but the menu goes beyond dessert. The restaurant is part of a small state chain and has other locations. There are soups, salads, and sandwiches. Prices are $5–$8.

In Pellston
Y **Dam Site Inn** (231-539-8851; www.damsiteinn.com), off US 31, 1.5 miles south of Pellston. The inn has been around since 1958 and is an old school dining place in the woods. The menu ranges from frog legs to seafood, lake fish, steaks, and chicken. Entrees are $15–$20.

✳ Selective Shopping

Most Petoskey shops are open year-round, but have limited winter hours. Call before you go in the off-season.

Grandpa Shorters (231-347-2603; www.grandpashorters.com), 301 E. Lake St., Petoskey. Open daily. The store has been a location for gift shops since 1880, when Native American Chief Pe-to-se-ga purchased the building. The town was named in his father's honor. It's on the Downtown Walking Tour. Nearby Petoskey Street ran to the bay in 1900 and was lined with souvenir shops and oriental bazaars. These days, Shorters carries on that tradition and also sells Petoskey stones, jewelry, craft items, and moccasins.

Symmons General Store (231-347-2438), 401 E. Lake St., Petoskey. Open daily. Built in 1879, it was the first brick building in Petoskey and was constructed in an early Victorian Italianate style. The store is now a high-end deli and sells specialty food items, including cheese, oil, baked goods, and meats.

Back to Nature (231-439-9135), 207 Howard St., Petoskey. Open late May–early Sept. A good source for polished Petoskey stones and garden sculptures.

Ciao Bella!! Garden & Home (231-487-0623), 409 E. Lake St., Petoskey. An unusual mix of art items for gardens and homes, including artworks, garden statues, and dishes.

GALLERIES **Indian Hills Gallery** (231-347-3789), 1581 Harbor-Petoskey Rd. (MI 119), Petoskey. Open daily in summer. You'll see a lot of so-called Native American arts and crafts items throughout northern Michigan, but this is the real thing. Michigan is the land of the Ojibwa, and there are traditional items from tribe members. There is a jewelry department, with items made by tribe members throughout the nation, and a bookstore with a collection of Native American materials that deal with arts, clothing, and the lives of natives.

Gaslight Gallery (231-348-5079; www.gaslightgallery.net), 200 Howard St., Petoskey. Gallery owners Keith and Mary Ellen Lapp have put together a gallery of contemporary art not usually found in northern Michigan. There are limited editions prints, one-of-a-kind jewelry, glassware, pottery, sculpture, and furniture by Herman Miller. The gallery has

nationally known artists, along with local ones.

BOOKSTORES **McLean & Eakin Booksellers** (231-347-1180), 307 E. Lake St., Petoskey. There is a large selection of Hemingway books and biographies about the writer, along with a large selection of local history, nature, and Great Lakes lore books, and the usual bestsellers and summer beach books. The store brings authors to Petoskey for talks and workshops during summer months.

Horizon Books (231-347-2590; www.horizonbooks.com), 319 E. Mitchell St., Petoskey. Open daily, 8–10. This smaller northern Michigan chain of bookstores has a good selection of regional books set in and about Michigan. During summer, they bring in many regional authors for book signings and readings. It's a good place to start, if you're interested in the history of the Little Traverse Bay region.

✳ Special Events

Late June **Gallery Walk** (231-347-4150), downtown Petoskey. A walking tour of art galleries.

Late July **Art in the Park.** The event brings artists to Pennsylvania Park, with items ranging from pottery and jewelry to paintings and photographs.

Mid-August **Festival on the Bay.** Live music, a triathlon, bay cruises, arts and crafts in downtown Petoskey.

Early October **Fall Kids Fest,** downtown Petoskey. Local kids parade in their Halloween costumes.

HARBOR SPRINGS

Located on the north side of Little Traverse Bay, the city has a reputation as being one of the most well-to-do communities in the state and boasts many million-dollar lakefront homes. It has a population of 1,567, but that swells during the Memorial Day–Labor Day summer season. Its many upscale shops are only open in the summer, and their owners head for Florida in the fall.

This playground of the wealthy once had a large concentration of Native Americans and was called L'Arbre Croche. It was founded by Jesuit priests, who established a school here. French traders renamed it Petit Traverse, or Little Traverse. The village was eventually called Harbor Springs in 1880.

Boats started bringing summer visitors to the harbor in the late 19th century, and a train once ran to Petoskey every 30 minutes during the summer season. To keep those boats safe Little Traverse Lighthouse was constructed on Harbor Point. It's a private residence, but it can be seen from the harbor area.

GUIDANCE **Harbor Springs Chamber of Commerce** (231-526-7999; www.harborspringschamber.com), 368 E. Main St. Open daily in the summer season, Sun.–Thur., 11–4, and Fri.–Sat., 11–5.

MEDIA *Harbor Light* (231-526-2191; www.harborlightnews.com), 211 E. Third St., Harbor Springs, MI 49740. The weekly paper is a good source of local events and news.

MEDICAL EMERGENCY **Northern Michigan Hospital** (1-800-248-6777; www.northernhealth.org), 416 Connable Ave., Petoskey. Call 911.

✳ To See & Do

❧ **Andrew Blackbird Museum** (231-526-0612), 368 E. Main St., Harbor Springs. Open year-round, Mon.–Sat. The museum is in a building used as the first post office in Harbor Springs and is dedicated to preserving the heritage of Native Americans. There are displays of arts and crafts. Blackbird (1815–1908) was an Ottawa Indian who lived in the house from 1858 until his death. He was a tribal leader and wrote a history of his people, *History of the Ottawa and Chippewa Indians of Michigan*. The book was the first such account written by a Native American.

❧ **Michigan Fisheries Visitor Center** (231-348-0998; www.michigan.gov/dnr), 3377 US 31, Oden. Open late May–early Sept., 10–6. Open weekends other times of year. The fish hatchery opened in 1920 and was renovated into a visitor center in 2003. There is information about how fish are raised in a hatchery, and a guided hatchery tour. Families and groups can take special tours. Admission is free.

SCENIC DRIVES To see some of the better lakefront homes in Harbor Springs, take Zoll Street off East Main and follow it until it becomes Beach Drive. The homes, most of them white and built in the late 19th and early 20th centuries, were considered by their owners as summer cottages. They were constructed in an era before air-conditioning and face Little Traverse Bay, their lawns going down to the lake. Most of this is private property, and some of the side streets are closed to traffic. A bicycle would be a good way to make the tour.

✳ Outdoor Activities

BEACHES ✍ The **City of Harbor Springs Beach** is near Zorn Park in the downtown area. It has lifeguards, a beach house for changing, rafts, and white sand.

🐾 **Zoll Street Beach** is dog friendly and is good for swimming and for kayak access to Little Traverse Bay. Both beaches are free.

GOLFING **Boyne Highlands** (231-526-3000; www.boyne.com), 600 Highland Dr., Harbor Springs. There are four top-flight golf courses at the resort, Heather (designed by Robert Trent Jones), Arthur Hills, Moor, and Donald Ross Memorial (see *Resorts*).

BOATING **Harbor Springs Municipal Marina** (231-526-5355), 250 E. Bay St., Harbor Springs. There are 31 seasonal and 46 transient slips available. Services include rest rooms, showers, water, pump-out, and launching.

BICYCLE RENTALS **Touring Gear Bike Shop** (231-526-7152; www.tourings gearbikes.com), 108 E. Third St., Harbor Springs.

A COTTAGE ON LAKE MICHIGAN

KAYAKING The Outfitter (231-526-2621; www.outfitterharborsprings.com), 153 E. Main St., Harbor Springs. Open daily, 9:30–5:30. Kayak rentals, sales, and local information during the water months, and cross-country ski gear during winter.

FISHING Trout and Salmon Charters (231-347-3232), Petoskey and Harbor Springs.

SPORTING CLAYS Wycamp Shooting Preserve (231-526-6651; www.wycamp lakeclub.com), 5484 Pleasantview Rd., Harbor Springs. Sporting clays are available to the public by appointment. There are also fall hunts for upland birds and duck hunts.

HORSEBACK RIDING ✿ **North Country Farms** (231-539-8315), 3718 Amikly Rd., Pellston. The farm near Cross Village provides western-style riding.

✳ Lodging

Most lodging for Harbor Springs is located in Petoskey or along US 131, where there are many chain hotels and motels. Rentals are also available in Harbor Springs (see *Rentals*).

Colonial Inn (summer 231-526-2111, winter 305-734-5246; www .harborsprings.com), 210 Artesian Ave., Harbor Springs. Open late May–mid-Oct. The 40-room inn has been in operation since 1894, and has been run by innkeeper Tim Brown since 1968. It's a short walk to the waterfront, where the inn has an access point to the beach. Surrounding the inn is the Wequetonsing summer area, which is composed of turn-of-the-century Victorian summer homes. These are the only accommodations in the area, and it is difficult to find. The rooms are light and airy. Many of the roads, although public, are blocked to traffic. Rates are $109–$199.

⚭ **Birchwood Inn** (231-26-2151; www.birchwoodinn.com), 7077 Lake Shore Dr., Harbor Springs. This isn't your normal motel. The inn was built in the early 1960s as a corporate retreat for a potato chip company and has been preserved and renovated into a lodgelike place with wood-beamed ceilings and paneled walls. The main lobby has a fieldstone fireplace. A continental breakfast is served. There is an outside pool and garden. The rooms range from a single with a double bed to a two-bedroom suite. Rates are $59–$299.

BED & BREAKFASTS Inn at Crooked Lake (231-439-9984; www.innatcrookedlake.com), 4407 US 31, Oden. The inn is a restored 1906 cottage on Crooked Lake, near Harbor Springs, and has five rooms with private baths. The Woodlands suite has the original birch paneling and a two-person hot tub. The rooms have a cottage feel, and the dining area, where a gourmet breakfast is served, is wood paneled. At night, desserts are served in front of the fireplace. The front porch overlooks Crooked Lake, and swimming and boating are available. Rates are $100–$200.

Kimberly Country Estate (231-526-7646; www.kimberlycountryestate

HARBOR SPRINGS MARINA

.com), 2287 Bester Rd., Harbor Springs. This is more than a bed & breakfast, and it lives up to its name—an estate. The inn overlooks the Wequetonsing Golf Course and has suites with private baths and hot tubs. The public rooms are elegantly furnished and have the feel of an English country estate. Several of the six rooms have their own verandas and most have canopy beds. Two rooms have fireplaces. There is a two-night minimum stay and children aren't allowed. Rates are $175–$295.

RESORTS **Boyne Highlands** (231-526-3000; www.boyne.com), 600 Highland Dr., Harbor Springs. The ski/golf resort has various types of lodging available at its sprawling complex just north of downtown Harbor Springs. The main lodge has 165 rooms in an English-style country estate building, some of which sleep up to six. Condos, cottages, and townhouses are also available. The rooms are done in a contemporary style. They offer various golf and downhill ski packages. There are four golf courses at the Highlands (see *Golfing*).

RENTALS **Northern Lights Vacation Rentals** (231-347-8855 or 1-877-347-8855; www.harborpetoskeyrentals.com), 692 W. Conway, Harbor Springs, MI 49740.

Graham Management (231-526-9671; www.grahamrentalproperties.com), 163 E. Main St., Harbor Springs.

Up North Vacation Rentals (1-800-901-8922; www.vistupnorth.com), Glen Arbor (1-877-334-3345), 6445 Western Ave. or in Traverse City (1-800-901-8922), 441 E. Front.

* Where to Eat

DINING OUT The restaurants are open year-round, unless otherwise noted.

Y The New York (231-526-1904; www.thenewyork.com), 101 State St., Harbor Springs. Open daily at 5. There has been a restaurant on this corner since 1904 when the Leahy brothers, from New York, put together a hotel/restaurant called Leahy's New York Hotel, which consisted of a lobby, a bar for men only, and bowling alleys. The food ranges from classic Great Lakes whitefish to chicken, salmon, steak, and duck. The baby back ribs are also a good choice. There is a large wine cellar. Entrees are $16–$32.

Y Stafford's Pier Restaurant (231-526-6201; www.staffords.com), 102 Bay St., Harbor Springs. This is another one of the Stafford's restaurants. There are others in Charlevoix, Petoskey, and at Bay View, and all are topnotch. Lake fish and steaks take top billing here. The whitefish is cooked on an oak plank and is a local favorite. Lake perch are a favorite too, as are walleye. The chefs have taken cold-water lobster and put it on a Midwest plank for a new twist. Entrees are $25–$45. The Chartroom offers more causal dining and lighter meals, with Great Lakes fish and cherry-smoked ribs. Prices are $7–$25.

EATING OUT Juilleret's (231-526-2821), 130 State St., Harbor Springs. Established in 1895, this is the oldest family-run restaurant in Michigan. Closed Tuesdays. This small town café is a real relief from overly trendy restaurants with food that doesn't measure up to the décor. Inside, the restaurant is simply decorated, and it's the food that has been bringing people back for generations. The planked whitefish is crisp and enticing. There is an old-fashioned soda fountain inside. Prices are $8–$12.

Y Teddy Griffin's Roadhouse (231-526-7805; www.teddgriffins.com), 50 Highland Pike Rd., Harbor Springs. Open daily at 4. The stuff here is a step up from pub food, but the sports bar may just be the kind of place you're looking for after a day at the beach. The menu includes shrimp, burgers, pizza, and fried lake fish, along with a few entrees. Prices are $8–$16.

Y Bar Harbor (232-526-2671), 100 State St., Harbor Springs. The boating crowd can be found many nights at this beer and burger place across from the marinas on Lake Michigan. It's the local watering hole most nights. Prices are $8–$10.

Mary Ellen's Place (231-526-5591), 145 E. Main St., Harbor Springs. Open daily, year-round. This 1950s-style soda fountain and newsstand is a local favorite that serves omelets, homemade soup, chili, and soda fountain fare. Prices are $5–$6.

Y Turkey's Café & Pizzeria (231-526-6041), 250 E. Main St., Harbor Springs. This has been a local hangout for years, offering up bacon and egg breakfasts, solid sandwiches, and family dinners. Prices are $5–$10.

Woolly Bugger, Roaster of Fine Coffee & Internet Café (231-242-0592), 181 E. Main St., Harbor Springs. This is the place to catch up on your e-mail over fresh coffee. Pizza and other snacks are served.

CROSS VILLAGE

Once a thriving Lake Michigan lumber town, this small community now has fewer than 300 residents, but it is an important site for Native Americans. There were once more than 20 tribes living in the area, and Father Jacques Marquette, a well-known French Jesuit priest, endeared himself to the local Indians by placing a huge white cross on a bluff overlooking the lake, thus the town's name. A replica of the cross still stands on the bluff.

The 27-mile drive from Harbor Springs to Cross Village takes you through the "Tunnel of Trees," on MI 119, with the arching trees creating a tunnel. It's a favorite route for bicyclists, so watch out, the road is narrow. And take your time; it's a winding road that follows the Lake Michigan shoreline, which has some of the most expensive real estate in the state. The road is lined with million-dollar homes and fantastic views. There are numerous places to pull off and look at the lake. You may want to take CR 66, a paved country road, back to US 31 for a quicker return trip.

Legs Inn (231-526-2281; www.legsinn.com) 6425 Lake Shore Dr., is open daily May–late October. The casual dining tavern is the heart of Cross Village, and the eclectic design has been attracting visitors since the 1920s. It's a place that could only have been created in America.

The founder was a Polish immigrant who, tired for working in the auto plants in Detroit and Chicago, moved to northern Michigan in search of a place that reminded him of Poland. That is the story of Stanley Smolak, who was born in Kamionka, Poland, in 1887. Before he died, he had become a resort owner and had gained a reputation as a sculptor working in wood.

✳ Selective Shopping

ART GALLERIES There are about a dozen art galleries in Harbor Springs. Most are open daily late May–early September. Call for fall and winter hours.

Boyer Glassworks (231-526-6359), 207 State St., Harbor Springs. Harry Boyer creates hand-blown glass in the studio/gallery. Original paintings by Kathleen Boyer are also on display.

By the Bay (231-526-3964; www.bythebay.com), 172 E. Main St., Harbor Springs. Open Tues.–Sat., 10–5.

This place is for Great Lakes buffs who like nautical items. There is a good selection of Great Lakes shipping artworks and lighthouses. There are also clocks and other items with a nautical theme and books and maps.

Hramiec Hoffman (231-526-1011; www.hramiechoffman.com), 6911 MI 119, Harbor Springs. The gallery is devoted to Mary Hramiec-Hoffman's original artwork of northern Michigan cottage scenes. She captures dogs, children, and the landscape in the colors of summer.

Cross Village was an old Native American community composed of Ojibwas, and Smolak immediately became friendly with them when he arrived in 1921. With their influence, and inspiration from nature, he created what was to become the Legs Inn in the late 1920s when he built a souvenir shop and later a tavern. The outside is a near fantasyland, an almost castlelike lodge building. Inside are the many woodcarvings done by Smolak. The interior is dominated by four fireplaces, and the walls are done in rustic logs. Everywhere you look there is either a Native American item or one of Smolak's creations.

While it was long a tavern, these days it is a casual dining spot with a Polish influence. For folks who haven't been initiated, there's the Taste of Poland, which includes cabbage rolls, kielbasa, sauerkraut, and pierogis. There are also some vegetarian Polish dishes on the menu, but I wouldn't stray. The bigos, a Polish hunter's stew made with sauerkraut, cabbage, smoked sausage, and mushrooms and served with dumplings, was enough food for an entire day. There is music many nights.

If staying in the area, this would be the type of place you would want to try several times, including for lunch. While many restaurants are one-trick ponies, this place has enough diversity on the menu to make the dining possibilities nearly endless.

After a Polish meal, a good walk around town is probably needed. The inn maintains a delightful garden with a view of Lake Michigan, and there are several interesting gift shops within walking distance.

The inn has several remodeled cottages for rent. They are rustic, wood-paneled structures. Rates are $69 nightly and $695 weekly, peak season.

Knox Galleries (231-526-5377; www.knoxgalleries.com), 175 E. Main St., Harbor Springs. These bronzes are sure to attract men into the gallery, with their outdoorsy and historical themes. There are also paintings of outdoor scenes.

ANTIQUES SHOPS Most are open during summer months. Call for winter hours.

L'Esprit (231-526-9888; www.lesprit.com), 195 W. Main St., Harbor Springs. There is more than 4,500 square feet of French country furniture and accessories, along with architectural and garden items.

Joie de Vie (231-347-1400; www.joiedevieantiques.com), 1901 MI 119, Petoskey. There is a selection of European antiques and home décor.

JEWELRY **Becky Thatcher Designs** (231-526-9336; www.beckythatcherdesigns.com), 117 W. Main St., Harbor Springs. The jewelry styles are influenced by the northern Michigan landscape. There are other stores in Leland, Glen Arbor, and Key West.

BOOKSTORES Between the Covers (231-526-6658), 152 E. Main, Harbor Springs. Open daily. The community bookstore focuses on regional books, as well as best sellers and beach books.

✳ Special Events

Mid-June **Harbor Springs Waterfront Wine Festival.** Local wineries show off their products during the one-evening event on the waterfront. Wisconsin breweries and other wine makers are also represented. There is music, too.

July 4th Fireworks are lighted over the harbor at dusk. There is also a parade on Main Street.

Mid-July **Blissfest** (www.blissfest .org). The music festival is several decades old and is held annually at the Blissfest Festival Farm, 3695 Division Rd., Harbor Springs, MI 49740. The music is bluegrass, blues, Cajun, Celtic, folk, jazz, Latin, ethnic, and world.

Late September **Taste of Harbor Springs.** An outdoor food event that showcases local restaurants.

Early October **Harbor Harvest Festival.** Local artists and crafts people display their works and local farmers bring their produce to the daylong event at the waterfront tennis courts.

BOYNE CITY

This small town on Lake Charlevoix was first settled by a couple looking for their dream home. But it wasn't like the plush, lakefront homes that now grace the area, it was a shack. John and Harriet Miller arrived in Boyne City in 1856 from upstate New York, coming there because Harriet had dreamed of a house on the east end of a lake shaped like a bear. They first came to Northport along the Lake Michigan coast, and then heard about Lake Charlevoix. After persuading a ship captain to take them to the eastern shore, they found an abandoned shack on the lakefront and moved in.

These days there are no shacks, just high-end condos and homes on the shoreline. Much of the activity here involves boating, and there are private developments centered on the boating life and a public marina in the city's downtown area on Lake Street.

Although Boyne City is on the eastern shore of Lake Charlevoix, it's a Great Lakes port town. The lake has access to Lake Michigan in Charlevoix via the Boyne River.

Boyne is a real relief to visit after spending time in the nearby larger communities of Traverse City and Petoskey, which have both suffered from urban sprawl in recent years. Boyne is still a small Up North village with 3,500 residents that offers decent shopping and a quaint restored downtown area, but with an easy pace. A cyclist can easily negotiate the streets, even during rush hour. Parking isn't a problem in summer, either.

Boyne City is the service center for Boyne Country, which includes Walloon Lake, Boyne Falls, and East Jordan, all less than 10 miles away. Boyne Falls has a major downhill ski resort, which attracts winter visitors.

Boyne City has a decent selection of restaurants, a historic hotel (Hemingway slept here), and a good number of art galleries. The downside is that there are only two public beaches, and they're rocky. However, Young State Park nearby offers plenty of sandy beaches.

Like most northern Michigan towns, it started as a lumbering center in the 19th century, but between 1890 and 1910 tourism started to develop. Steamboats served Boyne, like most Great Lakes ports, connecting the small lumber town to places like Chicago, Detroit, and Cleveland.

Nearby is the town of Ellsworth, which has a very good bed & breakfast and two fine restaurants.

Horton Bay, or Horton's Bay as Hemingway spelled it, is a collection of several houses, a general store turned upscale deli, and a backwoods Hemingway museum. It's a must stop for Hemingway buffs. Some of his stories were set in the small burg.

GUIDANCE **Boyne Area Chamber of Commerce** (231-582-6222; www.boyne city.com), 28 S. Lake St., Boyne City. Open Mon.–Fri., 9–5. Look for a guide to the entire Boyne Country area.

GETTING THERE *By car:* Take US 131 to MI 75 or Boyne City Road and go 6 miles west. There is very little traffic in this area, even on summer weekends.

MEDICAL EMERGENCY **Charlevoix Area Hospital** (231-547-4024; www.cah .org), 14700 Lakeshore Dr., Charlevoix. Call 911.

ERNEST HEMINGWAY FISHED FROM THIS LAKE CHARLEVOIX BEACH.

WALLOON LAKE INN

☀ To See & Do

⌀ Visit the **Old City Park** next to the Boyne River. It's a classic old-style park with plenty of shade trees and a gazebo, where there are musical concerts on summer evenings.

⌀ **Historical Museum** (231-582-6597; www.gov.boynecity.com), 319 N. Lake St., Boyne City. Open late May–early Sept., Mon.–Fri. Railroads, logging, and community history are the subject of most exhibits. Admission is free.

Avalanche Mountain Preserve, 1129 Wilson St., Boyne City. Take a picnic lunch to the top of Avalanche Mountain. You must climb 462 steps, but there's a great view of Lake Charlevoix. There are 300 acres of woodlands.

☀ Outdoor Activities

CANOEING & KAYAKING The possibilities are limitless on Lake Charlevoix. Rentals are available at Young State Park (see *Green Space*). The Jordan River, which empties into Lake Charlevoix at East Jordan, is a good kayak and canoe river. Rentals are available at **Jordan Valley Outfitters** (231-536-0006), **Swan Valley Marina** (231-536-2672), **Swiss Hideway** (231-536-2341), and **Ward Brothers** (231-547-2371). The outfitters will arrange dropoffs and pickups along the river.

HORSEBACK RIDING ⌀ **Walloon Equestrian Center** (231-535-7171), 2900 Old State Rd., Boyne City. Summer day horse camps for kids.

FISHING The nearby Jordan River is considered a blue-ribbon trout stream, and Lake Charlevoix has stocked rainbow trout and other species.

GOLFING *See Petoskey, Charlevoix, Boyne Falls, and Harbor Springs.*

GREEN SPACE Young State Park (231-582-7523; www.michigan.gov/dnr), 02280 Boyne City Rd., Boyne City. The 563-acre park has beach access to Lake Charlevoix and 240 modern campsites. Trails run through it, offering hiking in the summer and cross-country skiing in the winter. The park concession rents canoes, kayaks, and camping equipment. It also has gourmet coffees and home-made baked goods. There is a boat launch and picnic areas.

✳ Lodging

Also see Charlevoix and Petoskey.

Wolverine-Dilworth Inn (231-582-7388; www.wolverinedilworthinn .com), 300 Water St., Boyne City. Sue and Ray Christensen have come to the rescue of this historic hotel, reviving it and putting some spark in the food (see *Dining Out*). The hotel was built in 1911 by a group of area lumber barons who wanted a place to entertain guests from out of town. It's a registered historic hotel, and many rooms are decorated in Victorian style. There is a covered porch on which to lounge, and the lobby has an Arts & Crafts look. Rumor has it that Ernest Hemingway stayed here with his second wife. We're not certain, but if he did, he probably made use of the ornate Library Bar. Rates are $89–$139.

MOTELS Boyne City Motel (231-582-6701; www.boynecitymotel.com), 110 N. East St., Boyne City. This is an old school motel that has been nicely updated with fresh paint and restoration work. It has in-room refrigerators and wireless Internet. Rates are $50–$60.

The Brown Trout Motel (231-549-2791; www.browntroutmotel.com), 2510 Nelson Ave. (US 131), Boyne Falls. The 14-unit motel complex has a heated pool and spa area, which is attractive to downhill skiers at nearby Boyne Mountain. The rooms are clean and neat and many of them have knotty pine interiors. Rates are $60–$70.

RESORTS Boyne Mountain (231-549-6000 or 1-800-GO-BOYNE; www .boyne.com), 1 Boyne Mountain, Boyne Falls. The major downhill ski and golf resort offers various types of lodging, including hotel rooms, condos, villas, and cabins that sleep up to 12 people. The rooms are modern, clean, and have nice views of the surrounding downhill ski slopes. Wireless Internet is available.

✳ Where to Eat

DINING OUT ☿ Wolverine-Dilworth Inn (231-582-7388; www.wolverine dilworthinn.com), 300 Water St., Boyne City. Sue and Ray Christensen have brought a much needed full-menu restaurant to Boyne City, and in a historic setting. The dinner menu is pretty simple: steak, chicken, fish, and pasta. I liked the pan-fried walleye, which is served with potatoes and vegetables. Lunches include chicken strips, quesadillas, and burgers. Entrees are $10–$15.

Y **Lester's** (231-582-4500), 151 Ray St., Boyne City, MI 49712. Open daily, 11–11. Located in a historic railroad depot, this has been a perennial favorite in the community for years. The specialty is barbecued ribs and chicken. There are other items on the menu, but we'd stick with the barbecue. Entrees are $10–$15.

EATING OUT Horton Bay General Store (231-582-7827; www.hortons baygeneralstore.com), 5115 Boyne Rd., Boyne City. Open late Sept.–Oct. When Ernest Hemingway was a boy, there weren't any shopping malls to hang around when he wanted to get away from the nearby family cottage on Walloon Lake, so this general store sufficed. Young Ernest was often found on the front porch of the store. Chip and Claudia Lorenger, who also own J. D.s Market and Deli in Boyne City, are the current owners of store, which first opened in 1876. The couple has as much passion for food as for restoration work. They've added a rustic back dining room with an outdoor patio, where the menu has evolved since Hemingway's day. The best time to stop by is 4–6, when the couple serves up their deli delights. Try the smoked fish with homemade bread. Prices are $10–$15.

Y **Red Mesa Grill** (232-582-0049; www.redmesagrill.com), 117 Water St., Boyne City. Open Mon.–Sat. for lunch and dinner. The grill helps spice up eating in Boyne Country, with its Latin American menu that ranges from Peruvian armadillo eggs for appetizers to Costa Rican garlic steak for dinner. And there are tradition Mexican tacos and such. I liked

their take on walleye; it's topped with roasted corn salsa and baked in a cornhusk. There's another Red Mesa in nearby Traverse City. Entrees are $12–$18.

Roberts Restaurant (231-82-9927), 216 N. Lake St., Boyne City. Open daily. This is where the locals meet for bacon, eggs, and potatoes or sausage gravy. They make their own bake goods and soups. Prices are $5–$8.

Rennie's Restaurant (231-582-3311), 5 W. Main St., Boyne City. Open daily, 7–10, May–Oct. This is a new entry in the area, and it's open for breakfast, lunch, and dinner. Fresh biscuits and bread are for breakfast. For lunch there are burgers, but also a veggie sandwich for nonmeat eaters. For dinner, there is pasta, chicken, ribs, and seafood. Entrees are $10–$20.

Y **Boyne River Inn** (231-582-6768), 229 Water St., Boyne City. Open daily. The classic main street family tavern is a favorite of locals, who sent me to the Friday fish fry. Perhaps it was a bad night for fish. It was overly fried and pretty greasy. Next time I'll try the burgers. Prices are $5–$11.

✳ Entertainment

Y **The New Tannery** (231-582-2272; www.thenewtannery.com), 220 S. Lake St., Boyne City. Open Wed.–Sat. The place takes its name from a tannery that once operated during the late 19th and early 20th century in Boyne City. It's one of the few places around with entertainment. There are karaoke nights. The food is basic tavern fare, ribs, chicken, and burgers. There is a children's menu. Entrees are $12–$14.

✳ Special Events

Mid-May **The National Morel Mushroom Festival** (231-582-6222; www.morelfest.com). The weekend event celebrates the morel mushroom, which has legions of culinary fans. There is a mushroom hunt, a carnival, and mushrooms for sale.

July 4th The **Horton Bay 4th of July Parade and Fun Run** is the stuff of legend. The quirky event attracts thousands to this hamlet near Lake Charlevoix with a population of just a few folks. The only business in town is the Horton Bay General Store, were Ernest Hemingway hung around when he was a boy.

EAST JORDAN

Strollers in the Midwest often walk on one of the town's products—sewer grates. The East Jordan Iron Works long ago got involved in making them, and they grace the streets of many cities and towns. But you shouldn't think of sewers representing this small town of about 2,500 on the south arm of Lake Charlevoix and at the mouth of the Jordan River.

Boating, swimming, and camping are the main summer activities, and downhill skiing in the winter keeps the restaurants and motels filled. The nearby Jordan River is a blue-ribbon trout stream that attracts anglers.

GUIDANCE **East Jordan Chamber of Commerce** (231-536-7351; www .ejchamber.org), 100 Main St., Suite B, East Jordan, MI 49727. Open Mon.–Fri., 9–5.

✳ To See & Do

✎ ☂ **Raven Hill Discovery Center** (231-536-3369; www.ravenhilldiscovery center.com), 4737 Fuller Rd., East Jordan. Open daily in summer. The center focuses on giving children and adults a better understanding of art and nature. There are outdoor sculptures, science and technology displays, and a room filled with live animals such as snakes and lizards. There is also an adjacent nature trail. Admission is $7.

✳ Lodging

East Jordon doesn't have a lot of lodging. Charlevoix, 14 miles north, has more hotels and motels. Also, try Boyne Falls, Boyne City, and Petoskey, which are 7 to 10 miles away.

BED & BREAKFAST Jordan Inn (231-536-9906; www.jordaninn.com), 288 Main St., East Jordan, MI 49727. The inn has four suites and two

HOUSE ON THE HILL BED & BREAKFAST

TAPAWINGO RESTAURANT

rooms, all of which have a cottage feel and are decorated with furnishings ranging from French country to Victorian. Most rooms have king-sized beds, and some have a view of Lake Charlevoix. There is a restaurant (see *Dining Out*). Rates are $90–$125.

✳ Where to Eat

DINING OUT ♈ **Jordan Inn** (231-536-9906; www.jordaninn.com), 288 Main St., East Jordan. The historic inn has rooms (see *Bed & Breakfasts*) and a restaurant. Breakfasts of omelets, crepe-style pancakes, and lighter items are available to the public as well as inn guests. Lunch includes salads, soups, and sandwiches. For dinner, there are three-to five-course meals, which include seared duck breasts with pink peppercorn sauce and poached salmon. Prices are $15–$25.

EATING OUT ♈ **Lumber Jack Grill** (231-536-2191; www.lumberjack grill.com), 101 Main St., East Jordan. Open daily. This family-style pub has been a local favorite for years, and serves breakfast, lunch, and dinner. Fare ranges from burgers to prime rib, and of course there's the almost required fish fry on Friday. They do serve more healthy food in the form of wraps. Prices are $6–$15.

♈ **Murry's Bar & Grill** (231-536-3395; www.murrysbar.com), 115 Main St., East Jordan. Open daily spring and summer. Located near the marina, this family-style pub has a deck overlooking Lake Charlevoix. Burgers are the mainstay here, but there are some surprises, like a perogie (a potato, and cheese appetizer). Entrees are $16–$18.

CHARLEVOIX

Every town has its motto, and they are usually forgettable, but not so with this community, which calls itself "Charlevoix the Beautiful." Located between Lake Michigan and Lake Charlevoix, it lives up to its moniker and has long been a summer retreat for the well-to-do and boaters, who find a safe harbor from Lake Michigan in Lake Charlevoix.

The city of nearly 3,000 is named for Pierre Francois Xavier de Charlevoix, a French explorer who once stayed a night on nearby Fisherman's Island. The area was home to many Native Americans, but by the 1850s there were enough white people to cause some problems. Beaver Island, offshore of Charlevoix in Lake Michigan, was home to a group of Mormons, one of whom, Jesse Strang, had named himself King Strang, which angered the local residents. Strang was assassinated on June 20, 1856, and non-Mormons from the mainland were blamed, which led to what came to be known as the Battle of Pine River. Strang's followers landed on the mainland and engaged in a skirmish with the local residents.

Eventually, things calmed down, and Charlevoix, with its good harbor, became a summer destination for Chicago residents, many of whom built what are called Mushroom Houses, a sort of Arts & Crafts home that looks like a mushroom.

But it wasn't just the middle class who came. It's rumored that Al Capone, the Chicago gangster from the 1920s, had a safe house in Charlevoix.

GUIDANCE Charlevoix Chamber of Commerce (231-237-9410; www .charlevoix.org), 408 Bridge St., Charlevoix. Open Mon.–Fri., 9–5.

GETTING THERE *By car:* The major artery through town is US 31. Try taking MI 72 to US 31 or MI 66 from US 31.

GETTING AROUND Driving, walking, and bicycling are pretty much the only way. There's no public transportation in town.

LIBRARY Charlevoix Public Library (231-547-2651; www.charlevoixlibrary .org), 220 W. Clinton St., Charlevoix, MI 49720. Open Mon.–Sat. A good source of local history material.

MEDICAL EMERGENCY Charlevoix Area Hospital (231-547-4024; www.cah .org), 14700 Lakeshore Dr., Charlevoix. Call 911.

✳ To See & Do

Beaver Island Boat Co. (231-547-2311 or 1-888-446-4095; www.bibco.com), 103 Bridge Park Dr., Charlevoix. Open April–Dec., with two to four trips weekly. The trip to the island in Lake Michigan on the car ferry takes about two hours. Some people just spend the day on the island, while others opt for a longer stay. There are hotels and motels on the island and restaurants (see Beaver Island). You can take your vehicle, a bicycle, and canoes and kayaks. The boat also runs an excursion along the Lake Michigan shoreline to Mackinaw. Cost is $140 for a vehicle round trip and $42 for adult passage round trip.

∅ **Ironton Ferry,** Ironton. Take a car ferry from Ironton, just south of Charlevoix, across a narrow spot in Lake Charlevoix. It saves a bit of time if you are going to Boyne City, but it's also fun, and a nice way to see the lake.

∅ **Harsha House Museum** (231-547-0373; www.chxhistory.com), 103 State St., Charlevoix. Open mid-June–early Oct., Mon.–Sun., 1–4. Among the exhibits is Ernest Hemingway's original marriage license to his first wife, Hadley Richardson. They were married in Horton Bay, near Charlevoix. There are old photos of the area and restored Victorian rooms. The museum was built in 1891 and was donated to the Charlevoix Historical Society in 1979.

⊙ **Castle Farms** (231-237-0884; www.castlefarms.com), 5052 N. MI 66, Charlevoix, MI 49620. The stone farm complex was built in 1918 by Albert and Anna Loeb. Albert was the acting president of Sears, Roebuck and Company, and his dream was to build a model farm using the newest farm equipment from Sears. The castlelike buildings were based on stone barns in Normandy and the house was modeled after the French Renaissance Chateaux. Loeb died in 1924 and his son, Ernest, ran the farm until 1927, when an agricultural depression forced the family to sell the property. It is now used for antique shows, a rodeo, a fiber arts festival, and other events. Self-guided tours of the estate and its gardens are available. Cost is $6.

✳ Outdoor Activities

BEACHES *∅* **Fisherman's Island State Park** (231-547-6641; www.michigan .gov/dnr), 16480 Bell's Bay Rd., Charlevoix. This place is a little gem, with its 5 miles of undeveloped Lake Michigan shoreline. The 2,678-acre park isn't an island; it's just named for Fisherman's Island, which is a short distance offshore from the picnic area. The 3-mile hiking trail is used for cross-country skiing in winter. There are 81 rustic campsites. The fee is $10 a night, and a state park sticker is required for entrance, $20.

∅ **Lake Michigan Beach in Charlevoix.** This small beach is a bit hard to find, but worth the effort. Head west from downtown Charlevoix, along Park Avenue or the Pine River Channel. Turn off US 31 and wind through the neighborhood of older cottages until you get to the beach. It has white sand, and the water is shallow. There is playground equipment, picnic areas, lifeguards, and an excellent view of the Charlevoix Lighthouse.

∅ **Depot Beach on Lake Charlevoix.** The water is warmer, and the waves are toned down from the Lake Michigan beaches. There are lifeguards, playground equipment, rest rooms, and picnic areas. Follow Mercer Boulevard east off US 31. The beach is near an old train depot, which is now a historical museum.

∅ **Ferry Avenue Beach on Lake Charlevoix.** The water is warmer than in Lake Michigan, and the beach has a shallow, sandy area for kids. It has playground equipment, a concession stand, and rest rooms. Take Stover Road east off MI 66 or Belvedere Avenue from downtown.

SAILING TOURS **Sunshine Charters** (231-547-0266; www.sunshinecharters .com), 408 Bridge St., Charlevoix. Sailboat cruises and charters on Lake Charlevoix.

TRAILS North Point Nature Preserve. The 27-acre preserve has many trails running through it. Take Mercer Road north off US 31 to Pleasant Street, turn left onto Mt. McSauba, and then turn right before the dirt road. The preserve is on the left.

BOATING City of Charlevoix Marina (231-547-3272), downtown Charlevoix. The city maintains a yacht marina on Round Lake, which has access to Lakes Michigan and Charlevoix. It has electricity, water hook-ups, showers, and rest rooms.

BOAT LAUNCHES The Lake Charlevoix facility is next to Ferry Beach at the end of Stover Road off MI 66. There are ramps and parking. Another ramp is on the south arm of Lake Charlevoix in Ironton off MI 66. There are two boat ramps with parking and access to Lake Michigan. They are located at the end of Lake Shore Drive near the St. Marys Cement Co. and on US 31 north of Lexalite.

GOLFING Belevedere Golf Club (231-547-212; www.belvederegolfclub.com), 5731 Marion Center Rd., Charlevoix. The course was designed by Scotsman William Watson and was opened in 1927. It offers challenging 3 and 4 pars, with 5 pars that reward aggressive play.

Charlevoix Country Club (231-47-9796; www.chxcountryclub.com), 9600 Clubhouse Dr., Charlevoix. A members-only club.

Dunmaglas Golf Course (231-547-4653; www.dunmaglas.com), 9031 Boyne City Rd., Charlevoix. A par-72, 18-hole course with views of Lakes Michigan and Charlevoix.

Antrim Dells Public Course (1-800-872-8561; www.antrimdellsgolf.com), 12352 Antrim Dells Dr., Ellsworth. An 18-hole course, with a wooded back nine.

A LAKE MICHIGAN BEACH AT CHARLEVOIX

SPORTING CLAYS **Charlevoix Rod & Gun Club** (231-547-2785; www .charlevoixrodandgun.com), US 131, 1 mile north of Charlevoix. The sporting clays course is open to the public.

✳ Lodging

You'll find some of the better accommodations for the entire region in Charlevoix.

Weathervane Terrace Inn & Suites (231-547-9955 or 1-800-552-0025; www.weathervane-chx.com), 111 Pine River Lane, Charlevoix. The distinct stone building on the Pine River leading from Lake Michigan to Lake Charlevoix has been a northern Michigan landmark for decades. Its restaurant (see *Dining Out*) has long been a destination for diners. Rates are $58–$299.

BED & BREAKFASTS **Aaron's Windy Hill Bed & Breakfast** (231-547-2804; www.aaronswindyhill.com), 202 Michigan Ave., Charlevoix. This turn-of-the-century home has eight rooms, all with private baths. Open May–Oct. This is your basic B&B: the rooms are clean, neat, and adequately furnished, but nothing special. There is a view of the drawbridge and it's close to downtown shopping. The wraparound front porch would be a good place to spend an afternoon. Rates are $65–$150.

Bridge Street Inn (231-547-6606; www.bridgestreetinn.com), 113 Michigan Ave., Charlevoix. Innkeepers John and Vera McKown have come to the aid of this 1895 home, formerly known as Baker Cottage. The home was originally designed to accommodate summer guests, and it shows. The rooms are spacious for a B&B, and they are decorated in a cottage, country style with a touch of Victorian. All have private baths and TV sets. It's less than a block to a Lake Michigan beach. Rates are $100–$140.

Horton Creek Inn (232-582-5373 or 1-866-582-5373; www.hortoncreek innbb.com), 05757 Boyne City Rd., Charlevoix. This newer cedar log home on 60 acres has six rooms, all decorated in a rustic, Up North style. There is a pool and hot tub. The rooms are wood paneled and have hand-carved wood furniture like you'd see in an Adirondack lodge. There are walking paths on the grounds, and bicycling the country roads is a great pastime. Rates are $135–$250.

The Inn at Grey Gables (231-547-2251; www.innatgreygables.com), 306 Belevedere Ave., Charlevoix. The inn, like other 19th-century homes in the area, was built in 1887 as a cottage and was part of the Belvedere Club, a summer colony on the south side of Round Lake near Lake Charlevoix. It has been a B&B since 1998 and has been extensively remodeled. There are seven rooms, all with private baths and decorated with country-style furniture. The rooms are tasteful but not cluttered, and they are large enough for modern tastes. Breakfasts include French toast, quiche, muffins, and fruit. Rates are $74–$200.

MacDougall House Bed & Breakfast (231-547-5788; www.michigan bandb.com), 109 Petoskey Ave., Charlevoix. This Victorian-era cottage has five rooms, each with a private bath. The rooms have a frilly, almost too Victorian feel, and we'd be doubtful that many men would be comfortable in them, apart from Room 5, which has a more masculine feel. There is a full, hot breakfast, with fruits, pancakes, omelets, and French toast. A house specialty is Scottish shortbread. Rates are $68–$108.

In Ellsworth
The House on the Hill (231-588-6304; thehouseonthehill.com), 9661 Lake St., Ellsworth, about 20 minutes from Charlevoix. The seven-room B&B has rooms in the main house and a carriage house. All have private baths and are well decorated. I liked the carriage house rooms the best. All have private entrances and a view of the gardens. Many people stay here and eat at The Rowe Inn or Tapawingo in Ellsworth (see *Dining Out*). Rates are $175–$200.

✴ Where to Eat

DINING OUT ⅋ **Stafford's Weathervane Inn** (231-547-4311; www.staffords.com), 106 Pine River Lane, Charlevoix. Open daily. This venerable restaurant is under the ownership of Stafford's, which also runs the Perry Hotel in Petoskey and the Bay View Inn. You can dine inside or on an outside deck along the Pine River while watching boats navigate the drawbridge. Its roof is shaped like a gull's wing. I liked the way they've made use of local foods. My pick is the morel-encrusted whitefish, both local foods. The menu also includes steaks, pasta, ribs, and chicken. Entrees are $21–$29.

⅋ **Grey Gables Restaurant** (231-547-9261; www.greygablesinn.com), 308 Belvedere Ave., Charlevoix. Open daily for dinner. The small menu has some surprises for this area, such as the hazelnut and mustard seed–crusted whitefish. There are also ribs, chicken, steak, and lamb at this 1875 inn. Entrees are $19–$25.

⅋ **Mahogany's Fine Dining** (231-547-3555), 9600 Clubhouse Dr., Charlevoix, located at the Charlevoix Country Club. Open for dinner Tues.–Sat. Steak, seafood, and walleye in a country-club setting. Prices are $15–$22.

In Ellsworth
⅋ **The Rowe Inn** (231-588-2365; www.roweinn.com), 6303 C 48, Ellsworth. Open daily for lunch and

ALCOVE CAFÉ

dinner. From its rural location, this place has gained a statewide reputation since it opened in 1972, and it has one of the largest wine lists in the state. The menu changes, but its mainstays are beef, veal, lake fish, duck, and lamb. Dining is casual. Reservations are usually needed. Entrees are $20–$39.

♈ **Tapawingo** (231-588-7971; www.tapawingo.com), 9502 Lake St., Ellsworth, about 20 minutes from Charlevoix. Open daily for dinner, and lunch in summer. When you first pull into the parking lot, this destination restaurant looks more like a private home than a legendary eating establishment. Tapawingo is constantly on the list of top Michigan restaurants. The owner/chef is Harlan "Pete" Peterson. The menu includes rabbit, salmon, halibut, steak, pasta, and lamb, but changes daily. Reservations are required. Entrees are $50–$65.

EATING OUT ♈ **Landings Restaurant** (231-547-9036), MI 66 near the Ironton Ferry, Charlevoix. Open daily for lunch and dinner, late May–early Sept. Very casual dining aimed at the boating crowd on Lake Charlevoix. It's near a marina. There are burgers, perch, walleye, and sandwiches. You can dine on a deck and watch the boats, which can dock at the restaurants. Prices are $8–$12.

♈ **Giuseppe's Italian Grill** (231-547-2550), 757 Petoskey Ave., Charlevoix. Open daily for lunch and dinner. There are always plenty of cars parked in this place for the family-style Italian and American dishes. It looks more like a roadhouse, but the offerings are a bit up from that, with

pasta, steaks, and whitefish. Prices are $15–$22.

♈ **Villager Pub** (231-547-4374), 427 Bridge St., Charlevoix. Open daily. This is where you'll find the locals munching on burgers, fried fish, and other pub fare. It's a good place to get in touch with what's going on in town. Prices are $6–$10.

♈ **Whitney's of Charlevoix** (231-547-0818), 305 Bridge St., Charlevoix. Open daily. The oyster bar has fresh seafood flown in daily. There are also steaks, pasta, and New England clam chowder. There is a deck and occasional entertainment. Prices are $8–$12.

✳ Selective Shopping

Harwood Heritage Gold (231-547-2038), 61 Parsons Rd., Charlevoix. Call for hours. Run by the Parsons Farms, the store sells pure maple syrup, which has been made on the farm for more than 80 years.

ART GALLERIES **Elements Gallery** (231-547-5820), 107 Bridge St., Charlevoix. Open daily, May–Oct.; call for winter hours. Contemporary arts and home décor take center stage in this small downtown gallery, which features pottery, glass, paintings, and some furniture.

Bier Art Gallery (231-547-2288), 17959 Ferry Rd., Charlevoix. Open daily, May–Oct.; call for winter hours. Located in an old schoolhouse, the gallery has a view of Lake Michigan and displays the works of regional and national artists. Much of the work is contemporary, and includes wood pottery and glass.

BEAVER ISLAND

Thirty miles off the Lake Michigan coast, Beaver Island was once the only kingdom in America. From 1848–1856 James Strang led a band of Mormons who settled the island, building roads and farms and logging the forests. The island wasn't a backwater spot in those days. Almost everything that moved on the Great Lakes did so by ship, many of them steamers, and the island was a major refueling port.

During his reign, Strang, who had proclaimed himself king, and his followers banished non-Mormons from the island, and resentment grew on the mainland and on Mackinac Island, which Beaver Island had eclipsed as a refueling stop for ships. Legal attempts were made to oust him, but they failed. However, by 1856, things started to sour on the island, and he was assassinated by two disgruntled followers.

Following the assassination, a mob from Mackinac Island drove the Mormons from the island, and it was opened for settlement. Irish fishermen started to arrive, and they sent word back to family and friends in the old country about "America's Emerald Isle." More Irish fishermen arrived, and to this day the island has a strong Irish heritage.

By the 1890s, overfishing had taken its toll, and a decline followed, but the islanders hung on to their ways, and even through the 1940s fishing was a prime commercial activity on the island. Logging and farming were also important.

By the 1970s tourism had become important, and now construction is the top island industry, with second homes springing up. Visitors are attracted by the island's slow pace, beaches, public lands, and views of Lake Michigan. Television reception isn't good, Internet access is spotty, and newspapers don't arrive until the afternoon on the ferry.

The island is truly a sparsely populated and little-visited place. St. James, where the car ferry docks, is the only village on the island, and this is where most of the 550 or so year-round residents live. Most of the island's restaurants, lodging places, and services are located in St. James. There is one bank and one grocery store. On summer weekends, there may be 2,000–3,500 visitors on the island, which is 15 miles long and 6 miles wide.

Some of the restaurants and lodging establishments are open year-round, but basically the island closes down from late December through April, when the ferryboat stops running. There is year-round air service.

GUIDANCE **Beaver Island Chamber of Commerce** (231-448-2505; www .beaverisland.org), 26180 Main St. Open daily on weekdays. They have some good island maps available, along with information on lodging and restaurants. The chamber's Web site has a list of homes for rent.

MEDIA *The Beaver Beacon* (231-448-2476; www.beaverbeacon.com), P.O. Box 254, Beaver Island, MI 49782. The lush monthly magazine keeps you in touch with news and events on the island. Their Web site is a good resource.

STAYING CONNECTED **Beaver Island District Library** (231-448-2701; www .beaverisland.org), 400 Donegal Bay Rd. Open daily on weekdays, year-round. Internet access is available, although you have to sign up to reserve a time. It's a good source for information on the island's rich history.

GETTING THERE *By boat:* **Beaver Island Boat Co.** (231-448-2210; www.bibco .com), 103 Bridge Park Dr., Charlevoix. Open April–Dec., with two to four trips weekly. The trip on the car ferry takes about two hours. Some people just spend the day on the island, while others opt for a longer stay. You can take your vehicle, a bicycle, and canoes and kayaks. The boat also runs an excursion along the Lake Michigan shoreline to Mackinaw. Cost is $140 for a vehicle round trip and $42 for adult passage round trip.

By air: **Beaver Island Airport** (231-448-2750), 28215 Airport Rd. If you have your own plane, you can fly here. **Island Airways** (231-448-2071; www.island airways.com) offers flights from Charlevoix and Traverse City.

GETTING AROUND Just because you can bring a vehicle, doesn't mean you have to. A bicycle would be a good alternative. Most lodging places have vehicles to shuttle your luggage, and car rentals are available on the island.

MEDICAL EMERGENCY Call 911.

✴ To See & Do

❧ **Marine Museum** (231-448-2479), 38105 Michigan Ave. Open May–Oct. Exhibits tell the story of the island's shipping history. The port was once thriving, with ships stopping to resupply, and commercial fishing was at its peak.

THE BEAVER ISLAND FERRY

The Old Mormon Print Shop Museum (231-448-2254), 26275 Main St. Open May–Oct. It was built by the followers of James Strang, the island's Mormon king, and was used to print religious texts. It's now the museum for the Beaver Island Historical Society and has a focus on the island's Irish immigrants and on Native Americans, who once had fishing villages here.

✳ Outdoor Activities

BEACHES Much of the island is pubic land, but not all beaches are. If there are no signs marking it as private land, chances are it's a public beach. One prime one is **Pebble Beach** near St. James.

SCENIC DRIVES There are 100 miles of road on the island. Take a tour starting on East Side Drive, which takes you to the South End Road and then north again on West Side Road. The east- and south-side drives go basically along the lakeshore. There are numerous abandoned farms, some dating to the Mormon days.

BOATING **Beaver Island Marina** (231-448-2301) is a full-service marina in the harbor at St. James with transient and seasonal slips.
Beaver Island Municipal Dock (231-448-2252) is in the harbor at St. James and has boat slips for visitors.

CRUISES **Bonadeo Boat Charter** (231-448-2489), St. James Harbor. The service offers half-day and daylong cruises to outer islands, along with pickups and dropoffs for those camping on the outer islands.

PADDLING The opportunities are nearly limitless along the island's coast or in the inland lakes. I would take my boat to the east side of the island, where the waters are generally calmer.
Inland Seas School of Kayaking (231-448-2221; www.inlandseaskayaking .com), P.O. Box 437, Beaver Island, MI 49782. Open May–Sept. The school offers instruction and guided kayak trips around the island.

BICYCLING With 100 miles of lightly traveled roads and a relatively flat terrain, this is a haven for cyclists. If you don't bring your bike, rentals are available.
Lakesports (231-448-2166), near the ferry dock, rents bikes, kayaks, sailboats, and camping gear.

ECOTOURS **Beaver Island Ecotours** (231-448-2194). Open late May–early Aug. There are driving and walking, inland lake, biking, and hiking and camping tours.

GOLFING **Beaver Island Golf Course** (231-448-2301; www.beaverislandgolf .com). A nine-hole course.

DRIVING **Gordon's Rentals** (231-448-2438), 25578 Lake Dr. Open year-round. A source for SUVs and vans.

❋ Lodging

The island basically shuts down from late Dec.–April, when the car ferry doesn't run. Few places are open year-round.

Beaver Island Lodge (231-448-2396; www.beaverislandlodge.com), 38210 Beaver Lodge Dr. The 15-room lodge has standard motel-style rooms and suites, many with a view of the lake. Some suites offer a full kitchen. Nina's Restaurant is inside (see *Eating Out*). The innkeepers are Nina Simpson-Jones and Ray Cole. Rates are $65–$145.

Emerald Island Hotel (231-448-2376; www.emeraldislandhotel.com), 37986 Kings Hwy. Open year-round. The hotel is fairly new and has 16 units. The efficiency units have two queen beds and a kitchen. The suites have two bedrooms and a kitchen and can sleep six. The rooms have cable TV and private baths. No pets and no smoking. Rates are $100–$130.

MOTELS Laurain Lodge (231-448-2099; www.laurainlodge.com), 38085 Beaver Lodge Dr. The innkeepers at this lodge are Larry and Theresa Laurain. Rowboats on nearby inland lakes come with the rooms, which are basic

WHITNEY OYSTER BAR

motel units. There are also house-keeping units, some with two bedrooms. There is cable TV. The surrounding gardens are lovely. Rates are $110–$125.

RENTALS There are a large number of homes and cottages for rent on the island. Check out www.beaverisland .org for listings.

CAMPING There are two established campgrounds, St. James Township and Bill Wagner Peaine Township. Also, much of the southern portion of the island is part of the Pigeon River State Forest and all such lands are open to camping. Check with the DNR first at www.michigan.gov/dnr.

St. James Township Campground. There are 12 primitive sites with pit toilets and hand pumps. It's off Donegal Bay Road, 1 mile from the harbor. Cost is $5 a night.

Bill Wagner Peaine Township Campground. There are 22 rustic campsites with pit toilets and hand pumps. It's on the east side of the island, 7 miles south of St. James Harbor on the shores of Lake Michigan.

❋ Where to Eat

EATING OUT ❢ **Nina's Restaurant** (231-448-2396; www.beaverisland lodge.com), 38210 Beaver Lodge Dr. Open daily. Located in Beaver Island Lodge (see *Lodging*). This place has the largest menu of any restaurant on the island, and the food ranges from grilled chicken to steak, prime rib, roast duck, whitefish, perch, and salmon. It's casual dining, but with tablecloths. There are appetizers and a decent wine list. They offer free shuttle service from the marinas. Entrees are $13–$25.

Ϋ Donegal Danny's Pub (231-448-3000), 26420 Carlisle Rd. Open daily, year-round. A friendly Irish bar with pub food and beer on tap. There is seating outdoors. Prices are $8–$10.

Ϋ Shamrock Restaurant & Pub (231-449-2278), 26245 Main St. This place bills itself as the oldest pub on the island. They serve traditional pub fare, but dinners are available. White-fish, pork, chicken, and steak are the mainstays. Entrees are $13–$19.

MARKET McDonough's Market (231-448-2733; www.mcdonoughs market.com), 38240 Michigan Ave. Open daily. This is the only market on the island and serves the local residents during winter. There is a full line of groceries, meats, produce, beer, wine, and liquor. It's a bit of a general store, and also offers movie

rentals, hardware, toys, and lottery tickets.

✳ Selective Shopping

Beaver Island Apiaries (231-370-0929; www.beaverislandapiaries.com), East Side Drive north of Pebble Beach. The beekeepers have found the island a perfect place and they harvest honey and sell beeswax products such as lip balm and other cosmetic items.

Beaver Island Jewelry (231-448-2205; www.beaverislandjewelry.com). Open May–Sept. with various hours, so call ahead. Handcrafted glass lampwork beads and jewelry: There are dogs, frogs, necklaces, and bracelets. Beads are for sale. The owner, Nancy Peterson, also offers bead jewelry making classes.

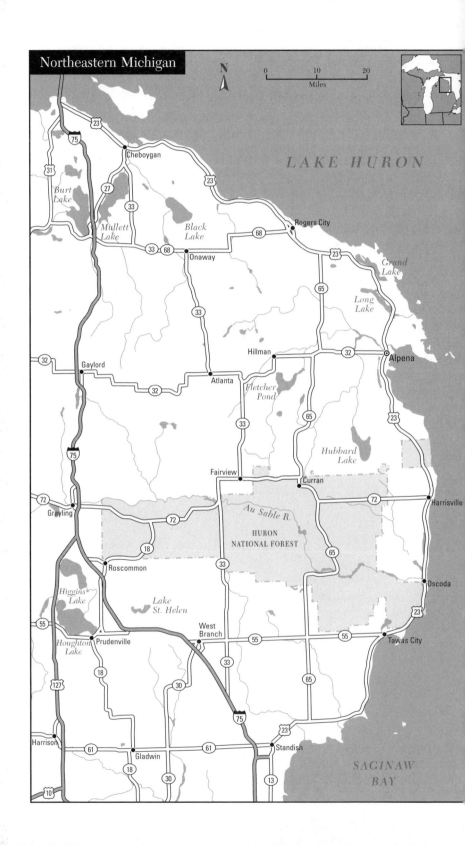

Northeastern Michigan
N
0
10
20
Miles
LAKE HURON
SAGINAW BAY
Cheboygan
Rogers City
Onaway
Hillman
Alpena
Gaylord
Atlanta
Fairview
Curran
Harrisville
Grayling
Roscommon
Oscoda
West Branch
Prudenville
Tawas City
Harrison
Gladwin
Standish
Burt Lake
Mullett Lake
Black Lake
Grand Lake
Long Lake
Fletcher Pond
Hubbard Lake
Au Sable R.
HURON NATIONAL FOREST
Higgins Lake
Lake St. Helen
Houghton Lake
75
23
31
27
33
68
65
32
72
18
55
127
30
61
10
13

Northeast

NORTHEAST

Stretching for more than 200 miles along Lake Huron on the state's east coast are the communities that bill themselves as "The Sunrise Side." The region is much less popular than the Lake Michigan coast, partly because it doesn't have the white, sandy beaches of the west coast.

There are fewer restaurants and lodging options, but the prices are much less than on Lake Michigan. Most lodging is in mom-and-pop motels, and there are few fine dining spots. Most restaurants are either family style or pubs.

The traffic and pace are much slower on this side of the state. Except for some summer weekends, US 23 along Lake Huron is rarely crowded. Much of the land is in the Huron-Manistee National Forest, and there are plenty of campgrounds and recreation areas. Also, a lot of land is owned by large hunting camps, which manage it for deer hunting in the fall.

The major influence on the region is the Au Sable River, which starts in the Grayling area and flows to Lake Huron, emptying at Oscoda. In the 19th century, loggers cut white pine and in the spring floated it down the Au Sable to Oscoda, where ships towed it to the lumber mills of Bay City and Saginaw.

The Au Sable eventually became a legendary river for fly anglers throughout the Midwest, and it was the birthplace of many fly patterns now used throughout the nation. Anglers still flock to the Au Sable for the predictable fly hatches, and numerous river guides float it in elegant wooden Au Sable boats, which are a cross between a canoe and a rowboat.

Fishing and hunting are major activities in the region. There are charter trips for salmon and trout, and mid-November brings the rifle deer season, which is nearly a state holiday in Michigan.

The region is very lightly populated. The major city is Alpena, a blue-collar town in the woods that had been dependent on the cement industry for jobs. The others communities are small beach towns with only a few thousand residents. Cottage development came quickly to the Lake Huron coast because of its proximity to Detroit, so much of the shoreline from Au Gres to Oscoda is privately owned, but once past there it opens up and the drive is much more inviting.

When traveling to the region, make sure you don't leave town without at least a half tank of gas. Stations are few and far between. There's also a well-known dead spot for cell phones north of Oscoda.

TAWAS & OSCODA

Duuring the 19th century, Tawas and Oscoda were home to sawmills, and their ports were busy shipping lumber to Chicago and other Great Lakes cities, but by the early 20th century much of the white pine was gone. The final blow came in 1911 when a series of forest fires burned from Lake Michigan to Lake Huron. It was partly caused by the lumbering practices of the day, which left the forests littered with tinder-dry slashings that burned easily.

There are photos of bedsteads set up in Lake Huron, where people sought refuge from the fires. One story has it that the entire town of Metz in northeastern Michigan fled the fires on a train, but they were forced to stop, and many took refuge in a railroad water tower. The heat was so intense that they boiled to death in the tower. When driving through the towns, you'll notice that few buildings date from before the fire.

Oscoda is the literary birthplace of the Paul Bunyan legends, which were stories told by French-Canadian loggers and written down by Oscoda newspaperman James MacGillvary starting in 1906, the first being "The Round River Drive."

NEARBY VILLAGES

Mio
The little burg is home to the Kirtland's warbler, a rare, endangered songbird that lives in jack pine that has burned. Birdwatchers from around the nation come here for tours and perhaps a sighting. Mio is also a destination for fly anglers who want to fish the big waters of the Au Sable River, which starts here, and many fishing guides operate from here.

To be blunt, there is not much to do in Mio if you're not a birdwatcher, angler, or canoeist attracted to the Au Sable. There are a few motels, and a couple of restaurants along MI 33, but little else. Better lodging can be found in Grayling or Oscoda, about 40 minutes east and west of Mio.

There is a large Amish community just north of Mio in the Fairview area, and on occasion you'll find a buggy parked alongside the road selling baked goods or quilts, but there are no craft stores or such. These folks pretty much keep to themselves.

Other Towns

There are a dozen or so more small towns in Oscoda, Alcona, Iosco, and Ogemaw counties, but a traveler will find little more than a gas station or convenience store. The notable exception is West Branch, a major stop on I-75, which has chain hotels, restaurants, and an outlet mall. It's the regional shopping hub for the area.

GUIDANCE **Tawas Bay Area Chamber of Commerce** (1-800-55-TAWAS; www.tawas.com), 402 E. Lake St., Tawas City. **Oscoda Convention and Visitors Bureau** (989-739-0900; www.oscoda.com). In Mio, **Chamber of Commerce for Oscoda County** (989-826-3331; www.oscodacounty.org).

Huron-Manistee National Forest Service (989-739-0728; www.fs.fed.us), 5761 N. Skeel Rd., Oscoda. Open Mon.–Fri., 8–4:30. Much of northeastern Michigan is U.S. Forest Service land and is open to the public. The Forest Service has information on recreational activities on the land, including hunting and fishing. It's a good source for maps.

GETTING THERE *By car:* The major artery along the Lake Huron coast is US 23. On weekends it can get crowded, and MI 65, an inland route, is a good alternative.

By air: **MBS International Airport** near Saginaw provides decent service. Also, **Bishop Airport** in Flint and Detroit's **Metro Airport** are good alternatives. It's about a three-hour drive to Tawas from Metro, and about an hour and a half from Bishop.

THE AU SABLE RIVER NEAR OSCODA

MEDICAL EMERGENCY **St. Joseph Hospital** (989-800-362-9404), 200 Hemlock, Tawas City. This is the major hospital in the area. Dial 911.

WHEN TO COME The best months are late May through October. The area is a hotbed of cross-country skiing in winter.

✳ To See & Do

The Tawas and Oscoda areas are about 30 miles apart, but there is little traffic on US 23, and virtually none on the county roads, so take note when planning trips in the area that travel time is short.

⌀ **Lumberman's Monument Visitor Center** (989-362-8961), intersection of River and Monument roads, Oscoda Township. Located on the banks of the Au Sable River, the huge bronze memorial to the state's lumber era sits on a bluff. It was constructed in 1932, and has developed into a tourist site. There are lumbering exhibits, including a replica of a logjam, crosscut sawing of logs, and a Wanigan, which was a floating cook shack used on the Au Sable when loggers were floating trees downriver in the spring.

⌀ **Iargo Springs** (989-739-0728). Located on River Road along the Au Sable near Oscoda, the springs were considered a holy place by Native Americans and offer a view of the Au Sable River valley from a 30-foot observation deck. There are 294 steps down to the river, where the springs that help feed the river can be seen.

⌀ **Tawas Point State Park** (989-362-5041; www.michigan.gov/dnr), 686 Tawas Beach Rd., off US 23. Located at the tip of Tawas Point, the park offers camping, a sandy, shallow beach area, and the Tawas Point Lighthouse. Some have referred to the point as the Cape Cod of the Midwest. It's a nice sandy split of land jutting into Lake Huron, but it's nothing like Cape Cod. The park has 183 acres and is a pleasant place to spend an afternoon at the beach.

✳ Outdoor Activities

SCENIC DRIVES The River Road Scenic Byway parallels the Au Sable River for 22 miles from Oscoda through the Huron-Manistee National Forest. Along the way there are stops at Lumberman's Monument, Iargo Springs, Eagle's Nest Overlook, and the Canoe Memorial. Boardwalks, hiking trails, and camping are available as well.

CRUISES On Charity Island **Charity Island Lighthouse** (989-876-8929; www .charityisland.net), Charity Island. Open mid-June–Sept. The 50-foot *Northstar* makes trips over to Charity Island in Lake Huron to the island lighthouse, where dinner is served in the 1857 facility. Visitors receive a tour of the lighthouse and dinner. The boat docks in Au Gres.

⌀ **Au Sable River Queen Cruises** (989-739-7351), 1775 Eastside River, Oscoda. Open May–Oct. The *Au Sable River Queen*, a paddle-wheel watercraft, provides cruises on the Au Sable, including evening dinner trips.

AU SABLE RIVER QUEEN

FISHING Charter fishing for salmon and trout are available in Tawas and Oscoda.

FLY-FISHING The Au Sable River is one of the prime trout streams in the nation, and much of it runs through Iosco County before it empties into Lake Huron at Oscoda.

Bob Linsenman's Au Sable Angler (989-826-8500; www.ausableangler.com), 479 S. MI 33, Mio. Open daily, April–Nov. Call for winter hours. It's about 45 miles from the Tawas/Oscoda area to Mio, where the trophy waters of the Au Sable start. Linsenman is the author of numerous fly-fishing books, including *Trout Streams of Michigan,* published by The Countryman Press. He has taught many people to fly fish, and his shop is a good place to start or pick up local information and flies. He and other guides take anglers on drift boat trips on the Au Sable in quest of trophy trout.

CANOEING & KAYAKING The Au Sable River is a top paddling destination in Michigan, and many people head to Grayling for a trip, but the waters down-stream from Mio are wide and deep and support more canoeists. There is a lot of friction between fly anglers and paddlers on the river, but don't let that stop you from taking a trip. Simply be courteous and quiet when you come upon an angler, and there will be few problems. From late May through early September the river is crowded. Early May, September, and October are good months to come. The weather can be good, and the crowds fewer.

In Mio

CANOE LIVERIES Gotts' Landing (989-826-3411; www.gottslanding.com), MI 33, Mio, on the Au Sable River. Open spring–late fall. The livery offers trips that last anywhere from a few hours to a few days (to Oscoda). There is also a fly-fishing shop and guides are available. A few cabins nearby are for rent from the landing.

Hinchman Acres Resorts (989-826-3267; www.hinchman.com), 702 MI 33, at the Au Sable River, Mio. Open spring–late fall. They have canoes, kayaks, rafts, and tubes for rent, and cabins are available.

BICYCLING Apart from US 23 and MI 65, there is little traffic in the region, and bicycling is a good way to see the back roads.

GOLFING **Red Hawk** (989-362-0800; www.redhawkgolf.net), 350 W. Davison Rd., East Tawas. An 18-hole course in the woods.

✳ Lodging

All establishments are open year-round unless otherwise noted.

Manor House (989-739-1977; www.manorhouse-oscoda.com), 399 N. US 23, Oscoda. Located near the mouth of the Au Sable River, the inn offers some of the better accommodations in the area. The 11 rooms have private decks and a view of Lake Huron. Some rooms have gas fireplaces, hot tubs, and large-screen TVs. All are modern and done in a contemporary style. Rates are $105–$160.

Redwood Motor Lodge (989-739-2021; www.redwoodmotorlodge.com), 3111 US 23, Oscoda. There are 34 rooms and eight cottages at this beachfront complex, which includes a restaurant. The rooms have air-conditioning and cable TV. There are 200 feet of beach, an indoor pool, hot tub, and sauna. Rates are $55–$116.

BED & BREAKFASTS

In Tawas
East Tawas Junction (989-362-8006), 514 W. Bay St., East Tawas. There are five rooms, all with private baths, in this Victorian home overlooking Tawas Bay. The innkeepers are Don and Leigh Mott. This place is a real find in this area, which isn't known for its B&Bs. The rooms have cable TV, wireless Internet, and private baths. The second-story rooms have coffee machines, and one suite has a sitting room, a private deck, and a private entrance. Rates are $109–$150.

In Oscoda
Huron House Bed & Breakfast (989-739-9255; www.huronhouse.com), 3124 US 23, Oscoda. Although this place bills itself as a B&B, it's more like an inn, with 13 rooms on the first and second floors. There is good access to a sandy beach and a nice deck. Rates are $165–$195.

RESORTS **Tawas Bay Beach Resort** (989-362-8601; www.tawasbaybeachresort.com), 300 US 23, East Tawas. This is a former Holiday Inn, and it has 103 rooms with coffee makers, wireless Internet, and cable TV. It has

THE MANOR INN

good access to a sandy beach next to the boat dock. Topsider's Lounge is in the complex (see *Dining Out*). Rates are $100–$170.

CABINS **Timberlane Resorts** (989-248-9634; www.timberlaneresorts .com), Tawas Beach Rd., East Tawas. The seven knotty pine cabins are on the point, which is a sandy beach area near Tawas State Park. The cabins are older, but clean, and have a good location. Most have two bedrooms and some have gas fireplaces. Rates are $120–$360.

MOTELS **Coleman's Resort** (989-362-3962; www.colemansresort.com), 1045 Bay Dr., Tawas City. There are one- and two-bedroom cabins with knotty pine interiors, equipped kitchens, microwaves, cable TV, and picnic tables. There is a sandy beach and play equipment for kids. Weekly rates are $550–$675.

✳ **Where to Eat**

DINING OUT ♈ **Lakewood Shores Resort** (989-739-2073; www.lake woodshores.com), 7751 Cedar Lake Rd., Oscoda. The country club–style resort offers one of the few upscale menus in the region, with steaks, ribs, chicken, pasta, and seafood. There are rooms available and golfing. Entrees are $18–$22.

EATING OUT ♈ **Topsider's** (989-362-8601), 300 East Bay St., East Tawas,

located in the Tawas Bay Beach Resort (see *Lodging*). The hotel-style restaurant is next to the beach and offers steak, chicken, seafood, and pasta. Prices are $8–$15.

♈ **Wiltse's Brew Pub** (989-739-2231; www.wiltsebrewpub.com), 5606 F 41, Oscoda. Open daily for breakfast, lunch, and dinner. It's one of only a few brewpubs in the region and offers decent, but limited entrees for dinner. There are Great Lakes fish such as perch and walleye, steaks, some seafood, chicken. and pasta. Entrees are $15–$18.

♈ **Chumbs Food & Spirits** (989-362-3681), 105 W. Westover, East Tawas. Open daily for lunch and din-ner. Pub fare and a bit more. There is some entertainment on weekends. Prices are $8–$15.

The Perfect Pickle (989-362-8482), 214 Newman St., East Tawas. Open daily for lunch and dinner. Burgers and other pub fare in a basic tavern. Prices are $5–$8.

✳ **Selective Shopping**
Wooden Nickel Antiques (989-739-7490), 110 Park St., Oscoda. Open daily late May–early Sept., but call first. Antiques and collectibles are on display in this small shop.

Time After Time Antiques (989-362-2298), 729 MI 55, Tawas City. The shop features glassware, furni-ture, and jewelry.

ALPENA, ROGERS CITY & CHEBOYGAN

T his 55-mile stretch of US 23 along Lake Huron is sparsely populated, except for Alpena, which has about 11,000 people. Alpena and Traverse City are the commercial hubs of northern Michigan, and while Grand Traverse Bay gets more visitors, Alpena's Thunder Bay is just as inviting. As with most Up North towns, Alpena has its roots in logging, but it is now known for limestone mining and the manufacturing of concrete blocks.

Nearby Rogers City has a population of about 3,300 and also has a limestone quarry. It is a busy Great Lakes port because of the quarry operations.

Cheboygan has a population of about 5,200, and it has become a retirement community for many seniors. Its location near the Straits of Mackinac makes it a viable alternative to the touristy Mackinaw City.

GUIDANCE **Alpena Area Chamber of Commerce** (989-354-4181; www.alpenachamber.com), 235 W. Chisholm St., Alpena.
Rogers City Chamber of Commerce (989-2535; www.rogerscitychamber .com), 292 S. Bradley Hwy., Rogers City. Open Mon.–Fri., 12–5.
Cheboygan Chamber of Commerce (231-627-7183; www.cheboygan.com), 124 N. Main St., Cheboygan.

MEDIA *The Alpena News* (989-354-3111; www.thealpenanews.com). The regional daily paper has news on events along the Lake Huron coastline.

GETTING THERE *By car:* The major artery through the region is US 23.

MEDICAL EMERGENCY **Alpena General Hospital** (989-356-7000; www.alpena regionalmedicalcenter.org), 1501 W. Chisholm, Alpena. This is the major hospital for the region. Call 911.

✳ To See & Do

✒ ⊤ **Besser Museum for Northeast Michigan** (989-356-2202; www.besser museum.org), 491 Johnson, Alpena. Open daily, Tues.–Sat. The museum is dedicated to the arts, history, and science, and there is no place like it in the region. The galleries have works by artists, sculptors, and potters. There are also historical exhibits depicting logging, farming, Native Americans, and commercial fishing. There is a planetarium.

🚢 **Thunder Bay National Marine Sanctuary** (989-356-8805; www.thunder bay.noaa.gov), 500 W. Fletcher St., Alpena. There are more than 100 shipwrecks in Alpena's Thunder Bay, and the sanctuary protects them from scavengers taking relics. There are displays at the Great Lakes Maritime Heritage Center, where the sanctuary is located. Divers can view the wrecks, but nothing can be brought up. There are glass-bottom boat tours of the ships and seven lighthouses in the area that can be toured. The center is a good place to start.

CANOEING & KAYAKING Thunder Bay provides a sheltered shoreline, with miles and miles of paddling possibilities.

✳ Lodging

Most lodging is found in motels along US 23. All establishments are open year-round unless otherwise noted.

Big Bear Lodge (989-354-8573), 2052 US 23, Alpena. The lodge has been remodeled and has a woodsy look. The rooms have wireless Internet and refrigerators and some have kitchenettes. Rates are $50–$60.

EATING OUT There is a dearth of good restaurants in the region. The establishments are open year-round unless otherwise noted.

In Alpena
🍸 **John Lau Saloon** (989-354-6898), 414 N. Second Ave., Alpena. Open daily. Alpena's oldest saloon serves lunch and dinner. It's mostly pub food

JOHN LAU SALOON

and burgers, but there are handcrafted beers in this brewpub. Prices are $8–$10.

Surf's Café (989-354-8841), 113 S. Second Ave., Alpena. Light lunches and cappuccino and espresso coffees. One of the few such places in the region.

In Ossineke

Υ **Rosa's Ristorante Italiano** (989-471-5517), 12087 US 23, Ossineke. There is a full Italian menu, along with steaks and seafood. Prices are $8–$12.

In Hawks

Υ **The Cobblestone Restaurant** (989-734-4688; www.nettiebay.com). Located in Nettie Bay Lodge, Hawks, the restaurant offers gourmet steak, fish, and chicken dinners by reservation only. Prices are $20 and up.

✳ Selective Shopping

The establishments are open year-round unless otherwise noted.

Art in the Loft at Gallery 109 (989-356-4877), 109 N. Second Ave., Alpena. This is one of only a few fine arts galleries featuring contemporary artists in the region. It's a community-based, nonprofit gallery that showcases local artists.

C. Leigh's Favorite Things (989-727-2362), 13822 Hubbard Lake Rd., Hubbard Lake. Open most days May–Nov. Located in an old postmaster's house, the antiques shop also features collectibles.

GAYLORD

Gaylord is home to many Up North activities, with golfing, 59 inland lakes, the Pigeon River Country State Forest, and several top-quality trout streams located nearby. The town has long been a stopping place for travelers because it's about one tank of gas away from the populated areas of southern Michigan.

To take advantage of that, town planners in the 1960s produced an Alpine theme for the downtown architecture. At one time it may have been cute, setting Gaylord apart from other northern communities, but these days the theme park look is a fading allure, and many of the sturdy brick buildings from the early 20th century simply look as though that have received a Swiss facelift.

But that hasn't stopped Gaylord from becoming the country club of northern Michigan, with more than a dozen golf courses within 30 minutes of town. In the winter, many of those courses host cross-country skiers.

Like much of northern Michigan, the history of Gaylord's settlement lies in the development of the timber and railroad industries. But because of its inland location and lack of access to a major river, the lumber firms didn't arrive in the area until the late 1860s, and it wasn't until the 1870s that railroads arrived and Gaylord came to life. The town itself is named for a railroad attorney of the time.

The city also makes much of its location on the 45th parallel. But most residents don't need to be reminded that they're closer to the North Pole than the Equator—the area can receive between 80 to 160 inches of snow and winter temperatures average in the 20s and 30s while summer temperatures only hit the 70s.

In the summer, the Au Sable, Sturgeon, Pigeon, and Black rivers provide trout anglers with hundreds of miles of streams to ply their sport. And the numerous inland lakes offer swimming and angling opportunities.

Elk-viewing is another attraction The Pigeon River area, about 10 miles north of Gaylord, is home to the largest elk herd east of the Mississippi.

GUIDANCE **Gaylord Area Convention & Tourism Bureau** (989-732-4000 or 1-800-345-8621; www.gaylord-mich.com), 101 W. Main St., Gaylord. The visitor center is located in an Alpine-style building downtown. The bureau is a good

source of rental information about lodging that ranges from rustic cabins to
upscale resorts. There is also an online room reservation system at the Web site.
Vacation and golf planners are available, as are snowmobile trail maps. A walking
tour map of Gaylord is also available.

GETTING THERE *By car:* There are two freeway exits off I-75 to Gaylord. The
downtown exit is often snarled in traffic during summer months. A good alternative is to use the exit for US 27, south of the downtown exit. Traffic is much
lighter there.

By air: See Getting There, Traverse City.

MEDICAL EMERGENCY **Otsego Memorial Hospital** (989-731-2100; www
.otsegomemorialhospital.org) 825 N. Center Ave., Gaylord.

✳ To See & Do

Downtown Walking Tour. Stop at the chamber of commerce (see *Guidance*)
and get a map. In the 1960s Gaylord adopted an Alpine village look in deference
to a Swiss firm that once owned a plywood plant in town. Most businesses complied with the program.

✍ ↑ **Call of the Wild Wildlife Museum** (989-732-4336 or 1-800-835-4347;
www.gocallofthewild.com) 850 Wisconsin Ave., Gaylord. The museum, filled
with stuffed animals in glass cases with replicas of their habitat, is an old side-of-
the-road tourist stop that dates from the 1950s. It has been updated over the
years, and it now doubles as a fudge and gift shop. There are polar bears,
weasels, wolves, and wolverines, along with more common animals. Admission is
$6 for adults, $5.50 for seniors, and $4 for children.

✳ Outdoor Activities

ELK-VIEWING **Pigeon River Country State Forest** (989-732-3541; www
.michigan.gov/dnr). The 95,000-acre wilderness area is about 10 miles north of
Gaylord off I-75 at Sturgeon Valley Road. It is home to the largest elk herd east
of the Mississippi. The DNR has set up elk-viewing areas, and September is the
best month. There are rustic campsites, cross-country ski trails, and backpacking
trails. The Pigeon, Sturgeon, and Black rivers offer brook trout fishing. The area
is open for hunting, and there is an annual elk hunt.

Otsego Lake State Park (989-732-5485; www.michigandnr.com), 7136 Old 27
S., Gaylord. The 62-acre park offers a half-mile-long sandy beach on Otsego
Lake that has play equipment. Two-thirds of the 155 campsites are in the North
Campground and the rest are in the South Campground closer to the lake.

FLY-FISHING The Gaylord area is in the heart of the best fly-fishing country in
Michigan, and anglers head for the Au Sable, Manistee, Pigeon, Sturgeon and
Black rivers, all of which are about 30 miles from Gaylord. There are two well-
established fly-fishing resorts: **Fuller's North Branch Outing Club** (989-348-
7951; www.fullersnboc.com), 6122 E. County Rd. 612, Grayling, and **Gates' Au**

Sable Lodge (989-348-8462; www.gateslodge.com), 471 Stephan Bridge Rd., Grayling. Both are located on the Au Sable River system and have fly shops. They offer guided trips in wooden Au Sable River drift boats. (Also see *Lodging*, Grayling.)

✴ Lodging

There are more than a dozen chain motel/hotels in Gaylord, most along the downtown exit from I-75.

RESORTS AND GOLF COURSES

Otsego Club and Resort (989-732-5181; www.otsegoclub.com), 696 E. Main St., Gaylord. The resort is open to the public during summer months and offers a 36-hole golf course, restaurants (see *Dining Out*), and lodging. The complex dates from the late 1930s and has 117 rooms and townhouses with kitchen facilities and condos. In the winter, it is a members-only club with downhill skiing. Rates are $100–$200.

Marsh Ridge (989-732-5552), 4815 Old 27 S., Gaylord. There is an 18-hole course, accommodations, and a restaurant at this complex. Rooms, suites, condos, and lodges are available for rent. The condos and lodge have kitchens and several bedrooms.

During winter, they offer snowmobile rentals. Rates are $89–$475.

Treetops (989-732-6711), 3962 Wilkinson Rd., Gaylord. There are 81 holes of golf on courses designed by Rick Smith, Tom Fazio, and Robert Trent Jones, Sr.; 238 hotel rooms and condos; and three restaurants. In winter there are 23 downhill ski runs. Lodging is in the lodge, which has remodeled rooms, Internet access, and large-screen TVs (some rooms have sitting space); the inn, where the rooms have patios or balconies; condos, which have two and three bedrooms and full kitchens; and chalets, with two and three bedrooms and kitchens. Golf packages run from $139–$460.

RENTALS Northern Michigan Vacation Rentals (989-735-4050; www.northernmichiganvacationrentals.info).

CAMPGROUNDS Beaver Creek Resort (989-732-2459), 5004 W. Otsego Lake Dr., Gaylord. There are cabins and 63 campsites on this 80-acre parcel in the woods, which features a clubhouse with a fireplace, cable TV, workout center, lounge, indoor pool, and sauna.

Big Bear Lake State Forest Campground (989-732-3541), Meridian and Little Bear Lake roads, Gaylord. Michigan's state forest campgrounds are a real deal. They are usually in out of the way places, and the sites are taken on a first-come, first-served basis. There are 30 rustic sites here,

OTSEGO CLUB

some of which can accommodate larger trailers. There is a hand pump and outhouses.

✳ Where to Eat

DINING OUT The eating establishments are open daily unless otherwise noted.

Ⓨ **Otsego Club** (989-732-5181 or 1-800-752-5510; www.otsegoclub .com) 696 MI 32, Gaylord. There are two fine restaurants at the Otsego Club Resort & Conference Center, the Duck Blind Grill (casual) and the Pontresina (more formal). The resort has its roots in the Otsego Ski Club and dates to 1939. Because of its history as a private club, the restaurants have a warm, worn feeling, but the menus are contemporary. Entrees are $15–$25.

Ⓨ **The Sugar Bowl** (989-732-5524), 216 W. Main, Gaylord. Open for lunch and dinner. The restaurant was started by the Doumas family in 1919 and its current owner, Robert Doumas, continues the tradition at this well-worn eatery in downtown Gaylord. It has gone through many changes over the years but keeps people coming back with its traditional American menu of steaks, seafood, and pub fare. Prices are $8–$20.

Ⓨ **Bennethum's Northern Inn** (989-732-9288), 3917 Old 27 S., Gaylord. Open daily for lunch and dinner. There is a decent wine list for this area, and the food offerings range from fish and chips to seafood, pasta, and steaks. The place has a North Woods ambiance. Entrees are $15–$22.

EATING OUT Ⓨ **Jac's Place Grill** (989-732-5552), 4815 Old 27 S., Gay-

BOB LINSENMAN'S AU SABLE ANGLER IN MIO

lord. Open daily for breakfast, lunch, and dinner. Burgers, steaks, seafood, fried perch, and duck are on the menu. Entrees are $15–$25.

Ⓨ **Timothy's Pub** (989-732-9333), 110 S. Otsego Ave., Gaylord. This is where the locals gather for the traditional Friday fish fry and burgers. Prices are $8–$10.

Ⓨ **Diana's Delights** (989-732-6564), 143 W. Main St., Gaylord. Open for breakfast, lunch, and dinner. Another locals' favorite for daily specials, soup, sandwiches, and desserts. There is beer and wine. The breakfasts are large. Prices are $8–$12.

THE SUGAR BOWL RESTAURANT

GRAYLING

The Au Sable and Manistee rivers are the lifeblood of this small town in the central Lower Peninsula, and the community itself took its name from the grayling, a trout-like fish that was once abundant in the Au Sable River.

Fly anglers and canoeists make up most the visitors, and they are at odds over the use of the river, which is narrow until it reaches Mio. Conflicts between anglers and paddlers break out quite often, especially when boaters make a lot of noise. Canoeists often tie several canoes together and float down the river, banging their crafts on rocks. If you're looking for a better place to canoe, try the Au Sable River in Mio (see Mio), where the river is wider.

The other perennial conflict is between anglers and the National Guard, which has an 80,000-plus-acre training camp in the area. Loud helicopters, planes, and artillery practice disturb the peace and quiet of the river.

If you are not planning on fly-fishing or canoeing, there's really not much to do here. There are a few mom-and-pop motels and several restaurants, but little else. A few lodges and bed & breakfasts are on the Au Sable. Much of the streamside property between Grayling and Mio is in private hands, and there are some old fly-fishing lodges. Gaylord, about 30 miles north, is more of a resort community.

GUIDANCE Grayling Chamber of Commerce (989-348-2921; www.grayling chamber.com), 213 N. James St., Grayling. Open daily, weekdays. A good source of snowmobiling maps.

GETTING THERE *By car:* Grayling is located on the I-75 business loop.

STAYING CONNECTED Cell phones work in most areas, including along the Au Sable and Manistee rivers. A few hotels/motels have Internet access.

MEDICAL EMERGENCIES Mercy Hospital (989-348-5461), 1100 Michigan Ave., Grayling. Call 911.

✳ To See & Do

❧ **Grayling Fish Hatchery** (989-348-7386; www.graylingfishhatchery.com), 4890 W. North Down River Rd., Grayling. Open daily late May–early Sept. The

hatchery was founded in 1914 in an effort to restore grayling to the Au Sable **139**
River. The state ran it until the 1960s, when it was abandoned, but volunteers
started restoring it in the mid-1990s and it has been an attraction ever since.
Children can feed the fish in the concrete troughs. Admission is $2.50 for adults
and $1.50 for children.

GRAYLING

✏ **Hartwick Pines State Park** (989-348-7068; www.michigan.gov/dnr), on MI
93, 3 miles from I-75, 4116 Ranger Rd. The park has 85 acres of old-growth
white pine that was spared from the loggers' axes in the 19th century and donated to the state by Karen Michelson Hartwick, who was the daughter of a lumber baron. The trees, some of which tower more than 300 feet, are the main
attraction. There is also a logging museum that preserves the methods used by
19th-century lumberjacks. The nearly 10,000-acre park is open to cross-country
skiing in the winter and hiking in the summer. Campsites and rustic cabins are
scattered throughout the park.

THE AU SABLE AND MANISTEE RIVERS

The headwaters of both rivers are just north of Grayling, and Native Americans used them to cross the Lower Peninsula from Lakes Michigan and
Huron, paddling up one river, portaging to the other, and continuing their
trip. During the logging era, lumberjacks floated logs down the rivers, caus-
ing much erosion and harming the spawning grounds of fish. Grayling were
once so plentiful in the river that the town took its name from them, but
overfishing made them extinct here.

Fly anglers discovered the rivers in the late 19th century, and they have
been a hotbed of fly-fishing ever since. Grayling is the birthplace of many fly
patterns that are now popular across the country. Grayling was also the
birthplace of Trout Unlimited, which is now a national conservation group
with chapters nationwide.

Both rivers, particularly the Au Sable, are lined with old fishing lodges,
many that have been kept in the same family for nearly a century. Others
have been turned into public lodging. One portion of the Au Sable's main-
stream is known as the "Holy Waters" because it regularly produces the
insect hatches relied on by anglers.

Fishing access to the Au Sable can be difficult, especially for new
anglers. Trout Unlimited chapters sell guidebooks that are available at
Gates' Au Sable Lodge (see *Fly-Fishing,* Grayling.)

A good place to start is on the Mason Tract near the village of Roscommon, where the Au Sable's south branch runs through this large parcel of
public land. There are many access points off a two-track road here. A
handy guide is *Trout Streams of Michigan,* by Bob Linsenman and Steve
Nevala (The Countryman Press).

OLD LOGGING EQUIPMENT AT HARTWICK PINES STATE PARK

✳ Lodging

FLY-FISHING LODGES Fuller's North Branch Outing Club (989-348-7951; www.fullersnboc.com), 6122 E. County Rd. 612, Grayling. Henry Ford, and perhaps Ernest Hemingway, stayed in this historic fly-fishing and hunting lodge on the banks of the North Branch of the Au Sable River. There are 12 restored rooms in this B&B, which also has a fly shop and guide services. Although fly-fishing is the top pursuit, there is also upland bird hunting in the fall. Todd Fuller is the top guide. Rates are $99–$135.

Rayburn Lodge B&B (989-348-7482; www.rayburnlodgebnb.com), 1491 Richardson Rd., Grayling. The lodge was built in the 1930s and is on the "Holy Waters" of the Au Sable. Anglers can step right from the property into the river. Breakfast is a big meal for anglers heading out for a day on the river. The lodge is a rustic log building with a massive fieldstone fireplace and a billiards room. Reservations are required. Rates are $95–$125.

Wyandotte Lodge Canoe & Outfitters (989-348-8354), 1320 S. McMasters Bridge Rd., Grayling. The log lodge has eight rustic rooms and several cabins with kitchens. There are dog kennels for upland bird hunters and access to the Au Sable River.

GATES' AU SABLE LODGE

They also offer canoe and kayak rentals. Fly-fishing guides are also available. Rooms run $60 and cabins $88.

Borchers Au Sable Canoe Livery and B&B (989-348-4921; www.canoe borchers.com), 101 Maple St., Grayling. The six-room inn is a good place to stay if you're planning a canoe trip on the Au Sable. Rooms are decorated country style, and three have private baths, while the others are shared. Rates are $72–$92.

Gates' Au Sable Lodge (989-348-8462; www.gateslodge.com), 471 Stephan Bridge Rd., Grayling. The Gates family has run this complex since 1970 and it's now in the able hands of Rusty Gates, who is also a local environmental activist. Along with the Anglers of the Au Sable, he has fought legal battles over oil and gas drilling near the Au Sable. The inn is Orvis-endorsed and offers guided trips on the Au Sable. It has 14 motel-style rooms, a suite, a fly shop, and a small restaurant that is used mostly by inn guests. The fly shop has some of the best patterns for the entire state. Wireless Internet is available. Reservations are usually needed. Rates are $60–$90.

✳ Where to Eat

EATING OUT All establishments are open daily, year-round unless otherwise noted. There are better dining options in Gaylord, which is about 30 miles north on I-75 (see *Dining Out, Gaylord*).

Y ✿ **The Moose Pub** (989-348-4331), 2552 S. I-75 Business Loop, Grayling. Open Mon.–Sat. for lunch and dinner. There is a log cabin feel to this recently remodeled place, and the menu has improved, too. This is pub food, but they've kicked it up a notch for this area with steak, pork chops, salads, whitefish, pasta, and prime rib. Prices are $10–$15.

Y **Spike's Keg O' Nails** (989-348-9587), 301 N. James St., Grayling. Spike's is nearly a legend with fly-fishermen in the area. There are also a scattering of National Guardsmen from the nearby camp, tourists, and bikers. Nobody much goes the weekend without a Spike burger. There is also other pub food. Prices are $5–$8.

Grayling Restaurant (989-348-2141), 211 E. Michigan Ave., Grayling. A small, family-style place with great breakfasts. Prices are $6–$8.

✳ Special Events

Late July **Au Sable River Canoe Marathon** (989-348-4425; www .ausablecanoemarathon.org). The 120-mile canoe race from Grayling to Oscoda is the longest nonstop canoe-only race in North America and attracts thousands of spectators along the route.

HOUGHTON LAKE &
HIGGINS LAKE

Houghton Lake is the largest inland lake in Michigan, and between it and Higgins Lake to the north is one of the oldest weekend resort areas in the state. Both lakes are surrounded by weekend cottages, with many dating back to the 1920s and '30s, when this area was pretty much as far north as you could get in a weekend.

The major towns are Houghton Lake and Prudenville, which are on the south shore of Houghton Lake. These represent the commercial hub of the area, basically a collection of mom-and-pop motels and restaurants. There are many small resorts with cabins.

GUIDANCE **Houghton Lake Tourism Bureau** (989-366-8474), 4482 W. Houghton Lake Dr., Open daily, weekdays. A good source for cabin rentals on the lakes.

GETTING THERE *By car:* One reason for the area's popularity is that it is located at the junction of two highways, I-75 and MI 27. It's 190 miles to Detroit, 130 to Grand Rapids, 310 to Chicago, and 250 to Fort Wayne.

MEDICAL EMERGENCY Call 911. (See *Medical Emergency*, Grayling.)

✳ To See & Do
❀ **Civilian Conservation Corps Museum** (989-348-6178), Roscommon, near the North Higgins Lake State Park on N. Higgins Lake Dr. Open daily late May–early Sept., 10–4. The exhibits center on the Civilian Conservation Corps (CCC), which was a public works program during the Great Depression of the 1930s. Members lived in camps in northern Michigan and planted 484 million trees and built roads, bridges, and buildings.

Fireman's Memorial, CR 103, Exit 239 off I-75, Roscommon. The memorial is dedicated to firefighters who have died in the line of duty. There are various events held during the year.

Gallimore Boarding House & Richardson Schoolhouse, downtown Roscommon. Open late May–early Sept., Sat.–Sun. The 1880s boardinghouse was used during the lumbering era and later. There are three rooms decorated in period furniture.

Houghton Lake Historical Village (989-366-9124; www.houghtonlakehistory .com), 1701 MI 55, Prudenville. Open late May–early Sept., Fri.–Sat., 12–4. There are 11 restored 1800s buildings, including a schoolroom town hall, dress shop, general store, doctor's office, barbershop, and homestead. Various special events are held.

Margaret Gahagan Preserve (989-275-3217), Southline Rd., off MI 18, Roscommon. Margaret Gahagan was a Michigan newspaperwoman who worked at Detroit daily papers in the 1940s. In the 1950s she moved to northern Michigan and started the *North Woods Call*, a conservation publication. The 10-acre preserve is the site of her cabin on the South Branch of the Au Sable River. It's open to the public from dawn to dusk.

Wellington Farm Park (1-888-OLD-FARM; www.wellingtonfarmpark.org), Military Rd., Roscommon. Open daily late May–Oct., 10–5. The 60-acre farm is a working replica of a midwestern farmstead from the 1930s. A farm market here sells produce from the farm.

✳ Lodging

All establishments are open year-round unless otherwise noted.

East Bay Lakefront Lodge (989-366-5910; www.eastbaylodge.com), 125 12th St., Prudenville. Randy and Lorrie Krause are the innkeepers at this landmark lodge on Houghton Lake. They offer rooms and cottages, and there's a sandy beach and dock. The main lodge has 27 rooms, most decorated country style, and the cottages have kitchens. There is wireless Internet and a lobby with a fireplace. Rates are $50–$120.

BED & BREAKFAST **Springbrook Inn Bed & Breakfast** (989-366-6347; www.springbrookinn.com), 565 W. Branch Rd., Prudenville. Matt and Kathy Grover are the innkeepers at this modern log-style inn. There are eight rooms, each with a king-sized bed, hot tub, bath, balcony, and cable TV. Rates are $169–$229.

✳ Where to Eat

EATING OUT The establishments are open year-round unless otherwise noted.

Ⓨ **Blue Bayou Spirits & Eatery** (989-422-2000), 100 Clearview Dr., Houghton Lake. Open daily. Located in the Comfort Inn, the hotel-style restaurant offers Cajun-style lunches and dinners, and it has a view of Houghton Lake. Prices are $10–$15.

Ⓨ **Kilkare Inn** (989-366-5254), 3942 W. Houghton Lake Dr., Houghton Lake. Open daily. Pub food and burgers are the fare in this local's tavern. There is a dance floor, pool, and darts. Prices are $8–$12.

Southeast

DETROIT

ANN ARBOR

DETROIT

espite southeastern Michigan's urban woes and the financial troubles of the Big Three, Detroit is a riverfront city that's receiving a lot of good attention lately, with a new river walk and new gambling casinos. The region is home to about 3 million people spread out in four counties and includes lush, upscale suburbs such as the Grosse Pointes, Birmingham, and Bloomfield Hills. Small towns that were once in the country have been swallowed up by urban sprawl.

Detroit's entertainment districts, Greektown and Mexicantown, are vibrant at night, and the newer sports stadiums built for the Tigers and Lions bring people downtown. The Detroit Red Wings play downtown too, and attract fans not only from Michigan, but also from much of southern Ontario.

Detroit was founded in 1701 by Frenchman Antonine de la Mothe Cadillac. The city's name means "a strait of water linking two larger bodies of water." Fort Detroit was a fur-trading post, but it also had a strategic location because it controlled shipping access to the upper Great Lakes. One geographical oddity is usually pointed out: When you cross the border to Windsor, Ont., you're actually headed south. It's the only place in the nation where you come from the north to enter Canada.

The British took control of Detroit in 1760, only to lose it to the U.S. during the Revolutionary War. The British retook it in the War of 1812, but it was returned to the U.S. after the war.

During the 19th century, Detroit became the center for iron stove manufacturing, and other mechanical works that set the stage for it to become a hotbed of auto manufacturing in the early 20th century. In the 1890s, a young Henry Ford was enticed to leave the family farm in Dearborn and come to Detroit to work at an Edison electrical generating plant. He started tinkering with an automobile and eventually got the thing to run. Ford wasn't the inventor of the automobile, but he had knack for efficient manufacturing and the Ford Motor Co. sold many people their first cars.

One of his pet projects was **The Henry Ford, Museum and Greenfield Village**, now collectively called The Henry Ford. It attracts about 1.5 million visitors annually (see *Museum Villages*, What's Where in Michigan).

Getting around Detroit is difficult. There is no effective mass transit in either the city or suburbs, and you have to call to get a cab. It's best to rent a car; remember, this is the Motor City.

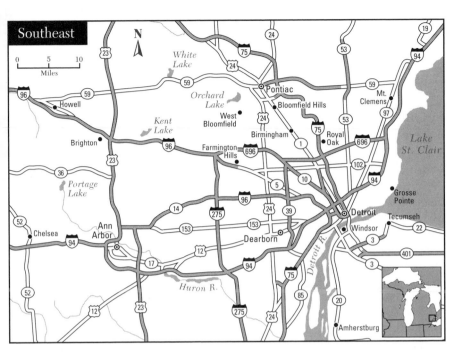

The suburbs are where the action is. Royal Oak has long been the hangout for the hip crowd, and has many restaurants, bars, and entertainment venues. Birmingham has some of the most expensive houses in the area and is home to many specialty shops and nightspots. Dearborn is another hotspot for restaurants and entertainment. It also has the largest concentration of people from the Mideast in the nation, and has an Arab business district, with many restaurants.

GUIDANCE **Detroit Visitors and Convention Bureau** (1-800-DETROIT; www.visitdetroit.com). Open Mon.–Fri. during normal business hours. There is much information about the new gambling casinos, along with maps and guides to the city.

GETTING THERE *By air:* **Metro Airport** (www.metroairport.com) is the largest in the state and is a hub for Northwest Airlines. It's about 30 minutes from downtown Detroit and about 45 minutes from the northern suburbs. A new terminal constructed several years ago has eased congestion. There's no mass transit running to the airport, but all the major car rental firms have facilities.

By bus: **Greyhound** (313-961-8011; www.greyhound.com), 1001 Howard St., Detroit. Operates service to the city.

By car: The major freeways leading to Detroit are I-75, I-94, and I-96. The beltway system is comprised of I-275 and I-696. Freeway speeds can be frightening to nonresidents—about 70 mph in the slow lanes. Merging onto a freeway can

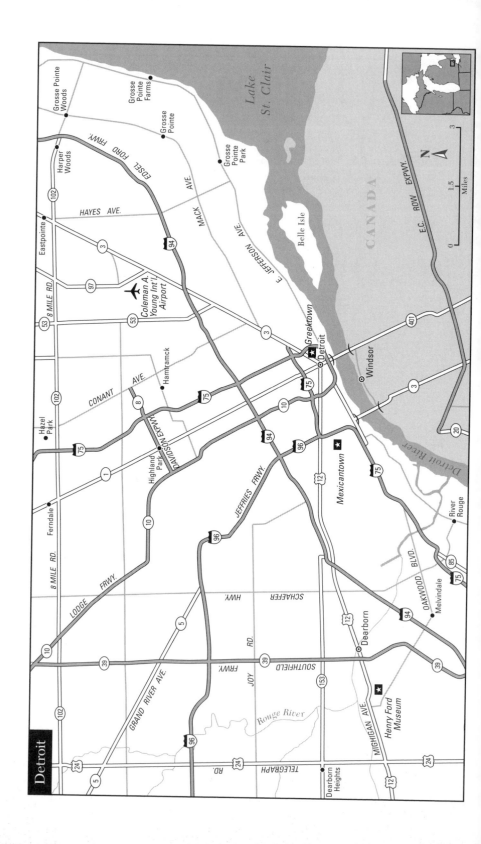

Detroit

be a harrowing experience. It's up to you to find a break in the traffic. Don't expect anybody to slow down for you.

By train: There is daily **Amtrak** (1-800-USA-RAIL; www.Amtrak.com) service from Detroit to Chicago. There are also stops in Ann Arbor and Dearborn, apart from downtown Detroit.

GETTING AROUND Driving is the only viable way to travel in Detroit. There is no mass transit system and finding a taxi can be difficult. Renting a limo may be a good option for larger groups. There is a light rail system, the People Mover, which connects a few buildings in the downtown area. But watch out, it stops operating by about midnight, and you might find yourself stranded. The city bus system is difficult to use and it may not be possible to get to a suburban location.

PARKING Downtown Detroit has plenty of parking spots in paid structures. However, if you're new to town and going to an entertainment venue, it would be best to take advantage of valet parking services because you don't want to be wandering around the streets at night looking for your car. The new gambling casinos in Detroit have onsite parking.

✳ To See & Do

Greektown is the liveliest area of downtown and is relatively safe. It's on Monroe Street and is near Ford Field, where the Detroit Lions play, and Comerica Park, where the Tigers play. It is lined with Greek restaurants, shops, and bars. The restaurants can be very crowded, and many from the Greek community in Detroit go there to eat on Sunday afternoons. They say that's when the best lamb is served.

GREEKTOWN

Fox Theatre (313-983-6000; olympiaentertainment.com), 2211 Woodward Ave., Detroit. The theater opened in 1928 and for many years it was an art deco movie palace, the first to have live sound. By the 1960s it had become run down, and was eventually closed, but it was restored in 1988 by Mike Ilitch, owner of the Little Caesar's Pizza chain. The theater is now an entertainment venue for performers and the 10-story building is used by the Ilitch family for its pizza business offices.

Gem Theater (313-963-9800; www.gemdetroit.com), 333 Madison Ave., Detroit. The theater dates from 1903, but hasn't always been at this site. It was moved there in 1997, and is now a venue for stage productions. The long-running *Escanaba in da Moonlight,* by Michigan actor Jeff Daniels, has been a mainstay production.

Music Hall (313-963-2366; www.musichall.org), 350 Madison St., Detroit. Located in the city's theater district, the Music Hall has been the only building dedicated to musical performances. It has been home to the Detroit Symphony, Michigan Opera Theatre, and is used by many musical performers in Detroit.

Detroit Institute of Arts (DIA) (313-833-1454; www.dia.org), 5200 Woodward Ave., Detroit. The building, constructed in 1927, now houses more than 100 galleries. One of the more controversial exhibits when it was first painted was a set of murals by Diego Rivera that depicted factory life in an unflattering light. Edsel Ford, the son of Henry, and president of Ford Motor Co. at the time, was involved with the DIA at the time, and the murals were deemphasized for a long period of time. The collection includes American, European, modern, and contemporary art, along with African, Asian, and Native American works. In the col-

FORD FIELD

lection is Vincent van Gogh's "Self-Portrait."

Cranbrook Art Museum (1-877-GO-CRANBROOK; www.cranbrook art.com), 39221 Woodward Ave., Bloomfield Hills. Open Wed.–Sun., 11–5. The museum is part of the Cranbrook Educational Community, which includes an art academy, Institute of Science, and other educational programs. The museum is filled with the works of contemporary artists like Lynda Bengils, Mark Dion, Bruce Nauman, Gilles Peress, Alexis Rockman, Bill Viola, and Dandrea Zittel. It also focuses on design and architecture. It is also worth seeing the art

THE HENRY FORD, MUSEUM AND VILLAGE

deco Saarinen House and garden, which was the home and studio designed by Eliel Saarinen, a Finnish American architect who served as the resident architect at Cranbrook from 1925 to 1950. Admission is $7 for adults and $5 for students.

Charles H. Wright Museum of African American History (313-494-5800; www.maah-detroit.org), 315 E. Warren Ave., Detroit. Open Mon.–Sun. The museum pays tribute to the contributions made by African Americans to the country. A permanent exhibit, "We Rise," traces the African American experience in coming to America and their struggles. Cost is $8.

🐾 **Detroit Zoo** (www.detroitzoo.org), 12 Mile and Woodward Ave., Royal Oak. Open daily, 10–5. The zoo has been updated over the years, and has good displays of penguins, monkeys, and birds. The Arctic Ring of Life exhibit explores the relationship between Arctic people and wildlife, and includes an early 1900s Inuit village, along with polar bears, arctic fox, and seals. Visitors can see the animals diving and swimming in the Polar Passage, a tunnel under the swimming area. Admission is $11 for adults and $7 for children.

Pewabic Pottery (313-822-0954; www.pewabic.org), 10125 E. Jefferson Ave., Detroit. Open Mon.–Sat., 10–6. Detroit was the birthplace of Pewabic-style tiles and pottery, which was part of the Arts & Crafts movement in the early 20th century. Mary Chase Perry Stratton founded Pewabic Pottery in 1903 and it has been housed in the current building since 1911. The pottery has a baked-on glaze and is for sale in the museum store. There are also exhibits and tours.

Windsor. The Canadian city offers many dining possibilities and has casino gambling. Access is via the Ambassador Bridge or through the Detroit-Windsor Tunnel. Backups on the bridge are common, especially since 9/11 and partly between the bridge handles 27 percent of the trade between the U.S. and Canada. The tunnel is a better bet, although access is a bit tricky. The tunnel is off Jefferson Avenue near the Renaissance Center. A passport will eventually be needed to cross the border.

✳ Lodging

Most lodging in Detroit is in chain hotels and motels. Some alternatives are also listed here.

In Downtown Detroit

Detroit Marriott at the Renaissance Center (313-568-8000), Renaissance Center. At 72 stories, this is the largest building in Detroit, with 1,298 guest rooms. The glass building gives visitors a good look at the Detroit River and surrounding city and the Canadian countryside across the border. The complex is huge and houses many General Motors employees. It was built in the early 1970s at the height of the modern architecture movement, and many critics say it's a confusing place to find your way around. There is some truth to this, as there really isn't a main entrance or central place where you can orientate yourself. Also, getting to restaurants and other places downtown is difficult. It's too far to walk, and there isn't any public transit system. There are restaurants and shops in the vast complex, which dominates the Detroit skyline. Rates are $280 and up.

Atheneum Suites Hotel and Conference Center (313-962-2323), 1000 Brush Ave. If you need to stay downtown, this place offers a more intimate alterative to the Renaissance Center. It is in the Greektown entertainment district. The major sports arenas for the Detroit Tigers and Lions are nearby. The hotel has 174 suites. Rates start at $200.

Courtyard by Marriott (313-222-7700; www.marriott.com) 333 E. Jefferson Ave. The large hotel with 260 rooms caters to many business travelers and is near the Renaissance Center. The rooms have cable TV, in-room pay movies, and WebTV and Internet service. Sweet Lorraine's Restaurant is located inside. Rates are $200 and up.

Hotel Pontchatrain (313-965-0200), 2 Washington Blvd. The landmark hotel is located close to the Detroit River in the heart of the business district, and it has good views of the river and Windsor. Rates are about $200.

Hilton Garden Inn (313-967-0900), 351 Gratiot Ave. This is one of the city's newer hotels, and it has 198 guest rooms, a pool area, and a fitness center. There are in-room refrigerators, coffee makers, and Internet access. It's close to the sports stadiums and Greektown. Rates run about $200.

In Dearborn

The Dearborn Inn (313-271-2700; www.marriott.com), 20301 Oakwood Blvd., Dearborn. Like many things in Dearborn, Henry Ford had a hand in this. The hotel was built in 1931 on Ford Motor Co. property and was near an airport. Ford made planes in those days. These days, the airport is gone and the 228-room, colonial-style inn is on 23 acres near The Henry Ford Museum. Lodging is available in the hotel, in two lodges, or in five guest homes. The rooms have cable TV, voice mail, hair dryers, coffee makers, and wireless Internet. There are restaurants in the lodge. Rates run about $200.

The Ritz-Carlton (313-441-2000), 300 Town Center Dr., Dearborn. The modern hotel is close to Ford Motor Co. World Headquarters and near Fairlane Shopping Mall. The rooms have wireless Internet access and cable TV.

Courtyard by Marriott (313-271-1184), 5200 Mercury Dr., Dearborn. The complex has 133 rooms and 14 suites and is located near the Ford World Headquarters. The rooms have air conditioners, coffee makers, cable TV, and Internet access. There is a restaurant and cocktail lounge.

BED & BREAKFASTS Detroit isn't a good town for B&Bs, but there are a few.

Inn on Ferry Street (313-871-6000), 84 E. Ferry St. There are 42 rooms in the inn, which is actually four restored Queen Anne homes and two carriages houses on one of Detroit's historic streets. The rooms and suites have air-conditioning and computer data ports. The inn is near Wayne State University and the Detroit Institute of Arts. Rates are $149–$259.

The Inn at 97 Winder (313-832-1538; www.theinnat97winder.com), 97 Winder St., Detroit. The 1870s, 11,000-square-foot brick Victorian mansions are near Detroit's sports arenas and comprise the largest remaining Victorian mansions in Detroit. They are in the Bush Park area, which was home to many wealthy Detroiters in the late 19th century. The 10-room inn has been extensively renovated and is furnished with many antiques. All rooms have baths. Rates are $245–$325.

✳ Where to Eat

The best options in the Detroit area are in Greektown, Mexicantown, Royal Oak, and Dearborn. Royal Oak has been the hotspot for entertainment and dining for more than a decade and has about 50 restaurants. There are a good number in Birmingham.

DINING OUT All restaurants are open daily for lunch and dinner unless otherwise noted.

Y **The Lark** (248-661-4466), 6430 Farmington Rd., West Bloomfield. Whenever a Detroit publication publishes a list of the area's best restaurants, the Lark is on it. It's owned by James and Mary Lark who are there often, making sure everything runs smoothly. Dinner here isn't something you take lightly. Reservations are required, and a suit and tie are usually needed. A typical main course would be grilled Atlantic sea bass with artichokes, fennel, and orange sauce or grilled veal medallions with king crab and roasted herb gnocchi. They maintain their own herb garden and there's a pastry chef. The wine list is one of the largest in the Midwest. Entrees are $75–$80.

Y **Carl's Chop House** (313-833-0700; www.carlschophouse.com), 3020 Grand River Ave., Detroit. Open daily. The venerable steakhouse is the oldest in Detroit and has been at the same location for more than 60 years. It has the longest bar in the city, at 64 feet. Neither the menu nor the décor have changed much over the years. It's pretty traditional food: beef, chops, and seafood. Entrees are $25–$30.

Y **Caucus Club Restaurant** (313-965-4970), 150 W. Congress, Detroit. Open Mon.–Sat. The old school, clubby restaurant opened in 1952 in the Penobscot Building and has been serving lunch and dinners to judges, lawyers, bankers, and stockbrokers ever since. Barbra Streisand performed here in 1961 and it was one of her first paying jobs. The menu has been updated a bit, but it still focuses on ribs, steak, burgers, and fish. Entrees are $18–$27.

DETROIT

Ÿ **Mario's** (313-832-1616), 4222 Second, Detroit. This is one of the last supper clubs of its era, and it has been at this location since 1948. The emphasis is on Italian pasta dishes such as linguine with lobster marinara sauce, but there are steaks, fish, seafood, and veal on the wide-ranging menu. I've never seen this many menu items. There are more than a dozen fish and seafood dishes and 16 veal dinners, and about 75 different offerings. Entrees are $20–$36.

Ÿ **Roma Café** (313-831-2253), 3401 Riopelle St., Detroit. Open Mon.–Sat. for lunch and dinner. Located in the Eastern Market, this Detroit favorite serves Italian food to dedicated customers. This is the city's oldest restaurant and the waiters still wear tuxedoes. The building dates to 1888, and in 1890 the Marazza family opened a boardinghouse here, catering to farmers who were bringing their produce to the nearby Eastern Market. Mrs. Marazza started cooking for them, and opened the Roma Café that same year. It has been run by members of the Sossi family since about 1918. Pasta and veal dishes are at the heart of the menu, but there are also seafood and beef dishes. Entrees are $20–$30.

Ÿ **The Whitney Restaurant** (313-832-5700; www.thewhitney.com), 3321 Woodward Ave., Detroit. Located in a 52-room mansion built in 1894 by lumber baron David Whitney, it cost $400,000 to build at the time. The restaurant has a large menu that features American dishes, pastas, and seafood. The chef uses many Michigan food products, including perch, walleye, and cherries in the entrees. There are also steaks, chicken, and seafood. Entrees are $19–$44.

Ÿ **The Rattlesnake Club** (313-567-4400), 300 River Place, Detroit. Open Mon.–Sat. Jimmy Schmidt has been one of Detroit's top chefs for several decades and he holds forth here with contemporary American food. The place has a good view of the Detroit River. Meat, fish, and poultry are the main dishes. Entrees are $20–$30.

Sweet Georgia Brown (313-965-1245), 1045 Brush, Detroit, in Greektown. Open daily for lunch and dinner. The menu is contemporary American and features a small, but unique selection of entrees, such as cornmeal-crusted sea bass, bronzed barbecued salmon, and sea scallop and shrimp penne. Entrees are $24–$38.

EATING OUT Ÿ **Traffic Jam & Snug Restaurant** (313-831-9470), 511 W. Canfield St., Detroit. Over the years, this place has morphed from a college burger and beer bar into an upscale restaurant. The list of entrees is small, but well selected and includes Detroit Delmonico, Caribbean jerk chicken, and Hawaiian Islands salmon. Entrees are $11–$17.

Ÿ **Xochimilco Restaurant** (313-843-0179), 3409 Bagley, Detroit. This place has been the anchor restaurant for Detroit's Mexicantown for years, and it keeps drawing crowds, even late at night. There is a full range of Mexican food. Prices are $8–$10.

Ÿ **Ginopolis' on the Grill** (248-851-8222), 27815 Middlebelt, Farmington Hills. Greek family-owned restaurants were once common in Detroit and its suburbs, but they've become less so. Pete and Johnny Ginopolis keep the tradition alive with their grill. Their specialty is Montgomery Inn ribs. They also do well with Greek-style amb. Entrees are $20–$24.

Lafayette and Senate Coney Islands (313-964-8198), 118 and 114 W. Lafayette Blvd. Detroit. Open 24 hours. These two places, located adjacent to each other, were founded by members of the same Greek family and have been dishing out Detroit's version of the Coney Island hot dog for nearly 100 years. Noisy Greek waiters are eager to take your order no matter what time of day. Plenty of college kids have sobered up here at 3 AM. Prices are $3.

In Greektown

Y **Laikon Café** (313-879-7058), 596 Monroe St., Detroit. Open Wed.–Mon. There are fancier places in Greektown, but none like this one. This is where Greek Americans from the area come to celebrate religious holidays, birthdays, and other events. For several decades, a parrot in the place chatted with customers. At one point, a reporter at a Detroit newspaper found himself a bit short on money when he was having dinner there and he scooped up the tip from the previous occupant of the booth. The parrot caught him and squawked: "Put the money down." The reporter complied, but held a grudge against the parrot for about 30 years and never lived down the story. But when the parrot died, the reporter got a bit of revenge. A wise city editor assigned the now old reporter the task of writing the parrot's obituary. The food here is classic Greek home cooking: lamb and rice, chicken, and large salads similar to what you'd have in a Greek home. Prices are $10–$20.

Y **New Hellas Café** (313-961-1999), 583 Monroe St., Detroit. Open Tues.–Sun. This is one of the most popular places in Greektown, and it has the flaming Greek cheese that has been a hit with non-Greeks, but which is rarely served in a Greek home. The other dishes—lamb, moussaka, and stuffed grape leaves—are all authentic. Prices are $10–$20.

Y **Pegasus** (313-964-6800), 558 Monroe St., Detroit. Open Mon.–Sat. There are classic Greek dishes, but also American food in this more upscale restaurant. If you're a garlic lover, try the scordalia; the half-garlic, half-potato spread separates Greeks from non-Greeks. For those new to the ethnic dishes, try the Greek trio, a combination of spanakoteropeta, moussaka, and pastitsio. All are authentic. Prices are $8–$27.

✳ Selective Shopping

There is virtually no shopping in Detroit apart from at the Renaissance Center, which has a few specialty shops.

DuMouchelle Art Galleries (313-963-6255), 409 E. Jefferson Ave., Detroit. The gallery has been owned by the DuMouchelle family since 1927 and has been an institution in Detroit. It specializes in fine arts and is an auction house for furnishings, crystal, paintings, and jewelry.

Detroit Antique Mall (313-963-5252), 828 W. Fisher Freeway, Detroit. Open Tues.–Sun. This place is packed with a lot of junk, but there are some finds, too, if you're willing to sort through the stuff. There are art deco items, old doors, woodwork, and a large collection of vintage hardware for those restoring homes.

ANN ARBOR

Ann Arbor is a quintessential small liberal college town, where the University of Michigan Wolverines regularly draw more than 100,000 people on Saturdays for football games. The downtown streets are filled with restaurants, taverns, and upscale coffee shops catering to students and returning alumni. Ann Arbor has become a regional "downtown" and its restaurants and entertainment events are the drawing card. The Ann Arbor Art Fair in mid-July attracts thousands. The city is dominated by the University of Michigan, which was founded in 1815 and has nearly 40,000 students.

The Huron River, which runs through Ann Arbor; small lakes nearby; and the gently rolling terrain have enticed many to move to the area. Michigan is a research university and a large employer. Ann Arbor's business district centers on Main Street, which is lined with late-19th-century brick commercial buildings that have been turned into trendy shops, coffee houses, bars, and loft apartments.

GUIDANCE **Ann Arbor Area Convention & Visitors Bureau** (734-995-7281; www.annarbor.org), 120 W. Huron St. Open Mon.–Fri., 8:30–5. The bureau is a good source of information about local events and restaurants.

MEDIA *The Ann Arbor News* (744-994-6860; www.annarbornews.com). There are entertainment and restaurant listings and plenty of stories on U-M sports.

GETTING THERE *By car:* Ann Arbor is at the junction of two major highways, I-94 and MI 14. It's about 40 minutes from Detroit and about 30 minutes from Metro Airport.
By air: See Metro Airport, Detroit.
By train: **Amtrak** has regular service from Detroit and Chicago.

PARKING It can be difficult downtown, but there are lots and structures to try. The police vigorously enforce the parking meter system.

MEDICAL EMERGENCY **University of Michigan Health System** (734-936-4000; www.umich.edu), 1500 E. Medical Center Dr. Call 911.

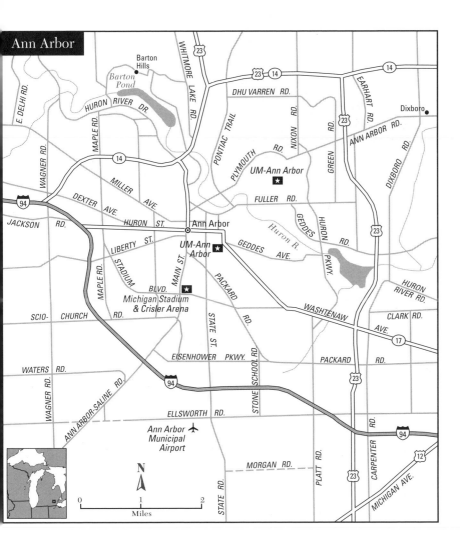

Ann Arbor

✳ To See & Do

Gerald R. Ford Presidential Library (734-205-0555; www.fordlibrary museum.gov), 1000 Beal Ave. Open Mon.–Fri., 8:45–4:45. President Ford was born in Grand Rapids, where the Gerald R. Ford Museum is located (see Grand Rapids), but graduated from the University of Michigan, and the library is on campus. It contains the core of his papers from his tenure as president from 1974–1977. These are accessible to scholars, the media, and the public.

Hill Auditorium (734-764-8350; www.umich.edu), 825 N. University Ave. The auditorium has been the venue for classical and contemporary music and was designed by Albert Kahn, an influential Detroit architect.

Underground Railroad Tours (734-994-6513; www.anotherannarbor .org). Southeastern Michigan was the end of the Underground Railroad, which

GERALD R. FORD PRESIDENTIAL LIBRARY

existed before the end of slavery in the U.S. Many African Americans found their way to Detroit and crossed over into Canada. Tours are offered to various sites.

FOR KIDS ♦ **Ann Arbor Hands-On Museum** (734-995-5439; www.aahom.org), 220 E. Ann. Open Mon.–Sat., 10–5, and Sun., noon–5. There are about 250 exhibits, most of which children can get involved with, including science and technology learning systems. Admission is $7.

♦ **Domino's Petting Farm** (734-998-0182; www.pettingfarm.com), 24 Frank Lloyd Wright Dr. Open Mon.–Fri., 9:30–4, and Sat.–Sun., 10:30–5. Located at the world headquarters of Domino's Pizza, the farm allows children to pet animals. There are pony and hayrides on the weekends, and there is an extensive collection of farm animals not often seen. The sprawling headquarters is worth seeing. It was built by pizza king Tom Monaghan, who is devoted to the architecture of Frank Lloyd Wright. Admission is $5 for adults and $4.50 for children.

VILLAGES Chelsea, about 10 miles west of Ann Arbor on I-94. Actor Jeff Daniels is a native and he has put his hometown on the cultural map by building The Purple Rose Theater, which stages productions, some of which he appears in. His family owns the local lumberyard, and much of the building materials for the theater came from the family business. He is often seen walking the downtown streets or eating at the Common Grill, a local hotspot. The theater has helped the town, and downtown streets are filled with strollers who visit the shops and art galleries.

✳ Lodging

Most lodging can be found in chain hotels/motels along the freeway corridors on I-94 and US 23.

⊚ **Vitosha Guest Haus** (734-741-4969), 1917 Washtenaw Ave., Ann Arbor. This 10-room stone guesthouse is more of an inn than a bed & breakfast and would be a good place for a long stay. The rooms are large, all have private baths, and most have fireplaces. The stone building is an Arts & Crafts structure, and it is a relief from the Victorian frilliness that

dominates many Michigan B&Bs. Rates are $50–$150.

✳ Where to Eat

DINING OUT ⍭ **The Gandy Dancer** (734-769-0592; www.muer.com), 401 Depot St., Ann Arbor. Open Mon.–Sat. for lunch and dinner. This has been a local favorite for more than 25 years. It is located in an 1886 railroad station, which still has the original cobblestones and red oak ceilings. It's run by the Muer family, which has operated several Michigan restaurants for several generations. They are known for their seafood. There are also steaks, chops, pasta, and house-baked desserts. Entrees are $18–$25.

Y The Earle (734-994-0211; www.theearle.com), 121 W. Washington St., Ann Arbor. Open daily for lunch and dinner. This is a perennial local favorite with its brand of French and Italian dishes and cellar with more than 900 wines. Happy Hour offers some early, lighter dining possibilities. Entrees are $20–$30.

Y The Chop House (734-669-9977; www.thechophouserestaurant.com), 322 S. Main St., Ann Arbor. Open daily for dinner. Midwestern grain-fed beef is the specialty of this upscale downtown restaurant. There is a large wine list and a large offering of single-malt Scotches. They offer every different steak you can imagine, but there are a few fish, chicken, and pasta dishes on the menu. Reservations are recommended. Entrees are $30–$44.

Y Bella Ciao (734-995-2107), 118 W. Liberty St., Ann Arbor. Open daily for dinner. This is a small place, but it scores big when it comes to its Italian menu, which is more than just pasta. There's pancetta-wrapped shrimp with lemon-sautéed spinach and grilled polenta. Duck, beef, Amish chicken, and veal are also on the menu. There is a large wine list. Entrees are $19–$26.

In Chelsea

Y Common Grill (734-475-0470), 112 S. Main St., Chelsea. Open Tues.–Sun. for lunch and dinner. Located in a restored 100-year-old building, the menu ranges from pastas to grilled steak and lighter fare. Owner/chef Craig Common is the author of a cookbook. There are lots of local favorites, including walleye and whitefish. The steaks are Angus beef. Actor Jeff Daniels's Purple Rose Theater is down the street, and he can be seen dining here on occasion. Entrees are $15–$27.

EATING OUT Y Metzger's German Restaurant (734-668-8987; www.metzgers.net), 305 N. Zeeb Rd., Ann Arbor. Open daily for lunch and dinner. The family-owed German restaurant has been a fixture in Ann Arbor for several generations and serves up traditional dishes such as sauerbraten, Bavaria veal, chicken livers, and prime rib. There are German wines and liquors. Entrees are $17–$22.

Zingerman's Bakehouse (734-761-7255; www.zingermansbakehouse.com), 422 Detroit St., Ann Arbor. This place has a near cultlike following, especially among University of Michigan graduates. It's an understatement to call it a deli—the sandwiches are all served on fresh Zingerman's bread. There are also many specialty food items. Prices are $8–$12.

Y Zingerman's Roadhouse (734-663-3663; www.zingermansroad

THE CHOP HOUSE

house.com), 2501 Jackson Ave., Ann Arbor. Open daily for lunch and dinner. This is part of the Zingerman's enterprises, which includes the deli downtown. It is a sit-down lunch and dinner place. There are many southern-style entrees, including pit-smoked beef brisket, eastern North Carolina pulled pork, spare ribs, and chicken-fried steak. Entrees are $15–$25.

Υ **Casey's Tavern** (734-665-6775), 304 Depot, Ann Arbor. Open daily for lunch and dinner. This is a popular neighborhood tavern with good burgers and a few weekly specials. It's near the Ann Arbor Amtrak Station and is a good place to wait for the train. Prices are $8–$10.

Υ **Café Shalimar** (734-929-9900), 211 E. Washington St., Ann Arbor. Open daily for lunch and dinner. The place to go for Indian food. They specialize in north Indian favorites and also offer Indian-Chinese specialties. Prices are $10–$20.

Υ **Lower Town Grill** (734-451-1213), 195 W. Liberty, Ann Arbor. Many bars in Ann Arbor are dominated by college students, and this is a good refuge from the loud music and crowds. The food is a bit up from pub fare. There are some good gumbos and soups on the menu and a few entrees. Some good beers are offered, but there isn't a wine list. Prices are $5–$10.

Fleetwood Diner (734-995-5502), 300 S. Ashley St., Ann Arbor. This classic metal dinner has been a hangout for the hip since it opened in 1949. You'll find a mixture of students, professors, and street people at its outside café on most warm days. The menu is burgers, fries, and regular coffee.

* Nightlife

Υ **Blind Pig & 8 Ball Saloon** (734-996-8555; www.blindpigmusic.com), 208 S. First, Ann Arbor. Open nightly. Since it opened in the early 1970s, this place has hosted some legendary blues and rock musicians, including Jimi Hendrix, John Lennon, Iggy Pop and the MC5, George Thoroughgood, and Bo Diddley. The bands change on Wednesday night. This is a bar, but there are limited choices.

Υ **Bird of Paradise** (734-662-8310), 312 S. Main St. Open daily. There is jazz downstairs and Zydeco and some Cajun music on the second floor. They serve a small menu of gumbos and sandwiches.

* Selective Shopping

The Ann Arbor/Chelsea area has more than 30 art galleries. Most are open daily, year-round unless otherwise noted.

In Ann Arbor
16 Hands (734-761-1110), 216 S. Main St., Ann Arbor. The works of more than 500 artists are on display in the shop, including fine art, decorative pieces, jewelry, and glass.

Ann Arbor Art Center (734-994-8004), 117 W. Liberty, Ann Arbor. The shop offers artwork, jewelry, ceramics, and paintings from local and regional artists. The gallery showcases different Michigan artists monthly.

Work Gallery (734-998-6178), 306 S. State St., Ann Arbor. The gallery houses exhibition space for students from the University of Michigan School of Art and Design. There is a variety of media, including paintings, photography, sculpture, and electronic media.

Washington Street Gallery (734-761-2287), 120 E. Liberty St., Ann Arbor. The gallery represents contemporary regional artists and features original fine art, including paintings, drawings, sculpture, ceramics, and glass.

BOOKSTORES **Shaman Drum** (734-662-7407; shamandrum.com), 311–315 S. State St., Ann Arbor. Open daily. The bookstore caters to the University of Michigan, but it also has many titles for other readers, and you'll always find a surprise here. The independent shop hosts book signings and readings by well-known authors.

West Side Book Shop (734-995-1891), 113 W. Liberty, Ann Arbor.

Open daily. There is a large selection of used and rare books, maps, and vintage photography.

In Chelsea

River Gallery (734-433-0826), 121 S. Main St., Chelsea. Open Tues.–Sat. The independently owned gallery has a focus on contemporary fine art, much of it done by local artists and sculptors. There are various artist showings during the year.

✳ Special Events

Late July The **Ann Arbor Art Fair** (www.artfair.org) attracts up to 500,000 people for the annual event, which has been held since 1960 in the downtown area.

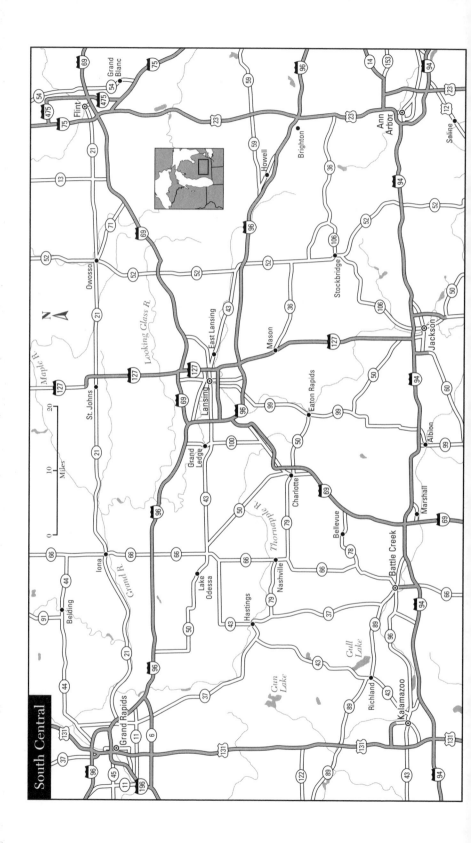

South Central

South Central

SOUTH CENTRAL

The south-central cities are home to many of the state's nearly 10 million residents. These are midsized communities, many of which are dependent on the auto industry and other manufacturing. Most are pleasant towns with sprawling suburbs.

Grand Rapids is close enough to Lake Michigan to have some attraction to travelers, and its revived downtown hosts many conventions. Lansing is the state capital and home to Michigan State University. Kalamazoo has a lovely downtown, with many art deco buildings and some good restaurants. It's also home to a major university. Battle Creek is the home of Kellogg's cereals. Jackson was the site of the state's largest prison, but that has closed, and the town is ailing. Flint is home to many General Motors plants, and it has been hard hit by the decline of the auto industry.

Each town has a scattering of good restaurants, particularly Grand Rapids, but lodging is mostly in chain hotels and motels. There are a few bed & breakfasts in villages near the larger towns. Marshall, near Battle Creek, is a historic town that's worth a visit. It has many older homes.

LANSING & EAST LANSING

The Lansing area is now home to the state capitol and Michigan State University. Michigan has two major universities with sports teams in the Big Ten, and this sparks some competitive rivalries between state residents. You'll often see MSU Spartan flags and U-M flags on the front lawn of the same house when the two football teams clash in the fall.

The city's first settlers arrived in 1836, enticed by the claims of two New York land speculators who platted a town called Biddle City and sold lots to unsuspecting folks from Lansing, New York. When they arrived, they found that the 65-block, so-called new city was underwater much of the year. Some left, but others stayed, found better land, and created the village of Lansing.

The village of roughly 20 souls dozed along for about 10 years, until a dispute broke out about where the state's capital should be located. Upper Peninsula residents wanted it in Calumet, then one of the largest urban areas of the state (see Calumet). The capital had been in Detroit since 1837, when Michigan became a state, but other cities thought Detroit was having too much influence on the rest of the state, and there was pressure to move it. There was also concern Detroit could be captured by the British, as it had in the War of 1812.

Large communities such as Ann Arbor, Jackson, and Marshall wanted the capital, and a political battle ensued. Out of frustration, Lansing was put forward, and the legislature compromised on it, perhaps thinking that it wouldn't happen. It did.

GUIDANCE Lansing Regional Chamber of Commerce (517-487-6340; www.lansingchamber.org), 112 East Allegan St., Lansing. Open weekdays, 8:30–5. The chamber offers a welcome packet with maps and guides.

MEDIA *Lansing State Journal* (517-377-1020; www.lansingstatejournal.com). The daily paper has information on events throughout central Michigan.

GETTING THERE *By air:* **Capital City Airport** (517-321-6121; flylansing.com), 4100 Capitol City Blvd., Lansing. The airport is serviced by Allegiant Air, Delta Airlines, and United. Most flights are connecters to Detroit, Chicago's O'Hare, and Minneapolis. Flights may be cheaper to Metro Airport in Detroit (see Detroit).

By auto: Lansing is about 90 miles from the Detroit area and is accessible via I-96. It's also serviced by I-69 from the south.

MEDICAL EMERGENCY Sparrow Hospital (517-364-1000; www.sparrow.org), Lansing. Call 911.

✳ To See & Do

Michigan Historical Museum (517-373-3559; www.michigan.gov), 702 W. Kalamazoo St., Lansing. Open Mon.–Fri., 9–4:30; Sat., 1–4; Sun., 1–5. The museum takes visitors through the state's history from prehistoric times through the 20th century, with exhibits of copper mining, a 1920s street, and a 1957 auto show. There are 26 permanent galleries on five levels, including a three-story relief map of Michigan. There is a strong focus on Native American history.

R. E. Olds Transportation Museum (517-372-0422; www.reoldsmuseum.org), 240 Museum Dr., Lansing. Open Tues.–Sun., 10–5, and Sun., noon–5. Ransom Olds developed the Oldsmobile, and the museum traces the city's involvement in the auto industry from 1883 to the present. Historic autos are on display, including the first Oldsmobile built in 1897. The collection includes a rare 1911 seven-passenger Oldsmobile touring car, of which only 825 were produced. Admission is $5 for adults and $3 for children.

State Capitol (517-373-2353; www.michigan.gov), Capitol Ave. at Michigan Ave. The state capitol, completed in 1879 and renovated in the 1980s, is one of many capitol buildings constructed after the Civil War that were designed by Elijah Myers. It is an example of Victorian architecture and decorative arts of

STATE CAPITOL

MICHIGAN LIBRARY AND HISTORICAL CENTER

the time. The building was a modern, fireproof structure. There is a glass-block floor that was innovative in its day. It's open to the public.

✳ Lodging

Most lodging in the Lansing area is in chain motels and hotels.

Wild Goose Inn (517-333-3334), 512 Albert St., East Lansing. The inn has six rooms, all with their own baths and different themes and five with hot tubs. It is located near Michigan State University. Breakfast is included. Rates are $109–$159.

EATING OUT The establishments listed are open daily unless otherwise noted.

Ƴ Beggar's Banquet (517-351-4573), 218 Abbott Rd., East Lansing. This is where Michigan State University students and their parents eat, and it has been a fixture near the campus since 1973. They offer pub food, but also entrees like whitefish, salmon, seafood, chicken, steak, and ribs. Prices are $10–$25.

Ƴ Coral Gables (517-1311), 2838 E. Grand River, East Lansing. This place has a long history of being a college hangout, going back to the 1930s, but these days it's more of a family restaurant where parents and students dine out. Entrees range from ribs to fish and chicken, and there's also pizza and burgers. Prices are $10–$20.

GRAND RAPIDS

This western Michigan city once had the reputation of being a dull, but large farm town. These days, the Grand Rapids region is home to about 700,000, and it has become the nightlife destination for much of western Michigan. The transformation came about when the city took advantage of the Grand River, which runs through the city.

Grand Valley State College and other smaller parochial schools have contributed to the vitality of the city. A downtown convention center attracts many events and the Amway Grand Plaza Hotel also has brought conventions to the city. Having Gerald Ford as a native son has helped, too, in the form of the Gerald R. Ford Presidential Museum.

The Ojibwa were the first to inhabit the area, and later on Europeans arrived to engage in the fur trade with the Native Americans. By the 1830s, immigrants started arriving from New York and New England, many of them attracted by the fertile farmland in the Grand River valley. Lumbering was also important, and Grand Rapids became the center of furniture manufacturing, which is still important today. It also became a railroad center.

Two newer industries have homes here. The Meijer chain of retail stores started in the region and has its headquarters here, and Amway began here and still has a major presence.

One note on eating out: The Grand Rapids area is heavily conservative Christian, with a large population of Dutch Reformed churchgoers, and many places are closed on Sundays.

GUIDANCE **Grand Rapids/Kent County Convention & Visitors Bureau** (616-459-8287; www.grcv.org), 171 Monroe Ave. NW, Ste. 700, Grand Rapids. Open daily, weekdays. A good resource for the entire region.

GETTING THERE *By car:* Two major freeways meet in Grand Rapids, I-96 and US 131. It's about two hours from Detroit.

By air: **Gerald R. Ford International Airport** (616-233-6000; www.grr.org), 5500 44th St. SE, Grand Rapids. This is the second largest airport in Michigan behind Detroit Metro, and it offers direct flights via many major carriers.

MEDICAL EMERGENCY **Butterworth Hospital** (616-391-1690), 100 Michigan   **169**
St. NE, Grand Rapids. Dial 911.

GRAND RAPIDS

✳ To See & Do

Frederik Meijer Gardens & Sculpture Park. Open Mon., Wed., Thur., and
Sat., 9–5; Tue., 9–9; and Sun., noon–5. Meijer was the founder of the Meijer
chain stores now located throughout the Midwest. The gardens combine the arts
and nature, and it takes from four to eight hours to see the park. Many of the
plants are native to the Midwest and are in outdoor gardens. A tropical conserva-
tory holds more than 500 species from around the world in natural settings such
as waterfalls. Admission is $16 for adults, $9 for students, $6 for children age
5–13, and $4 for ages 3–4.

Gerald R. Ford Museum (616-254-0400; www.fordlibrarymuseum.gov), 303
Pearl St. NW, Grand Rapids. Open daily, 9–5. The museum draws on holdings of
the presidential library system, the Smithsonian, and National Archives to tell
the story of President Gerald Ford, a Grand Rapids native. There is a replica of
the White House Cabinet Room as it existed during the 1970s when Ford was
president and a Watergate exhibit that focuses on the bungled burglary of the
Democratic offices that eventually forced the resignation of President Richard
Nixon and put Ford in the White House. Admission is $7 for adults and $5 for
students.

Grand Rapids Art Museum (616-831-1000; www.gramonline.org), 155 N.
Division Ave., Grand Rapids. Open daily. The museum was built in 2007 and
features local, national, and international artists. There is a museum store.
Admission runs $3.

⊘ Grand Rapids Children's Museum (616-235-4728), 22 Sheldon Ave. NE,
Grand Rapids. Open Tues.–Sat., 9:30–5, and Sun., noon–5. The hands-on museum allows children to learn on their own with various exhibits. A popular

FREDERIK MEIJER GARDENS

exhibit is a beehive visitors can view through a glass-block system to see the bees making honey and creating their home. Admission is $5.

⚘ **Van Andel Museum Center** (616-456-3977), 272 Pearl St. NW, Grand Rapids. Open Mon.–Fri., 9–4; Sat., 10–4; Sun., noon–4. The museum offers exhibits on nature, cultural heritage, Native Americans, the 19th-century urban landscape of Grand Rapids, and a 1928 carousel.

⚘ **Roger B. Chaffee Planetarium at Van Andel Museum Center** (616-456-3663), 271 Pearl St. NW, Grand Rapids. Multimedia sky and laser light shows are set to popular music. There is also a Digistar theater.

✳ Lodging

Grand Rapids is a big convention city, and many hotels are to be found downtown. Others are near the Gerald R. Ford Airport and along the freeway exits.

In Downtown

Amway Grand Plaza Hotel (616-774-2000; www.amwaygrand.com), 187 Monroe Ave., NW, Grand Rapids. The Amway incorporates the 1913 Pantlind Hotel in the 682-room complex. There are rooms in the Pantlind and in the modern glass structure that surrounds it. The hotel is the site of numerous conventions and is 29 stories. There are six restaurants (see *Dining Out*) in the complex, which includes fitness rooms, a pool, and spa facilities. The lobby feels like a step back into the 19th century. The Grand River is nearby, and it's within walking distance of downtown restaurants and shopping. Rates are $155–$200.

Courtyard by Marriott (616-242-6000), 11 Monroe Ave., NW, Grand Rapids. The hotel is connected to the Van Andel Arena and DeVos Hall, where many conventions take place.

THE PANTLIND HOTEL, NOW CALLED THE AMWAY GRAND PLAZA HOTEL

Its 207 rooms are in the heart of downtown, and it has an indoor pool and fitness facilities. The rooms have Internet service. Rates are $149.

✳ Where to Eat

DINING OUT ⟨ **The 1913 Room** (616-774-2000; www.amwaygrand .com) 187 Monroe Ave. NW, Grand Rapids. In the Amway Plaza Hotel. Open Mon.–Sat. for lunch and dinner. The menu is classic, with a French influence. The restaurant is rated one of the top eateries in Michigan in various rating systems. Entrees include filet of beef au poivre, Alaskan halibut, and saddle of rabbit. Entrees are $35–$40. The Grill at 1913 provides more casual dining. Steaks, chicken, and lamb are the heart of the menu. Entrees are $20–$36.

⟨ **Charley's Crab** (616-459-2500; www.muer.com), 63 Market St. SW, Grand Rapids. Open Mon.–Sat. for lunch and dinner and Sun. for brunch. The restaurant is in the Muer family, which runs several in Michigan and has a tradition of serving seafood. Prices are $15–$25.

EATING OUT **Grand Rapids Brewing Company** (616-285-5970; www .michiganmenu.com), 3689 28th St., Grand Rapids. The brewpub brews its own beers and serves up pub fare and a few entrees, including ribs, steak, salmon, and London broil in this large older building. Entrees are $18–$19.

KALAMAZOO, BATTLE CREEK
& MARSHALL

Because of its offbeat name, Kalamazoo has turned up in more popular songs than many larger cities, and it is also the subject of numerous jokes. Nobody knows where the catchy name came from, but it's suspected that Native American tribes gave the river the name, and the city adopted it.

Kalamazoo is a classic midsized midwestern town of about 77,000 residents and is home to Western Michigan University and Kalamazoo College. One of the larger employers is Pfizer, the large pharmaceutical maker created from Upjohn Co. Many smaller biotechnology firms are also located in the area.

Battle Creek, a town of about 53,000, is a small southern Michigan city along the I-94 corridor running from Detroit to Chicago, and it's the home of Kellogg's, the cereal maker. Historical home tours in Battle Creek and nearby Marshall draw many people. Marshall, a city of about 7,459, is one of the largest National Historic Landmark Districts in the nation, with 850 homes. A home tour in mid-September is a major event. The city was settled in 1830 and was named for John Marshall, the chief justice of the U.S. Supreme Court.

GUIDANCE **Kalamazoo Regional Chamber of Commerce** (269-381-4000; www.kazoochamber.com), 346 W. Michigan Ave., Kalamazoo, MI 49007. The chamber offers a visitor's guide from its Web site, with much regional information.
Marshall Area Chamber of Commerce (269-781-5163), 424 E. Michigan Ave., Marshall. Open Mon.–Fri., 8:30–4:30, and Sat., 10–3. The chamber is a source of maps to historic homes in the town and also handles information about the home tour in September.

GETTING THERE *By car:* I-94, the major east-west freeway in southern Michigan, runs through Kalamazoo, Battle Creek, and Marshall.
By air: The nearest large commercial airport is in Grand Rapids (see Grand Rapids).
By train: There is daily **Amtrak** service on a train that runs between Detroit and Chicago, with a stop in Kalamazoo.

MEDICAL EMERGENCY Bronson Methodist Hospital (269-341-7654; www.
bronsonhealth.com), 601 John St., Kalamazoo. Call 911.
Battle Creek Health System (269-966-8000), 300 N. Ave., Battle Creek. Call
911.

✷ To See & Do

In Kalamazoo
Bell's Brewery and Eccentric Café (269-382-2332; bellsbeer.com), 355 E.
Kalamazoo Ave. Bell's was one of the first microbreweries in the Midwest and it's
now one of the largest. It was started in 1983 as a home-brewing supply shop,
but expanded into brewing in 1985. Its beers are found in stores in the Midwest
and beyond. There are brewery tours on Saturdays.

In Marshall
Honolulu House Museum (269-781-8544; www.marshallhistoricalsociety.org),
107 N. Kalamazoo Ave., Marshall. Open May–Sept., Thur.–Sun, noon–5. The
home was built in 1860 by Judge Abner Pratt, who was the U.S. Consul to the
Hawaiian Islands. He had it constructed as a copy of the executive mansion he
lived in while in Honolulu. It's a bizarre blend of Italianate, Gothic Revival, and
Polynesian influences. The home was slated to be knocked down and replaced
with a gas station in 1951, but was purchased by Harold C. Brooks. It is now
owned by the Marshall Historical Society, which is continuing renovations to recre-
ate how it looked in the 1880s. Admission is $5 for adults and $4 for children.

G.A.R. Civil War Museum (269-781-8544; www.marshallhistoricalsociety.org),
402 E. Michigan Ave., Marshall. Open June–Aug. on Sat. noon–4. The hall was
built in 1902 as a meeting place for veterans of the Grand Army of the Republic.
The building is now owned by the city and houses artifacts from the Civil War,
Spanish-American War, and World Wars I and II. Admission is $2.

DOWNTOWN KALAMAZOO

✳ Lodging

Most lodging for the area is found in chain hotels/motels along the I-94 corridor.

In Marshall

The National House Inn (269-781-7374), 102 Parkview, Marshall. The inn is the oldest operating hotel in Michigan. It is a designated State Historical Site and is on the National Register of Historical Places. It was built in 1835 and used by stagecoach travelers between Detroit and Chicago, as it was the halfway point at the time. It eventually became a railroad hotel, and then an apartment house. It was reopened as an inn in 1976. There are 15 rooms and suites, all furnished with Victorian furniture, some of which are reproductions. The rooms have private baths and air-conditioning. A full breakfast is served. Barbara Bradley is the innkeeper. Rates are $105–$160.

✳ Where to Eat

DINING OUT

In Marshall

Ⴘ **Schuler's Restaurant and Winston's Pub** (269-781-0600), 115 S. Eagle St., Marshall. The Schuler fa-mily has been in the restaurant business for about 100 years, much of it at this historic building in Marshall. For years German and traditional midwestern fare took top billing on the menu, but it has expanded in recent years to more fish and chicken. You can still get pork, beef, and whitefish, and there's also a pub menu. Entrees are $22–$26.

EATING OUT

In Battle Creek

Ⴘ **Clara's on the River** (269-963-0966; www.claras.com), 44 N. McCamly St., Battle Creek. Open daily for lunch and dinner. Located in an 1888 train depot, the casual dining restaurant features steak, seafood, chicken, and ribs. Some dishes have a Cajun influence. Entrees are $12–$20.

Ⴘ **Arcadia Brewing Company** (269-963-9690; www.arcadiabrewingcompany.com), 103 W. Michigan Ave., Battle Creek. Open Mon.–Sat. for lunch and dinner. Arcadia is a fairly large working microbrewery producing British-style ales that are distributed in the Midwest. The Battle Creek pub is an offshoot of the brewery operation, and it offers burgers, barbecue, and pizzas. Prices are $8–$18.

A HISTORIC HOME IN MARSHALL

FLINT

T his town is hard to love. It has all the problems of Detroit, and none of the attractions. Flint is a kind of no-man's land. It's technically in the Saginaw Valley, but it has little to do with Saginaw, Bay City, and Midland. It is a factory town located on the edge of the Thumb—too far from the Detroit area to be part of the southeastern Michigan mix of older cities and well-to-do suburbs.

The city's claim to fame is that it was the birthplace of General Motors, which was created by the somewhat eccentric William C. Durant, who managed the Buick plant in 1908 and went on to found the auto giant. Durant lost control of GM twice in his life and eventually was ruined by the Stock Market Crash of 1929. He spent the last years of his life running a bowling alley in town. Flint was home to many auto plants, but starting in the late 1970s the city was hit with auto layoffs and hasn't recovered.

Grand Blanc, a Flint suburb, has become the center of some lodging and restaurant activity in recent years. Most of these services in Flint can be found along I-75, which is a major north–south artery in Michigan.

GUIDANCE **Flint Area Convention & Visitors Bureau** (810-231-8900; www .flint.com), 316 Water St., Flint. Open Mon.–Fri. during business hours. A source of information on convention and business meeting planning.

✴ To See and Do

Alfred P. Sloan Museum (810-237-3450; www.flint.org), 1221 E. Kearsley St., Flint. Open daily on weekends 10–5 and weekends noon–5. The museum is for auto buffs, and there are plenty of vintage Buicks and other General Motors autos on display. Flint was the birthplace of General Motors and the United Auto Workers, and exhibits depict the evolution of both. Many neon signs and period commercial goods from roadside attractions are on display.

✴ Lodging

Avon House Bed & Breakfast (810-232-6861), 518 Avon St., Flint. The three-room B&B was built in 1893 and has a Victorian theme throughout, with many antiques in the rooms and the parlor. There is a sitting area with a television and VCR on the second floor. The two bathrooms are shared. The house is near downtown Flint, and there is off-street parking. Rates are $50–$60.

Wingate Inn of Grand Blanc (810-694-9900), 1359 Grand Pointe Court, Grand Blanc. The hotel has 82 rooms, which have phones, data ports, coffee makers, and 25-inch cable TV. There is a 24-hour business center and a spa area and pool.

EATING OUT ϒ **Redwood Lodge** (810-233-8000), 5304 Gateway Center, Flint. Open daily for lunch and dinner. The brewpub has a lodgelike theme and serves grilled beef, pork, and wild game. There is a wood-fired pizza oven, and they have a decent wine list. Prices are $8–$15.

SAGINAW VALLEY AND THE THUMB

BAY CITY, SAGINAW & MIDLAND; FRANKENMUTH

This area of Michigan is heavily agricultural, especially in the Thumb, while the Tri-Cities—Bay City, Saginaw, and Midland—are industrial and port communities, where General Motors and Dow Chemical are the major employers.

Midland has a sprawling Dow Chemical complex, where the giant firm has its headquarters. It's a company town, with Dow's stamp on city and cultural affairs. Saginaw, with a population of about 60,000, is the largest, and with General Motors plant closing, it has been hit hard economically. The urban landscape here has been beset by typical city problems. Bay City is a former lumber town, with many fine old houses, but it's also a General Motors town, and auto layoffs have hurt it too.

The rural farmlands in the Thumb have had their troubles, too, as the farm economy goes up and down, but the predominantly German and Polish American farmers have retained a tenacious grip on family farms. The area is one of the top producers of sugar beets and beans in the nation.

Generally, this isn't a well-traveled region. Much of the Saginaw Bay shoreline is mucky, and it lacks the sandy beaches of northern and western Michigan. There are exceptions around Caseville in the Thumb, where sandy beaches can be found. Also, much of the Saginaw Bay shoreline is in private hands, and there are many family cottages and year-round homes on it.

Frankenmuth in Saginaw County is one of the top tourist destinations in the state, with its signature chicken dinners and one of the largest Christmas ornament stores in the world.

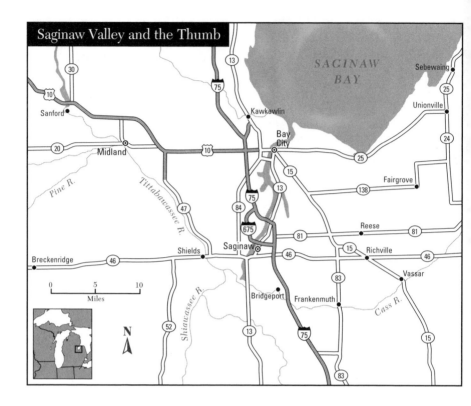

Saginaw Valley and the Thumb

SAGINAW BAY

Sebewaing
Unionville
Sanford
Kawkawlin
Bay City
Midland
Fairgrove
Pine R.
Tittabawassee R.
Reese
Breckenridge
Shields
Saginaw
Richville
Vassar
Miles
Bridgeport
Frankenmuth
Shiawassee R.
Cass R.

N

BAY CITY, SAGINAW & MIDLAND

For some reason, somebody started calling Bay City, Saginaw, and Midland the Tri-Cities area. It must have been a joke: The three towns have very separate identities and assets, and they've never been one unit. All are about 10 miles apart and are in different counties.

Midland is a town more attuned to the arts, Saginaw is a factory town, and Bay City is a bit like Brigadoon, a place that time forgot. It was once a sprawling lumber mill town in the 19th century, and has retained some of that heritage. But it's also a factory town. Much in Bay City has remained unchanged since the end of the lumber era in about 1920.

Bay City's main street, Center Avenue, is lined with the ornate Victorian mansions of lumber barons who once lived there. Because the town languished for many years, older commercial buildings survived intact, and a newer entertainment district now thrives along Midland Street on the city's west side.

Bay City and Saginaw are river towns, and development followed the water, with lumber mills along the banks. Both communities thrived during the 19th century when white pine logs were floated down the Saginaw River.

Bay City's Water Street was once a brawling place filled with vice that attracted lumberjacks in the spring after the logging drives. With money in their pockets, they supported the saloons and houses of prostitution, including one saloon that had a trap door in the floor to help the management get rid of unruly patrons.

But things have settled down, and most residents of this town of about 35,000 work at nearby General Motors or Dow Chemical Company plants. However, with easy access to the Saginaw Bay, Bay City has become a boating center, with marinas providing slips for people from as far away as the Detroit area. Walleye fishing in Saginaw Bay is very good, and attracts anglers from throughout Michigan.

The riverfront is in an age of transformation, with river walks, parks, and marinas being developed, but there are still remnants of its heavy-industry past. Hulking old empty factories, a shipyard, junkyard, and oil tanks still dot the river landscape. Bay City has escaped the urban decay that has hit many Michigan communities, and the neighborhood business district still thrives. Kids still ride their bikes to baseball practice, and older folks feel comfortable walking the streets. It reminds many of mythical Bedford Falls in the movie, *It's a Wonderful Life*.

GUIDANCE **Bay Area Chamber of Commerce** (989-893-4567; baycityarea .com), 901 Saginaw St., Bay City. A source of information about the city and Saginaw Bay area. **Saginaw County Chamber of Commerce** (989-752-7161; saginawchamber.org), 515 N. Washington Ave., Saginaw. A source for information on restaurants and lodging in Saginaw County. **Midland Area Chamber of Commerce** (989-839-9901; www.macc.org), 300 Rodd St., Midland. All are open Mon.–Fri. during business hours.

GETTING THERE *By car:* Bay City, Saginaw, and Midland are an easy two-hour drive from the Metro Detroit area via either I-75 or US 23. Weekend summer traffic can be difficult on Friday nights and Sunday afternoons when Michigan folks are on their way Up North or back home. Traffic on weekdays is fairly thin. *By air:* **MBS International Airport** (989-695-5555; www.mbsairport.org), 8500 Garfield Rd., Freeland. The airport serves the Saginaw Valley and much of central Michigan with flights offered on Northwest and United. There are few direct flights, and most passengers will be routed through Detroit, Cleveland, or Chicago.

MEDICAL EMERGENCY **Bay Regional Medical Center** (989-894-3000), 1900 Columbus Ave., Bay City. **St. Mary's** (989-907-8000), 800 S. Washington Ave., Saginaw. **Mid Michigan Medical Center** (989-839-3000), 4005 Orchard Dr., Midland.

SAGINAW BAY VILLAGES Stretching east from Bay City on MI 25 are the

DOWNTOWN BAY CITY

villages of **Sebewaing, Bay Port, Caseville,** and **Port Austin,** on the tip of the Thumb. While much of the Thumb is devoted to agriculture, these communities are beach towns, each with populations of 2,000 or less. You'll find a few decent restaurants, and there are many cabins and cottages for rent in this area. Caseville is more of a destination than the other communities because of Albert Sleeper State Park, which offers one of the best beaches in the area (see *Outdoor Activities*).

✳ To See & Do

In Bay City

❧ **Bay County Historical Museum** (989-893-5733), 321 Washington Ave., Bay City. The community-based museum offers a few exhibits focusing on the development of the community and Bay City's role as a port.

Bay City State Park (989-684-3020; www.michigandnr.com), 3582 State Park Dr., Bay City. This isn't the best beach on Lake Huron, but it's passable. Much of the water is mucky. There is a mile of sandy shoreline and more than 2,000 acres of wetland woods, meadows, and marshlands, making it a good place for migratory birds. There are 193 campsites.

In Midland

❧ **Dow Gardens** (989-631-2677), 1809 Eastman Ave., corner of Eastman Avenue and West Street Open daily, from 9 to one hour before sunset. The 110-acre garden was established in 1899 by Herbert H. Dow for his family and friends. The plantings include annuals, perennials, trees, and rhododendrons. Admission is $5 for adults and $1 for students.

The Tridge, downtown Midland. The three-way bridge over the Tittibawasee River is worth a stop if you're in Midland. It's just behind the downtown area.

FORMER LUMBER BARON HOMES

The Bay Port Fish Co. (989-656-2121), 1008 First St., Bay Port. There are free, guided tours of this commercial fishing operation, which has been here since the early 1900s. Call first.

✳ Outdoor Activities

FISHING Saginaw Bay is a destination for walleye anglers.

HUNTING Saginaw Bay is a prime area for duck and goose hunting in the fall. The low marshlands attract migrating birds. **Fish Point State Wildlife Area** (989-2511; www.michigan.gov), 7750 Ringle Rd., Unionville, is a prime hunting spot.

Fish Point Lodge (989-647-2631; www.fishpoint-mi.com), 4130 Miller Ave., Unionville. Doug and Christine Deming run this historic lodge on Saginaw Bay, which offers lodging and guided wildfowl hunts. The lodge was founded by Deming's grandfather, a commercial fisherman and duck-hunting guide in the early 1900s.

Sleeper State Park (989-856-4411; www.michigan.gov/dnr), 6573 State Park Rd., Caseville, off MI 25. The 700-acre park has one of the best beaches on Saginaw Bay. It's sandy and has shallow waters for kids. Camping is available, as are boat-launching facilities. There are mountain bike trails, and in the winter, cross-country skiing.

✳ Lodging

The Tri-Cities don't have a lot of lodging or restaurant options. There are some chain hotels/motels along I-75 and US 10, which run through the region.

In Bay City
Bay Valley Hotel & Resort (989-686-3500), 2470 Old Bridge Rd., Bay City. The resort hotel has 145 rooms, a fine-dining room (see *Dining Out*), a pool and spa area, and a golf course. The hotel caters to many corporate meetings and conferences and is the only such place in the general area. We'd be more comfortable attending a conference here than bringing the kids for a weekend. The rooms are comfortable and have in-room coffee, irons and boards, hair dryers, and wireless Internet. Rates are $70–$90.

In Saginaw
Montague Inn (989-752-3939; www.montaqueinn.com), 1581 S. Washington Ave., Saginaw. Sugar beet growing is big in the Saginaw Valley, and the original owner of this Saginaw mansion turned beet residue, of which there is plenty, into hand creams and soaps. The home, which features 17 rooms, was built in the early 1930s and is now owned by innkeeper Chinu Mridha. Room packages run $180–$270.

In Bay City
The Angel's Lair B&B (989-893-6411; www.angelslairbnb.com), 900 5th St., Bay City. The 1880s Victorian home has been restored, including the 10-foot angel on the roof. This five-room B&B is located on one of Bay

KESWICK MANOR IN BAY CITY

City's historic residential streets and is in a quiet neighborhood. Their rooms have air-conditioning, and one has a hot tub. Rates are $95–$185.

Keswick Manor (989-893-2845), 1800 Center Ave., Bay City. Center Avenue is Bay City's main drag, and it's lined with the homes of lumber barons and historic churches. This home was built in 1898 and has four rooms and suites, one with a hot tub. Rates are about $100.

In Bay Port
Sweet Dreams Inn Victorian Bed & Breakfast (989-656-9952), 9695 Cedar St., Bay Port. The 1890s Victorian mansion overlooks Saginaw Bay and has seven rooms and a wraparound screened-in veranda. Rates are $60–$150.

In Port Austin
Krebs Beachside Cottages (989-856-2876: www.krebscottages.com), 3478 Port Austin Rd., Port Austin. Open May–Nov. There are eight updated cottages along a sandy stretch of Saginaw Bay. The cottages sleep up to eight guests and have fully equipped kitchens and cable TV.

There are picnic tables and grills outside. Weekly rates, in season, are $700–$1,400.

The Garfield Inn (989-738-5254), 8544 Lake St., Port Austin. There is a small pub inside the inn, which has six rooms, three with private baths and three with shared baths. Rates are $95–$135.

In Caseville
Crew's Lakeside Resort (989-856-2786; www.crewslakesideresort.com), 4750 Port Austin Rd., Caseville. These seven knotty pine cottages have between 1,400 and 1,600 square feet of space and have two bedrooms and bathrooms. Each has a fully equipped kitchen, cable TV, gas fireplaces, and queen-size beds. Rates are $125–$150.

Lake Vista Motel & Cottages (989-738-8612; www.lakevistaresort.com), 168 W. Spring St., Port Austin. The motel units and a few cabins have access to a Lake Huron beach. The rooms are basic but clean and the grounds well groomed. Room rates are $100–$160, and cottages run about $800 a week.

RENTALS The Cabins of Caseville (989-531-2347; www.snlprop.com), 5949 Port Austin Rd., Caseville.

Dale's Private Cottage Rentals (989-874-5181; www.daleslakefront cottages.atfreeweb.com), 4744 Port Austin Rd., Caseville.

✳ Where to Eat
DINING OUT There are few fine-dining opportunities in the region.

In Bay City
Ⴤ **Heatherfields Restaurant** (989-686-3500), at Bay Valley Hotel &

Resort, 2470 Old Bridge Rd., Bay City (see *Lodging*). Open daily for breakfast, lunch, and dinner. Steaks, chops, veal, and salmon are the mainstays here. The entrees are standard country-club fare, but you're not going to find much else in this area. There is a good wine list. Entrees are $18–$25.

In Port Austin

ϒ The Farm Restaurant and School of Cooking (989-874-5700), 699 Port Crescent Rd., Port Austin. Open May–Oct., 5–10. The Farm serves up many midwestern foods, cooking from scratch and using herbs and produce from its 5-acre garden. A farmer's style Swiss steak, pan-seared salmon, pork chops, and whitefish are on the menu. For dessert there is a bread and butter pudding. Entrees are $20–$25.

EATING OUT

In Saginaw

ϒ Jake's Old City Grill (989-797-

8325; www.jakesforsteaks.com), 100 S. Hamilton St., Saginaw. Open Mon.–Sat. for lunch and dinner. Located in Saginaw's historic Old Saginaw area of downtown, the grill serves steak, chops, seafood, chicken, pasta, and vegetarian entrees. Prices are $10–$20.

In Bay City

Krzysiak's House Restaurant (989-894-5531), 1605 Michigan Ave., Bay City. Open daily for breakfast, lunch, and dinner. This place is a local favorite that features authentic Polish food. The portions are large. The Big Don is a breakfast served on a pizza pan, and it includes bacon, eggs, pork chops, and steak. It's a novelty meal, and no one person could be expected to eat it. Prices are $8–$12.

Atrium (989-891-1600), 1100 Water St., Bay City. The menu has a European flavor, with many German dishes, including schnitzels, sausages, sauerbraten, and hot German potato salad. There are also many European beers on hand. Prices are $10–$20.

FRANKENMUTH

Frankenmuth could only happen in America. A German American family sets up shop in an old hotel in an off-the-beaten-track town, and instead of serving German food, it picks an American classic, fried chicken, to make its centerpiece meal. The result is one of Michigan's biggest tourist attractions.

Generations of Michigan families make an annual pilgrimage to Frankenmuth for the fried-chicken dinners and a walk around town to see the various shops and attractions. On Mother's Day, it's packed to the rafters. The central attractions are two restaurants, both owned by the Zehnder family: Zehnder's, housed in a colonial building, and the Bavarian Inn, which is across the street in a Bavarian-style building. Both serve pretty much the same food, but Michigan devotees of Frankenmuth have their favorites and will tell you at great length which is better and why.

Another mainstay in town is Bronner's, where it's Christmas every day. The Midwest is awash in billboards for this place, and it is indeed a destination for folks who make Christmas a year-round holiday. It was founded in 1945 by Wally

Bronner, who opened a small Christmas trimming business, and has grown over the years to the point that it's now on a 45-acre plot on the southern edge of town.

It's hard to believe, but the store is open 361 days a year, and it sells only Christmas decorations ranging from nativity scenes to stockings, trees, and just about anything in between. Stop by in July, and you'll find a good number of customers.

For some, Frankenmuth, with its "Little Bavaria" and total tourist town looks, is a bit too much. However, one event, "The Bavarian Festival" in early June, actually attracts area residents of German ancestry and doesn't just appeal to tourist buses filled with senior citizens. There is a beer tent and polka bands.

Most of the action is on Main Street, where the two restaurants are located. Dozens of shops line the street, offering gifts that range from plates reading "God Bless our Trailer" to quilts and sausages and cheese. The shops are comfort food for shoppers, and reflect midwestern values of home and hearth. You won't find many unique items, but browsing through the shops is a good way to work off your fried-chicken lunch or dinner.

Although the shopping may not seem exciting, it is a family-friendly town where you can let the kids roam and not have to worry about what they're exposed to. The Zehnder family has exercised a great deal of control over what goes in along Main Street, so there aren't any vulgar T-shirt shops or tacky attractions that suck money out of parents' wallets. The town is also free of carnival rides and theme parks.

While many of the tourist attractions are man-made, Frankenmuth does have a real German heritage, dating back to the 1840s when immigrants found the Saginaw Valley farmland a fertile place for family farms. They brought with them the sugar beet, which is refined into sugar. The harvest takes place in November, and the area's rural roads are filled with semi-trucks loaded with beets for what the locals call the "sugar beet campaign," as though it was a part of World War II.

MAIN STREET

www.frankenmuth.org), 635 S. Main St., Frankenmuth. Open Mon.–Fri., business hours.

* To See & Do

Bavarian Inn Glockenspiel Tower, outside the Bavarian Inn. The Zehnder family has pretty much built the tourist town of Frankenmuth and has given the community this delightful moving clock. At 11, noon, 3, 5, 9, and 10 PM, figurines reenact the legend of the Pied Piper of Hameln. For road-weary parents of small children, this is a good place to park them for some entertainment.

Holz-Brucke Covered Bridge, located behind the Bavarian Inn. This 239-foot-long wood bridge crosses the Cass River in Frankenmuth and is based on an authentic 1820 design. It weighs 230 tons. It was opened in 1980 and carries vehicle traffic. It's thought to be the only wood-covered bridge built in the 20th century. Crafted from Douglas fir, it was put into place by a team of oxen. The project was undertaken by the Zehnder family, which owns the restaurants.

Bavarian Belle (1-866-808-2628; www.bavarianbelle.com), River Place, Frankenmuth. The stern-paddlewheel vessel offers tours of the Cass River, which runs through town. Open Memorial Day–Labor Day, Mon.–Sun. The cost is $8 for adults and $4 for children 12 and under.

Thunder Bay Mining Company (1-866-808-2628; www.bavarianbelle.com), River Place, Frankenmuth. For under $20 a family can spend time looking through and picking gems out of a bucket and learning how to identify them.

Grandpa Tiny's Farm (989-652-5437; www.grandpatinysfarm.com), 7775 Weiss St., Frankenmuth. Open daily, April–Oct. A historically correct re-creation of a family farm circa 1900, the homestead gives kids and adults an idea of how farm families lived. The barn is filled with cattle, sheep, and chickens, all domestic animals that helped feed families. The surrounding fields are tilled using horse-drawn equipment. Admission is $5, and children under 2 are free; $20 maximum for a family.

Tompkins' Orchard and Country Store (989-823-2891; www.tompkins orchard.com), 5966 W. Sanilac Rd., MI 46 at Vassar Rd. Open daily, June–Nov. The Thumb farming community of Vassar is just down the road from Frankenmuth, and the orchard offers families a chance to pick apples, cherries, plums, peaches, pears, and apricots in season. The country store offers farm produce and there's a bakery. This is a great place to take kids during the fall harvest.

WEDDINGS **The Frankenmuth Wedding Chapel** (989-652-7311; www .frankenmuthweddingchapel.com), 130 W. Tuscola, Frankenmuth. Various packages for those who want to tie the knot with a Bavarian flavor.

GOLFING **The Fortress Golf Course** (1-800-863-7999; www.zehnders .com/new-site/golf-course), 950 Flint St., Frankenmuth. An 18-hole, par-72 course.

SOUTH CENTRAL

✳ Lodging

Note: Most of Frankenmuth's hotels and motels cater specifically to families and large groups of tourists, especially senior citizens. (See Bay City and Saginaw for other options.)

Frankenmuth Bavarian Inn Lodge (989-652-7200), One Covered Bridge Lane, Frankenmuth. The 360-room inn is close to downtown and has large rooms and suites, many with hot tubs, and a family center with an indoor water park that has five pools. It's a popular retreat for families during winter. Rates are $100–$200.

✳ Where to Eat

DINING OUT Zehnder's of Frankenmuth (1-800-863-7999; www.zehnders.com), 730 S. Main St. Open daily, 11–9:30. This is an amazing operation. The Zehnder family has been serving up fried chicken on an almost industrial basis since the 1940s, and it is still excellent. A bakery is on the premises and the bread is always fresh. Try the fruit bread. One wonders how they can keep the quality up with thousands of dinners served on a Sunday. Zehnder's alone

ZEHNDER'S RESTAURANT

serves 840,000 pounds of chicken a year, 628,000 pounds of cabbage, 111,000 pounds of vegetables, and 26,000 pounds of coffee. In 1986, it served 5,916 people in one day. Extra chicken is available on request, but they don't let you take it out. One tip, avoid Frankenmuth on Mother's Day; it's terribly crowded. German food is also on the menu. Entrees are $12–$22.

Frankenmuth Bavarian Inn (989-652-9941 or 1-800-228-2742; www .bavarianinn.com), 713 S. Main St., Frankenmuth. Open daily, 11–9:30. The Zehnder family, which runs Zehnder's across the street, also owns the Bavarian Inn, and the only real difference between the two places is the décor. The Bavarian Inn was once Fischer's Hotel, but was rebuilt in a Bavarian style. Zehnder's retains its Mt. Vernon–like colonial feel. The dinners are served family style, and never vary in quality. The menu is pretty much the same at both restaurants: all-you-can-eat chicken, homemade breads and preserves, chicken noodle soup, salads, dressing, giblet gravy, mashed potatoes, buttered noodles, hot vegetables, and ice cream. You can also get steak, seafood, and German food. Entrees are $12–$22.

Freeway Fritz (989-777-8730; www .bavarianinn.com), 6560 Dixie Hwy., Bridgeport. Located off I-75 just south of Saginaw, the restaurant is owned by the Bavarian Inn of Frankenmuth. It offers fried chicken carryouts and has a small eating area. The chicken here is just as good as in Frankenmuth. It has become a popular alternative to fast-food restaurants for Michigan cottage owners who stop by on their way Up North to stock up on food for a weekend. There are good side dishes of cole law and other comfort foods. Prices are $10–$15.

Selective Shopping

Bronner's Christmas Wonderland 989-652-9931; www.bronners.com), 25 Christmas Lane, Frankenmuth. Open daily, except Christmas. Walley Bronner opened a Christmas store in his family store in 1945, and it has since morphed into a 96,000-square-foot complex on 45 acres that attracts more than 2 million visitors. Travelers in the Midwest frequently see billboards for the place, which is open 361 days a year. But until you walk in the front door, it's simply hard to believe that a single store can make it on Christmas decoration sales, especially one this size. But even in July you'll find patrons looking at the 6,000 different kinds of ornaments and 500 styles of nativity sets. Here are a few numbers about the place: 100,000 individual lights in the salesroom, 1.3 million glass ornaments, and 135,000 light sets sold annually, and 700,000 feet of garland.

Willi's Sausage Company (989-652-9041; www.willissausages.com) 316 S. Main, Frankenmuth. Located outside of the big tourist walking area, the shop offers 100 different sausages, many of them German style and locally made. Bratwurst is a Michigan favorite, as popular as hot dogs are in other parts of the country. This is a great place to stock up on them, especially if you're headed to a northern Michigan cottage for a week.

Frankenmuth Cheese Haus (989-652-6727; www.frankenmuthcheese haus.com), 561 S. Main, Frankenmuth. Open daily. German immigrants in Michigan had a way with cheese spreads, and this shop makes its own, everything from chocolate to jalapeno flavored. My favorite is horseradish, which seems more classically German than the others. Frankenmuth cheese, a local product, is a yellow, almost cheddarlike cheese that's worth a taste.

✿ Zehnder's Splash Village (1-800-863-7999; www.zehnders.com/new -site/hotel), 1365 S. Main, Frankenmuth. Unless you have kids, this hotel/water park isn't for you, but if you do have young ones it's a great place to let them run around. The hotel has 152 rooms and 63 suites, all modern, fully equipped rooms with cable TV. But the real feature is the 30,000-square-foot water park with rides and attractions for kids. For adults, there are whirlpool hot tubs. There is a shuttle bus to Zehnder's restaurant. Rates are $129–$314.

Special Events

Mid-May World Expo of Beer (1-800-386-3378; www.frankenmuth festivals.com). Beer tasting and more polka music.

Early June Bavarian Festival (1-800-386-3378; www.frankenmuth festivals.com), held in early June. The event features plenty of beer and German music and attracts many area residents with German backgrounds.

Late September Oktoberfest (1-800-386-3378; www.frankenmuth festivals.com), held in late September. Plenty of beer, polka music, and Canadians, who show up by the busload for the event.

LAKE VIEW

Straits of Mackinac

MACKINAW CITY

MACKINAC ISLAND

ST. IGNACE

STRAITS OF MACKINAC

Mackinac Island is the state's top tourist attraction. It lured the first Victorian travelers here with its views of Lakes Huron and Michigan and cool summer breezes as early as the 1830s, when it was still a rough, frontier fur-trading outpost. Tourist hotels started to develop in the 1850s, but it wasn't until the opening of the Grand Hotel in 1887 that the island became a top attraction.

Mackinaw City and St. Ignace are the jumping-off points for people heading to the island, and they're filled with restaurants and hotels/motels. Both have boat docks for the watercraft that take people to the island.

The island attractions are its historic buildings, a fort built by the British, its views of the Mackinac Bridge, and the lack of auto traffic. It's ironic that the top tourist attraction in a state where autos were developed is one without vehicles. They were banned at the turn of the 20th century as job insurance for the carriage drivers who had long taken visitors around the island. Transportation on the island is by foot, horse, carriage, or bicycle.

The Grand Hotel, with its 660-foot porch overlooking the lakes, defines the island. It was built by railroad and steamship barons to entice people to travel here. There was no air-conditioning at the time, and the porch offered cool breezes during summer. Fudge also became a popular dessert during that era, and the island became so well known for the treat that tourists here are still known as "fudgies."

The hotel has been used for movie sets since the 1940s, but perhaps the best-known one was *Somewhere in Time*, which starred Christopher Reeve and Jane Seymour. It was a romance set in the early 1900s that has Reeve traveling back in time, where he meets and falls in love with Seymour. The 1980 movie wasn't a huge success, but it has become a cottage industry on the island, where it's shown nightly in some hotels, and there's even a gift shop that specializes in movie memorabilia.

The gazebo used in the filming of the movie has become a popular place for weddings, and since the death of Reeve, a plaque honoring him has been placed on it. Because of its romantic Victorian ambiance, the island has become a popular place for weddings. There are various venues for them (see *Weddings*, Mackinaw City), and many of the hotels cater to couples getting married.

However, before Victorians strolled the lakefront, the Straits had a less gentle

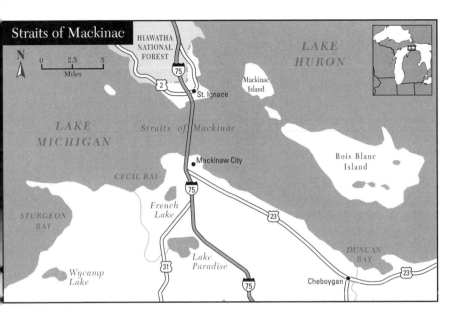

Straits of Mackinac

start. For centuries it was a gathering place for French-Canadian fur traders and Native Americans and was fought over by the French and British, and later Americans, because it controlled the entrance to Lake Michigan and the lucrative fur trade.

The French controlled much of the Great Lakes until 1763, when they were defeated by the British and made their exit from North American. During the Revolutionary War, the British found it difficult to defend the mainland at Fort Michilimackinac at Mackinaw City, so they moved to Mackinac Island in 1783 and constructed a stone fort from which their cannons controlled boat travel in the Straits. The island was turned over to the U.S. in 1796, but was recaptured for a brief time during the War of 1812. It wasn't until 1815 that the Americans were firmly established on the island.

As they say these days, the fur trade was the economic engine of its time in the Great Lakes, and Europeans and Native Americans depended on it. Each summer, Indians and French-Canadian trappers brought the furs to the island for a rendezvous, which was a sort of open air market where they traded furs for rum, brandy, muskets, blankets and pots, and other needed goods.

John Jacob Astor, the first American millionaire, established the American Fur Company on Mackinac Island in the early 19th century, giving him control of much of the Great Lakes fur trade. Astor eventually went into real-estate development in New York City, making him the Donald Trump of his era.

Fort Mackinac was kept in operation at first because of fears that the British, and later the Canadians, would invade, but those fears vanished. The fort had so little strategic importance that during the Civil War only one soldier was left to man it. In 1875, the island became a national park, and the fort was eventually decommissioned in the 1890s.

Because it was part of a national park, and later Mackinac State Park, the fort never was abandoned, and its buildings have been the subjects of extensive preservation work, along with others in the village of Mackinac Island.

The tourist season runs from May through October, and most island businesses are closed in the winter; however, about 300 residents stay during winter, and there is some tourism. A few bars and one lodge stay open, catering to the locals and the few visitors.

Snowmobiles are used to access the island when the ice between the mainland and the island is thick enough to support them. During colder winters the snowmobile trail is marked with Christmas trees.

The island is a mix of public and private lands. Much of the island is composed of Mackinac State Park. There are many private homes with views of the Straits. The state of Michigan maintains a mansion for use by the governor.

MACKINAW CITY

W hen you first arrive here, it looks like a collection of motels and restaurants, but there's more to see and do here than first meets the eye. Get out of the car and take a stroll or bike ride along the shoreline and you'll find a lighthouse, a great view of the Mackinac Bridge, and a historic, restored fort.

GUIDANCE **Mackinaw City Chamber of Commerce** (231-436-5574; www .mackinawchamber.com), 216 E. Central Ave. and Mackinaw Crossings Mall, Mackinaw City, MI 49701. The chamber maintains two offices, with the one in Mackinaw Crossings Mall open May–Oct. Open daily, 9–5.

GETTING THERE *By car:* I-75 is the most direct route. It's about 4½ hours from Detroit, and about 6 hours from Chicago. If you're looking for scenic, but much longer routes, try US 23 along Lake Huron or US 31 along Lake Michigan. From the Upper Peninsula, access is via I-75, which goes across the Mackinac Bridge. Mackinaw City is small enough that you can walk most everywhere. There is little traffic, and a bicycle could be handy.
By air: **Pellston Regional Airport** (231-539-8423; www.pellstonairport.com), on US 31, just north of Pellston. Northwest Airlines runs linking flights from Detroit Metro to this small airport. Rental cars are available. There is also a similar small airport near Sault Ste. Marie (see Sault Ste. Marie).

PUBLIC REST ROOMS They are everywhere. Most people here are tourists; the most restaurants and other buildings have public rest rooms. The visitor center under the bridge is a good stop.

WHEN TO COME Mackinaw City revolves around trips to Mackinac Island, mid-May–mid-Oct. Apart from a few exceptions; the town is virtually deserted in the winter months.

MEDICAL EMERGENCY **Mackinac Straits Hospital** (906-643-8585), 220 Burdette St., St. Ignace. Call 911.

✳ To See & Do

Mackinaw City is a May–Oct. town. Most attractions are open those months unless otherwise noted.

Old Mackinac Point Lighthouse (www.mackinacparks.com), next to the Mackinac Bridge. The castlelike lighthouse was built in 1892 and was in operation until 1957, when the Mackinaw Bridge opened and its lights took the place of the lighthouse. The building has been restored to its 1910 appearance. A fog-signal building constructed in 1907 is part of the complex. Inside, interpreters conduct tours. Admission is $22 for adults, $13.25 for youths 6–17, and free for children under 5.

Historic Mill Creek (www.mackinacparks.com). Open daily, 9–4. Mill Creek is a restored mill that provided timber for constructing buildings on Mackinac Island in the 1790s. A small stream provided power for the mill, and there are demonstrations. The mill is in a 625-acre state park that includes a 3.5-mile nature trail. Admission is $7.50 for adults, $4.50 for youths 6–17, and free for children under 6.

⊙ **Icebreaker** *Mackinaw* (231-436-9825; www.icebreakermackinawmuseum .org), 131 S. Huron Ave., Mackinaw City. For more than 60 years the U.S. Coast Guard Cutter *Mackinaw* was a common sight on the Great Lakes, clearing shipping channels during colder months and doing general work during other times. It has been replaced with a new vessel and is now in a museum where visitors can see how the officers and crew lived and worked on the craft. It was launched in 1944 and was decommissioned in 2006. Getting around the ship requires safe shoes. Admission is $10 for adults and $5 for children 6–17; a family pass is $25.

MACKINAW CITY LIGHTHOUSE

HISTORIC WALK Nearly 40 markers guide a walker through the history of Mackinaw during a short stroll through the downtown area. I did it on a bicycle, and it worked out well. The markers and kiosks tell visitors about the early pioneers of the village, shipwrecks in the Straits, and railroad and boat transportation. Car-carrying ferryboats once crossed the Straits between Mackinaw City and St. Ignace. Also, motorists made the run from Chicago and Detroit in 1913 and were the first tourists to reach the town.

THE BRIDGE The Mackinaw Bridge celebrated its 50th anniversary in 2007. A small visitor center run by the state is located right under the bridge. There is a park nearby where you can sit on a bench and look at the structure, which was opened in 1957.

WEDDINGS The Mackinaw area is a popular place for weddings, especially Mackinac Island. It's a very wedding friendly place. One of the most popular spots is the Somewhere in Time Gazebo on Mackinac Island. The movie was filmed on the island in 1979, and the gazebo was built for use in the movie. But there are other public venues available for weddings.

∞ **Somewhere in Time Gazebo** (906-847-3328; www.mackinacparks.com), on Mackinac Island.

∞ **Mission Church** (517-373-4289; www.mackinacparks.com), Mackinac Island. The church is the oldest surviving church building in Michigan and was constructed in 1829 by island residents. It is an example of New England Colonial church style.

∞ **Church of St. Anne's at Fort Michilimackinac** (517-373-4289; www.mackinacparks.com), Mackinaw City. The church is a reconstruction of a Roman Catholic church built in 1743 and used by French-Canadians.

∞ **Historic Mill Creek** (517-373-4289; www.mackinacparks.com), Mill Creek State Park, Mackinaw City. The restored lumber mill is the setting.

∞ **Fort Mackinac** (517-373-4289; www.mackinacparks.com), Mackinac Island. The venue is the 1780 Revolutionary War–era fort that overlooks the village of Mackinac Island and its harbor.

∞ **Old Mackinac Point Lighthouse** (517-373-4289; www.mackinacparks.com), Mackinaw City. The lighthouse was constructed in 1892 and is restored to its 1910 appearance.

✳ Outdoor Activities

Bicycling is a prime activity in the area, and there are plenty of opportunities. Downtown Mackinaw City is best seen on a bicycle, and traffic isn't an issue if you stay off US 23 and US 31. One good ride is a 22-mile round trip from Mackinaw City to Wilderness State Park, west on County Road 81 (CR 81), which can be accessed just west of the bridge. The route follows the Lake Michigan shoreline, and there are several beaches along the way. Once in the park, get a map. There are various trails to follow with many along the lakeshore.

FERRY BOAT

CANOEING & KAYAKING The best place for these activities is at Wilderness State Park (see *Green Space*), but you can basically put in just about anywhere you have public access to the shoreline. This isn't a place for novice paddlers, though. The winds can kick up quickly in the Straits, and high winds are often present, even during summer months.

GREEN SPACE Wilderness State Park (231-436-5381; www.michigan.gov/dnr), 903 Wilderness Park Dr., Carp Lake. The 10,512-acre park offers 26 miles of Lake Michigan beaches, hiking, and camping. There are 250 modern campsites in two units, six rustic cabins, and three rustic bunkhouses for rent. For mountain bikers, there are 16 miles of trails. In the winter, many of the trails are cross-country ski routes. A boat launch and Lake Michigan access site are available. Many of the rustic cabins are located on Lake Michigan, where you have your own beach. The cabins fill up quickly, and reservations are recommended. The state Department of Natural Resources, which runs the state park system, maintains a good Web site for reservations (www.midnrreservations.com).

✳ Lodging

BED & BREAKFASTS Brigadoon of Mackinac City (231-436-8882; www .mackinawbrigadoon.com), 207 Langlade St., Mackinaw City. Open April–Oct. Innkeeper Sherree Hyde has a little gem of a place tucked away on a side street. The eight suites are decorated Victorian style, are spacious, and offer a needed relief to staying in the basic motel rooms that are pretty much standard in Mackinaw City. Some rooms have separate sitting areas and bedrooms, and one suite has a hot tub. Many rooms have a view of Lake Huron. They don't say children aren't allowed, but they do bill themselves as being adult-preferred accommodations. It's a short walk to the boat docks. Rates are $165–$255.

⊙ **Deer Head Inn** (231-436-3337; www.deerhead.com), 109 Henry St., Mackinaw City. Open year-round. Innkeepers Barry and Nancy Dean have turned this home into a delightful, although small, B&B. The five rooms have an outdoorsy feel, and one is actually named the Hemingway Room. Another is decorated with a bear skin. Each room has a private bath, fireplace, television, and wireless Internet. The inside of the Arts & Crafts house has a contemporary feel and would appeal to folks who don't like the antique fussiness of Victorian-style places. The home is one of the oldest in Mackinaw City, built in 1913 by Samuel Smith, who was a banker, lumberman, and hotel owner. A third generation has operated the home as a B&B since 1998. A full breakfast is served in the Orchard Dining Room, where some of the home's original Arts & Crafts furniture is still being used. Wedding friendly. Rates are $100–$225.

MOTELS Huron Avenue is home to many motels, some owned by chains, others by individuals. Most are, clean, basic rooms, and many are within walking distance of downtown shopping and the boat docks where the ferries depart for Mackinac Island.

Bridgeview Super 8 Motel (231-436-5252; www.mackinaw-city.com), 601 N. Huron. This isn't your typical Super 8. The large, log-style hotel has clean rooms, many with balconies that offer a view of the Mackinaw Bridge and Mackinac Lighthouse. It's within walking distance of downtown restaurants and shopping and the ferry docks. There is an indoor pool and spa area. Rates are $108–$238.

Best Western Dockside (231-436-5001; www.mackinaw-city.com), 505 S. Huron, Mackinaw City. While this is a chain, they have adopted a North Woods feel with the use of wood paneling in the public rooms. The rooms are large, clean, and well furnished, but nothing special. Part of the attraction is the 1,200 feet of Lake Huron beach access from the hotel. There is an indoor pool and whirlpool. For those with large families, there are 1,000-square-foot suites. Many of the rooms have balconies that overlook Lake Huron. Shopping, restaurants, and the Mackinac Island boat docks are all within walking distance. Rates are $159–$369.

⚓ **Econo Lodge Bayview** (231-436-5777), 712 S. Huron, Mackinaw City. The rooms have TV, HBO, and a pool and spa area. There is a laser show at night for kids and a 1,400-foot beach for them to run on. There is also an exercise room. The Mackinac Island boat docks and downtown shopping and restaurants are all within walking distance. Rates are $45–$208.

Super 8 Motel Beachfront (231-436-711; www.mackinaw-city.com), 519 S. Huron Ave., Mackinaw City. The location is very good, within walking distance of the Mackinac Island boat docks and downtown shopping and restaurants. There is a

1,400-foot beach, an indoor pool and spa area, and lakefront rooms with balconies. Rates are $48–$278.

✸ Where to Eat

DINING OUT Mackinaw City restaurants are generally open daily May–October, unless otherwise noted.

♈ **Audie's Restaurant** (231-436-5744; www.audies.com), 314 Nicolet St., Mackinaw City. Open daily, year-round. This became a favorite when a companion and I stopped here late one January evening after deciding not to try crossing the Mackinaw Bridge at night. We walked in not long before 10 PM, when the kitchen was scheduled to close, and they kept it open for us. The place is one of the few open year-round in the Mackinaw area, and it's popular with local residents. And they have good taste in food. We had smoked trout as an appetizer and whitefish for dinner. The fish was perfectly cooked, and it was impressive. As the only game in town, they knew they had a couple of hungry guys and could have tossed anything out there and we would have eaten it. But they took the time to do everything right. There are actually two restaurants here, a family room with moderately priced meals and the Chippewa Room, which features more upscale meals and a bar. They also serve breakfast and lunch. In the Chippewa Room, you'll find meals

FORT MICHILIMACKINAC

Fort Michilimackinac (www.mackinacparks.com) presided over the first economic boom in the history of the Great Lakes—the fur trade. In the 1700s, beaver hats were the fashion statement of the day, and traders and trappers met annually at the Straits to trade fur.

The trappers included Native Americans and French-Canadians. The French built Fort St. Phillippe de Michilmackinac in 1715 as part of their empire in North America, and they controlled the lucrative fur trade. But by 1763 the British had pushed the French out of North America and claimed the fort for England. During the Revolutionary War, the British found the fort vulnerable to attack by Americans and moved their troops to a new fort on Mackinac Island. The British occupied the island fort until 1796, when it was turned over to the U.S. The British recaptured it during the War of 1812, but held it only briefly.

The structure that now stands is a re-creation of how the fort and village looked during the British occupation of the 1770s. There are 13 buildings and reenactors perform scenes from the past during daily demonstrations from mid-May through October, playing the parts of British soldiers, traders, and women who tended to the domestic tasks of the day. There are various events during the summer months.

The fort entrance is at the visitor center under the Mackinaw Bridge. Admission is $10 for adults, $6 for youths 6–16, and free for children under 6.

unusual for the area, including herb-encrusted lamb, duck, and stuffed morel mushrooms. Entrees are $18–$35.

EATING OUT Admiral's Table (231-436-5687), 502 S. Huron Ave., Mackinaw City, MI 49701. This is the type of place to take a family after spending the day walking around Mackinac Island or before the ferry sails. Beef, chicken, and whitefish form the backbone of the menu, and it's simple and hearty food. Entrees are $15–$17.

Ŷ **Dixie Saloon** (231-436-5449; www.dixiesaloon.com), 401 E. Central Ave., Mackinaw City. This has been a traditional stopping spot because it was at the end of the Old Dixie Highway, a federal road that ran from Florida and ended in Mackinaw City. The saloon has its origins in the 1890s, and although the building it now occupies is much newer, it does retain its heritage with old photos on the walls. It's a fun place built with logs, giving it an Up North feeling. It's across the street from the ferryboat docks that service Mackinac Island. The ribs are a top attraction. Entrees are $15–$22.

Anna's Country Buffet (231-436-5195), 416 S. Huron Ave., Mackinaw City. The all-you-can-eat buffet is a deal for a hungry family. Whitefish and roast beef are there for the adults, along with a bar. Entrees are $10–$15.

Ŷ **Historic Depot Restaurant** (231-436-7060), 248 S. Huron Ave., Mackinaw City. It's really not that historic; it's actually in Mackinaw Crossings, a mall area, but it blends in very well with the city's main street. It's another place to take the family after you've gotten off the boat after a day on

Mackinac Island. The food is pretty standard: steaks, ribs, seafood, and pub food for lunch. Entrees are $10–$15.

Ŷ **Nona Lisa's Italian Ristorante** (231-436-7901; www.nonnalisa.com), 312 S. Huron Ave., Mackinaw City. This casual Italian dining spot with a bar is a good addition to the restaurant mix in the village. The pizzas are baked in a brick oven and are much better than the normal side-of-the-road pizza parlor around here. Various types of pasta are on the menu, and you can create your own. There are stuffed portabella mushrooms and calamari, both dishes you don't often find around here. Prices are $10–$15.

MARKETS Bell's Fishery (231-436-7821), 229 S. Huron Ave. This isn't just a retail operation, it's an actual fishing operation operated by the Little Traverse Bay Bands of Odawa Indians, which have a fishing treaty with the federal government. It's a good place to stop for maple-smoked fish, a favorite in the Great Lakes. Fresh fish is also sold.

Mackinaw IGA (231-436-5502), 101 E. Central Ave. This is the place to go if you're cooking for yourself. It's a small market, but it has a nice selection of deli meats.

✳ Selective Shopping
Most shops are open from May–October unless otherwise noted.

Devon's Delight (231-436-7885; www.devonsdelight.com), 128 S. Huron Ave., Mackinaw City. Located in the Mackinac Bay Trading Company building. Fudge has been consumed by tourists on Mackinac Island since the 1880s, so much so that visitors are often referred to as "fudgies," and it seems like you can't walk a block without passing a fudge shop. But this place is worth seeking out. They have classic Mackinac Island fudge in various flavors, but they also make caramel corn, homemade jams, and handmade chocolates. Part of the fun is in watching the candy makers work with the copper kettles to concoct the sweets.

Woodland Creek Furniture (231-436-8522; www.woodlandcreek furniture.com), 128 S. Huron Ave., located in the Mackinac Bay Trading Company. Open daily and year-round, 10–6. We've all seen rustic furniture sitting in shops by the side of the road, and well, it certainly looks rustic. Woodland Creek has taken the rustic look and given it a contemporary appearance. Much of the furniture seems inspired by Adirondack furniture, and my favorite was a console table trimmed with birch bark. The cost was amazingly low at $495. There are also pieces decorated with hammered copper. A large number of the pieces are one of a kind, and Michigan craftsmen make many of them. The store also has locations in Traverse City and Kalkaska.

Views of the Past (231-436-7793; www.viewsofthepast.com), 148 S. Huron Ave. This is one of two such historical photographic galleries owned by Jack Deo; the other is in Marquette. Deo acquired the historical collection of Childs Art Gallery, which was founded in the 1860s by Brainard F. Childs and included many 19th-century scenes from across northern Michigan. Deo also purchased the archives of other northern Michigan photographers. You could look through the photos for hours.

There are hardened-looking loggers and miners, proud business owners, Model T dealers, kids fishing, and people generally enjoying life during the Victorian era. The prints are for sale and are relatively inexpensive. There are about 100,000 images and looking at them reveals much about the lives of everyday people.

Mackinac Bay Build Your Bear (231-436-5940), 312 S. Huron Ave. Located in the Mackinac Bay Trading Company. This place has been around for several years now and has become fairly popular in Michigan. It's an opportunity for people to design and dress their own teddy bears. They get their own names and birth certificates.

Alice's Kandy & Korn (231-436-5183; www.aliceskandyandkorn.com), 512 S. Huron Ave. Open daily and year-round, 9–5. This little shop goes beyond the normal fudge sold in the area, and there are other sweets made by hand, including hand-dipped chocolates.

Coffman Hardware (231-436-5650; www.coffmancaseknives.com), 227 Central Ave. Open year-round, daily. This old-time hardware store dates from the 1880s and sells regular hardware to the locals. It's worth a stop just for the atmosphere. These days, there are plenty of camping items and fishing and hunting gear. They are the largest dealers of W. R. Case knives in the state.

Jim Wehr's Mackinaw Outfitters (231-436-4066; www.mackinawout fittersstore.com), at Mackinaw Crossings Mall. Open year-round. There are 30,000 square feet of outdoor gear, including fishing and hunting equipment, clothing, and camping items. Inside is a 10,000-gallon aquarium containing various species of Great Lakes fish.

BOOKSTORES **The Island Bookstore** (231-436-2665; www.island bookstore.com), 215 E. Central Ave., Mackinaw City. Local history, legend, and Great Lakes books are top sellers here. There is also a good selection of children's books about the Great Lakes and Native American lore. It's a small place, but they have a good selection of the best sellers and beach books. There is a small coffee shop, so you can have a seat while you flip through a book. Internet access is available.

True North Books & Gifts (231-436-4000), 226 S. Huron Ave., Mackinaw City. The Hollywood movie *Somewhere in Time*, which was filmed on Mackinac Island in 1979, has become somewhat of a cottage industry in the Straits area. This bookstore and gift shop specializes in memorabilia and gifts based on the movie. There is a great kid's section with a focus on Michigan, and there are plenty of coffee-table books on lighthouses and other Great Lakes subjects. Local history books are also big sellers, along with regional authors.

MACKINAC ISLAND

T he island in the Straits of Mackinac is the state's top tourist destination and has good views of the lakes and the Mackinac Bridge (see Straits of Mackinac).

GUIDANCE **Mackinac Island Tourism Bureau** (1-800-454-5227; www .mackinacisland.org), P.O. Box 451, Mackinac Island, MI 49757. Look for the bureau's kiosk on Main Street when you get off the boat.

GETTING THERE *By boat:* Over the years, I've taken several of the ferry lines to Mackinac Island, and there really isn't much difference between them. Three ferries currently operate from Mackinaw City and St. Ignace, and the prices are about the same. The ferries run from 7:30 AM to 10 PM and take about 20 minutes. **Arnold Transit Co.** (231-436-5542 or 1-800-542-8528; www.arnoldline .com), 801 S. Huron Ave. **Shepler's Mackinac Island Ferry** (231-436-5023 or 1-800-828-6157; www.sheplersferry.com), 556 E. Central Ave. **Star Line Mackinac Island Ferry** (231-436-5045; www.mackinacferry.com), 711 S. Huron Ave.
By air: **Mackinac Island Airport** (906-847-3231), Airport Rd., Mackinac Island. If you have a small plane, you can fly here, but there are no commercial flights.

GETTING AROUND There are no autos on the island, so you'll have to get around by foot, bicycle, or horse-drawn carriage. If you're staying at the Grand Hotel, or a few other upscale inns, the hotel sends a carriage to pick you up from the boat. Also, even the smaller, less-expensive hotels will send a carriage to pick up your luggage.
By bicycle: Many folks bring their own bicycles over to the island on the ferries. Unless you are very attached to your own, however, it's not worth it. There are plenty of bikes of all sorts to rent on Main Street for about $4 an hour, and sometimes less for an entire day.
Walking: Most sites on Main Street and in the surrounding village area can be reached on foot, including the fort. Make sure to wear good walking shoes.
Horse carriages: Tours of the island are offered, and there is horse-drawn taxi

service. The taxi service is located on Main Street and cabs are radio dispatched, so you'll need to call from the taxi stand. Fares are about $4 per person. For information, call 906-847-3713.

WHEN TO COME The island's season runs from early May through late October, with June, July, and August the most popular times to visit. September is an overlooked month: the weather is still usually warm and the island isn't crowded. Actually, May can be cold in Michigan, and it usually doesn't fully warm up until late May.

MEDICAL EMERGENCY Mackinac Straits Hospital & Health Center (906-643-8585; www.mshosp.org). The center runs a facility on the island. Call 911.

✳ To See & Do

Mackinac Island Carriage Tours (906-847-3307; www.mict.com), Mackinac Island. Located on Main Street across from the Arnold Transit Dock. A carriage tour offers you a good chance to get a look at the island without walking or peddling. The nearly two-hour tour takes you past the Grand Hotel and other attractions. While you can walk to most places, the Grand Hotel would be difficult for some to reach on foot. Cost runs $23 for adults and $9 for children. A white wedding carriage is available for $400 an hour.

Jack's Livery Stable (906-847-3391; www.jacksliverystable.com). You can drive your own carriage around Mackinac Island for the day or just for a few hours. This allows you to stop and see the sights or even take a trip around the island, about 8 miles. The livery also rents saddle horses. Rates are $54 per hour for a two-passenger buggy; $66 per hour, four passenger; $78 per hour, six passenger; and $35 per hour for a saddle horse.

DOWNTOWN

FORT MACKINAC

Fort Mackinac (www.mackinacparks.com), Main St. Sitting on a bluff overlooking the village, and with a commanding view of the entire Straits area, you can see why the British built the fort here during the Revolutionary War. It was turned over to the U.S. at the end of the war, but was retaken by the British briefly during the War of 1812. In total, it was in service for more than 115 years.

The buildings are in excellent shape because the fort was turned over to the state of Michigan and never abandoned like other forts. It has long been a tourist attraction, even when it was still manned by soldiers.

The fort is part of the Mackinac State Historic Parks, which include Colonial Fort Michilimackinac, the village of Mackinac Island historic downtown, Mackinac Island State Park, and Mill Creek (see Mackinaw City).

Fort Mackinac has long been the subject of preservation efforts by the state. In one of the more amusing incidents, the state tore down a rest room in the 1950s, thinking it had been added at some point and wasn't part of the original fort. It was later discovered that a fort doctor had ordered the flush toilets built in the 19th century for health reasons and it was used by soldiers in the 1890s. There is also a bathhouse in the fort, with tubs that were used by the soldiers.

The fort's jail is worth seeing. At one point, miscreants were chained in a cellar. Also, there is a display about one soldier, with photo, who got into many altercations with his superior officers and spent plenty of time in the lockup. At one point, someone smuggled him a bottle of Irish whiskey, and he was able to get drunk in jail.

Reenactors play the parts of soldiers at the fort in the 19th century, and one of the most popular daily activities is the firing of a cannon. The reenactors are well versed in life at the fort during the 1880s and can answer questions.

Cindy's Riding Stable (906-847-3572; www.cindysridingstable.com), Market St. Eighty-three miles of roads and trails in the 2,500-acre Mackinac State Historic Park are open to horseback riding. You can't use a horse to tour the historic districts of the village, just the backcountry roads and trails.

Historic downtown. Stretched mostly along Market Street, which runs parallel to Main Street, are restored buildings that were in use in the 1700s and 1800s, when the island was the hub of fur-trading activity in the region. A ticket to Fort Mackinac gives access to the structures or you can buy a separate pass at the fort.

From our modern-day perspective, life at the fort appears a remote existence, but actually the island was well served by steamships during the shipping season, and soldiers enjoyed beer from Milwaukee in the post recreation building while they played pool. Also, many tourists started showing up in the 1880s, making the island a hub of activities. There were many saloons in the village during that era, and some soldiers spent their evenings there. There is also a roller-skating rink in the village where the soldiers sought amusement.

One of the newer exhibits is on 19th-century medicine in the 1829 post hospital, the oldest hospital building in Michigan. There is a giant microscope and medical and surgical equipment. Admission is $10 for adults, $6 for children 6–17, and free for children under 6.

FORT MACKINAC

American Fur Company Store. Established by John Jacob Astor, the store served as a trading place for furs among Native Americans and others who trapped. Astor became America's first millionaire, partly based on his fur-trading activities in the Great Lakes. The store has been restored to the way it looked during the early part of the 19th century. On the store grounds is the Dr. William Beaumont Museum. (One of Detroit's largest hospitals also bears his name.) Beaumont was stationed at the fort in 1822 when Alexis St. Martin, a French-Canadian voyageur, was brought to him with a shotgun wound to the stomach. The wound, which left an opening in his stomach, never healed.

Beaumont was able to watch the digestive system at work for a good number of years.

Mission Church. The Presbyterian church dates to 1829 and was built by evangelical Protestants, who also supported a mission school for American, French-Canadian, and métis students. The church was active until 1937. It was partly restored in the early 19th century, and later restoration was done in the 1980s.

Main Street is lined with stores of all kinds, including fudge shops. The stores offer every type of Mackinac Island souvenir you can imagine. Chances are you'll soon tire of them. The more interesting shops and historical buildings are one block over.

Indian Dormitory. The building was used as the headquarters of the American Indian Agency, which was responsible for dealing with native issues in the upper Great Lakes. Indians would gather at the building to receive annuity payments from the government. Later, the building served as the island's public school through the 1960s. It is not open to the public.

McGuipin House. It's suspected that this distinctly French-Canadian home was moved from the mainland in 1780, when the British moved Fort Michilimackinac to the island during the Revolutionary War. Exposed sections of the walls show the original lathe, plaster, layers of wallpaper, paint colors, and an area that may have contained a Catholic shrine.

Biddle House. Built in the late 18th century and purchased by Edward Biddle in 1832, the home was occupied by the family for several generations. Biddle came from a prominent family and took up residence on the island after the War

MACKINAC ISLAND

Canadian/Indian). The home is restored to the era when Biddle lived in it, and
there are living history demonstrations of early 19th century crafts.

GREEN SPACE **Mackinac Island State Park** (www.mackinacparks.com). About
80 percent of the island is parkland and open to visitors. Dozens of footpaths
crisscross the 1,800-acre park. Most visitors use MI 185, which follows the
shoreline around the island, about 8 miles total. It's open to bicycles, walkers,
and horse-drawn vehicles. Trails take visitors to landmarks such as Arch Rock
and Sugar Loaf. There is no admission charge.

✳ Lodging

There are usually plenty of rooms
available on the island. Prices for
some of the better places can break
the $200-a-night mark. Many people
opt to stay in Mackinaw City or St.
Ignace, where there are plenty of
motel rooms and the prices are much
lower.

The Grand Hotel (1-800-33-
GRAND; www.grandhotel.com). The
hotel opened in 1887, and over the
years it has come to define Mackinac
Island. Mark Twain lectured here,
and the 1979 movie *Somewhere in
Time* was filmed here, sparking new
interest in the hotel. But it wasn't the
first movie. In 1949 Esther Williams,
an actress who started in movies
showcasing her swimming abilities,
filmed *This Time for Keeps* at the
hotel, making plenty of use of its
swimming pool. The Michigan Central Railroad, Grand Rapids and Indian Railroad, and the Detroit and
Cleveland Steamship Navigation
Company built the hotel to meet the
demand for accommodations on the
island when it was becoming a tourist
destination in the 1880s. When it
opened, its 660-foot porch, reportedly
the largest in the world, was the main
attraction. It still is. Visitors flock to
see it, and the hotel now charges an
entrance fee to walk on it. Perhaps
the best deal at the hotel is high tea in
the late afternoon. For $20 you get
access to the porch, along with tea.
The rooms all have baths and have
been updated over the years, but they
still retain their Victorian feel. Breakfast and a five-course dinner are
included in the price of a room. And
during a three-day stay, you'll never
have the same meal. Wine is included,
as is the tip. The restaurant is open to
nonguests (see *Dining Out*). There is
an evening dress code: coats and ties
for men and dresses or pantsuits for
women. Rates are $220–$665.

Mission Point Resort (906-847-
3312; www.missionpoint.com), 6633
Main St. This place is out of the hustle and bustle of the village, and it has
a view of Lake Huron. It's a great
place to sit outside and watch the lake
freighters pass by. The 242-room
resort has a heated pool, sauna, steam
room, and spa services. Many of the
rooms have a lake view. The grounds
are country-club style. Many of the
guests can be found on the 18-hole
putting course, which is near the lake.
The rooms and suites are upscale and
well decorated, and there is a hot-tub
suite. High-speed Internet is offered.
Rates are $239–$289.

STRAITS OF MACKINAC

HISTORIC INNS Haan's 1830 Inn Bed & Breakfast (906-847-6244; www.mackinac.com/haans). The Greek revival home was built on the foundations of a fur-trader cabin brought from the mainland during the Revolutionary War. The inn's 10 rooms are furnished with antiques and one has a four-poster double bed. There is a balcony, and the front porches invite you to enjoy a summer evening. Rates are $100–$200.

∞ **The Inn at Stonecliffe** (906-847-3355; www.theinnatstonecliffe.com). Located in the northwest portion of the island, the inn is away from the activity of the village and is a good place to stay if you're looking for peace and quiet. However, if you're there for sight-seeing, you're going to have to walk, bike, or take a carriage ride into town. The inn is composed of two buildings, Cudahy Manor and the Summer House. The Summer House has 33 studio suites furnished in a summer cottage style. The suites have air-conditioning, a refrigerator, microwave, coffee maker, television and Internet connection. There is a whirlpool suite. Breakfast is included, and dinner buffets are available. Cudahy Manor is a turn-of-the-century Tudor mansion with 16 rooms, many with a view of the Straits. Reservations are recommended. Rates are $85–$325.

Harbourview (906-847-0101; www.harborviewinn.com), Main St., three blocks from downtown. For those who want to stay close to the village, this is a good spot. The house was built for Madame La Framboise, a fur-trade pioneer who hosted such guests as Alexis de Tocqueville at her home. It's located next to St. Anne's Church, which served many of the French-Canadians on the island. The harborside rooms have the best views of the harbor of any B&B. All rooms have private baths, and some have balconies. The carriage and guesthouses offer more privacy and outdoor whirlpools. Rates are $89–$299.

Metivier Inn Bed & Breakfast (1-866-847-6234; www.metivierinn.com), Market St. The inn was built by Louis Metivier in 1877 and was a private home for about 100 years. Metiver was a French-Canadian who settled on the island and engaged in barrel making for the commercial fishing industry. The 22 rooms have a French and English country style, and there are wonderful windows in the turret rooms. The comfortable porches are a great place to spend a summer afternoon. Wireless Internet service is available. Rates are $85–$315.

Inn on Mackinac (www.4mackinac.com), Main St. Parts of the inn date to 1867, but most of the rooms have been updated and all have private baths. The front porch is a great place to sit and have coffee in the morning. The interior matches its exterior Victorian look, and some of the rooms can be a bit cramped, but the public rooms are a better place to spend your time. The inn is close to the historic downtown area. Rates are $89–$330.

HOTELS Chippewa Hotel (1-800-241-3341; www.chippewahotel.com), Main St. The hotel has long been a favorite of boaters who tie up at the docks. There are rooms and suites overlooking either the harbor or Main Street. Although it's an older building, the rooms have been renovated, most in a Victorian style. There are rooms with hot tubs. It's in the heart of downtown, and you're near restaurants and shopping. Rates are $95–$515.

Hotel Iroquois (906-847-3221; www.iroquoishotel.com), Main St. This 1904 hotel may not be the hippest place on the island, but it takes you back to another era when people stayed longer and strolled along the beach. The location is great. You have a view of the Straits, and it's on a quiet end of Main Street, which has less activity. There are 46 rooms and suites, all done Victorian style. Like many older hotels, the rooms are a bit smaller than what modern-day people are accustomed to, but you're going to be spending most of your times outdoors or in the hotel's public rooms. If you need more space, there's a two-bedroom suite. Rates are $165–$625.

Murray Hotel (1-800-4-Mackinac; www.4mackinac.com), Main St. The Murray is about 120 years old, and while it may not be for some, it has a good location near Fort Mackinac and allows visitors to experience a bit what it was like for 19th-century tourists. Some of the rooms show their age, so if you're into décor this isn't the place for you. I found the rooms adequate and would stay here again because most of your time is spent outdoors, not in the room. The hallways are filled with historic photos and artwork. There is an outdoor deck and whirlpool. Rates are $69–$280.

Island House Hotel (1-800-626-6304; www.theislandhouse.com), Main St. Built in 1852, it was the first summer hotel on the island. The 96-room hotel is on the list of Historic Hotels of America, National Trust for Historic Preservation. As with many historic buildings, the hotel fell on

hard times in the 1950s and '60s, and it was thought that it would be demolished. However, local business people banded together in the early 1970s and the hotel was renovated and restored. The result is an older hotel with modern rooms. The front porch is the place to be, with its view of the Straits. There are traditional rooms and suites. Rates are $165–$600.

Lake View Hotel (906-847-3384; www.lake-view-hotel.com), Main St., across from the boat docks. Parts of the historic hotel date to 1858, but it has been restored and added to over the years, most recently in 1983. Most of the 85 rooms have been updated and are modern, with private baths. There is a pool, whirlpool, and sauna. The front porch is a great place to spend a late afternoon after sightseeing. Rates are $99–$405.

Lilac Tree Hotel & Spa (1-866-847-6575; www.lilactree.com), Main St. If you're tired of the older, historic inns and B&Bs on the island, this is the place to stay. The modern building has a Victorian curbside look, but the structure is newer. The rooms are all suites, and there's a major focus on weddings. The rooms have a contemporary feel and are larger than most on the island. The spa services offer massage, hot stone treatments, facials, manicures and pedicures, body wraps, and hot tubs. Rates are $130–$330.

Pontiac Lodge (906-847-3364; www.pontiaclodge.com), on Hoban St., just off Main. For those wishing to visit the island during winter, this is one of the few places open. There are 10 rooms and two 2-bedroom suites. The rooms are serviceable, but aren't like the plush accommodations you'll find elsewhere on the island. Looking at the place makes you ponder the possibility of a winter trip and cross-country skiing on the island. Horse-drawn sleigh rides are also offered in winter. Rates are $85–$350.

∞ **Main Street Inn** (906-847-6530; www.mainstreetinnandsuites.com), Main St. This is a newer building with a Victorian face. It offers eight rooms and suites, including a honeymoon suite with a hot tub. With the many weddings on the island, this would be an ideal place for the wedding party to stay. The rooms have irons and ironing boards to make sure everybody's clothing is neat for the big day. There are hair dryers and terrycloth bathrobes. Its location near the boat docks makes it a good meeting place. Rates are $85–$375.

Windermere Hotel (906-847-3301 or 1-800-847-3125; www.windermere hotel.com), Main St. This place is a favorite of ours. It's on a quiet part of Main Street, away from the daily noise of tourists making their way through town, and near the Straits of Mackinaw. It has been a hotel since 1904, and it retains the original charm of the area. The view from the porch is one of the best on the island. The 26 rooms have private baths, but no television sets or telephones, a benefit because you can detach yourself from daily life and get a better glimpse of the Victorian era. The rooms are simple, but tastefully decorated. Rates are $85–$255.

RENTALS **Mackinac Resort Management** (1-800-473-6960 or 906-847-3407; www.sunsetcondos.com), P.O. Box 849, Mackinac Island, MI 49757. The firm handles condos and home rentals on the island. Home rentals can range from $4,000–$8,000 a month.

✳ **Where to Eat**

DINING OUT **The Fort Tea Room** (1-800-33-GRAND; www.grand hotel.com), at the Grand Hotel. Eating lunch or dinner in the Fort Tea Room is a good way to see the hotel if you're not staying there. The dinner grill menu includes steak and grilled Michigan whitefish. Chicken and lamb are on the menu, along with a high-class burger. The grilled polenta with wild mushroom stew is a good bet. Entrees are $13–$36.

The Gate House (1-800-33-GRAND; www.grandhotel.com). Located at the bottom of the Grand Hotel hill, the bar/restaurant is a new addition to the historic hotel complex and offers casual dining in a less formal atmosphere than the hotel. The fare is a step up from most pub food and includes ribs, steak, veal, fish and chips, whitefish, and chicken. There are also burgers and chicken sandwiches. The dessert menu is enticing; try the Grand Hotel pecan ball with fudge sauce. Entrees are $15–$26.

The Jockey Club (1-800-33-GRAND; www.grandhotel.com). The restaurant is located in the clubhouse at the Grand Hotel golf course and offers full dinners along with sandwiches. Steaks, whitefish, and lobster top the menu, but there are some creative dishes to be found. The beer-braised buffalo short ribs sounded like a good, different choice. Entrees are $18–$40.

Goodfellows (906-847-3384; www .lake-view-hotel.com). Located in the Lake View Hotel, the bar/restaurant offers casual, upscale dining inside or on an outdoor deck. The bar area offers a full menu in a pub atmosphere. Lamb is offered, which is uncommon for the island, and there are fish and chicken dishes. Breakfast and lunch are also served. Prices are $10–$20.

EATING OUT **Pink Pony Bar & Grill** (1-866-847-6575; www.chippewa hotel.com), Main St. Located on the first floor of the Chippewa Hotel, the bar and grill offers up pub food and full dinners in its Harbor View Dining Room, which has a view of the harbor. There is an outside deck. Its convenient location makes it a good place to meet for lunch. My favorite here was the cherry barbecue salmon. The burgers and smoked pork sandwiches were a great choice for lunch. Pasta and chicken are also on the menu. This place gets pretty wild in July when the annual Port Huron to Mackinac sailboat races take place. The deck is a good spot for watching the boats arrive. Entrees are $16–$23.

1852 Grill Room (906-847-3463; www.theislandhouse.com). Located in the Island House Hotel, the grill offers a full dinner menu. Local whitefish is a specialty, and there is an awesome prime rib and baby back ribs. Lake Michigan perch are also on the menu. Entrees are $20–$32.

Patrick Sinclair's Irish Pub (906-847-8255; www.patricksinclairs.com), Main St. The old-fashioned pub was a real find on the island. The fish and chips are a standard here, along with shepherd's pie. Prices are $8–$12.

Jesse's Chuckwagon (906-847-3775), Main St. This small, storefront diner is hard to find, but it's worth the search. This is where the locals go to have a quick breakfast before work. You don't have to ask for a second cup of coffee. Prices are $5–$8.

MARKET **Doud Market** (906-847-3551), Main St. Located near the fort,

this is the only food source on the island, selling fresh meats, vegetables, fruits, beer, wine, and liquor. There is a small deli counter and salad bar where you can get lunch.

✳ Entertainment

Horn's Gaslight Bar & Restaurant (906-847-6154; www.hornsbar.com), Main St. Located downtown, it's a good place to meet friends. Bands and DJs make this a lively spot at night. The food focus is on American and Southwest dishes. For wings fans, this is the place to go on the island. It features most of my favorite pub foods, including fajita steak and chicken. Prices are $6–$17.

✳ Selective Shopping

Most shops are spread out along Main Street and are concentrated near the boat docks, where most everyone arrives on the island. The shops are open May–October unless otherwise noted.

The Balsam Shop (906-847-3591; www.balsamshop.com), Main St. Open April–Nov., with some winter hours. This place is a cut above most of the gift shops on the island. There is a decent selection of history books about the island, cookbooks, and Lilac Festival posters and related gifts. Cross-country ski rentals are available.

✐ **The Butterfly House** (906-847-3972; www.originalbutterflyhouse .com), behind St. Anne's Church, off Main St. The exhibit includes an 1,800-square-foot tropical garden filled with butterflies from around the world. There is also an exhibit of exotic insects from around the world. This is a fun place to take children, and there's a gift shop.

Lilacs & Lace (906-847-0100; www
.liacsandlace.com). Located in the
Carrousel Shops on Market Street,
the shop sells jewelry, teapots, and
other items that relate to the large
number of lilacs on the island. The
broken china jewelry is enticing. It's
made by Linda and Tim Carrigan,
who turn broken china into bracelets,
necklaces, and earrings. There are
also prints of island scenes by regional
artists.

Freshwater Foods (906-847-3567;
www.freshwaterfoods.com), Main St.
This small company has its operations
in St. Ignace on the mainland and
produces dessert toppings, sauces,
chutneys, and other items. The firm
uses Traverse City area cherries in
many of its products.

Michigan Peddler (906-847-6506;
www.michiganpeddler.com), Main St.
The focus is on Michigan products in
this shop. There is a good supply of
local history books, many published
by Michigan State University. Food,
glassware, Petoskey stone jewelry, and
other Michigan-made items are on
the shelves. There is a good selection
of Michigan wines.

Scrimshanders (906-847-3792; www
.scrimshanders.com), in the lobby of
the Chippewa Hotel, Main St. While
many of the shops on the island are
aimed at women, here's a place where
guys can spend some time looking at
nautical scrimshaw carvings on knives,
driftwood, money clips, letter open-
ers, and other items.

Mackinac Outfitter (906-847-6100;
www.mackinacoutfitter.com), Main
St., in the Bay View Inn building.
Open year-round. The island is a center for boating, and this is where you
can get the gear you need. The shop
has everything from sunglasses and
clothing to marine hardware. They
also sell winter sporting goods, and
they're the people to check with for
kayaking around the island.

Mackinac Lapidary (906-847-1040;
www.mackinaclapidary.com), located
in the Carrousel Mall near Market
Street Frank Bloswick, Jr. creates
Mackinac-themed custom jewelry in
the shop. He uses Petoskey stones
(the state stone) for many items and
depicts horses and carriages, lighthouses, and other local icons. There is
a bead shop for those who make their
own jewelry.

BOOKSTORE The Island Bookstore
(906-847-6202; www.islandbook
store.com), Main St. If you are coming to the island for the first time, this
should be your first stop. The store,
and its sister shop in Mackinaw City
(see *Bookstores*, Mackinaw City), has
many books about the island, the
Great Lakes, Native America lore, the
Mackinaw Bridge, and local history.
There is a good selection of children's
books about the island.

ART GALLERY Maeve's Arts (906-
847-3755; www.maevecroghan.com),
Market St., Mackinac Island. Hours
and days vary, so call first. During the
summer Maeve splits her time
between the island store and Campbell's Gallery in Grand Marais in the
Upper Peninsula. During the winter
months she spends time in California.
The results are landscape paintings of
Michigan and California, done in a
contemporary style and with vivid colors. A visitor familiar with the Upper
Peninsula will easily pick out her
landscapes of the rugged Lake Superior shoreline.

✳ Special Events

There are almost weekly events on the island. Check www.mackinac.com for a complete list. Here are some of the most popular.

Early June **Mackinac Island Lilac Festival** (www.mackinacislandlilac festival.com). Lilacs are in bloom this time of year here. Various music events are associated with the festival.

Mid to late July Two sailboat races, one from Chicago and the other from Port Huron, are among the most attended events on the island. The Chicago-to-Mackinac race is held in mid-July, and the Port Huron event later that month. See www.byc.com for the Port Huron race and www .chicagoyachtclub.org for the Chicago race.

Early August **Annual Mackinac Island Fun & Games Horseshow** (www.mackinac.com). The event at Great Turtle Park is hosted by the Mackinac Horsemen's Association.

Late August Grand Hotel Labor Day Jazz Festival, (www.mackinac.com).

ST. IGNACE

O f the three Straits of Mackinac communities, St. Ignace is a real town where many of the people who work on Mackinac Island live. It's also the oldest, founded in 1671 by Father Marquette and named for St. Ignatius Loyola, the founder of the Jesuit order. It too was a bustling fur-trading town, with a long history of Native American settlements (see Straits of Mackinac).

These days, it's still a hub of activity and a jumping-off place for travelers to the Upper Peninsula. Interstate 75 continues its northerly route for 50 miles to Sault Ste. Marie, US 2 starts here and heads west across the U.P., and MI 123 heads north from here to Tahquamenon Falls. Many savvy Mackinac Island travelers opt to cross the bridge and stay in St. Ignace. The pace seems slower, and accommodations are often cheaper in this town of 2,678.

GUIDANCE **St. Ignace Visitors Bureau** (906-643-6950; www.stignace.com), 6 Spring St., St. Ignace, MI 49781. Open Mon.–Fri., 9–5. A source of information about walking tours, Mackinac Bridge events, and local restaurants and hotels.

Michigan Welcome Center St. Ignace. Open year-round, 8–5. The state operates one of its major travel centers just north of the Mackinaw Bridge tollbooth on I-75. The center has information about the Straits area and much of the Upper Peninsula.

GETTING THERE *By car:* Follow I-75 north to the Mackinaw Bridge (toll $2.50), and take the first exit for St. Ignace after passing the tollbooth.

MEDIAL EMERGENCY **Mackinac Straits Hospital & Health Center** (906-643-8585; www.mshosp.org), 220 Burdett St., St. Ignace. The center offers 24-hour emergency care and has a facility on Mackinac Island. Call 911.

✴ To See & Do

Most venues are open from late May through early October unless otherwise noted.

Museum of Ojibwa Culture (906-643-9161; www.stignace.com), 500 N. State St., St. Ignace. Open daily, 11–5. The museum and grounds are located on a site long used by the Ojibwa, on State Street near Lake Huron. The museum tells the story of the Ojibwa's epic migration from upper Canada across the northern Great Lakes to get away from European influence. The Huron Indians are also represented on the grounds with a longhouse. The Ojibwa are also known as the Chippewa. The British, and later Americans, came up with Chippewa from the French, Ojibwa. The real name for the people is the Anishinabek. The museum site is also used for informal teaching sessions between tribal elders and young people. The museum gift shop next to the museum offers real items made by Native American and other regional artists.

MUSEUM OF OJIBWA CULTURE

BEACHES

Brevort, Epoufette, and Naubinway. Stretching for about 50 miles west of St. Ignace are some of the best Lake Michigan beaches in the Upper Peninsula, and most are open to the public.

It's very informal here. Just find a beach you like, pull off US 2, and park. There are also U.S. Forest Service campgrounds near the beach between Brevort and Epoufette and near Naubinway. Don't expect to find much in the way of services in these towns. What you see while driving along US 2 is what you get. Some of the small motels and restaurants seem to be in business one year and out the next.

However, there are some excellent pasty shops along the road, and they're usually a good option. Also, a lot of commercial fishing is done in this area. Check out the fishing boats in Naubinway, which is the bigger town. Many of these fisheries offer smoked fish at roadside stands along US 2, and it's another good option for lunch or dinner. There are no fast-food restaurants or man-made attractions for kids, as you often find near beach areas.

The beaches are sandy and shallow and the water is warm, making them good places for kids. There is some private property, so look for the NO TRESPASSING signs. However, there is enough beach for everyone, and they're rarely crowded. One note: a Michigan Supreme Court ruling allows walkers to stroll in front of private beachfront property just as long as they stay as close as possible to the water line. No fees or parking permits are required to use the beaches, but there are fees in the campgrounds.

GAMBLING Kewadin Casino (1-800-KEWADIN; www.kewadin.com), 3015 Mackinac Trail, St. Ignace. Open daily, year-round. The casino/hotel resort complex offers gambling, decent hotel rooms, and a good restaurant. It's operated by the Sault Band of the Chippewa Indians.

✳ Lodging

Many major hotel/motel chains are represented along State Street from downtown St. Ignace to the Kewadin Casino, a gambling complex owned by Native Americans. There are usually plenty of rooms, many with a lake view.

BED & BREAKFASTS Colonial House Inn (906-643-6900; www .colonial-house-inn.com), 90 N. State St. The Victorian-style home overlooking the Straits of Mackinac, and near the Mackinac Island boat docks, has been a bed & breakfast since 1940. There are six rooms. Much of the place has been renovated, and each room has a private bath. The rooms have a Victorian theme. There is also an adjoining 12-room motel, and breakfast is available to motel guests. The porch is large and has a terrific view of the water and the boats headed to the island. No children under 14 are allowed in the inn.

Rates for the inn run $89–$155 and for the motel $59–$79.

HOTELS The Boardwalk Inn Hotel (906-643-7500; www.boardwalkinn .com), 316 N. State St. The inn dates from 1928 and is a good example of an old travelers' hotel. The innkeepers, Jim and Kayla Krug, have decorated the rooms in a country style. The rooms are larger than what you'd normally expect. Breakfast is in the Fireside Room. Indoor bicycle storage is available. Rates are $69–$135.

☙ **Birchwood Motel** (906-643-7738; www.stignace.com/lodging), 1899 I-75 Business Loop. This mom-and-pop motel is a little off the beaten track, but it's close to the Kewadin Casino. My single room was a bit cramped, but then again I was sharing it with two hunting dogs. The rooms were clean enough for me. The grounds are nicely landscaped and the owners friendly. Several of the rooms have kitchenettes. Rates are $60–$75.

Upper Peninsula

UPPER PENINSULA

Once you cross the Mackinac Bridge or the state line near US 2 in the western Upper Peninsula, you've entered the most remote area of Michigan, one that's peopled with folks who call themselves Yoopers and thrive on spending their winters in one of the snowiest regions of the nation. As one Yooper friend told me, "Winters separate the visitors from the natives."

It's a large, sparsely populated peninsula, with 328,000 people living in an area of 16,452 square miles—an area the size of Connecticut, Delaware, Massachusetts, and Rhode Island combined. Most people here live in Marquette, Sault Ste. Marie, and Iron Mountain, the U.P.'s largest cities.

The Mackinac Bridge, which connects the Upper and Lower Peninsulas, was opened in 1957. Before that, the U.P. was so isolated that it developed its own identity and Yooper culture. Some U.P. residents opposed the bridge when it was built and for years after pushed for U.P. statehood.

Once in the U.P., the fast-food restaurants fade from the roadside scene, replaced by pasty shops and smoked-fish stands. And apart from a few of the larger towns, there are hardly any chain hotels/motels. Cell phones often don't work so check your plan before you come, and if you're a public radio listener, the signals die away unless you can pick up 98.3 from Sault Ste. Marie or 90.1 from Marquette.

You've entered a semi-wilderness where about 80 percent of the land is publicly owned or is owned by lumber companies that allow public access. There are only 50 miles of freeway: I-75, running from the bridge to Sault Ste. Marie, and the two major east–west arteries, US 2 and MI 28, both two-lane blacktop roads in most places.

Beyond the big towns, most accommodations are found in housekeeping cabins and small motels. I'd suggest that you look at the cabin listings herein. Apart from North Woods taverns and occasional family-style restaurants, there aren't a lot of places to eat, and cooking for yourself is a good option. This isn't to say that there aren't some upscale hotels in the U.P. The Landmark in Marquette and the Chippewa in Sault Ste. Marie fill that bill.

There are three regions in the U.P.—the eastern, central, and western—and the top attractions are mostly spread out along the Lake Superior shoreline. These include the Soo Locks in Sault Ste. Marie, where lake freighters navigate

LAKE FREIGHTER ENTERS THE LOCKS

he St. Mary's River, the Tahquamenon Falls, Pictured Rocks National
Lakeshore, Seney National Wildlife Refuge, and Isle Royale National Park in
Lake Superior. Outdoor recreational opportunities are endless. Most of the
peninsula is like a nature preserve, and there are black bear, deer, moose, and
even a healthy wolf population.

Travel in the U.P. is fairly easy. There is little traffic on most roads and the
distances may look long, but you're going to be doing the speed limit at most
times. Another issue is getting fuel. There aren't a lot of gas stations, and just
because there's a town on the map doesn't always mean there's a station. It's best
to fill up when you can. Also, four counties along the Michigan/Wisconsin border
in the western U.P. are on Central Standard Time, not Eastern Standard like the
remainder of the state.

The three U.P. regions are fairly distinct. The eastern portion is fairly flat,
mostly wooded, and sparsely populated; in the central region the Marquette area
is the most populated and has rugged hills where iron is still mined, while the
Keweenaw Peninsula is fairly well populated and has rugged hills where copper
was mined and rocky shorelines on Lake Superior; and the western U.P. has few
people and a rugged landscape. Most western U.P. residents live along the 128-
mile-long border with Wisconsin.

EASTERN UPPER PENINSULA

SAULT STE. MARIE; PARADISE; HESSEL, CEDARVILLE, DE TOUR & DRUMMOND ISLAND

SAULT STE. MARIE

The Soo, as Michigan people call it, is one of oldest towns in the U.S., dating to 1688, when it was founded by the French, who then ruled Canada. However, it had long been a gathering place for Native Americans, who stopped here to portage their canoes around the rapids in the St. Mary's River, a 21-foot drop from Lake Superior to Lake Huron. Its location made it important during the fur-trading era because it controlled access to Lake Superior, and the French and British fought for control of it numerous times. It wasn't until 1820 that it officially became part of the U.S.

The rapids made it impossible to sail large craft north into Lake Superior, and ships were built in the lower Great Lakes, sailed to the Soo, and portaged overland to Superior. The British built a lock for ships, but it was destroyed in the War of 1812, and it wasn't until 1855 that the Americans built one. Since then, four locks on the American side have been built and improved on.

The locks are a major tourist attraction, especially for shipping buffs who keep track of the names of Great Lakes ships. On a busy summer afternoon, a ship going through the locks can attract several hundred spectators. It's quite a sight to watch a 1,000-foot-long freighter gently edging into a lock and then being raised or lowered.

But after you have watched the ships for a while, there really isn't a lot to do in town. Portage Street, which runs along the boat-viewing area, is crammed with T-shirt and souvenir shops and a few restaurants. Actually, Sault Ste. Marie, Canada, across the river is much larger; it has more than 74,000 residents, while the American Soo has just 14,000.

GUIDANCE **Sault Ste. Marie Chamber of Commerce** (906-632-3301; www .saultstemarie.org), 2581 I-75 Business Spur, Sault Ste. Marie, MI 49783. Open Mon.–Fri., business hours.

GETTING THERE *By car:* The Soo is the only major town in the Upper Peninsula that's accessible by freeway. The 50 miles from the bridge to the Soo represent the only stretch of freeway in the U.P.

By air: **Chippewa Country International Airport** (906-495-5631; www .airciu.com). Mesaba, an air link for Northwest Airlines, offers daily flights to and from Detroit. It's the only commercial airport in the eastern Upper Peninsula. A shuttle service is available at the airport.

Getting fuel: There are few gas stations on the freeway between St. Ignace and the Soo.

When to go: The Soo pretty much operates from late May through Oct., and many of the tourist-related businesses are closed during the off-season. The shipping season runs from the ice breakup in the spring until early December.

MEDICAL EMERGENCY **War Memorial Hospital** (906-635-4460; www.war memorialhospital.org), 500 Osborn Blvd. Call 911.

✳ To See & Do

Most attractions are open from late May through October unless otherwise noted.

Native American Reservations. There is a strong Native American presence in the Sault Ste. Marie area. A small Chippewa Reservation is located on Sugar Island, and nearby Brimley has the Bay Mills Indian Reservation, which is larger. There are Indian-owned gambling casinos in both the Soo and Brimley.

The Soo Locks are operated by the U.S. Army Corps of Engineers. The best place to start is at the visitor center on Portage Street. A short film covers the history, and the exhibits give a visitor an overview on how the system works. Admission is free. The locks are closed in the winter when the shipping season ends, usually in December.

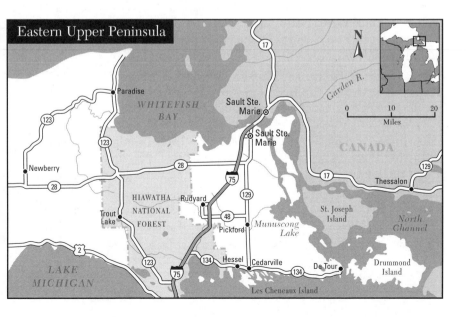

Eastern Upper Peninsula

UPPER PENINSULA

Museum Ship Valley Camp (906-632-3658 or 1-888-744-7867; www.thevalley camp.com), 501 E. Water. The museum is a Great Lakes freighter that once was home to 29 crewmembers. There are 100 exhibits in the ship, including two lifeboats from the *Edmund Fitzgerald,* the last freighter to sink in the Great Lakes, in Lake Superior on Nov. 10, 1975. Admission is $14 for adults and $6.50 for children 6–16.

Tower of History (906-632-3658 or 1-888-744-7867; www.thevalleycamp.com), 326 E. Portage, Sault Ste. Marie. The 210-foot tower offers a good view of the locks and St. Mary's River. The tower was built in 1968 by the Catholic Church as the Shrine of the Missionaries and was supposed to be part of a larger complex that was never completed. It was donated to the Sault Historic Sites in 1980 and has been operated as the Tower of History ever since. A museum in the bottom level deals with local and Native American history. Admission is $6 for adults and $3 for children.

Water Street Historic Block, located one block off the main drag near the locks, on Water Street near Portage Avenue. Community and business leaders lived on this block in the early 19th century, beginning with John Johnston, one of the first Europeans to settle in the area. A native of Ireland, he was an early fur trader who married the daughter of a Chippewa Indian leader. The couple moved to the Sault in 1793 and constructed the house now on display. Henry Rowe Schoolcraft, the first Indian agent in the area, also lived in a house here. His writings on Native Americans inspired Longfellow to write his epic poem, *Hiawatha.* Don't miss the Ojibwa burial ground, which is marked with a monument and a newer, ornate metal fence with arrows on it. The Ojibwa have marked out the traditional burial ground and occasionally have services there.

River of History Museum (906-632-3658 or 1-888-744-7867; www.thevalley camp.com), 209 E. Portage Ave. Exhibits in this former post office building chronicle the history of the St. Mary's River and the Soo. There are 11 galleries with local artifacts from Native Americans, French fur traders, and Americans who built the locks and engaged in trade. Admission is $5.50 for adults and $2.75 for children.

Soo Locks Boat Tours (906-632-6301; www.soolocks.com), Dock 1, 1157 E. Portage Ave., Dock 2, 515 E. Portage Ave. Open May–mid-Oct. The best way to see the locks is on a boat tour. The two-hour cruise takes sightseers through the locks, and the tour boat raises and lowers along with the lake freighters passing through. There is also a cruise to the St. Mary's River Lighthouse. Rates are $19.50 for adults, $9.50 for children 4–12, and free for children under 3.

Sugar Island. Take the car ferry to the small island in the St. Mary's River. It's home to a Native American reservation. The area has long been populated by what Americans call Ojibwa or Chippewa Indians. French missionaries Claude Dablon and the better-known Jacques Marquette founded a mission at the Soo in 1688. There is a good Ojibwa museum in St. Ignace (see *To See & Do,* St. Ignace).

GAMBLING **Kewadin Casino** (1-800-KEWADIN; www.kewadin.com), 2186 Shunk Rd., Sault Ste. Marie, and at other locations in the Upper and Lower

Peninsulas. Casino gambling is legal on reservations in Michigan, and the Chippewa have taken advantage of the laws. There are slot machines, card games, and roulette. There is also a hotel and restaurants (see *Dining Out*).

Bay Mills Resort & Casino (906-248-3715; www.4baymills.com), 11386 W. Lakeshore Dr., Brimley. The Chippewa own and operate a casino and resort hotel with three restaurants and a golf course. The 144-room hotel is sleek and modern, with decent restaurants.

MARINA George Kemp Marina (www.thevalleycamp.com), 485 E. Water, Sault Ste. Marie. The public marina can accommodate vessels up to 75 feet and has fuel available.

✳ Lodging

Most lodging can be found on the I-75 business spur leading into Sault Ste. Marie. Most are chain hotels and motels. I found little to recommend on Portage Street, which is the main drag next to the locks. One may try Sault Ste. Marie, Canada, which is just across the St. Mary's River. It is larger than the American town. At some point a passport will be required for travel to Canada.

🏨 Ramada Plaza Hotel Ojibway (906-632-4100; www.ramada.com), 240 W. Portage Ave., Sault Ste. Marie, MI 49783. The hotel has a long history in the Soo and is still known to most as the Ojibway Hotel. Built in 1927, it is the best place to stay in the Soo. President Bush stayed here in 1992. It has a view of the locks and first-class accommodations. For an older hotel, the rooms are very modern and have been updated. The restaurant (see *Dining Out*) has a good view of the locks. High-speed Internet service is available. There is a pool and a workout room. Rates are $118–$199.

MOTELS Lockview Motel (906-632-2491 or 1-800-854-0745; www.lockview.com), 327 W. Portage Ave. If you're interested in staying near the locks, this was the best motel I found

within walking distance. They are basic rooms, nothing special, but they are clean and the furnishings are better than what you'd expect. There are 47 units. Actually, the cottages in the back of the property were the most intriguing and would be good for a family. Rates are $55–$76.

CAMPING Brimley State Park (906-249-3422; www.michigan.gov/dnr), 9200 W. Six Mile Rd., Brimley, MI 49715. The 160-acre park is located on the shores of Whitefish Bay. The beach is sandy and the water relatively warm for Lake Superior. It's possible to swim from June–Aug. Camping is available, and there is a boat launch and a playground. The park takes telephone reservations for campsites.

Lime Island Cottages (906-635-5281; www.michigan.gov/dnr), Sault Ste. Marie Forest Management Unit, 2001 Ashmun, Sault Ste. Marie. The state Department of Natural Resources rents rustic cabins on Lime Island overlooking the St. Mary's River. The two- to three-bedroom cabins can sleep up to eight people, and there is limited solar power available. There are also platform tent campsites on the island. Visitors need to charter a boat for the 3-mile trip from the

BISHOP BARAGA HOUSE

mainland to the island. Cabins run $65 and tent sites $15.

✳ Where to Eat

DINING OUT ☿ **Freighters Restaurant/Captains Pub and Grille** (906-632-4100; www.ramada.com), 240 W. Portage Ave., Sault Ste. Marie. Open daily, year-round. Located in the Ramada Plaza Hotel Ojibway (see *Lodging*), the two restaurants offer the best eating options near the Soo locks. The food is nothing special, but when compared to what's available nearby it's a stand out. The menu is filled with standard North Country fare like whitefish, perch, and steak. The Captain's Pub offers soups, salads, and sandwiches. Entrees $15–$20.

☿ **Dream Catchers** (1-800-KEW-ADIN; www.kewadin.com) Open daily. Located in the Kewadin Casino (see *Gambling*). Food and service in the U.P. are often uneven because there isn't a consistent stream of customers, so the Native American gambling casinos are often a good bet for a restaurant meal. The Indians have put together a menu that will attract even nongamblers. Ribs and steaks are part of the mainstay, along with whitefish and trout. The Field & Stream Combo

was my favorite, a pan-roasted rainbow trout with a 5-ounce sirloin steak, grilled shrimp, and vegetables. Breakfasts and lunches are also served. Entrees are $10–$15.

In Brimley

☿ **Stacy's Restaurant at Bay Mills Resort & Casino** (906-248-3715; www.4baymills.com), 11386 W. Lakeshore Dr., Brimley. Open daily. Steaks, seafood, and ribs are the mainstay for the gambling crowd. It's one of the best places for steak in the eastern Upper Peninsula. There is also a full menu, with pasta, chicken, and pub-style sandwiches, along with local whitefish. This would be a good destination for a family with different tastes looking for a night out. Entrees $15–$20.

EATING OUT ☿ **Goetz's Lock View Restaurant** (906-632-2772), 329 W. Portage Ave. Don't let the 1950s tourist look fool you, this really is one of the better places to eat in town, especially for breakfast. Founded in 1945, the first owners used to go across the street to the St. Mary's River to catch whitefish for their fish sandwiches. Those types of sandwiches are still sold for lunch and dinner. The service was good. Prices are $6–$10.

PARADISE

Located on Lake Superior's Whitefish Bay, this community of only several hundred residents is mostly a collection of motels and restaurants, catering to visitors to nearby Whitefish Point and Tahquamenon Falls. There are hundreds of miles of snowmobile trails, and it's a popular destination.

Most accommodations are basic motel rooms, and the restaurants are simple places that serve pub food and family-style food to people who have spent most of their day outdoors seeing the sights or at the beaches between Paradise and Whitefish Point. If you're looking for better lodging or meals, they are to be had at Sault Ste. Marie or Newberry. The latter is about 45 miles away and the Soo about 55 miles. There is little traffic in the area, so the drives don't take long.

Eating out can be difficult here, and many people simply buy food in nearby Newberry or Sault Ste. Marie and bring it with them. A good solution would be to rent a cabin where there's at least a grill. Apart from a few souvenirs, there is virtually no shopping.

GUIDANCE **Paradise Chamber of Commerce** (906-492-3219; www.paradise michigan.org), P.O. Box 82, Paradise, MI 49768. It's a good source for snowmobile maps.

GETTING THERE *By car:* Paradise is 44 miles north of the Mackinaw Bridge on MI 123. Driving is the only way to get there.

Getting fuel: We'd suggest buying gas in Sault Ste. Marie or Newberry. There is a station in Paradise, but the cost is usually higher.

MEDICAL EMERGENCY **Helen Newberry Joy Hospital** (906-293-9200; www .hnjh.org), Newberry. It is 45 miles away, but it's the closest hospital. Call 911.

✳ To See & Do

At Whitefish Point

🚢 **Shipwreck Museum** (1-888-492-3747; www.shipwreckmuseum.com), Whitefish Point. Open mid-May–late Oct. The *Edmund Fitzgerald*, which sank nearby in Whitefish Bay on Nov. 10, 1975, was the last Great Lakes freighter to go to the bottom, and it's the focus of the museum. The point is a good place for ship-watching, and a sandy beach stretches for several miles from the museum to Paradise. The museum is the centerpiece, with its exhibits on Great Lakes shipping, diving, and artifacts. The lighthouse can also be toured. Admission is $10 for adults, $7 for children 6–17, and $28 for families.

GREAT LAKES SHIPWRECK MUSEUM

🚢 **Tahquamenon State Park** (906-492-3415; www.michiganandnr.com),

41382 W. MI 123, Paradise. The nearly 50,000-acre state park is home to the upper and lower Tahquamenon Falls, a top tourist attraction. The upper falls is one of the largest east of the Mississippi. It has a drop of nearly 50 feet and is more than 200 feet across. The lower falls is 4 miles downstream and is less dramatic. It's a series of five small falls swirling around an island. If the name Tahquamenon sounds familiar, it's from Longfellow's epic poem, *Hiawatha*. There is no evidence that Longfellow was ever in the area, though. The park has extensive hiking trails that are used for cross-country skiing in the winter.

✳ Outdoor Activities

BEACHES An 11-mile stretch between Paradise and Whitefish Point is basically one long, sandy beach. The waters in Whitefish Bay tend to be warmer than in other parts of Lake Superior.

BICYCLING The possibilities are unlimited. There is very little traffic in the area, and virtually no trucks, so even the state roads are good bets. One of the best trips is from Paradise to Whitefish Point, about 22 miles round-trip; MI 123 is flat, and the route follows the lakefront.

HIKING *See Tahquamenon State Park.*

TAHQUAMENON FALLS

FISHING AND HUNTING The Tahquamenon River is open to fishing for trout   **227**
and other species. Check with the DNR for access points. A set of county maps
is also helpful. There are hunting opportunities for bear, deer, ruffed grouse, and
woodcock. Check with the DNR for seasons and license information.

✳ Lodging

Most lodging in Paradise is in smaller, independently owned motels and cabins along Lake Superior.

Best Western Lakefront Inn & Suites (906-492-3770; www.best westernmichigan.com), MI 123. The inn is a great addition to the accommodations in Paradise, and the newer-style, large rooms, many with a view of Lake Superior, are a real standout here. It's the only nice place to stay in the area. There is a beach for swimming and an indoor pool, sauna, and hot tub. Free wireless Internet is provided. Rates are $50–$100.

MOTELS Curley's Paradise Motel (906-492-3445 or 1-800-236-7386), MI 123 at Whitefish Point Rd., Paradise. The innkeepers are William and Lynda Ferguson, and they offer standard, clean motel rooms with decent showers. There are also cabins for rent, which can sleep up to eight, and they look a lot more interesting than the motel rooms. The ability to cook in a cabin is a real plus in Paradise, which isn't exactly "paradise" when it comes to eating out. Rates are $50–$75.

✳ Where to Eat

DINING OUT ⅋ Tahquamenon Falls Brewery & Pub (906-492-3300), located on MI 123 near the entrance to Tahquamenon State Park. Closed in late spring and late fall; call for dates. Owner Lark Carlye Ludlow has pulled off something just short of a miracle in this neck of the woods—a fine restaurant and brewpub in an area that usually doesn't support such upscale endeavors. Although the menu is slightly limited, they do offer everything from appetizers to entrees. You won't find anything like this within 25 miles. They serve the North Country standards, steak and whitefish, but there is also brochette of charbroiled shrimp. Pub-food standards such as buffalo burgers and whitefish and sandwiches are on the menu, too. Entrees are $15–$20.

EATING OUT ⅋ Yukon Inn (906-492-3264), 8347 N. MI 123, Paradise, MI 49768. Open daily. The classic Up North family tavern serves pub-style food. Prices are $5–$10.

⅋ Little Falls Inn Red Flannel (906-492-3529), 8112 N. MI 123, Paradise. Open year-round. This is one of the few places in Paradise where you can actually get a full dinner with a salad. It's a northern style menu with whitefish and steak. Prices are $5–$12.

Paradise Pizza Factory (906-492-3663), 8165 N. MI 123, Paradise. Open daily, 4–10. It's the only one in town; a basic pizza place to take the kids.

North Star Bakery 906-658-3537; www.exploringthenorth.com/north star/bakery), located in the woods 13 miles north of Newberry on MI 123. Open mid-May–Oct.; hours vary. Joanne and Paul Behm make sourdough bread in a wood-fired brick oven at a backwoods location. There are 17 types of European-style breads, but not all are available daily.

Picking up a loaf and making a stop at a convenience store for meat and cheese may be a better option than relying on local restaurants.

HESSEL, CEDARVILLE, DETOUR & DRUMMOND ISLAND

Most visitors to the Upper Peninsula cross the Mackinaw Bridge and head west or north to the shores of Lake Superior, but those folks miss the Hessel, Cedarville, Drummond Island area, which The Nature Conservancy has called one of the last great places in the western hemisphere.

The landscape is not as stunning as it is along the rocky shores of Lake Superior, or dramatic as it is along the north edge of Lake Michigan to the west, but it has a diversity that one could spend a week or two discovering. There are two historic lighthouses, several Nature Conservancy wildlife areas, a 75-mile kayak trail in Lake Huron, miles of deserted beaches, hiking, bird-watching, and camping. The little-used side roads make for great bicycling. What the area doesn't have is also noteworthy—not a single fast-food place or chain restaurant along the stretch on MI 134 from I-75 to Drummond Island. The communities of Hessel and Cedarville provide food and lodging, mostly in the form of family-owned cabins and taverns/restaurants.

The focal point is on Lake Huron's north shore and the 36 Les Cheneaux Islands off the coast of the mainland. The islands shelter the communities from Great Lakes storms and make for good swimming and canoeing and kayaking. The area isn't a true wilderness, but is an accessible place to spend time outdoors, walking the beach, taking woodlands hikes, bicycle touring, or simply sitting on a beach and reading or watching the boats pass.

Drummond Island is the largest of the more than 900 islands in the Great Lakes and is home to about 1,000 year-round residents, but that more than doubles in the summer. Even then, the island's 136 square miles are fairly uncrowded, and most people stick to the western end near the Four Corners, where much of the service businesses are located. More than two-thirds of the island is state land, so there is plenty of space to roam, especially on the east end.

Most of the beaches are limestone and not sandy. If you're looking for a beach vacation, you're better advised to stay on the mainland east of DeTour, where there are splendid stretches of sandy, little-used beaches. There are, however, a few resorts with sandy beaches.

GUIDANCE **Les Cheneaux Islands Chamber of Commerce Welcome Center** (906-484-3935; www.lescheneaux.net), 670 MI 134, Cedarville. Open daily, weekdays.

Drummond Island Tourism Association (906-493-5245 or 1-800-737-8666; www.drummondislandchamber.com) Located at the Four Corners, the intersection of MI 134 and Townline Road, about 7 miles east of the ferry dock.

GETTING THERE *By car:* Exit I-75 at MI 134 and head east. The communities are spread along the state road, and most lodging places and eating establishments are located on it. Traffic is light and there are few trucks.

The Drummond Island Ferry (906-297-8851 or cell 906-235-3170) runs 24 hours, early April–early Jan. The ferry leaves DeTour on the mainland hourly from 6:40 AM for the 20-minute ride to the island. The cost is $8 for a car and driver, and $2 for each additional passenger. Round-trip

THE DRUMMOND ISLAND FERRY

passage is paid during the ferry ride to the island. There are no advance ticket sales or reservations. Campers, trailers, and larger trucks pay additional fares ranging up to $18 for a motor home.

MEDICAL EMERGENCIES **Drummond Island Medical Center** (906-493-5221) 33896 S. Town Line Rd., Drummond Island. Call 911.

✳ To See & Do

✐ ⬥ **Les Cheneaux Historical and Maritime Museums** (906-484-2821; www .lescheneaux.org). Open daily, late May–early Sept. The Historical Museum is on Meridian Road, one block south of MI 134, and the Maritime Museum is four blocks east of MI 134 on Lake Street. The museums have exhibits depicting the history of the communities and their nautical heritage.

LES CHENEAUX MARITIME MUSEUM

⇧ **Mertaugh's Boat Works,** on the waterfront in Hessel. The Les Cheneaux Islands are home to one of the largest concentrations of wooden boats in the nation, and the boat works is the oldest Chris-Craft dealer, dating to 1925. Stop by and watch as wooden boats are restored.

✳ Outdoor Activities

BEACHES Take MI 134 east from Cedarville toward DeTour. There are numerous sandy beaches on Lake Huron. Unless there are signs saying otherwise, all are on public land.

BICYCLING The terrain is flat, there's little traffic, and MI 134 follows Lake Huron, making it a good route.

CANOEING, KAYAKING & RENTALS **Woods & Water Ecotours** (906-484-4157; www.woodswaterecotours.com), 20 Pickford Ave., Hessel. Guided kayak tours of Les Cheneaux Islands, Lake Huron. Jessie Hadley, the owner operator, has worked in the conservation field for more than a decade and will put visitors in touch with the area's wildlife on the islands and its Native American history. The tours are nature based and are done via hiking, biking, and kayaking.

On Drummond Island
The sheltered bays offer good kayaking and canoeing. Rentals are available at **Arnold's Landing** (1-888-252-2650), **the Drummond Island Resort & Conference Center** (906-493-1000), **Drummond Island Yacht Haven** (906-493-5232), and **Fort Drummond Marine** (906-493-5471).

FISHING **Dream Seaker Charters & Tours** (1-888-634-3419; www.dreamseaker.com). Charter fishing trips and lake tours.

✳ Lodging

In Hessel
Hessel Bay Sunset Cabins (906-484-3913), 3347 W. Lake St., Hessel. The six cabins on Lake Huron have beach access and offer canoes and kayaks. The comfortable cabins feature full kitchens, two bedrooms, and a living room. There is a lake view from all cabins. The cabins are located near the west entrance of the Les Cheneaux Islands and are within walking distance of restaurants and shops in Hessel. Rates are $118 daily, $815 weekly.

Lindberg Cottages (906-484-2440; www.hesselbayresorts), Hessel. Open year-round. Located on the water-front, the 11 cottages have one to four bedrooms, fully equipped kitchens, coffee makers, microwaves, and grills. There is beach access. The wooden, North Woods–style cabins have plenty of room. No pets. Summer rates are $215 daily, $1,410 weekly.

In Cedarville
Spring Lodge Cottages (906-484-2282), Four Mile Block Rd. between Hessel and Cedarville. Open May–Oct. The 20 cottages overlook Snows Channel. There is a beach with a sandy bottom. It's an old school resort with a common room. The cabins come with cable TV, coffee mak-

ers, and microwaves, and are equipped to handle anglers. Rates are $650–$800 per week.

Les Cheneaux Landing (906-484-2558), Four Mile Block Rd., between Hessel and Cedarville. There are 11 sportsman–type cabins with log interiors. Boat rentals are available. Rates are $400–$775 per week.

BED & BREAKFAST

Les Cheneaux Inn (906-484-2007), 243 Hodeck St., Cedarville. Open May–Oct. Two second-floor rooms share a bath and sitting room in this older, remodeled home. Rates are $80–$90.

On Drummond Island

Y **Drummond Island Resort and Conference Center** (906-493-1000; www.drummondisland.com) 33494 S. Maxton Rd. The resort was built as the private refuge of Domino's Pizza chain owner Tom Monaghan in the 1980s, but has since gone public. The center is on 2,000 acres and offers 40 rooms in the log hotel and 30 one- to five-bedroom cottages with fireplaces and kitchens. Some have hot tubs. The center offers free kayaks, canoes, mountain bikes, cross-country skis, and snowshoes. Rates run $118–$154.

Fort Drummond Marine & Resort (906-493-5359; www.fortdrummond marine.com) 36183 S. Whitney Bay Rd. This is a boater's refuge, with five housekeeping cabins offering two, three, and four bedrooms. The orientation is lakefront, with neat, clean cabins and grills and fire pits on a sandy beach. It's a great stop on a boating trip in the island area. Rates run $400–$500 per week.

Lake View Resort (906-493-5241; www.lakeview.sault.com) 32033 E. Tourist Rd. Off a little-traveled road,

the Lake View offers eight modern cottages with a view of Potagannissing Bay. The rooms are clean and neat and offer kitchens. Boat rental is included in the price of a room and 7.5-, 10-, and 15-horsepower engines are available. The small resort is a family-type place run by Steve and Karen Kemppainen. It is a good place to let the kids roam while you relax by the water or do some fishing. Rates run $440 per week.

✳ Where to Eat

EATING OUT

In Hessel

Y **Hessel Bay Inn** (906-484-2460), 186 Pickford Ave., Hessel. Open daily for breakfast, lunch, and dinner, mid-April–Oct. This is where the locals eat. There is casual dining inside or on the deck. The menu runs from sandwiches to steak and seafood. Prices are $5–$20.

In Cedarville

Y **Snows of Les Cheneaux** (906-484-3370), MI 134, Cedarville. Open daily for breakfast, lunch, and dinner. Steak, Great Lakes fish, and Italian food are on the menu of this locals' place, with knotty pine paneling and murals. There is the traditional Friday fish fry. Prices are $5–$15.

Y **Fisher's Channel Marker** (906-484-2995), MI 134, Cedarville. Open late May–early Sept. The fare is steak, fish, pizza, and pasta in this spot near the Cedarville Harbor. Occasional entertainment. Prices are $8–$20.

Pammi's Restaurant (906-484-7844), corner of MI 134 and MI 129, Cedarville. Open daily for lunch and dinner. It's one of the few places that serves espresso and cappuccino coffees. For lunch there are wraps and portobello chicken, items not usually found around here. Dinners include a fish fry on Friday and local walleye. Prices are $5–$15.

On Drummond Island

Ÿ **Bayside Dining** (906-493-1014), Maxton and Tourist rds. Open late May–Sept. and weekends the rest of the year. Located at Drummond Island Resort (see *Lodging*), this full-service restaurant is your best bet on the island. There is whitefish, pasta, pork loin, and steaks on the menu, which also features appetizers. Prices are $10–$25.

Ÿ **Chuck's Place** (906-493-5480), Johnswood Rd., 6 miles east of Four Corners. Open daily. The folks who live here come in year-round. It's the local North Woods tavern with burgers, beer, and some entrees. Prices are $7–$15.

Ÿ **Bear Track Inn** (906-493-5090), Town Line Rd. between the village and Four Corners Rd. Open daily. This is the local gathering place for hearty breakfasts. Prices are $5–$8.

✳ Selective Shopping

The stores are open year-round unless otherwise noted.

Creekside Herbs & Art (906-484-2415), 752 North Blindline Rd., Cedarville. The arts and gardens merge here. There is a display gar-

den, regional and local contemporary art, herbal products, and gifts. Owners Wendy Wagoner and Tammy Patrick offer native Michigan plants and feature work by local crafts people, including hand-blown glass, jewelry, pottery, hand-turned wood bowls, and Native American art. The sweetgrass Christmas ornaments and birch-bark frames are especially attractive and have a Michigan feel.

BOOKSTORES **Safe Harbor Books** (906-484-3081; www.safe-harbor-books.com), 16 East Hwy. (MI 134), Cedarville. Open Mon.–Sun. This is a full-service shop that has best sellers, plus a good selection of local authors. Book signings are held during summer.

The Village Idiom (906-484-3533; www.villageidiom.net), MI 134, Hessel. Open daily, late May–early Sept. The store has second-hand books and many titles on fishing, hunting, and birding.

✳ Special Events

In Hessel

Early August Antique Wooden Boat Show & Festival of the Arts (www.leschenaux.org). Nearly 200 restored watercraft from as far away as California and Florida are on display, along with the works of local artists at the public marina in Hessel.

CENTRAL UPPER PENINSULA

NEWBERRY; GRAND MARAIS; MUNISING; MARQUETTE AREA, INCLUDING NEGAUNEE & ISHPEMING; BIG BAY; KEWEENAW PENINSULA; HOUGHTON & HANCOCK; CALUMET & LAURIUM; COPPER HARBOR & ISLE ROYALE NATIONAL PARK

Stretching along Lake Superior from Grand Marais to Munising, the Pictured Rocks National Lakeshore is the defining geographical feature of the region, and also the top tourist attraction.

Visitors drive County Road H-58 (CR H-58) from Grand Marais to Munising, stopping along the way to see such features as Miner's Castle, a rock formation, and the Log Slide, a place near Grand Marais where loggers once rolled timber into the lake and floated it to nearby mills.

The North Country Trail, which follows the Lake Superior shoreline, attracts backpackers and canoeists and kayakers who explore the Pictured Rocks. Campers make heavy use of the area, and anglers fish for coaster brook trout and other species in the big lake.

The other top attraction is the Seney National Wildlife Refuge, where bird-watchers walk the trails.

This is big country and it's sparsely populated, so I follow the half-tank rule: Never leave a town with less than a half tank of gas. There are stretches of 25 miles or more where you won't see a gas station.

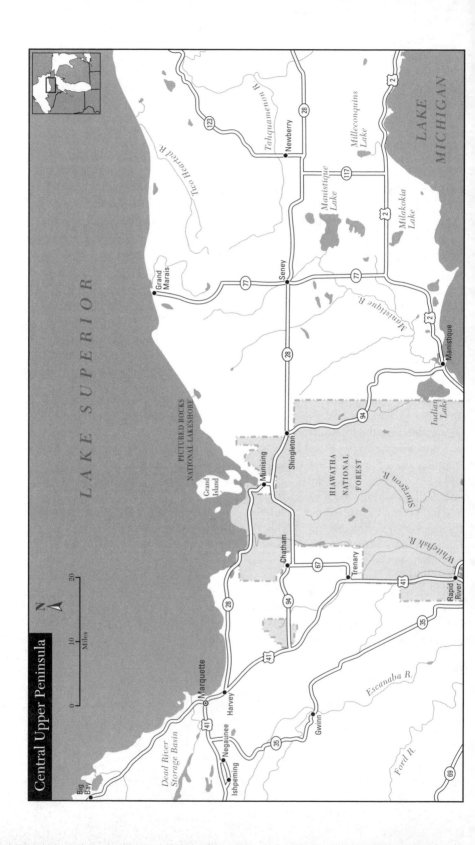

With a population of about 2,600, Newberry is the major town in the region and it's where many local residents come to shop. Tourism and prisons are major industries here. The state has a large correctional facility, which provides many local jobs. The town is also a jumping-off place for Tahquamenon Falls, a major tourist attract (see Paradise). The village was a major lumber baron headquarters in the 19th century, but it's now a sleepy little town with a few businesses. In the winter, it's a major destination for snowmobilers.

GUIDANCE **Newberry Area Chamber of Commerce** (906-293-5562; www .newberrychamber.net), corner of MI 28 and MI 123. Open daily, weekdays.

GETTING THERE *By car:* It's about a 1½-hour drive from the Mackinaw Bridge via I-75 to MI 123, and MI 28. The latter is a major east–west artery through the U.P.

✳ To See & Do

❧ **Tahquamenon Boat Service and Toonerville Trolley** (906-876-2311), 5883 CR 441, Newberry. Open May–Sept. The service offers boat trips to Tahquamenon Falls and rides through the woods on a narrow-gauge railroad.

❧ **Tahquamenon Logging Museum** (906-293-3700), MI 123, 1.5 miles north of Newberry. Open daily, May–Sept. A collection of logging-related exhibits from the region, including a replica of a logging camp kitchen.

In Seney
Seney National Wildlife Refuge (906-586-3800; www.fws.gov/Midwest/Seney/ Contact), 1674 Refuge Entrance Rd., Seney, off MI 77. Open May–Oct. The

ERNEST HEMINGWAY GOT OFF THE TRAIN AT THIS RAILROAD BRIDGE OVER THE FOX RIVER IN SENEY DURING THE TRIP ON WHICH HE BASED HIS FAMOUS SHORT STORY, "THE BIG TWO-HEARTED RIVER."

marsh area attracts birdwatchers from throughout the Midwest, and there are several trails and ponds where the birds land. The refuge was established in 1935 for the protection of migratory birds and other wildlife. Early in the 20th century developers tried to drain the area and sell it as farmland, but farming was impossible, and the land reverted to state ownership. Hiking, canoeing, hunting, and fishing are allowed on the refuge, which is one of the top tourist destinations in the U.P.

✳ Lodging

In Newberry

Falls Hotel (906-293-8621; www .fallshotel.com), 301 Newberry Ave., Newberry. The 25-room hotel, built in 1915, has been refurbished without losing its historic feel. The well-updated rooms have private baths and a suite is available. Rates are $60–$100.

Zellers Village Inn (906-293-5114), MI 123, Newberry. The accommodations in the 20-room motel are lush for this area. There are phones, air-conditioning, and cable TV, and the rooms are modern and clean. A decent family-style restaurant is located in the complex. Rates are $60.

BED & BREAKFAST The MacLeod House (906-293-3841), 6211 CR 441. The three-room B&B is in a restored 1898 Victorian home that's filled with antiques. The rooms have private baths. The innkeepers are Cheryl and Frank Cicala. It's one of the few such places in the region. No pets. Rates are $75–$105.

In Curtis

Chamberlin's Ole Forest Inn (906-586-6000; www.chamberlinsinn.com), Curtis. The inn was a hotel built for the railroad in the late 19th century and has been turned into one of the better restaurants in the region. The 12 guest rooms are clean and well furnished, and eight have private baths.

There is a hot tub in one suite. Rates are $130–$150.

At the Mouth of the Two-Hearted River

Rainbow Lodge (906-658-3357), 9706 CR 423. Located about 40 minutes north of Newberry, the lodge is pretty much all you'll find north of the village. There are six rooms in the motel and several cabins. It's pretty rustic; there's no power and the lodge makes its own with a wind generator. There is a small store, and the lodge offers canoe trips on the Two-Hearted River. Rates are $50–$60.

✳ Where to Eat

DINING OUT

In Curtis

⟨ Chamberlin's Ole Forest Inn (906-586-6000; www.chamberlinsinn .com), Curtis. Open daily for lunch and dinner. The inn has been a destination for years for many in the central U.P. It's one of the few fine-dining establishments to be found in the region. The menu has Michigan favorites such as steak, pasta, and chicken, along with Great Lakes fish. But there is also a breast of duckling. Appetizers include baked goat cheese with crabmeat and fried oysters. Rooms are available (see *Lodging*). Prices are $15–$25.

In Newberry

Y **Timber Charlies** (www.timber charlies.com), 110 Newberry Ave., Newberry. Open for breakfast, lunch, and dinner daily. This classic North Woods tavern serves up big burgers, steaks, chicken, and ribs for sportsmen and women who have spent their days in the woods. Prices are $6–$15.

Y **Falls Hotel** (906-293-8621; www .fallshotel.com), 301 Newberry Ave., Newberry. This place has been cleaned up and refurbished, and it's a relief to see it doing better. It had fallen on hard times. The hotel is a community landmark, built in 1915. Rooms are available (see *Lodging*). The food is standard northern Michigan fare: steak, lake fish, and chicken, along with burgers and other pub food. Prices are $10–$15.

GRAND MARAIS

There are no traffic lights, fast-food places, coffee shops, Internet cafés, chain hotels, or specialty shops in this end-of-the-road town of 300 on the shores of Lake Superior. It serves as a jumping-off spot for people exploring the nearby Pictured Rocks National Lakeshore. You'll find one gas station, two grocery stores, three taverns, and a few small family-owned motels and cabins.

Commercial fishing and logging were the principal industries that brought people to Grand Marais in the late 19th century, and the town hit its peak population of about a thousand in 1900. A railroad ran 25 miles south to Seney, connecting the community with the outside world, but by 1911 the pine was gone and the lumber industry departed, taking the railroad with it. The population declined to about 200, until MI 77 was built to Seney. By the 1930s, a few tourist cabins started to appear, but tourism didn't fully bloom until 1957 when the Mackinac Bridge opened.

Life revolves around "the Bay," as locals call it, and along Lake Avenue, an extension of MI 77, where most businesses are located. When you ask directions, people simply point to where you want to go.

In the summer, anglers, campers, hikers, backpackers, birdwatchers, bicyclists, canoeists, and kayakers are drawn to the 67,000-acre Pictured Rocks National Lakeshore, which stretches 30 miles along Lake Superior from just west of Grand Marais to Munising.

This is open country. The state and federal governments own most of the land, so it's open to the public unless posted. If you have the time and inclination, and four-wheel drive, try one of the many two-track dirt roads that lead into the woods. You'll find solitude.

✳ To See & Do

Historic Walking Tour. Pick up a booklet entitled *"Promenade Through the Past"* for $1 at the Bayshore Market and follow the guided historic walking tour of Grand Marais. The first stop is the best—the Pickle Barrel House, which was

A PERFECT DAY IN GRAND MARAIS

8:00 AM. Coffee and a homemade muffin with friends at the West Bay Diner and Delicatessen. Buy sandwiches to take out for the day's activities.

9:30 AM. Spend the morning paddling Grand Sable Lake looking for eagles, beaver, and sandhill cranes.

Noon. A shore lunch on Grand Sable Lake.

1:00 PM. Spend time on the Lake Superior beach at Grand Marais Harbor, swimming and watching sailboats.

3:00 PM. Bicycle ride through Grand Marais to see the 19th-century homes.

5:00 PM. Fly-fish the Sucker River for rainbow trout.

8:00 PM. Grill whitefish for dinner with friends at a picnic table at the cabin.

9:30 PM. Nightcap at the Lake Superior Brewing Co. and exchange stories with other tourists and locals.

11:00 PM. Watch the skies for the Northern Lights.

built in 1926 by William Donahey, creator of the Teenie Weenie children's characters featured in the comic strip he drew for the *Chicago Tribune.*

✲ **Au Sable Light Station** (906-494-2669; www.nps.gov/piro/), CR H-58, 12 miles west of Grand Marais. Tours daily, July–Sept., 12–4. Park at the Hurricane River Campground and walk about 1.5 miles east to the restored 1874 lighthouse built to warn Great Lakes sailors of the Au Sable Reef. A National Park Service guide/historian conducts tours and can describe the isolated lives of 19th-century lighthouse keepers. The keeper's quarters and light tower were restored by the Park Service and are furnished with period furniture, tools, and other articles. Shipwrecks can be seen along the beach. Admission is $2 for adults and $1 for children under 12.

✲ **Gitche Gumee Agate and History Museum** (906-494-2590; www.agate lady.com), E21739 Brazel St., Grand Marais. Open July–Aug., Mon.–Sat., 2–8. The museum, run by Karen Brzys, is filled with an eclectic mix of local history and agates and is a good first stop for visitors searching for agates along Lake Superior. The museum is next to a 33-foot-long fishing tug. Also on display are items used by lumberjacks and commercial fishermen in the 19th and early 20th century. Admission is free.

✳ Outdoor Activities

CANOEING & KAYAKING Grand Sable Lake, CR H-58, 2 miles west of Grand Marais. Located in the Pictured Rocks National Lakeshore, this inland lake is free of most powerboat traffic. There is a well-hidden, unimproved boat launch that some local anglers are able to use for motorized craft, but for the most part it's used by kayakers and canoeists. A paddling trip around the lake takes about

MINER'S CASTLE IN THE PICTURED ROCKS NATIONAL LAKESHORE

four hours. The east shore has been home to sandhill cranes for the past several years. Beaver are active.

SWIMMING **Grand Marais Harbor,** MI 77 and CR H-58. The area offers a public beach with free changing facilities and rest rooms. The sandy harbor is shallow and needs to be dredged on occasion to ensure that boats can dock there, but because it's not deep, it offers warmer water to bathers than most U.P. beaches. There are no lifeguards. Savvy local swimmers head a couple of miles east on CR H-58 to Cemetery Road, park at the road's end, and use the beach at the mouth of the Sucker River. The water is warmer here.

BICYCLING There is very little traffic in Grand Marais, making it a haven for cyclists. A sturdy mountain bike is more useful than a 10-speed because many of the roads are gravel and the two-track forest roads are dirt or sand. Try a ride out to Grand Marais Point, which is basically the end of MI 77. There is a Coast Guard station and several old fishing boats on the spit of land. There are no convenience stores outside of Grand Marais, so make sure to carry water. Also, bring extra tires, tubes, and a repair kit, as there are no bike shops in town.

FISHING Licenses are available at the Bay Shore Market on MI 77. A special stamp is required for catching trout in streams or in Lake Superior.
Captain Jim's Charter Boat (906-287-0545) offers fishing and sight-seeing trips on Lake Superior in the Grand Marais area from mid-April–October. Trips range from $390–$600. The boat is 25 feet long, and its owner, Captain Jim Lowry, is licensed by the Coast Guard. As of this edition, it was the only charter boat service offered out of Grand Marais.
Lake Superior offers angling for whitefish on the pier at the end of MI 77 on Grand Marais Point. June is the best month.

Grand Sable Lake, CR H-58 in the Pictured Rocks National Lakeshore, offers bass, pike, and lake trout.

Sucker River, CR H-58, east of Grand Marais. Despite its name, the small stream holds brook and rainbow trout for the angler. The stream is open to fly-fishing and bait and lure angling. Fall and spring offer steelhead and salmon runs. A Michigan fishing license with a trout stamp is required. Park near where the river crosses CR H-58 and try wading to the holes upstream and down. It's mostly public land.

❋ Lodging

There are no chain hotels or motels in Grand Marais, and no B&Bs, but there are many independent motels, cabin-style resorts, and homes available for rent. Many of the better cabins are booked a year ahead, with families returning to the same one each year, so call early. Unless otherwise noted, they're all open year-round.

MOTELS North Shore Lodge (906-494-2361; www.exploringthenorth .com/welkers/resort), 22020 Coast Guard Point, Grand Marais. Closed mid-March–mid-May. Located at the tip of the point, the lodge is the most complete resort in the area, offering 42 traditional motel rooms and house-keeping cabins. A full-service restaurant/bar offers breakfast, lunch, and dinner (see *Eating Out*). There is an indoor pool, sauna, and hot tub, but the real attraction is a large sandy beach on Lake Superior that's within walking distance. Some rooms have a lake view, others a bay view. The rooms are clean and comfortable and offer cable TV. Rates are $80–$100.

CABINS ✂ ❀ Hilltop Cabins and Motel (906-494-2331; www.exploring thenorth.com/hilltopgm/cabins), N 14176 Ellen St. near CR H-58. About a half-mile east of the center of town, this family-owned complex offers a five-unit motel with kitchenettes and eight housekeeping cabins. The owners, John and Jeanette Bauknecht, have renovated many of the rooms and have added a new three-bedroom log cabin that overlooks Lake Superior. There is a deck, picnic tables, grills for cooking, and a fire pit for evening campfires. Both John and Jeanette know the area and are willing to share information. The rooms don't have phones or Internet access, but if you need to make a call or want to check your e-mail, just ask and they'll be happy to let you use their computer or phone. Rates are $65–$150.

Sunset Cabins (906-494-2693), off CR H-58 on Lake Superior, east of Grand Marais. These are quintessential Up North cabins with beach access and a view of Lake Superior. Many of the cabins have been hand-crafted by the owner, Craig Winnie, and are mostly wood paneled. It's a quiet location off the main road, with plenty of room to roam. Call early for reservations because the small resort tends to attract the same people yearly, and sometimes there are no vacancies. The five cabins sleep up to six and come with kitchens, TV, and laundry facilities. Rates are $100–$125 per night, or $660–$750 weekly.

❋ Where to Eat

EATING OUT There are few options in Grand Marais, and all are listed here.

☿ **Lake Superior Brewing Co.**
(906-494-2337), 14283 Lake Ave.,
Grand Marais. Open daily. This traditional North Woods brewpub is filled
with animal mounts and examples of
cut agate rocks from the Lake Superior beaches. The brewpub is the
source of handcrafted beer (try the
Puddingstone Light) and burgers and
pizza, and also local information.
Strike up a conversation at the bar,
and there's no telling to whom you
may be talking—an artist, poet, a sci-
entist working in the nearby Pictured
Rocks National Lakeshore, or a lum-
berjack who has spent the day in the
woods. The menu occasionally moves
above tavern fare, and whitefish,
steak, and chicken dinners are
offered. The tavern was called the
Dunes Saloon for many years and
many people still refer to it by that
name. Prices are $10–$15.

☿ **North Shore Lodge** (906-494-
2361; www.exploringthenorth
.com/welkers/resort). 22020 Coast
Guard Point. Open mid-May–mid-
March. It closes at the end of the
snowmobile season and reopens in
May. This is the closest thing Grand
Marais has to a full-service eating
establishment, and it's the only place
in town offering breakfast, lunch, and
dinner. The crowd is mostly made up
of tourists staying at the motel/cabin
resort (see *Lodging*). The fare is fairly
standard for breakfast and lunch, but
in the evenings try the whitefish if it's
on the menu. There is still one commercial fisherman plying his trade in
the area, and his fresh fish is often
offered. Prices are $10–$15.

West Bay Diner (906-494-2647),
Veteran Ave., Grand Marais. Open
daily for breakfast and lunch. The
restored diner is one of the few places

for breakfast in town and features
home-baked breads and rolls and
skillet-style breakfast dishes. Prices
are $5–$8.

The Bay Shore Market, on Lake
Ave., offers basic items, such as meat,
vegetables, canned goods, and beer,
wine, and liquor. The wine selection
in the U.P. can be thin, but the market does offer a few decent wines
with a cork. Don't laugh. Some don't.
It also carries charcoal for grills.
Hours run 7 AM–11 PM.

IGA Market, on Lake Ave., offers a
full selection of meats, cheeses, fresh
vegetables, pasta, and most basic
canned goods. There is often a selection of crusty breads, but it varies
from day to day. This is an end-of-the-
road town and delivery trucks don't
always makes stops, so stores can be
out of certain items. There is a decent
selection of wines, beers, and liquors.
Hours run 7 AM–9 PM.

✳ **Selective Shopping**
Campbell Street Gallery (906-494-
2252; www.maevecroghan.com) 14281
Campbell St. Open various hours,
May–Oct.; call first. The gallery is
housed in the oldest commercial
building in Grand Marais, an 1883

LAKE SUPERIOR BREWING COMPANY

two-story wood structure, and it's the only real art gallery in the area. It features oil paintings by artist Maeve Croghan, who owns the gallery, and works by others from around the globe. Croghan splits her time between Grand Marais and San Francisco, and her art reflects the landscapes of both places, plus Tuscany, Italy. Her work captures the colors and shapes found along the Lake Superior shoreline.

✳ Special Events

Mid-August Annual Music and Arts Festival (www.grandmarais .com). Live music is a rarity in Grand Marais, except during this event, which features blues, jazz, folk, bluegrass, and mountain music outside. There are arts and crafts booths, but the main focus is the music. This is usually the only weekend of the summer when it's difficult to find a room in town, so call ahead for reservations.

Mid-July Great Lakes Sea Kayak Symposium (www.GLSKS.org). Sponsored by the Great Lakes Sea Kayak Club, the annual event features techniques of sea kayaking, equipment use, regulatory issues, first aid, and great destinations. Classes are held at Grand Marais High School and in the harbor. There is a registration fee, and forms are available at the group's Web site.

MUNISING

There were early attempts at iron mining in Munising, but a large boom never materialized as it did to the west in Marquette, so this community sat quietly until the late 19th century when a town was eventually developed and became a logging center. A paper mill still employs many residents.

In summer, the town caters to outdoor people who hike and sightsee in the nearby Pictured Rocks National Lakeshore or take the boat trip along the lakeshore. The boat dock on Lake Superior is the busy place in town.

Don't expect much in the way of fine dining in Munising. It doesn't have the traffic needed to supply that clientele. Most restaurants are basic family-style restaurants catering to the crowds headed for boat trips and to those headed to Grand Island, which is a semi-nonmotorized national recreation area just west of town. Cyclists and hikers have this island, larger than the much-visited Mackinaw Island, all to themselves.

Also near Munising is the town of Christmas, which has its own post office, and people use it to mail their Christmas cards so they can be postmarked "Christmas."

Waterfalls and outdoor pursuits are common activities in the area, and snowmobiling is popular in the winter. Hikers and sightseers in the Pictured Rocks use Munising as a service town after long days in the woods.

GUIDANCE Munising Chamber of Commerce (906-387-2138; www.munising .com), MI 28 East, Munising. Open daily, weekdays. It's a good source of snowmobile maps and there are guides to the many nearby waterfalls.

WATERFALLS There are 17 waterfalls accessible via short walks in the Munising area. The **Munising Visitors Bureau's** Web site (www.munising.org) offers a look at them. Here is a short list of the best and easiest to see. **Alger Falls,** on the east side of MI 28, is just east of Munising. Visible from the road is **Chapel Falls,** located in the eastern portion of the Pictured Rocks National Lakeshore Park. **Miners Falls** is off CR H-58, which goes through the park. Take the Pictured Rocks Trails to see **Memorial Falls,** a small waterfall near Munising on CR H-58 just east of Munising Avenue. Turn right on Nestor and follow the signs to **Munising Falls** in town; follow MI 28 to Sand Point Road, head north, and watch for signs.

SHIPWRECK TOURS **Shipwreck Tours** (906-387-4477), 1204 Commercial St., Munising. Open June–Oct. The Alger Underwater Diving Preserve offers sights of long sunken ships and diving tours in the 113-square-mile state preserve. The clear waters of Lake Superior offer good views of the ships that lie on the bottom, the oldest of which sank in 1856. Capt. Peter Lindquist offers the boat tours, and also diving tours to six wrecks. The dive shop offers air service and scuba rentals. There are morning, afternoon, and night dives. Rates are $27 for adults, $11 for children under 12, and free for children under 5.

Pictured Rocks Cruises (906-387-2379; www.picturedrocks.com), Munising City Pier. Open daily, late May–mid-Oct. Over the years I've hiked and canoed along the Pictured Rocks and have realized that a boat tour is the best way to see the grandeur of the weathered rocks along Lake Superior. The nearly three-hour cruise takes you on a 37-mile trip past Lovers Leap, Grand Portal, Miner's Castle, and Indian Head. The evening cruise is probably the best, with the sun

PICTURED ROCKS NATIONAL LAKESHORE

GRAND ISLAND

Hiawatha National Forest Service Visitor Information Center (906-387-2512; www.fs.fed.us/r9/forests/hiawatha/recreation/hiking/grand-island-trail/ index), west of Munising, off MI 28, at the end of Grand Island Landing Road. This is a 13,500-acre haven for cyclists, who can follow a 23-mile trail around the island, and for kayakers who want to spend the day paddling in Lake Superior. The beaches range from sandy to 300-feet-high, wave-cut sandstone cliffs. The island was settled in 1846 as a trading post for the Ojibway Indians and has escaped major development, but there are private landowners and some vehicle traffic. Much of the island is accessible only by foot or bicycle. The trails are maintained to low standards, so expect rough riding. For canoeists and kayakers, the island is only a half-mile from shore, and the route is protected from the rougher Lake Superior waves by the island. There are 17 designated campsites, most along the shoreline. The island is a great destination for a multiday kayak or canoe trip. Bring water, as there is only one hand pump at Murray Bay and surface water must be boiled before drinking. Fishing, hunting, and trapping are allowed. A bus tour around the southern portion of the island is run by the **Grand Island Ferry Service** (906-387-3503; www.grandislandmi.com/tours) from mid-June–Labor Day. The service also runs the daily boat service to the island from late May–early Oct. During the winter, the island is open to snowmobiling. Rentals are available at **Grand Island Sled Rentals** (906-387-2772), Munising.

setting on the rocks. Cost is $30 for adults, $13 for children 6–12, and free for children under 5.

Skylane Pictured Rocks & Grand Island Air Tours (906-387-5611; www .exploringthenorth.com/air/air), P.O. Box 544, Munising. The tours are by special arrangement and include flights over the Pictured Rocks and Grand Island Recreation Area, with views of the lighthouse and shipwrecks.

✳ Lodging

Establishments are open year-round unless otherwise noted.

☙ Alger Falls Cottage (906-387-3536; www.algerfallsmotel.com), E9427 MI 28, Munising. Open year-round. The two-bedroom cabin near the Pictured Rocks National Lakeshore sleeps up to six people and has a fully equipped kitchen, dining area, and comfortable living area. The bath has a tub and shower. There is an adjoining motel, but the cottage is nested in the woods and away from the comings and goings at the motel. It's close to Alger Falls and near snowmobile trails. Rates are $47–$68.

MOTELS Terrace Motel (906-387-2754), 420 Prospect, Munising. The

18-room motel is two blocks from MI 28, the major artery, and offers a quiet place. There is a sauna and an indoor repair area for snowmobiles. Rates are $36–$55.

Sunset Motel on the Bay (906-387-4574), 1315 Bay St., Munising. Basic motel units with a view of Lake Superior and beach access. Some rooms have knotty pine paneling and refrigerators and microwaves. Rates are $50–$60.

✳ Where to Eat

EATING OUT These establishments are open year-round unless otherwise noted.

The Navigator (906-387-1555), 101 E. Munising Ave., Munising. Open daily. The family-style restaurant serves breakfast, lunch, and dinner. There are homemade soups and full meals, with daily specials, including whitefish and steak. It's close to the dock for the Pictured Rocks boat tours. Prices are $8–$12.

Υ **Dogpatch** (906-387-9948; www .dogpatch.com). Open daily. If you can get past the name, this is a decent restaurant for this area, serving fish, steaks, chicken, pizza, burgers, and a breakfast buffet. You're going to find more on the menu here than at most places in this area. Prices are $8–$15.

MARQUETTE AREA, INCLUDING NEGAUNEE & ISHPEMING

With 1,841 square miles, Marquette is the largest county in Michigan. It is also the most populous area in the Upper Peninsula, with 64,634 residents. It serves as the unofficial capital of the U.P. and has a major university, along with a major regional hospital and other commercial services.

You can spend the day on a trout stream, hiking a backwoods trails, or kayaking in Lake Superior and not see another person, but by evening you can be having cocktails on the sixth-floor penthouse lounge of the Landmark Hotel.

This blend of semiwilderness with the urban landscape of the city of Marquette has helped place the community on the state list of "cool cities." In the winter, there is cross-country skiing and snowmobiling, and in warmer months, mountain biking and kayaking. Add Northern Michigan University and a revived downtown to the mix, and you have an enjoyable place to spend some time.

The region's roots are in iron ore, which is still mined. The ore was discovered in the 1840s, and mines sprung up in the surrounding communities of Negaunee, Ishpeming, Palmer, and Gwinn. Marquette became the shipping point for the ore, and you can still watch Great Lakes ore freighters being loaded in Lake Superior.

Winter is a special season in Marquette. It receives about 170 inches of snow annually and is one of the most populated cities in the nation with that much of the white stuff. There are downhill ski slopes nearby, and countless trails for cross-country skiing or snowshoeing. Also, there are hundreds of miles of snowmobile trails in the area and numerous lakes for ice fishing.

DOWNTOWN MARQUETTE

For some movie buffs, Marquette will have a familiar look, because it was the setting for the 1959 movie, *Anatomy of a Murder*, with Jimmy Stewart and Lee Remick. The Marquette County Courthouse, where the court scenes were filmed, is still in use, as is the tavern at the Thunder Bay Inn in nearby Big Bay, which was built by the director, Otto Preminger, for use in the movie. Legend has it that the director didn't think the inn had enough of a woodsy look, so he had the pine-paneled tavern built for filming scenes.

GUIDANCE **Marquette Country Convention & Visitors Bureau** (1-800-544-4321; www.marquettecountry.org), 337 West Washington St., Marquette. Open Mon.–Fri.

Marquette County Chamber of Commerce (906-226-6591; www.marquette.org), Ishpeming office (906-484-4841), 610 Palms, inside the U.S. National Ski Hall of Fame. Open Mon.–Fri.

MEDIA *The Marquette Mining Journal* (906-228-2500; www.miningjournal.net), 249 W. Washington, Marquette, is the largest daily paper in the Upper Peninsula, and it provides information about the city and the region.

Marquette Monthly (www.mmnow.com) is a delightful small free publication with lots of listings of regional events.

GETTING THERE *By car:* Marquette is pretty much at the east/west center of the U.P., on MI 28, which is one of only two main routes through the region. Apart from a short stretch of I-75 between St. Ignace and Sault Ste Marie, there are no other limited access roads. The only major road running east/west is US 2.

By plane: **Sawyer International Airport,** Gwinn, is less than 30 minutes from Marquette and is the major airport in the U.P., offering connecting flights to Chicago and Detroit.

By bus: **Greyhound Bus Lines** service the Upper Peninsula. The station is at 145 West Spring St., Marquette (906-228-8393).

STAYING CONNECTED NPR Radio (www.wnmu.publicbroadcasting.net). Northern Michigan University in Marquette is the major source for public broadcasting in the Upper Peninsula. It's at 90 FM. Other communities that broadcast the station in the U.P. are: Escanaba, 107.1 FM; Manistique, 91.9 FM; Menominee, 91.3 FM; Newberry, 107.3 FM; and Stephenson, 107.3 FM.

Ishpeming Carnegie Public Library (906-486-4381; www.uproc.lib.mi.us/ ish/) 317 N. Main St., Ishpeming. Open Mon.–Sat. This early 20th century building is worth seeing for the structure alone. Internet service is available.

The Peter White Public Library (906-228-9510; www.uproc.lib.mi.us), 217 North Front St., Marquette. Open daily. A $9 million renovation of the 1904 Beaux Arts building has left the feel intact but has turned the building into a modern information center. Travelers needing to check their e-mail will find the library a haven.

WHEN TO COME The best months for outdoor activities are June through September, but beware of the black flies in late June. September and October can provide some of the best weather, and the opportunity to see fall foliage. As with most of Michigan, avoid March and April.

THE MARQUETTE COURTHOUSE

MEDICAL EMERGENCY Marquette General Hospital (906-228-9440; 580 W. College Ave., Marquette. This is the largest hospital in the U.P. Call 911.

VILLAGES Ishpeming and **Negaunee** are old iron mining towns off MI 28 about 10 miles west of Marquette. They offer a glimpse of what life was like for miners in the 19th century. Marquette has morphed into a 21st-century, tourist-orientated college town, but the Ishpeming and Negaunee area has held onto its mining roots; there are still two iron ore mines nearby where many residents work. The towns developed around the mines, and Ishpeming has held the upper hand since the early 20th century, when about half of Negaunee was abandoned because underground mining made the ground unstable. Iron ore was first mined in the region in Negaunee in 1845 from the Jackson Mine, which eventually closed in the 1940s. The Cliffs Mine was established in 1867 and operated until 1967. These days it's a museum, but for 100 years it was the major employer and attracted thousands of European immigrants in search of work.

✷ To See & Do

Northern Michigan University (1-800-882-9797; www.nmu.edu). Tours of the campus are available upon request. However, the focal point of the school is the U.S. Olympic Education Center, which is one of only four such training centers in the country. It is located on the campus.

🏷 **The Superior Dome** (906-227-2850; www.nmu.edu), Marquette. It is on the campus of Northern Michigan University and is the world's largest wooden dome. Opened in 1991, it was built with 781 Douglas fir beams and 108.5 miles of fir decking. At a height equal to a 14-story building, it's part of the Marquette skyline.

"Anatomy of a Murder" tour brochure, available from the Marquette Country Convention & Visitors Bureau (906-228-7749; www.marquettecounty.org), 337 West Washington St.

🏷 **Marquette County History Museum** (906-226-3571), 213 North Front St. Open June–Aug, Mon.–Fri. The museum embraces the region's Yooper heritage with a special exhibit on what it means to be a Yooper. Photos, items used in the U.P., and stories are part of the display. Photos are well used to help tell the story of the wealth created by iron mining in the area during the 19th century. Admission is $3 for adults and $1 for students over 12.

🏷 **Marquette Maritime Museum** (906-226-2006; www.mqtmaritimemuseum .com), 300 Lakeshore Blvd. Open May–Oct., Mon.–Sun, 10–5. Housed in the old City Waterworks building, constructed of the distinctive local red sandstone, the museum keeps the shipping heritage of the region alive with its displays of lighthouse lenses from the region and displays of shipping-related items.

🏷 **Upper Peninsula Children's Museum** (906-226-3911; www.upcmkids.org), 123 E. Baraga Ave. Open year-round, daily. This is a hands-on museum where kids can climb around an airplane and giant heads and slide through an intestine. There are also informational programs. Admission: $20 per family or $4 per adult and $4.50 per child.

In Ishpeming

❦ **U.S. National Ski Hall of Fame and Museum** (906-485-6323; www.ski hall.com), 610 Palms, Ishpeming. Open Mon.–Sat., 10–5. The Scandinavians who came to the area in the 19th century to work in the iron mines brought their love and knowledge of skiing with them, making the area a hotbed for the sport. About 100 years ago, a group of area business people and skiers formed the National Skiing Association, making Ishpeming the home of organized skiing in the U.S. The Hall of Fame was established in 1954 and honors more than 350 skiers in the 20,000-square-foot building. There are also exhibits on the history of Nordic and alpine skiing.

❦ **Michigan Iron Industry Museum** (906-475-7857; www.michigan.gov), 73 Forge Rd., Negaunee. Open daily, May–Oct. The museum over the Carp River is on the site of the first iron forge in the Upper Midwest, the Jackson Iron Co., which made wrought iron from 1848–1855 from local ore. While the company eventually failed, other mines took over and iron ore is still produced in the area to this day. The 4,000-square-foot museum offers displays that depict the early years of iron mining. Admission is free.

❦ **Cliffs Shaft Mining Museum** (906-485-1882; www.me.mtu.edu), 501 W. Euclid St., Ishpeming. Open May–Sept., Tues.–Sat, 10–4. The iron mine was in operation from 1867 to 1967, and the buildings and equipment are being restored to give visitors a look at how mining operations were done during that era.

👕 ❦ **Negaunee Historical Museum** (906-475-4614; www.negauneehistory com), 303 E. Main St., Negaunee. Open Mon.–Sun. This small, community-based museum is located in an older home and includes a collection of clothing, furniture, photos, and other items from the 19th and early 20th centuries. An old dentist's chair doesn't look inviting. Admission: $3 for adults and $1 for children.

GAMBLING 🍸 **Ojibwa Casino** (1-800-560-9905 or 906-249-4200; www.ojibwa casino.com) 105 Acre Trail, Marquette. Open year-round, the gambling casino is one of numerous ones owned by Native American tribes in Michigan. It offers slot machines and table games. The casino runs an RV park for lodging and offers shuttle buses to area motels. There is a small snack bar and a gift shop that offers items made by Native Americans.

✳ Outdoor Activities

With an average of 170 inches of snow, Marquette County is a popular destination for snowmobilers. Local communities throughout the U.P. maintain trails. There are hundreds of miles of trails in the Marquette region, and maps can be obtained at the **Marquette County Convention & Visitors Bureau** (1-800-544-4321 or 906-228-7749; www.marquettecountry.org), 337 W. Washington, Marquette. At the bureau's Web site, there is a list of local businesses that rent snowmobiles.

GOLFING **Chocolay Golf Club** (906-249-3111; www.chocolaydownsgolf course.com), 125 Downs Dr. The 18-hole, par-72 course boasts a 29,000-square-foot putting green.

Gentz's Homestead Golf Course (906-249-1002), 353 Gentz Rd. A 9-hole, par-36 course.

Red Fox Run (906-346-7010), 217 Fifth St., Gwinn. An 18-hole, par-70 course.

Wawonowin Country Club (906-485-5660), 3432 CR 478, Champion. An 18-hole, par-72 course.

Greywalls Golf Course (906-225-0721; www.marquettefolgclub.com), 1075 Grove St. Greywalls is part of the Marquette Country Club and offers views of Lake Superior and the Pictured Rocks.

FISHING Lake Superior offers fishing for salmon, lake trout, whitefish, steelhead, and splake. Also, there are hundreds of inland lakes in the Marquette area that offer angling for panfish, bass, trout, muskie, northern pike, perch, and walleye. Rivers such as the Yellow Dog, Escanaba, and Laughing Whitefish offer prime fly-fishing. A good start for information is the state Department of Natural Resources, which has three offices in the region: Marquette (906-228-6561; www.michigan.gov/dnr), Ishpeming (906-485-1031), and Gwinn (906-346-9201).

HUNTING The Upper Peninsula, with thousands of acres of public land, offers hunting for deer, grouse and woodcock, turkey, waterfowl, and small game. Licenses are required and can be obtained at outdoor-related businesses and online at the state Department of Natural Resources Web site (www.michigan.gov/dnr).

BICYCLING *Bike Magazine* rated Marquette a top city nationally for biking in 2001, and for good reason. The Lake Superior shoreline, which was once the site of iron ore shipping, has been turned over to walkers and cyclists. The shoreline trail runs through the city, giving the cyclist a Lake Superior view the entire way. There is also a 3.6-mile loop on Presque Isle Park, which is along the route. Most of the beach areas along the route are public, and there are rest room facilities along the way. Traffic is light on most days in Marquette, and a bicycle is a good way to see the downtown area and harbor.

MOUNTAIN BIKING Michigan has done a good job of developing mountain bike trails in the state. The Marquette area is no exception. Try these areas: Harlow Lake, Sugarloaf, Hogsback Trail Systems, Presque Isle, Bog Walk, Vandenbom Nature Trail, and the Elliot Donney and McCormick Wilderness Tracts. The DNR office in Marquette is a good place to find trail maps and general information.

DOWNHILL SKIING **Marquette Mountain** (906-225-1155; www.marquette mountain.com), 4501 MI 533, Marquette. The ski resort offers one of the highest vertical drops in the Midwest, with an elevation of 1,357 feet. With ample snowfall, the resort averages 135 ski days a year.

CROSS-COUNTRY SKIING Marquette has nearly a dozen marked cross-country ski trails and ample snowfall, making it a destination for Nordic fans. Skiing is free unless otherwise noted.

Al Quall Recreation Area (906-486-6181 or 906-485-4332), Ishpeming. Groomed trails and toboggan rentals.

Anderson Lake Trail (906-346-9201), Escanaba River State Forest, off CR 557.

Blueberry Ridge Trails (906-485-1031), near CR 480 and CR 553. Groomed loops on a state pathway.

Kawbawgam Ski Trail (906-249-1448), Chocolay Township, MI 28, Kawbawgam Rd. A 1.5-mile beginner loop and a more difficult 3.9-mile loop around Lake Le Vasseur.

Maple Lane Ski Area (906-485-1636), off US 41 in Skandia, 15 miles west of Marquette at Maple Lane Farm off Kreiger Drive.

Marquette City Fit Strip (906-228-0460), on Seymour St. near Washington, Marquette. This trail is in the city and offers two loops, a 1.7 km. beginner and a 1.5 km. intermediate. The route is groomed for skating and diagonal stride.

Negaunee Community Center Ski Trail and Kivela Road Trail (906-475-7869), Kivela Rd., off US 41, Negaunee. A series of groomed trails.

Presque Isle Park (906-228-0460), Lakeshore Blvd., Marquette. There are a series of groomed trails in this Marquette city park on an island in Lake Superior.

✳ Lodging

The Landmark Inn (906-228-2580 or 1-888-752-6362; www.thelandmark inn.com), 230 N. Front St., Marquette. This elegant 62-room hotel is a real find in the U.P., especially after a few days in the woods. It's one of only a few U.P. hotels with a decent lobby and also boasts a penthouse cocktail lounge with a view of Lake Superior. The hotel opened in the 1930s, but by the early 1980s it was in decline and it closed in 1982. It was restored and reopened in 1997 by Christine Pesola, who owns and runs the hotel. Rates are $125–$269.

The Nordic Bay Lodge (1-800-892-9376 or 906-226-7516; www.nordic bay.com), 1880 US 41 S., Marquette. The 43-room lodge is the place to stay for those attuned to outdoor activities. The complex was built by Austrian natives Sepp and Annemarie Hoedlmoser and opened in 1966. The Austrian-style chalet buildings on 12 acres offer hiking and mountain biking and kayaking on nearby Lake Superior in the warm months, and snowshoeing and cross-country skiing in the winter months. This a great place to take a group or a large family because there are a number of accommodation options, ranging from a bunkroom with four beds to single and double rooms. Rates are $95.

Blueberry Ridge B&B (906-249-9246), 18 Oakridge Dr. The traditional B&B has three rooms and is furnished with comfortable homemade quilts and antiques. There is a large stone fireplace, and breakfast is served on fine china. Rates are $100.

COTTAGES **Johnson's Cottage on the Bay** (906-228-4569), 525 Erie Ave. The two-bedroom cottage is a great place for a family to stay, with queen beds and air mattresses for the kids. The kitchen is fully equipped and there's a deck and outdoor grill. It's not fancy and the décor is decidedly cottage, but it's a good alternative to a motel room. Rates: $150 per day, $875 per week.

MOTELS The U.P. isn't exactly a destination for upscale travelers, so there aren't a lot of mid to high-end places. **Cedar Motor Inn** (1-888-551-7378 or 906-228-2280), 2523 US 41 W., Marquette. This 43-room motel on the outskirts of Marquette is just the place to reorganize after camping. It has cable TV and wireless Internet access so you can check your e-mail. There are even housekeeping rooms with refrigerators and microwaves for snowmobilers and anglers on longer stays. Rates are $50.

In Ishpeming/Negaunee
Negaunee Union Station Depot Lodge (906-475-7939; www.union stationdepot.com), 212 Gold St., Negaunee. This historic railroad depot, built in 1910, has been renovated into lodging for travelers and can hold up to eight guests. The facility has kitchen service and can be rented by large groups. Rates range from $150–$175.

MOTELS **Best Western Country Inn** (1-800-528-1234 or 906-485-6345), 850 US 41, Ishpeming. The 60-room hotel is the largest in Ishpeming and offers travelers the basic modern inn experience with large rooms and an indoor pool. It's the kind of place where you can sprawl out and let the kids run around, so don't look for a lot of ambience. Rates run about $90.

Jasper Ridge Inn (906-485-2378), 1000 River Parkway. This newer hotel offers a variety of rooms, including whirlpool suites, and is adjacent to the Jasper Ridge Restaurant. The inn offers clean basic rooms for travelers. Snowmobilers can park their machines here and also ride into the surrounding area. This isn't the type of inn with a lot of atmosphere; it's a basic hotel. The focus here is on outdoor activities, and this is just a place to crash after a hard day outside. Rates are $60–$100.

Wonderland Motel (906-485-1044), 873 Palms Ave., Ishpeming. A mom-and-pop motel, it offers 11 rooms and a free continental breakfast. Although the rooms are small, it's a roof over your head and a hot shower. Rates are $50–$60.

RENTALS **Jasper Ridge Vacation Homes** (906-485-2378 or 1-866-875-4312; www.countryvillageresort.org), 850 US 41, Ishpeming. There are four homes for rent, most of which accommodate six to eight people and have 800 to 1,300 square feet of living space. All have decks. This is a great destination for a snowmobiling group or for several large families. Rates are $126 daily, $800 weekly.

✳ Where to Eat

DINING OUT ♈ **Vierling Restaurant & Marquette Harbor Brewery** (906-228-3533; www.thevierling.com) 119 S. Front St., Marquette. This brewpub offers pub food, but also fine dining in a casual atmosphere in a historic building. There has been a saloon/restaurant at this site for more than 100 years. The building received a facelift in the mid-1980s when its current owners, Kristi and Terry

Doyle, took over, but it still has an 1890s feel. The beer is made on site. The red ales were excellent, and there is a decent wine list. The local white-fish dishes are a real find after a day of U.P. road food, which typically consists of burgers and pizza. Entrees are $12–$20.

EATING OUT ⵚ **The Sweetwater Café** (906-226-7009; www.sweet watercafe.org), 517 N. 3rd St., Marquette. Open daily, 8–8. This place has all the bases covered with its bakery, restaurant, and bar. Breakfast here is a treat, with its freshly baked bread and other baked goods. The French toast is a great bet in the morning. Lunches with homemade soup, salads, and sandwiches are a welcome respite after a morning on the road. There is a small bar area, but it's not the type of place you'd want to spend an evening.

In Ishpeming/Negaunee
The Ishpeming/Negaunee area is fairly rustic, and there are no fine-dining restaurants. But a few places do offer decent food at reasonable prices. All are open year-round unless otherwise noted.

ⵚ **Jasper Ridge Brewery and Restaurant** (906-485-6017), 1035 Country Ln., Ishpeming. Open daily, 11–2. Ribs, steaks, chicken, and beer brewed on the premises are the staples here. The pub food is nothing special and you won't find fresh fish on the menu, but it's a good place for a hearty meal after a day in the woods. Also, it's the only brewpub around until you get to Marquette, about 15 miles away.

Country Kitchen (906-486-1074), 850 US 41, Ishpeming. Open daily. Most folks are in the area for outdoor

pursuits, and breakfast is a good start for the day. This family restaurant is the place to go for a moderately priced one. There is a salad bar during lunch and dinner hours. Burgers are large, but there are also homemade soups. Prices are under $10.

ⵚ **Congress Pizza** (906-486-4233), 106 N. Main St., Ishpeming. Open daily. This tavern/restaurant is a local hangout for Ishpeming, and has a long history of serving up brick-oven baked pizza. The menu is limited to pizza, cudighi sandwiches, and pizza fries. Cudighi is a locally made Italian sausage flavored with nutmeg. They don't even have it in Italy, my server told me. It's a tangy, spicy sausage and well worth trying. The tavern's history reflects that of Ishpeming. It was founded in 1934 by A. Louis Bonetti, an Italian immigrant, who came to work in the area iron mines and opened the tavern after the repeal of Prohibition, naming it for the U.S. Congress because it had voted to end Prohibition. Everything went well until 1951, when in the words of hometown writer John Voelker, author of *Anatomy of a Murder*, "A bullet from a deer rifle unerringly found its way into Louie's belly, he had been mistaken for a deer." The founder died the next morning, but his sons, Guido and Geno, carried on and kept the place going. Paul Bonetti now runs the Congress. Prices are $5–$10.

✳ **Selective Shopping**
Unless otherwise noted, all shops are open year-round.

Art U.P. Style (906-226-6154), 153A West Washington St., downtown Marquette. An art gallery with gifts, the shop features a series of prints of local landmarks, done by regional artists.

Eclectique Atelier (906-226-6649), 147 West Washington St., downtown Marquette. Local artist Catherine Brunet holds forth here with her collection of watercolors, mixed media, and oil paintings.

The Studio Gallery and Gifts (906-228-2466) 2905 Lake Shore Blvd. This small gallery features original paintings and prints, and there is a good selection of silver and gold jewelry. It's also the place to go for sculptures and contemporary home items.

BOOKSTORES Snowbound Books (906-228-4448; www.snowbound books.com), 118 N. Third St. Open Mon.–Sat. The shop isn't your typical college town bookstore. It's an independent bookstore presided over by Ray Nurmi, who opened the shop in 1984 with 10,000 used books, many of them his own. There are now more than 30,000 books, with a focus on Michigan, and the Upper Peninsula in particular. The collection ranges from novels by Jim Harrison and Marquette hometown favorite John Voelker, author of *Anatomy of a Murder,* to histories by local writers. **Chapter Two,** a part of Snowbound that stocks overruns, is nearby at 124 N. Third St. Open Mon.–Sat.

SPORTING GOODS Wilderness Sports Shop (906-485-4565), 107 E. Division St., Ishpeming. Open daily. The shop is what sporting goods

DA YOOPER TOURIST TRAP & MUSEUM

Da Yooper Tourist Trap & Museum (906-485-5595; www.dayoopers.com), 490 N. Steel St., Ishpeming, west of Marquette on US 41, south side of highway. Open Mon.–Sun. At least they're honest about the place—it isn't a fine-gift shop. This throwback to the era of roadside attractions is filled with gag gifts that portray the life of so-called Yoopers, rustic locals who spend their days hunting deer and avoiding work and their nights drinking beer. Don't be put off by its junkyard looks. Outside you're met by Big Gus, the largest working chainsaw in the world. There is a plaque inside from the *Guinness Book of World Records* to say so. Other outside exhibits rely on outhouse humor and deer getting their revenge on deer hunters. This demented version of what it's like to be a Yooper is the creation of Jim "Hoolie" DeCaire. A personal favorite is the Yooper Quarter Pounder, a wood contraption with a hammer that pounds on a quarter. Some of the items may raise taste issues for parents with children. The shop features CD recordings by a locally well-known musical group, Da Yoopers, who produce comedy/musical numbers that exploit the Yooper character. Many of the songs are about deer camp, which is a tradition for many in the region. For newcomers to the U.P., it's a good place to get a handle on the quirky nature of Yooper culture.

stores used to be, a place that's jammed with equipment and outdoor clothing to help you enjoy nature. It's also a place that offers information about what to do and where to go in the area. Cross-country ski and snowshoe rentals are available.

Country Village Ace Hardware (906-485-1870), 1150 Country Ln., Ishpeming. This is the place to go for snowmobile rentals, trail information, and maps. A series of trails from here will take you deep into the nearby Huron Mountains, to Lake Superior, and into the surrounding countryside.

✴ Special Events

Late June Hiawatha Music Festival (906-226-8575; www.hiawatha music.org) Tourist Park, Marquette. This outdoor music and arts festival brings traditional music to the central Upper Peninsula.

Early August Art Faire & Renaissance Festival (e-mail: contact@ish peminggrenfest.com), Lake Bancroft Park, Ishpeming. Arts and crafts booths and Renaissance period entertainment are provided. The park is adjacent to the Cliff Shaft Mining Museum and close to Lake Bancroft.

BIG BAY

This is where Marquette folks go to get away from the city and spend weekends at their cottages on Lake Independence or strolling the Big Bay on the Lake Superior shoreline.

The town of 265 residents is at the end of Country Road 550 (CR 550) about 25 miles northwest of Marquette. Even during summer, there are few people here and you can bicycle or walk along the main streets without fear of traffic. There is one small gift shop, three places to eat at last count, and one general store/gas station. Those interested in quaint shops or trendy restaurants should head elsewhere.

The big attraction is the Huron Mountains, which offer opportunities for hiking, mountain biking, fishing, and hunting in warmer months, and snowmobiling and cross-country skiing in the winter. The mountain range is small by most standards, only rising to about 1,900 feet in elevation.

North of town is the exclusive Huron Mountain Club, with its Adirondack-style homes in a compound that's off-limits to all but its membership, which reads like a who's who of the Midwest. There are 50 rustic homes on its 20,000 acres in the Huron Mountains. Henry Ford and his descendants have been members, but because it's private and exclusive, there's no public membership list. It was so exclusive that Henry Ford had trouble joining in the 1920s, and Big Bay actually remains off the beaten track today because of his efforts to join. At the time, the state wanted to build a major road, MI 35, along the Lake Superior shoreline through the Huron Mountains, but club members were opposed. Ford saw his opportunity and bought property along the proposed route and opposed the road-building efforts. He was successful, and eventually was able to join the club in the late 1920s.

Ford also bought a lumber mill and the landmark Thunder Bay Inn, which was used in the filming of *Anatomy of a Murder* in 1959 and is still open today. Ford eventually sold the inn and the lumbering operation was turned into a bowling pin factory.

The mountains are characterized by steep slopes and rocky ledges. County Road 510 (CR 510) from near Big Bay to US 41 is a good route to follow to get a view of the landscape. It crosses the Yellow Dog River, a prime trout stream, several times. There are other roads going back into the mountains, but be careful. Some are okay with an auto, but others require a four-wheel-drive vehicle.

GUIDANCE **Marquette Country Convention & Visitors Bureau** (1-800-544-4321; www.marquettecountry.org), 337 West Washington St., Marquette, MI 49855.

Another handy Web site is **www.bigbaymichigan.com.** It maintains listings on sight-seeing, lodging, and services.

GETTING THERE *By car:* Big Bay is about 25 miles northwest of Marquette on CR 550.

Getting fuel: There is only one gas station in Big Bay, and none between there and Marquette, a distance of 25 miles. Gas prices are generally cheaper in Marquette.

MEDICAL EMERGENCY Call 911.

✳ Outdoor Activities

OUTFITTERS **Big Bay Outfitters** (summer, 906-345-9399 or winter, 906-250-2457; www.bigbayoutfitters.com) 300 Bensinger, Big Bay. Open daily in summer, 8–6; open Fri.–Sun. in winter. This historic building once served as Big Bay's township hall, fire department, and jail, but it now houses 2,500 square feet of retail space, with products ranging from live bait to local art and a paddle sport shop called "Anatomy of a Canoe." There is also outdoor gear, local flies for the fly angler, and other fishing gear. The shop is a great source of outdoor information and has good maps for getting around. The small complex is operated by Kristi Mills and Bill Kinjorski. Both know the area well, are friendly folks, and are good sources of local information. A small coffee shop, the Big Bass Café, is in the building. They rent fishing boats, pontoons, canoes and kayaks, and mountain bikes and also offer tour and guide services.

CHARTERS **Uncle Ducky Charters** (906-228-5447; www.uncleducky.com), 434 E. Prospect St., Marquette. Charter boat fishing for salmon, steelhead, and walleye with licensed captains. The charter boat firm also offers shoreline tours and lighthouse tours and guided and unguided canoe and kayak tours of area rivers and lakes.

TOURS **Marquette Country Tours** (906-226-6167), Marquette. Fred Huffman offers waterfall and mountaintop tours throughout Marquette Country. There

WILDLIFE-VIEWING

The back roads and trails around Big Bay are good places to look for wildlife such as deer, eagles, fox and other small game, and birds, along with large predators like black bear and wolves.

The gray wolf has made such a tremendous comeback since being reintroduced to the Upper Peninsula in the 1970s that it has been taken off the Endangered Species List and is now managed by the state of Michigan. Although sightings are rare, they're not unheard of. While traveling through a remote U.P. area with a wildlife official, I saw one crossing a road. Another time, I saw one bound across a road in the western U.P., chasing a deer. If you see a wolf, consider yourself lucky.

Black bear are common in the U.P. and are seen regularly. Don't get between a mother and her cubs—it's a dangerous place to be. Bears don't have good eyesight and often can't see you, so make noise to warn them that you're around. Moose sightings are common too.

are also gold-panning tours, along with canoeing, hiking, snowmobiling, snowshoeing, and cross-country tours.

BICYCLING Since Big Bay is an end-of-the-road town, there's no through traffic, making the roadways tremendous routes for cyclists. Mountain biking through the Huron Mountains is popular, but should be attempted only by the most fit because of the steep grades. Bike rentals are available at **Big Bay Outfitters** (see *To See & Do*).

FISHING The Yellow Dog River is considered a prime trout stream. Lake Independence offers opportunities for inland lake fishing in small boats, and Lake Superior offers fishing for salmon, steelhead, lake trout, and whitefish.

✳ Lodging

Thunder Bay Inn (906-345-9376; www.thunderbayinn.com), 400 Bensinger. The inn, opened in 1910 by lumber barons, was used as a warehouse, general store, office, and barbershop until 1917, when the Brunswick Co. turned it into a company store and added rooms on the second floor for loggers. In 1940 it was bought by Henry Ford, who had it renovated to serve as a retreat for himself and his executives. It fell on hard times during the 1970s, but was

purchased and renovated in the mid-1980s. These days, it's called a bed & breakfast inn. It has 12 rooms, all with baths, that are reminiscent of the 19th century. The floors are a bit creaky, but this is an old warehouse. The rooms have period furniture and are comfortable. (*See Eating Out*.) Rates are $76–$130.

Big Bay Point Lighthouse Bed & Breakfast (906-345-9957; www.big baylightouse.com), #3 Lighthouse Rd., Big Bay. Perched on the rocky shore of Lake Superior, this B&B is a great place to get away from the world. The seven-room inn opened in 1986. While the rooms have baths, they don't have televisions or phones. There is a common living room, library, and sauna. The lighthouse is on a secluded 40-acre parcel, which offers hiking trails. The innkeepers are John Gamble and Jim and Linda Gamble. There are fireplaces in some rooms. If you're looking for more space, try the keeper rooms. The Northern Lights can be seen throughout the summer. Rates are $106–$187.

MOTELS **Big Bay Depot Motel** (906-345-9350), on Lake Independence, CR 550. This motel offers a bonus for Big Bay—five rooms with kitchens. Eating options are scarce, limited to two tavern/restaurants and a small breakfast and lunch spot. Cram's General Store, which offers groceries, is nearby. The rooms are clean and have an old-cabin feel. There is a small dock on the lake and a good view of the water. Rates are $50–$60.

Big Bay Motel (906-345-9444), 96 Bensinger, Big Bay. There is little ambience at this 12-unit motel, but it is a roof over your head and it's a short walk to the business district. The building is newer and there are telephones and cable TV in the rooms. It's a good destination for snowmobilers, who will find a heated garage in which to make repairs to their machines. Rates are $40–$60.

RENTALS For families or groups staying for longer periods of time, cabin rentals are a good option. Almost all come with a kitchen. Here's a sampling.

Alder Bay Lodging (906-345-9914; www.alderbaylodging.com). Clarence and Yvonne Stortz handle rental cabins in Big Bay that range from a pricy cedar home called the Dickerson House to humble cabins that are just a step or two above camping. The **Whispering Wings** cabins are handled by Darlene and Clayton Turner (906-345-9467). The Dickerson House sleeps eight in style and has a fireplace, three baths, satellite TV, a fully equipped modern kitchen, and dining area. Rates are $350–$1,000 per week.

☙ **Shaw's Cabin** (906-249-1389), on Lake Independence, Big Bay. This small, two-bedroom cottage is a perfect place to spend time with children. It has a kitchen with basic appliances, including a microwave, toaster, and coffee maker, but don't expect more. There is a queen-sized bed in one room, two bunks in the other. The bath has a shower stall, and linens are provided. A rowboat and canoe are included. Rates are $450–$1,200 per week.

Dock of the Bay Cabins (906-345-9353), 301 Beamer Rd., Big Bay. Jack and Kim Bourgeois are your hosts at these rustic log townhouse-style lodges with 400 feet on Lake Independence. Both townhouses have two bedrooms, living and dining areas, and kitchens. The TV sets are small, but who wants to watch the tube when you have a view of the lake? The log structures have a long covered porch with picnic tables. There are grills and a fire pit outside. Rates are $475 per week.

STATE CABINS **Little Presque Isle Rustic Cabins** (906-228-6561; www.michigan.gov/dnr) CR 550 between

Marquette and Big Bay. The state offers rustic cabins for rent in state forests, most of which are walk-in types. The cabins are near Harlow Lake and Harlow Creek and are adjacent to 18 miles of hiking trails and 4 miles of Lake Superior beach. They sleep six. There is a hand pump outside for water and outhouses. Woodstoves provide heat, and there is no electricity. You need to bring your own cooking equipment, including a stove. Rates run $35 per night, $225 per week.

CAMPING **Perkins Park** (906-345-9353), CR 550, Big Bay. Open May–Oct. Marquette County operates this park on Lake Independence. It offers 30 campsites with full hook-ups, nine electric only, and 33 sites with no hook-ups. There are rest rooms, showers, a boat launch, swimming area, playground, picnic area, and dump station. Pets must be leashed. Reservations are suggested.

✳ Where to Eat

EATING OUT ⛾ **Thunder Bay Inn** (906-345-9376; www.thunderbay inn.com), 400 Bensinger, Big Bay. Open daily. The movie *Anatomy of a Murder* was filmed here in 1959, and it has been a cottage industry ever since. Sandwiches on the menu are named for characters in the movie, and the restaurant was ordered built

by Otto Preminger, the director, because the regular dining room didn't look enough like a North Woods bar. There is pizza, steak, and whitefish. Prices are $6–$10. (See *Lodging*.)

Hungry Hollow Café is adjacent to the general store and serves breakfast and lunch, but is closed at dinnertime. This is a basic ham-and-egg breakfast place, but most folks in town end up here because it's the only place in Big Bay to offer a full breakfast menu. Lunch brings burgers, soup, and sandwiches. Don't expect anything fancy. Prices are $5–$7.

Cram's General Store (906-345-0075; www.cramsgeneralstore.com), CR 550, Big Bay. Open daily. If you go to Big Bay, you'll find yourself at Cram's, which is the only gas station and grocery store in town. Owners Joe and Kathy Cram operate this old-time country store, which offers bread, milk, meat, produce, and beverages, along with local information. Coffee is in a Styrofoam cup, but it's hot, and this is one of the few places in town to get a cup in the morning. The store also offers an ATM machine, hunting and fishing licenses, movie rentals, auto parts, and a fax machine. There is also a selection of hardware and camping gear. If they don't have it, chances are you'll be driving to Marquette.

KEWEENAW PENINSULA

It's hard to believe that the Keweenaw Peninsula once was one of the most populous parts of the state, drawing thousands of European immigrants to work in the copper mines. It even had major urban areas with ornate commercial and public Victorian-style buildings. The region stretching from Houghton/Hancock to Copper Harbor is called Copper Country, and at its height in the late 19th and early 20th centuries it was the Silicon Valley of its time, producing wealth and technological innovations in the mines.

Native Americans were the first to mine copper, but it wasn't until the mid-1840s that serious mining took place. The copper discovery here preceded the California Gold Rush of 1849.

These days it's one of the most visited areas on the Upper Peninsula. Isle Royale National Park, 50 miles offshore in Lake Superior, draws thousands of visitors each summer, and Copper Harbor pretty much exists to service those going to the island.

Each summer also sees many people returning to Copper Country for family reunions. The region was the first stop in America for many Finnish, Italian, and French-Canadians who came to work in the mines. These folks formed the ethnic stew that became the basis for Yooper culture.

A SNOW METER ON THE KEWEENAW PENINSULA

The Cornish brought the pasty, a concoction of beef, potatoes, rutabaga, and carrots wrapped and baked in pastry. It made a good, solid lunch for hardworking miners. The Finns brought the sauna and the Italians, their cuisine.

The resulting accent from this collision of cultures can best be summed up in a bumper sticker commonly seen in the U.P.: SAY YA TO DA U.P., EH? To the untrained ear, it sounds a bit like a Canadian accent at first, but there are elements of Finnish, Italian, and German.

By the 1920s, mining was in decline and the last mine closed in 1967. These days tourism is mined like copper once was, and the Keweenaw has done a good job of marking its historic sites. Look for brown signs indicating old mines in the communities that once surrounded them.

Even the larger Calumet/Laurium area feels abandoned. The mining center once had a population of 60,000 to 70,000 from 1890 to 1910,

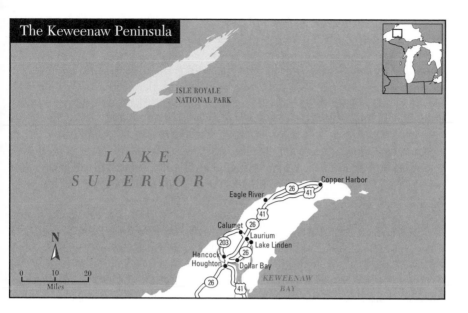

The Keweenaw Peninsula

ISLE ROYALE
NATIONAL PARK

LAKE
SUPERIOR

Copper Harbor
Eagle River
26
41
41
Calumet 26
Laurium
203
Lake Linden
Hancock
26
Houghton
Dollar Bay
26
KEWEENAW
41
BAY

N

0   10   20
Miles

but it now hovers around 7,000. The area looks like a living museum, and much of it is now part of a National Park Service Historic Park. Created in 1992, it covers 17 sites on the peninsula.

GUIDANCE **Keweenaw Peninsula Chamber of Commerce** (906-482-5340; www.keweenaw.org), 902 College Ave., Houghton, MI 49931. The chamber is a good first stop for those looking to explore the area. It has information about the largest community, Houghton/Hancock, and also about smaller ones spread throughout the peninsula.

GETTING THERE *By air:* **Houghton County Memorial Airport** (906-482-3970; www.houghtoncounty.org), 23810 Airpark Blvd., Calumet, MI 49913. **Mesabe** (1-800-225-2525; www.nwa.com) offers connecting flights to Minneapolis on a regular schedule. This is the only airport in this region of the U.P. The closest other commercial airport is in Marquette. Flights to Marquette are generally cheaper.

By car: It's really the only viable way to get around; MI 26 and MI 41 from MI 28 are the only routes to the peninsula. There are no freeways in the region.

Getting fuel: Many place-names on the state map aren't really towns, just deserted mining villages. There are gas stations in Houghton/Hancock, Calumet/ Laurium, and Copper Harbor. A good rule of thumb is to make sure you have at least half a tank of gas before leaving town. A full tank is better. Also, gas prices are less in the more established towns.

Traffic: Driving in the Keweenaw Peninsula is a fairly relaxing affair. Rush hour will produce some traffic in Houghton/Hancock, but nowhere else. There is very little truck traffic. Occasionally there is a traffic jam in Houghton/Hancock when the Portage Lake Bridge has been raised to allow a vessel to pass.

WHEN TO COME As with most of the U.P., April is the worst month. It's still winter, and you can expect some snow. May is iffy too, as there still can be a bit of snow. June through August is the best time, but starting in mid- to late June the black flies can be bothersome.

RADIO STATIONS Public Radio 90 (90.1 FM) from Marquette is the National Public Radio outlet for the central U.P. and has local content. However, the signal is weak in the Keweenaw. Minnesota Public Radio (91.1 and 92.7 FM) has stronger signals.

GREEN SPACE Gratiot River North (906-337-0782; www.northwoodsconservancy.com), Tanskanen Rd., Ahmeek. The 495-acre natural area is owned by the North Woods Conservancy and has hiking and biking trails, along with nearly 5,000 feet of beach, which is filled with agates, not sand. The area is adjacent to and accessible from the Gratiot River County Park, which has 100 acres of property, including 4,000 feet of Lake Superior shoreline. Access is free, but no fires, camping, or motorized vehicles are allowed.

Seven Mile Point, Sunset Bay Rd. off Five Mile Point Rd. There is a stunning 1,854 feet of Lake Superior shoreline in the form of sand, bedrock, and cobble. The 32 acres are open from mid-May to mid-Oct. during weekends. A $5 donation is requested.

Dore Woods, access from the Gratiot River North trailhead parking area at the end of Tanskanen Road.

HOUGHTON & HANCOCK

Houghton/Hancock is the principal community in the Keweenaw Peninsula, a role it has long played. The two cities are connected by a lift bridge that spans Portage Lake and provides the only access via US 41 to the northern portion of the region.

With about 11,000 residents, this is the largest Keweenaw community. It is home to Michigan Technological University, a science and engineering school founded in 1885 as a mining college.

Portage Lake was an inland body of water until the 1870s when canals were dredged to connect it to Lake Superior, allowing ships to avoid the dangerous route around the tip of the Keweenaw Peninsula.

Hancock was founded in 1859 when the Quincy Mining Company started operations, and it has a population of 4,323. Its turn-of-the-century downtown features many historical buildings, but the iconic building is the Quincy Mine shaft, which towers over the town on the banks of Portage Lake.

Finnish immigrants were so numerous in the 19th century in Hancock that they founded their own school, Suomi College, which is now known as Finlandia University.

MEDIA *The Daily Mining Gazette* (906-482-1500; www.mininggazette.com). This daily paper is a good source of information about the entire Keweenaw Peninsula.

MEDICAL EMERGENCY **Portage Hospital** (906-483-1000; www.portagehealth .org), 500 Campus Dr., Hancock. The only emergency room in the area. Call 911.

✳ To See & Do

Houghton Historic District, on Shelden Ave. in Houghton, looks much like it did in the early 20th century. A map for a walking tour is available at the Keweenaw Peninsula Chamber of Commerce.

The Portage Lift Bridge. Pedestrians can walk across it and get a good view of Portage Lake and both communities. This is a working bridge, and its center span is lifted for shipping.

∞ **Keweenaw Excursions** (906-482-0884; www.keeweenawexcursions.com). The boat is docked at the Dee Stadium, Houghton. Tours of Portage Lake and its canals are offered on the *Keweenaw Star,* a 110-foot, 149-passenger excursion vessel, which has a bar, dining room, and air-conditioning. There are daily sunset cruises Mon.–Sun, 7–9:30. Cost: $20 for adults and $12 for children 6–12. A July tour takes you to 10 lighthouses and includes a light breakfast and lunch. Cost: $125.

The Nara Nature Trail is 4 miles long and starts at the south end of Houghton and follows Portage Lake. The trail starts at Pilgrim Terrace Industries off US 41.

✒ **Quincy Mine** (906-482-3101; www.quincymine.com) US 41, Hancock. Open June–early Sept.; daily, 8:30–7, and Sun., 12:30–7. Tours of the surface and

FORT WILKINS STATE PARK

below-ground copper mining operations are offered. The museum is located in the No. 2 Shaft House, which was used from 1908 to 1931, and includes an exhibit of what role the shaft and rock house played in mining. Cost: $12.50 for adults, $7.50 for youths 6–12, and $11.50 for seniors.

✍ **Houghton County Historical Museum** (906-296-4121), 5500 Hwy. MI 26, Lake Linden. Open daily June–Sept., 10–4:30. The focus of the museum, run by the Houghton County Historical Society, is on the lives of the copper miners and their families in the 19th century. Kitchens, clothing, and logging memorabilia are on display. The museum is also involved in the Lake Linden & Torch Lake Railroad, a reconstruction of a narrow-gauge railroad that serviced area copper mines. Admission is $8 for adults, $6 for students and seniors, and $4 for children under 12.

✍ **Keweenaw National Historical Park** (906-337-3168; www.nps.gov/kewe), P.O. Box 471, Calumet, MI 49913. The park has two units, one in Houghton/ Hancock and the other 12 miles north in Calumet. They preserve the technical processes of mining, and the social and ethnic history of the people who worked in the mines for more than 100 years. Copper mining had its heyday from about 1860 to 1920. The historic park includes 17 sites on public and private lands. The Keweenaw Tourism Council provides information on the sites scattered across 100 miles of the peninsula.

✳ Outdoor Activities

CANOEING & KAYAKING Keweenaw Water Trails (906-377-4579 or 1-800-338-7982; www.keweenaw.info), Keweenaw Water Trail Association, Keweenaw Tourism Council, 56638 Calumet Ave., Calumet, MI 49913. Four water trails wind 47 miles from the Keweenaw Bay near Baraga to the north entrance of McLain State Park. The waterway includes Portage Lake and its canals leading to Lake Superior and into Torch Lake at the north end. Paddling allows you to see abandoned smelting and mining operations.

DOWNHILL SKIING AND SNOWBOARDING Mount Ripley (906-487-2340; www.skimountripley.com), MI 26, Ripley. This ski resort is owned and operated by Michigan Tech University in Houghton and offers beginner to advanced runs. With about 200 inches of snow a winter, it has some of the best natural snow conditions in the Midwest.

Mount Bohemia (906-937-2411; www.mtbohemia.com), near Lac La Belle, 39 miles north of Houghton/Hancock. This isn't a place for beginners. The vertical drop is 900 feet and the terrain is suggested for advanced or expert skiers.

BICYCLING AND RENTALS Traffic is very light throughout the entire Keweenaw, making it a haven for cyclists. North of the Calumet/Laurium area, there is virtually no truck traffic. Try a loop from McLain State Park off CR 203 to Copper Harbor and back. It's a 62-mile ride. Be prepared. There are bike shops in Calumet, Houghton, and Copper Harbor, but none elsewhere.

Keweenaw Adventure Company (906-289-4303; www.keweenawadventure .com) 145 Gratiot St., Copper Harbor. Open late May–Oct. Sam Raymond is a veteran outdoors person and offers bike rentals and repairs. It's the only such place on the tip of the Keweenaw (see Copper Harbor).

✶ **Lodging**

Lighthouse Inn (906-523-4137; www.jacobsvillelighthouse.com), 28741 Jacobs St., Lake Linden, MI 49945. Open daily, year-round. The 1869 lighthouse on Lake Superior has six rooms spread between the lighthouse complex and a new guesthouse. You can really get away here; there are no TV sets or phones in the rooms. Lighthouse devotees can stay in the original keepers' quarters. From shore, you can see across Keweenaw Bay to the Huron Mountains to the east. Rates are $150–$250.

Sheridan on the Lake Bed & Breakfast (906-482-7079; www .sheridanonthelake.com), 47026 Sheridan Place, Houghton. A contemporary home, this B&B run by Bill and Barbara Briggs is located on the shores of Portage Lake. It is near a golf course and cross-country ski and snowmobile trails. An outdoor Finnish sauna is available. Rates are $150.

Bayshore Inn (906-482-9010; www .bayshore-inn.com), 17629 Bay Shore Rd., Houghton. This three-bedroom, contemporary home isn't exactly what many B&B devotees are looking for. It's more of a rental home than an inn. There is a complete kitchen with appliances. Its location on an old farmstead is a plus, and it's on the canal portion of Portage Lake, close to Lake Superior. There is a boat dock, and kayaks are included. No credit cards. Rentals are mostly by the week, $950.

MOTELS **Travelodge** (906-482-1400; www.travelodgeofhoughton.com), 216 Shelden Ave., Houghton. This family-owned hotel offers a great location on Houghton's main drag, near the historic district and not far from the Isle Royale boat dock. There is a pool, sauna, and hot tub for weary hikers. The rooms are large—a benefit to backpackers who need a place to sort out gear—and cleanly furnished. Rates are $40–$60.

Super 8 Motel (906-482-2240; www .super8.com), 1200 East Lakeshore Dr., US 41 at Lake St., Hancock. You can walk to the Isle Royale boat dock from here. Rates are $65–$70.

Best Western Franklin Square Inn (906-487-1700 or 1-888-487-1700; www.houghtonlodging.com), 820 Shelden Ave., Hancock. There is a view of Portage Lake and the Quincy Mine shaft in Hancock. I've stayed here after long backpacking trips to Isle Royale, and it's a great place to rejoin the rest of the world. Rates are $84.

CABINS **Bridgeview Cabins** (906-482-1730, days, or 906-487-5507, evenings; www.bridgeviewcabins .com), 100 Navy St., Hancock. These two newer cabins are fully equipped with kitchens, cable TV, telephones, and wireless Internet. Each sleeps five to eight people. This is a popular place for snowmobiling, with trails running nearby. There is also a view of the Portage Canal. Housekeeping services are available. No pets. Rates are $100–$160.

CENTRAL UPPER PENINSULA

Oskar Bay Cabins (906-281-1841; www.oskarbaycabins.com), 52060 Canal Rd., Houghton. Perched on the shores of Portage Lake, these three cabins have decks on the water and feature two to three bedrooms. They have been remodeled, with wood paneling and newer bathrooms. Rates are $600–$900 per week.

RENTALS **Victorian Rental House** (906-482-0562; www.exploring thenorth.com/victorian/house), 2002 Reservation St., Hancock. This two-bedroom vacation home sleeps four and has a view of the Portage Lake Canal. There is a full kitchen with standard appliances, and a wrap-around porch. It would be a good place for snowmobilers in the winter or a nice place to rent while visiting students at Finlandia University or Michigan Tech.

CAMPING **McLain State Park** (906-482-0278; www.dnr.state.mi.us/ parksandtrails), 18350 Hwy. MI 203, Hancock, MI 49930. The 443-acre park has 2 miles of sandy beach on Lake Superior. Check the water temperatures before swimming, as lake temperatures can be cool even during summer months. The Keweenaw Waterway Lighthouse is located near the state park and can be toured. The state maintains one of its rustic cabins for rent. It sleeps eight, but you need to bring your own sleeping and cooking gear. The state Department of Natural Resources offers reservations, which are usually needed for the cabin. Campsites run $16–$26 and a cabin, $60. A $20 state park sticker is required for entry.

✳ Where to Eat

DINING OUT ☿ **The Library Restaurant and Brew Pub** (906-487-5882; www.librarybrewpub.com), 62 North Isle Royal, Houghton. Open daily. This brewpub with a view of Portage Lake offers some of the best food you'll find in the Keweenaw and has a full menu, including broiled lake trout, Jack Daniel's steak, and pub food. The Canadian walleye is another top pick, served with herbs and butter. For dessert, you can keep with the Jack Daniel's theme by ordering the bourbon-flavored, homemade chocolate-chip ice cream. Entrees $15–$20.

☿ **Spica Restaurant and Thirsty Fish Pub** (906-482-4882; www .spicahoughton.com), 820 Shelden Ave., Houghton, Best Western Franklin Square Inn. Open Mon.–Sun. This is the most formal restaurant you'll find in the region. The lake trout and Lake Superior whitefish are similar to what you'll find in other less upscale area restaurants, but the 8- or 12-ounce prime rib isn't to be found elsewhere. The Caribbean-style jerk chicken is a real find, too. Entrees are $16–$22.

EATING OUT ☿ **The Ambassador Restaurant** (906-482-5054), 126 Shelden Ave., Houghton. Open Mon.–Sat. Don't let the 1950s pizza parlor exterior fool you. Inside is an early 20th century building with impressive murals on the ceiling, painted by a traveling artist named Rohrbeck who, as legend has it, painted them in 1902 for free drinks. They were put into storage for 12 years during Prohibition. It's a local hangout, with pizza and Italian food. The lobster pizza is a favorite. They also feature a cudighi sausage sandwich. Cudighi is an Italian sausage flavored with nutmeg. However, the food takes second place to the décor. It's worth the price of a meal to gaze at the murals. Prices are $5–$15.

Ŷ **Gemignani's Italian Restaurant** (906-482-3020; www.gemignani.com), 512 Quincy St., Hancock. Open Mon.–Sat. Much of the menu is homemade at this family-owned business, including the sauce. Rudy and Celeste Gemignani have been in business since 1982, and also sell their spaghetti sauce spice to patrons. Seating is limited. Entrees run $10.

Ŷ **Douglass House** (906-482-2003), 517 Shelden Ave. Open daily. The building has been Houghton's social center since 1860, and the current building dates to 1900. There are vintage stained-glass windows and ornately carved, dark woodwork of the era. These days, a family-style restaurant named Amando's serves breakfast, lunch, and dinner here. The restaurant/bar has gone through several cycles in the last 30 years. The menu is less than inspired, but it's decent food for this area and ranges from Italian to basic midwestern meat and potatoes. You'll enjoy eating in the bar area for the décor. Entrees are $10–$15.

Ŷ **The Waterfront** (906-482-8494; www.thewaterfrontdining.com), 99 Navy St., Hancock. Open daily for lunch and dinner. Located in the Ramada Inn on Portage Lake, the bar/restaurant is one of the few places to offer entertainment on weekends. The menu includes steaks, ribs, and fish for adults, and hot dogs for the kids, making this a good choice for families. A decent Cobb salad provides an alternative for those who have suffered an overdose of burgers

and pizza on the road. For the very hungry, there's a 5-pound hamburger. Entrees $10–$15.

◊ Ŷ **Quincy's** (906-482-2118), MI 26, Dollar Bay. Open daily. Named for the old Quincy Copper Mine nearby, this pub serves up decent burgers, steak, and Italian food in a knotty pine, North Woods–style family tavern decorated with old photos of area mines and tools. The service here was good for the region. Entrees are $10–$20.

The Lunch Bag Food Fudge & More (906-483-2335), 503 Shelden Ave., Houghton. Open Mon.–Sat. The name pretty much says it all: soup and sandwiches. The soup is homemade and topnotch. It's a good place to pick up a sandwich for a day on the road, especially if you're headed toward Copper Harbor.

Kaleva Café (906-482-1230), 234 W. Quincy St., Hancock. Open Mon.– Sat. The locals here look up when a stranger walks in, but they're friendly. It was one of the best breakfasts I had in the area. It's a historic restaurant, in operation since 1918, but it has been remodeled into a new, clean version of the old café. There is a bakery, and they produce bread and pasties. Prices are $5–$8.

THE DOUGLASS HOUGHTON HOUSE

Ⓨ **Nutini's Supper Club,** 321 Quincy, Hancock. Open daily. I really wanted to like this old-school supper club, but I couldn't. The tavern was smoky and run down and had the usual bar crowd. The food is the standard area fare—whitefish, steaks, and ribs. You can get the same food in other restaurants in town for the same price, and in a much better atmosphere. Entrees are $15–$20.

Soumi Home Bakery & Restaurant (906-482-3220), 54 Huron St., Houghton. Open daily. Don't let the exterior fool you. The hand-painted sign on the outside could put some off, but go inside for the best breakfast in town. You'll find many locals ordering Finnish pancakes and baked goods. Try the Pannukakku, it's an oven-baked pancake that's filled with custard and served with warm raspberry sauce. They also feature the U.P. classic, the pasty. The bread is homemade, and there are lots of comfort foods on the menu. Prices are $4–$6.

FOOD STORES Many folks staying in cabins are doing their own cooking, so here are a couple of places to buy food. Also, there aren't many places in the U.P. to find a decent wine.

Jim's Foodmart (906-482-4080), 300 Pearl St., Houghton, near the Michigan Tech campus. Open daily. It's one of the few stores in the Keweenaw where you'll find a decent selection of wine. Because it's near the campus, there's a good selection of ethnic foods not normally found in the U.P. Prepared foods are available, including deli sandwiches and pasties.

✷ Selective Shopping

BOOKSTORES Book World (906-482-8192), 515 Shelden Ave., Houghton. Open daily. This isn't your cookie-cutter bookstore. Located on historic Shelden Avenue in downtown Houghton, it features a great selection of historical books on the Copper Country and has a focus on local authors. There are some lush photo histories of the area.

North Wind Books (906-487-7217) 437 Quincy, Hancock. Open Mon.–Sat. If you're interested in the history of Finland or in Finnish immigrants to the U.S., this is the place to go. It probably has one of the largest collections of Finnish-related books in the nation, including copies of the *Kalevala,* the epic poem of Finland, which was used as a model by J. R. R. Tolkien when writing *Lord of the Rings.* It also has a large selection of local history books, many of which are about copper mining and Native Americans.

✷ Special Events

Mid-June Bridgefest! (www.bridgefestfun.com). This community festival marks the birthday of the Portage Lake Lift Bridge, which connects Houghton and Hancock.

Early February Michigan Tech Winter Carnival (www.mtu.edu.com). Tech students tend to study engineering, and when they take up building ice sculptures, they have a technical edge.

LITTLE FINLAND

Boston has the Irish, New York the Italians, and the Upper Peninsula has the Finns, a relatively obscure ethnic group from Scandinavia who came in droves during the 19th and early 20th centuries to work in the copper and iron mines. The region resembled their homeland, with its deep forests, lakes, and cold winters, so they stayed.

They brought with them their saunas, thankfully, but more than that, they brought with them a word still used to describe them—*Sisu*, which translates into "to have guts."

They needed them. The Finns were relegated to the lowest paying, dirtiest, and most dangerous jobs in the mines. The Cornish, from Wales, were the expert miners who tended to be the mining captains, engineers, and foremen of the era. But many got out of the mines as soon as they had a little money and started small businesses and farms.

They intermarried so much with the local Ojibwa Indians that some now call themselves "Finndians." Jim Harrison, a Michigan novelist and poet, has written several books about the lives of this unique group of people, including his newest, *The Summer He Didn't Die*.

There were enough Finns in Houghton/Hancock by 1896 to found Suomi College, which eventually evolved into Finlandia University in Hancock. Many Finnish Americans visit the school to trace their genealogical roots and get in touch with their Finnish past.

The attraction is the **Finnish American Heritage Center & Historical Archive** (906-487-7557; www.finlandia.edu/Department/FAHC), 601 Quincy St., Hancock. Open Mon.–Sat., 8–4:30. Located on the campus of Finlandia University, the center offers exhibits that focus on the contributions of Finns to American culture, including the largest collection of Finnish American artwork in the nation. There are also genealogical materials.

The university's International School of Art & Design is a top attraction for students because it combines American and Finnish design ideas.

CALUMET & LAURIUM

When you arrive in this former mining town, it looks like a ghost town. There were about 60,000 people living here in 1900, and now there are just 7,000. Immigrants from nearly 40 countries flocked here for jobs, and it was a 24-hour-a-day town.

There were numerous copper mining operations in the Copper Range, which runs along the middle of the Keweenaw Peninsula, but the largest was in Calumet.

At first the mine owners and miners were close, but as mining became more industrialized, there was a hardening of the lines between workers and owners, and by 1913–1914 the miners went on strike. During that strike, a tragic incident took place in the Italian Hall on Dec. 24, 1913 that remains a controversy to this day. Miners and their families had packed the hall for a Christmas celebration, and during the festivities someone yelled, "Fire!" There wasn't one, but 73 people were killed in the ensuing rush to get out of the hall, and though it was never proven, the mine owners were blamed for the incident, which prompted folk singer Woody Guthrie years later to record "1913 Massacre."

Many miners left town after the incident, headed to new jobs that were opening up in the new, booming auto plants in Detroit, and mine profits started to dip. By the 1920s, the government stopped buying copper, and prices fell. Later, mining was hurt by the Great Depression, boomed a bit during World War II, and by the 1950s was ultimately proved to be unprofitable.

The sudden population decline gave the community a run-down, abandoned look, but during the 1980s restoration work on the Opera House and copper-baron mansions started to give the towns a new life.

GUIDANCE **Keweenaw Convention & Visitors Bureau** (906-337-4579), 56638 Calumet Ave., Calumet. Open year-round Mon.–Fri., 9–5. A good source for information on the entire peninsula, including maps.

MEDICAL EMERGENCY **Keweenaw Memorial Medical Center** (906-337-6500; www.kmmc.org), 205 Osceola St., Laurium. Call 911.

✳ To See & Do

✎ **The Calumet Theater** (906-337-2166; www.calumettheatre.com), 340 Sixth St., Calumet. Summer tours Tues.–Sun., unless there's a performance. The village of Calumet was so wealthy from the copper mining boom that it decided to build its own Opera House, which opened on March 20, 1900, with a touring Broadway production of Reginald DeKoven's *The Highwaymen*. Major performers such as Lillian Russell, John Philip Sousa, Sarah Bernhardt, and Douglas Fairbanks, Sr. performed there during its heyday. It eventually became a movie house, and in the 1970s it was restored for the village's centennial. The exterior was renovated in 1983. The Calumet Theatre Company now hosts 60–80 performances a year, including symphony, folk, jazz, opera, theater, dance, and community events.

Ÿ **Shute's Bar** (906-337-1998), 322 Sixth St., Calumet. This tavern, built during the copper mining boom in 1895, is thought to be Michigan's oldest known original tavern. The bar remains true to its working-class mining roots and is still a shot-and-a-beer place where locals gather. Stop by and see the elaborate ceiling, wooden bar, and the original stained-glass canopy over the bar.

✎ **Keweenaw Heritage Center at St. Anne's Church**, Scott and 5th Sts., Calumet. Open June–early Sept. Pick up a map for a walking tour of downtown Calumet here or at the Keweenaw Convention & Visitors Bureau (see *Guidance*). The church was built in 1900 to serve French-Canadian miners and was open until 1966. It has been renovated, along with many of the buildings in the downtown area. In 1900, the copper barons lived near their mines, and their ornate, Victorian homes are along Calumet Avenue.

CALUMET OPERA HOUSE

✎ **Coppertown USA Mining Museum** (906-337-4354; www.uppermichigan .com/coppertown), Red Jacket Rd., Calumet, MI 49913. Open daily, June–mid-Oct. This community-based museum offers a good look at how miners lived and worked during the late 19th and early 20th centuries. The museum is located in the old pattern shop of the Calumet & Helca Mine, and also houses the machinery used to bring copper up from the mines. Admission is $3 for adults and $1 for children.

✳ Lodging

BED & BREAKFASTS Laurium Manor Inn and Victorian Hall Historic Hotels (906-337-2549; www .laurium.info), 320 Tamarack St., Laurium. Owners Dave and Julie Sprenger have turned two copper king mansions into hotel-style accommodations and have also redone a 100-year-old miner's home into a cabin rental. The 45-room Laurium Manor is now a heritage site in the Keweenaw National Historical Park. The home boasts 13,000 square feet on four floors and has some of the original stained-glass windows intact. There is a wall-sized, built-in icebox made of marble. The dining room

seats 22 people. The three-story Victorian Hall Historic Hotel is across the street and is housed in a 7,000-square-foot home built in 1906. Julie has been deeply involved in local historical issues and homes and has information about the historic areas in Calumet/Laurium. Rates run $89–$135.

Oak Street Inn (906-337-7337; www.oakstreetinn.com), 808 Oak St., Calumet, MI 49913. The inn was built in 1879 and has seen a lot of tenants in its time, including grocery stores, saloons, houses of ill repute, and speakeasies, but these days it has been renovated into two suites of rooms with three bedrooms each, two baths, and full kitchens. The inn is near snowmobile trails. Rates are $125–$295.

Sand Hills Lighthouse Inn (906-337-1722; www.sandhillslighthouse inn.com), P.O. Box 298, Five Mile Point Rd., Ahmeek. These are top-notch accommodations for the area. The rooms have been restored to Victorian-era elegance and have been well-furnished with antiques by innkeeper Bill Brabotta. The light-house is on the National Register of Historic Places. There are eight rooms with king- or queen-sized beds and private bathrooms. Two have whirlpool tubs. Rates are $135–$200.

Y **Michigan House** (906-337-1910; www.michiganhousecafe.com), 300 Sixth St., Calumet, MI 49913. Lo-cated in the Michigan House Café & Brewpub in downtown Calumet, the inn offers two restored suites on the second floor. Both have small kitchens, private baths, and wireless Internet access. They are roomy places, with tables for dining or work. Although they have been restored, turn-of-the-century accents have been retained. Rates are $60–$75 nightly and $400 weekly. The suites are above the brewpub (see *Dining Out*).

❋ Where to Eat

DINING OUT The restaurants are open year-round unless otherwise noted.

Y **Michigan House Café & Brew-pub** (906-337-1910; www.michigan housecafe.com), 300 Sixth St., Calumet. Open daily. Located in the

LAURIUM MANOR INN

historic downtown area, the brewpub serves up some of the best meals in the Keweenaw. There has been a hotel/restaurant located on this site for more than 100 years. This is normal pub food, but my favorite was the cedar-plank trout, a Michigan specialty. Ribs, chicken, and pasta also are on the menu. Entrees are $11–$17.

EATING OUT ✐ **Jim's Pizza** (906-337-4474), 117 Sixth St., Calumet. Open daily. Located in the downtown historic area, the family restaurant is housed in an older building and serves up pizza and more. Entrees are $5–$10.

✳ Selective Shopping

Vertin Gallery (906-337-2200; www .vertingallery.com), 220 Sixth St., Calumet. Open daily. The gallery is a surprising find of original contemporary art, sculpture, woodworking, and pottery in this neck of the woods. Located in what was once a department store that operated at the site for nearly 100 years, the gallery features more than 60 artists, many of them local. Many of the images are of the Copper Country, and there's a special focus on pottery. The owner, Ed Grey, is a potter himself. One pen-and-ink drawing of a snowshoe caught my attention, along with carved fish. The four-story 1880s building itself is worth seeing, with its decorative cornices and red stone.

Omphale Gallery (906-337-2036; www.omphale.org), 431 Fifth St., Calumet. Open Mon., Wed., and Fri., 10–4, and Sat., noon–4. Staffed by volunteers, this not-for-profit cooperative gallery displays locally produced contemporary art. The exhibits change monthly and range from sculpture to the visual arts. Much of the artwork has local U.P. content.

Copper World (906-337-4016; www.calumetcopper.com), 101 Fifth St., Calumet. Open Mon.–Sat. Located in Calumet's oldest building, dating to 1869, this shop offers decorative items made from copper. Much of it reflects the North Woods landscape. There is also bedding, locally made thimbleberry jam, maple syrup, and pasty sauce, along with a selection of books by local authors and on the history of Copper Country. An amusing array of Finnish coffee mugs is on display.

BOOKSTORE **Artis Books & Antiques** (906-337-1534), Calumet. Open Tues.–Sat., 10–5. Located in Calumet's historic district, the bookstore has been in the rare book business for more than 25 years and is a great place to spend a rainy afternoon browsing through the titles on Michigan and Great Lakes history. There is a large selection of local history books and a fine section of hunting and fishing books.

COPPER HARBOR & ISLE ROYALE NATIONAL PARK

Copper Harbor is the northernmost community on the Keweenaw Peninsula, and the first one settled in the early 1840s when copper was discovered. These days, it's the resort hub for the peninsula and has most of the lodging and restaurants. It's also the jumping-off point for visitors taking the *Isle Royale Queen* to Isle Royale National Park, located 50 miles offshore in Lake Superior.

Copper Harbor was one of the first frontier mining towns in the nation, with the natural harbor making it a supply depot and gathering place for copper exploration parties. To watch over the rowdy prospectors, the U.S. government established Fort Wilkins in 1844, but it was abandoned two years later. It's now a state park.

Copper Harbor has the feeling of a northern outpost, not a town. For many years, it was virtually deserted during winter, but these days snowmobiling and cross-country and downhill skiing have allowed resort owners to stay open year-round. The area receives about 200 inches of snow during winter, which often lasts through late March.

Summer months bring hikers, bicyclists, berry pickers, and paddle-sport devotees to the town. The Keweenaw Water Trail, an established paddle trail around the peninsula, runs through the community.

✳ To See

✼ **Fort Wilkins State Park** (906-289-4215; www.michigan.gov), Copper Harbor, US 41. The state park is on 700 acres and offers visitors a look at what military life was like in the 1840s when there were soldiers stationed here for two years. The visitor center has information about nearby lighthouses and other attractions. Campsites are available. Open May–Oct. A $20 state park sticker is required for admission.

✼ **Copper Harbor Lighthouse** (906-337-2310; www.copperharborlighthouse.com) Fort Wilkins State Park, Copper Harbor. Open May–Oct. The lighthouse is accessible only by boat, and the Lighthouse Ferry Service offers trips to the lighthouse facility. The house itself was built in the 1860s, but the keeper's home was erected in the 1840s. Visible at the site is the keel of the *John Jacob Astor,* which was the first shipwreck on the Great Lakes in 1844. It was attempting to bring supplies to Copper Harbor, which was then a fledgling copper-mining town. The boat trip is a way to see the lighthouse as those in the 19th century did, when it was supplied by the water route. Admission is $14 for adults and $9 for children under 12. The lighthouse sunset tour runs $18.

✳ To Do

✼ **Delaware Copper Mine Tours** (906-289-4688; www.copperharbor.org), US 41, Delaware, 10 miles south of Copper Harbor. Open June–Oct., 10–5. Tom and Lani Pounter are area natives who actually own the mine. They bought it about 25 years ago and turned it into a tourist attraction. The Delaware operated from 1847 to 1887, during which time 8 million pounds of copper was mined

SCENIC DRIVES

Brockway Mountain towers over Copper Harbor, and at 735 feet it offers a good view of Lake Superior and the entire Keweenaw Peninsula. Signs in Copper Harbor point the way to Brockway Mountain Drive, and there are numerous places to pull off the road and take in the scenery. Bicyclists in good shape can make it to the top. Once on top you can come back the way you came or go down the other side of the mountain and take MI 26 back to Copper Harbor.

Take MI 26 (Lake Shore Drive) from Copper Harbor and follow it along 27 miles of Lake Superior shoreline through the villages of Eagle Harbor or Eagle River. The rocky shoreline looks much like that of Maine, but there are also sandy beaches along the way. Unless posted, it's all public land. There are miles of beaches with nobody on them. There is little traffic on the winding road, and it would be a good place for bicycling. In Eagle River, head back to US 41 and take the woods road back to Copper Harbor. The complete route is about 50 miles. Look for the snow-measuring sign on US 41. It will tell you how much of the white stuff the peninsula received in the past year, usually about 200 inches.

from five shafts that reached depths of 1,400 feet. The tours are self-guided, and while it only takes 45 minutes to go through the mine, some people spend hours.

✳ Outdoor Activities

BICYCLING & KAYAKING There are 20 miles of marked, designated mountain bike trails in the Copper Harbor area, and countless miles of old logging and mining trails that cross the Keweenaw. Also, there is very little vehicle traffic in Copper Harbor, even during the high summer season. A bicycle ride to the top of Brockway Mountain is possible for the very fit.

The Keweenaw Water Trail traverses the Lake Superior coast (see *Guidance, Houghton/Hancock*). Copper Harbor is a good refuge for kayakers and presents good, calm waters for paddling.

Keweenaw Adventure Company (906-289-4303; www.keweenawadventure .com) 145 Gratiot St., Copper Harbor. Open late May–Oct. There are tremendous bicycling, canoeing, and kayaking opportunities in the Copper Harbor area, but before you start out, check with Sam Raymond, the owner; he's a good source of local maps. The shop offers kayak lessons and trips to small islands in Lake Superior and to deserted beaches. Bike rentals and repairs are available. The next closest bike shops in the Keweenaw are more than 50 miles away in Houghton/Hancock.

GREEN SPACE **Estivant Pines Sanctuary,** Copper Harbor, 2.5 miles south of the intersection of MI 26 and US 41. The sanctuary holds the oldest living trees in Michigan, a stand of white pine that escaped the lumberman's axe and was at a good height at the time of the Civil War. The more than 100-feet-tall, 200-year-old trees are on a 400-acre preserve that offers two hiking trails.

Mary Macdonald Preserve at Horeshoe Harbor. The 1,433-acre preserve, owned by The Nature Conservancy, is difficult to get to and involves good car navigation skills and some walking, but the view of the bedrock shoreline makes the work worth it. From the intersection of MI 26 and US 41 in Copper Harbor, take US 41 east 2.5 miles until the pavement ends, and then follow the dirt road 0.89 mile to a two-track heading north. From there you can park and walk 2 miles to the beach or follow the two-track 1.2 miles until you find a sign at the trailhead. Look for black bear, rabbit, peregrine falcons, and ruffed grouse.

DIVING The Keweenaw Peninsula has about 140 shipwrecks offshore in Lake Superior, but only about 40 have been located and identified. They are in the **Keweenaw Underwater Preserve,** which was established by the state of Michigan in 1991 to protect the shipwrecks from salvage divers. The preserve attracts historians and recreational divers.

FISHING **Fred's Charters** (906-289-4849; e-mail, kraig@pasty.com). From Copper Harbor, the charter service makes trips for lake trout and salmon on Lake Superior on a 41-foot boat.

Copper Harbor in Lake Superior offers good fishing. Inland, Lake Fanny Hooe and Lake Manganese offer angling opportunities.

GOLFING **Keweenaw Mountain Lodge & Golf Course** (906-289-4403; www.atthelodge.com/golfing), US 41, Copper Harbor. A nine-hole, par-36 course, with alternative tee boxes offering an 18-hole round.

✳ Lodging

RESORTS ⅋ **The Mariner North** (906-289-4637; www.manorth.com), 245 Gratiot, Copper Harbor, MI 49918. The lodge/restaurant/bar complex would be a great destination for a snowmobile group. Most of the rooms are in log structures and some have two bedrooms, fireplaces, kitchens, whirlpools, queen-sized beds, and cable TV. The rooms are large and have comfortable furniture. The front porches are great places to hang out. (See *Eating Out.*) Rates are $78–$100.

⅋ **Keweenaw Mountain Lodge & Golf Course** (906-289-4403 or 1-888-685-6343; www.atthelodge.com), US 41, Copper Harbor. Open April–Oct. The 1930s lodge was built by unemployed copper miners during the Great Depression. There are eight motel rooms in the main building and 34 cabins with stone fireplaces. The knotty pine dining room and bar in the main lodge has a towering stone fireplace and is a cozy place to spend an evening. There is a restaurant (see *Eating Out*). Rates are $95 for rooms and $114–$144 for cabins.

The Pines Resort (906-289-4222; www.pinesresort.net), P.O. Box 122, Copper Harbor. It's one-stop shopping at this complex: restaurant, bar, motel, and cabin. This is a good place to stay

KEWEENAW MOUNTAIN LODGE

for folks headed to Isle Royale or for those engaged in outdoor activities in the area. The knotty pine cabins have kitchens and are clean. The motel rooms are newer, and there is a hot tub and sauna, along with wireless Internet service. Rates are $60–$110.

BED & BREAKFASTS AND INNS

Dapple-Gray Bed & Breakfast (906-289-4200 or 1-866-909-1233; www.dapple-gray.com), 13640 MI 26, Eagle Harbor. The four suites have a view of Lake Superior, a deck or balcony, and a private bath. There are telephones, satellite TV, and high-speed Internet. The rooms are furnished with antiques, and each has a theme: the Lincoln Bedroom, Americana Room, North Woods Room, and Seashore Room. Eggs Benedict are served at 9 AM on most days. Rates are $150–$250 per room, and the cabin rents for $1,000 a week.

Eagle River Inn (906-337-0666; www.eagleriverinn.com), 5033 Front St., Eagle River. This 12-room historic inn has a view of Lake Superior and is a great place to relax for several days. The rooms are clean and utilitarian and don't have fancy furnishings. The real attractions are the sunsets on Lake Superior. There are also condos with full kitchens for rent, with a minimum stay of two days. Wireless Internet access is available. No pets and no smoking allowed. Room rates are $85–$160.

Sand Hills Lighthouse Inn (906-337-1744; www.sandhillslighthouseinn.com), Five Mile Point, Box 298, Ahmeek. The lighthouse, listed on the National Register of Historic Places was one of the last manned on the Great Lakes. It was built in 1917. It was refurbished by innkeeper Bill Frabotta into a B&B in 1995 and has eight rooms, furnished in Victorian style, all with private baths. Two rooms have whirlpools, and some have views of Lake Superior. Rates are $135–$200.

BACKPACKERS TAKE A BREAK ON ISLE ROYALE

ISLE ROYALE NATIONAL PARK

Isle Royale National Park is a haven for backpackers, who hike the island off the coast of the Keweenaw Peninsula in Lake Superior. The park, which is the least visited in the system, is roadless and its bays and outer islands are only accessible by foot or boat.

There is a lodge, restaurant, and cabins in Rock Harbor, the island's service center, but that's it as far as accommodations. Michigan access is from Houghton or Copper Harbor by boat or plane. But for those hardy folks who make the trip, the island is a jewel. The 50-mile-long series of rocky ridges are home to wolf and moose populations that live in balance. The wolves feed on the moose, and when there are too few moose to support the wolf packs, their numbers go down, and those of the moose start to increase. Biologists and others have long studied the relationship between the two.

While moose are a fairly common sight, wolves are wary of humans. You can hear them howl at night, but you'll rarely see them during the daylight.

The island gets a bit crowded in early August, so try to come earlier if you're planning a trip. The two boats servicing the island run from early June through early September.

You can camp in tents or in Adirondack-style shelters. The wooden, screened shelters provide a welcome relief from insects at the end of the day, and picnic tables and outhouses are nearby.

Isle Royale National Park Service Headquarters (906-482-8753; www.nps .gov.isro/contacts), 800 East Lakeshore Drive, Houghton, MI 49931. The Park Service office is located next to the Ranger II dock, where many visitors catch the boat to the island. Knowledgeable rangers are on hand to answer questions, and there are maps and books about the island on sale, along with displays. It's a good place to stop for current information.

Rock Harbor Lodge (906-337-4993, summer, or 1-866-644-2003, winter; www.foreeverlodging.com), P.O. Box 605, Houghton MI 49931, summer; P.O. Box 27, Mammoth Cave, KY 42259, winter. The lodge is it when it comes to overnight accommodations and restaurant food. It offers basic, simply furnished, no-frills rooms with a view of Rock Harbor, and it has 20 cottages along a trail that runs to Tobin Harbor. The cottages sleep up to six and come with kitchenettes, cooking utensils, and dishware.

Rock Harbor Lodge Restaurant. Open daily, 7–7. The lodge runs the only restaurant in Rock Harbor, and it includes a dining room and the Greenstone Grill. Beer and wine are available. The grill offers food and snacks when the dining room isn't open. Prices are $12–$27.

Boats run from Houghton/Hancock and Copper Harbor from late May through early September. The *Ranger,* operated by the National Park Service, makes trips out on Tuesday and Friday and return trips on Wednesday and Saturday. Reservations suggested. One-way rates are $54 for adults and $24 for children. Group rates for more than seven are $47, and $21 for children under 12. Canoes and kayaks less than 20 feet cost $24, over that length $60. Boats less than 18 feet run $85 and boats 18–20 feet $135. The *Isle Royale Queen* (906-289-4437; www.isleroyale.com) runs from Copper Harbor on a daily basis. Reservations are requested and are needed during the high season from mid-July through mid-August. One-way rates in the high season are $62 for adults, $31 for children 11 and under, and $25 for canoes and kayaks. One-way fares from mid-May to mid-July and mid-August to September run $54 for adults and $27 for children. **Royale Air Service** (218-721-0405 or 1-877-FLY-ISLE; www.royaleair service.com) provides air service. You're allowed a 50-pound pack, and reservations are necessary. The flight from Houghton County Airport to the island takes about 35 minutes. Rates are $260, round-trip.

MOTELS Many visitors to Copper Harbor are backpackers headed to Isle Royale who are looking for a simple motel room. Here is a list of Isle Royale–friendly motels.

Brockway Inn (906-289-4588; www.brockwayinn.com), 840 Gratiot St., MI 26, Copper Harbor. Located at the base of Brockway Mountain, the inn is a family owned business that's open year-round. There are six units with cable TV and a few have hot tubs. Rates are $44–$67.

Minnetonka Resort (906-289-4449 or 386-672-1887 in winter; www.minnetonkaresort.com), US 41, Copper Harbor. This looks like an old side-of-the-road attraction, but the complex offers an array of overnight accommodations that suit many tastes and needs. The Astor House Motel offers basic rooms, with soundproofing and hot water heat. There are double beds in each room. Rates are $68–$80.

Bella Vista Motel, 160 Sixth St., Copper Harbor. This mom-and-pop motel, run by Mick and Judy Jukuri, is within walking distance of the Isle Royale boat dock and offers 27 simple rooms with one to two beds. Summer rates are $70–$85. There are also eight cottages with full kitchens. Rates are $62–$89.

King Copper Motel (906-289-4214) Copper Harbor. The 34-unit motel is located next to the Isle Royale boat dock. Rates are $50–$60.

Harbor Lights Inn (906-289-4741), US 41, Copper Harbor. With its sauna house, this is a good place for people who need a place to soothe aching muscles after a full day outdoors. The small rooms are adequate and basically furnished, but nothing more. It's a place for a good night's sleep and a hot shower. There are several campsites at the complex. Rooms are $60–$70 and campsites run $20.

✳ Where to Eat

EATING OUT Most restaurants are open daily late May–early September. Call for winter hours.

Ɏ **The Mariner North** (906-289-4637; www.manorth.com), 245 Gratiot St., Copper Harbor, MI 49918. Open for lunch and dinner. The Mariner complex offers accommodations (see *Lodging*) and a bar/restaurant. This modern resort offers steak, fish, and ribs in a dining room and tavern. Entrees are $10–$15.

The Tamarack Inn (906-289-4522), 512 Gratiot St., Copper Harbor. This friendly little restaurant, run by Bill and Bonnie Degowski, is a real find in Copper Harbor—a place that serves three meals a day. It's a good place for a hearty breakfast before a trip to Isle Royale, as the boat dock is a block away. The soup is homemade, and there's Lake Superior whitefish and trout. Large steaks and broasted chicken are on the menu. Entrees are $8–$10.

✳ Selective Shopping

Laughing Loon (906-289-4813), 240 First St., Copper Harbor. Open daily, 9–6. Laura Rooks has presided over this shop for more than 25 years and has turned it into a truly unique gift and craft shop. It rises above stuff like traditional lamps with moose painted on the shades that you so often find in northern Michigan. She has sought out Native American artists who produce baskets, moccasins, and other craft items. The native crafts people often put on seminars and appear at the shop.

The Jam Pot (www.societystjohn .com), 6500 MI 26, 3 miles east of Eagle Harbor. Open late May–late Oct., Mon.–Fri., various hours; Sat., 10–5. Monks from the Society of St. John produce the local favorite, thimbleberry jam, along with other jams and jellies and banked goods in this tiny shop along Jacob's Falls. Thimbleberries are native to the Copper Country and grow waist high along roadsides and other open country. They also offer fruitcakes and breads. The monks moved to their location in 1983 and are a Catholic monastery of the Byzantine rite. The traditional monks, clad in brown robes, embrace evangelical poverty, chastity, obedience, and stability of life.

The Wood'n Spoon, (906-337-2435), US 41, Mohawk. The making of thimbleberry jam takes on a religious aura in the Keweenaw Peninsula. Thimbleberries grow in very few places, but are abundant in the region. This small shop, 25 miles north of Houghton, features local jellies, jams, and syrups. They accept e-mail orders and have holiday mail-order programs.

✳ Special Events

Labor Day Weekend Fat Tire Festival (www.keweenawadventure.com). Bicycle races, live music.

WESTERN UPPER PENINSULA

IRON MOUNTAIN; IRON RIVER & CRYSTAL FALLS; IRONWOOD; WATERSMEET, LAND O'LAKES & PORCUPINE MOUNTAINS WILDERNESS STATE PARK

Detroit is actually closer to New York City than it is to the western Upper Peninsula, making this a remote place for downstate residents. Chicagoans are closer to this vast area, which has more than 1 million acres of federal and state forestlands, and they make up a large portion of the travelers here. This region is a destination for hunters, anglers, snowmobilers, and skiers.

The peninsula's interior is lightly populated, and most residents live in communities along the border with Wisconsin. The four major towns lie along a 128-mile corridor of US 2 that stretches through three counties. Much of the area is west of Chicago, and the counties are on Central Standard Time, rather than Eastern Standard Time, which causes some confusion for travelers.

Cell phones often don't work, and gas stations are few and far between, so it's best to fill the tank before leaving town. Internet cafés are almost nonexistent, and chain hotels/motels are some of the only places to offer wireless Internet access.

When you hit the road for this area, make sure your gear is in good condition, as it's difficult to get replacement parts. Iron Mountain is the largest town in the region and is the best bet for services. It also has the only commercial airport in the region.

The area was tied together by iron mining and the extensive railroad system needed to haul the iron to Great Lakes ports in the 19th and early 20th centuries. But both the iron and the rails are gone now, so it's hard to image that the region was once a bustling mining region. Most communities that sprang up near the mines are long gone, while others are now a collection of a few houses and a gas station.

GUIDANCE **Ottawa National Forest,** Iron River District (906-265-5139) 990 Lalley Rd., Iron River. Open daily, year-round. With more than 1 million acres in the western U.P., there are numerous district offices that offer information of

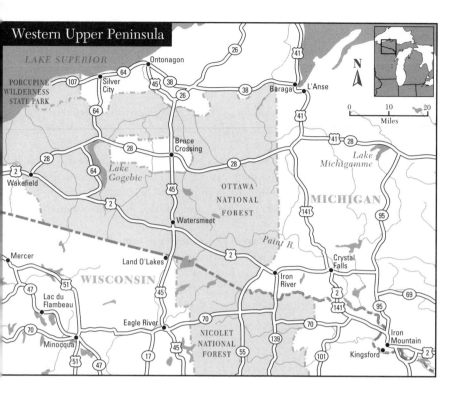

recreational opportunities in the forest. For a good overall view of the lands, check out the **Ottawa National Forest Visitor Center** (906-358-4724; www fs.fed.us/r9/ottawa), intersection of US 45 and US 2, Watersmeet. The center has displays of historical items, along with nature interpretive exhibits. The forestlands are in Gogebic, Ontonagon, Baraga, Houghton, and Iron counties. They are open to outdoor activities, including fishing, canoeing, kayaking, camping, cross-country skiing, and snowmobiling.

GETTING THERE *By car:* US 2 is the only major east–west route through the region. While the distances appear long on the map, there's little traffic.

By air: **Ford Airport** (906-774-4830; www.fordairport.org), Iron Mountain. There are flights from Milwaukee and Lansing. The fares are cheaper to Marquette, which is less than two hours away (see *Getting There,* Marquette).

WHEN TO COME June, July, and August are the best for warm-weather activities. Black flies can be bad in late June, and the ticks are out during warmer months.

IRON MOUNTAIN

The cities of Iron Mountain and Kingsford merged, but retain separate identities, one known for mining, and yes, the other for the charcoal that was once made here. With 14,000 residents, the town is the largest in the region and the commercial hub.

While many people have an image of the U.P. as filled with rustic, woodsy towns near a lake, Iron Mountain's neighborhoods actually make you feel as though you were in a 1950s ethnic Chicago neighborhood, with churches on every street corner and neighborhood bars and restaurants. This is due in large part to the fact that European immigrants were attracted to the iron mines and lumber mills during the 19th and early 20th century. Many were Italians, and their heritage is evident today in the large number of Italian restaurants.

GUIDANCE Dickinson County Area Chamber of Commerce (906-774-2002; www.dickinsonchamber.com), 600 S. Stephenson Ave., Iron Mountain. The chamber handles requests for information for most of the county and surrounding communities in Wisconsin. Open Mon.–Fri., 8–5. The chamber is part of the Dickinson Area Partnership, which hosts a good Web site with local information at www.ironmountain.org.

MEDIA *The Daily News* (906-774-4715; www.ironmountaindailynews.com). The small county daily paper serves Iron Mountain, Kingsford, and Norway, and is a good source of local events.

MEDICAL EMERGENCIES Dickinson County Hospital (906-774-1313; www .dchs.org), 1721 S. Stephenson Ave., Iron Mountain. Dial 911 for emergencies.

✳ To See & Do

✿ **Cornish Pump Museum** (906-774-1086), Kent St., two blocks west of US 2, Iron Mountain. Open late May–early Sept. The museum houses the largest steam engine built in the U.S., which was constructed to pump nearly 5 million gallons of water out of the Chapin Mine, one of the wettest iron mines ever worked. The Cornish Pump was put in place in the 1890s and was used until 1914 when an electric pump replaced it. Admission is $4 for adults and $2 for children 10–18.

MENOMINEE RANGE MUSEUM

✿ **Iron Mountain Iron Mine** (906-563-8077 or 906-774-7914; www .ironmountainironmine.com), US 2, Iron Mountain. Open daily, 9–5, early June–Oct. Underground tours are offered at this mine, which was in production from 1870 to 1945 and produced 22 million tons of iron ore. Admission is $7 for adults and $6 for children.

✏ **Amasa Museum** (906-822-7714), Pine St., off US 141, Amasa, 12 miles north of US 2. Open late May–early Sept. This community-based small museum gives visitors a glimpse of small town Upper Peninsula life in the late 1800s when logging and railroads were the chief economic engines of the day. The small, rural community was once a major hub for logging and railroading. There are displays of logging equipment and railroading. Free admission.

✏ **Millie Hill Bat Cave** (906-774-8530; www.michigan.gov/dnr), US 2, Iron Mountain, 1.8 miles from the US 2/US 141 intersection. The cave is owned by the city of Iron Mountain and offers bat-viewing and information on the value of bats. They feed on mosquitoes, of which there are plenty in the UP. More than 50,000 bats hibernate and breed in the cave, and it's one of the largest concentrations of bats in the Midwest. The bats migrate from Wisconsin, Minnesota, Ontario, and Michigan to spend their winters here. The best time for viewing is in April, and then in August and September, from dusk until about 1 AM.

✳ Outdoor Activities

CANOEING & KAYAKING **Piers Gorge,** near Norway, offers some of the best whitewater kayaking and canoeing in the Midwest, with a 10-foot waterfall that tumbles down the canyon walls of the Menominee River. Nearby, a nature trail offers a great view of the falls. Take US 8 off US 2 in Norway and go 2 miles south.

FLY-FISHING The Paint and Brule rivers are the top trout streams. **Northwoods Wilderness Outfitters** (906-774-9009 or 1-800-530-8859; www.northwoodsoutfitters.com), N4088 Pine Mountain Rd., Iron Mountain. These folks have the gear and knowledge needed to get you going in a kayak or canoe, or fly-fishing in the rivers of the western U.P. They sell river guides for the Michigamme, Brule, and Menominee rivers and also offer guided trips. In the winter, there is dogsledding and ice fishing.

BICYCLING & RENTALS The region is a mountain biker's haven, with thousands of miles of backcountry, paved county roads and rougher trails for the more hardy. But getting cycling equipment is tough. I found only two places to buy equipment, but both are knowledgeable about local roads and trails. **Mortl's Sports Center** (906-774-9519) 120 E. Main, Iron Mountain. Parts, gear and cycling information. **The Bike Shop** (906-265-2258), 216 Cherry St., Iron River.

GREEN SPACE **Fumee Lake Natural Area.** A parking lot is located at the east end of Fumee Lake on Upper Pine Creek Road, which is 1 mile north of US 2 between Norway and Quinnesec. The natural area offers 1,800 acres of land for nonmotorized activities. In winter, hiking trails around the lake are used for cross-country skiing and snowshoeing. The area is home to bald eagles and the common loon, along with 17 species of orchids.

✳ Lodging

Edgewater Resort Country Log Cabins (906-774-6244; www.edgewaterresort.com), N4128 N. US 2, Iron Mountain. The nine classic, 60-year-old cabins have been renovated and redecorated. They are on the Menominee River and include a boat slip. The cabins have fully equipped kitchens, laundry facilities, and cable TV. There is a playground and wading beach for kids. The river has bass, northern pike, walleye, bluegill, crappie, muskellunge, perch, rock bass, and brown trout. Weekly rates are $415–$625.

Timbers Motor Lodge (906-774-7600; www.thetimbers.com), 200 US 2 (S. Stephenson), Iron Mountain. The lodge is a very reasonable option and is close to restaurants. While the interior is a bit time worn, there is an indoor pool and sauna that are a relief after a hard day of driving. Free Internet access. Rates are $44–$116.

RESORTS **Pine Mountain Resort & Timber Stone Golf Course** (906-774-2747; www.pinemountainresort.com), N3332 Pine Mountain Rd., Iron Mountain. Sitting at the base of Pine Mountain, the resort offers downhill skiing in the winter and golf packages in the summer, making it one of the few four-seasons resorts in the region. There is also a restaurant and sports bar in the facility. The main building has 34 traditional hotel rooms and two suites, and there are 24 condos on the grounds.

Norway Mountain (1-800-272-5445; www.norwaymountain.com), US 2, Norway. With plenty of natural snow, the resort often offers skiing and snowboarding. There are two double chairlifts and one triple-chair. The ver-

tical drop is 500 feet. A trailside condo sleeps six. Rates are $119–$169.

✳ Where to Eat

DINING OUT The restaurants are open year-round unless otherwise noted.

Y **Fontana's Supper Club** (906-774-0044), 115 N. Stephenson Ave. (US 2), Iron Mountain. Closed Sunday. The classic supper club offers steaks, seafood, and Italian food in an old-school atmosphere. It's one of the few places around where you'll find a full menu. Entrees are $15–$20.

Y **Romagnoli's** (906-774-7300), 1630 N. Stephenson Ave. (US 2), Iron Mountain. Northern Italian food is a top draw. There are large steaks and other local favorites. Entrees are $15–$20.

In Spread Eagle

Y **El Capitan Supper Club** (715-696-3493), US 2, Spread Eagle, Wis. Homemade Italian food, steak, and seafood make up the menu. The portions are large. Entrees are $15–$20.

EATING OUT **Holiday Kitchen,** Iron Mountain, US 2. This family restaurant is nothing special, but it does serve a decent breakfast. There aren't a lot of restaurants in Iron Mountain, so I followed the locals to this place. The menu had fresh salads and home-style food. The meat loaf grinder, an Italian-style sandwich, was a good pick for lunch or dinner. There is a children's menu. Open daily for breakfast, lunch, and dinner. Prices run $5–$10.

B's Country Café (906-774-4401), 629 S. Stephenson Ave. (US 2), Iron Mountain. Don't let its looks fool you because this is the real deal when it

FONTANA'S SUPPER CLUB

comes to local, home cooking. The
wait staff knows the local patrons by
first name, and how they take their
coffee. There are daily specials for
breakfast and lunch, and the soup and
bread are homemade. A ham and
cheese omelet, the special, kept me
going all day. The décor dates from
the 1950s and '60s, and unlike at
chain restaurants there are flyers for
local causes pasted on the windows

and checkout counter. Prices are
$5–$8.

✳ Special Events

**Early August Woodtick Music Fes-
tival** (906-498-7723), CR 388, between
Powers and Hermansville. The Upper
Peninsula version of Woodstock has
attracted the Nitty Gritty Dirt Band,
the Marshall Tucker Band, and
Stephen Kellogg & the Sixers.

IRON RIVER & CRYSTAL FALLS

These two small communities are 16 miles apart, and they're the largest towns in
Iron County. Both have roots in iron mining and logging and now rely on
tourism. You'll find more restaurants and lodging in Iron River.

Iron River is at the center of a 6-mile stretch along US 2 where nearly two-
dozen iron mines once operated, and it's hard to believe streetcars once carried
miners and others along the corridor.

Iron ore was first discovered in the region in 1847, but it wasn't until 1873
that mining claims were filed. A railroad eventually was built by 1882, allowing
the iron to be shipped to Great Lakes ports.

Visitors to the area are beholden to the Italians, who came here as iron miners, because their legacy has left an imprint on the restaurant landscape of Iron
Country. There are several decent Italian restaurants in this community of less
than 2,000 people.

Crystal Falls is city of about 1,790, and these days it's known for having the largest living fungus in the world in a nearby forest. The nearly 100-ton fungus is the oldest living organism in the world and covers more than 30 acres. It received national attention in the early 1990s, and the community holds an annual fungus festival.

GUIDANCE Iron County Chamber of Commerce (906-265-3822; www .tryiron.org), 50 E. Genesee St., Iron River. Open Mon.–Fri., 8–4. The chamber handles duties for Iron River and Crystal Falls.

✻ To See

In Crystal Falls
❧ **Harbour House Heritage Center Museum** (906-875-4341 or 906-875-6026), 17 N. 4th St., Crystal Falls. Open late May–early Sept., Tues.–Sat., 11–4. The circa 1890 Queen Anne Colonial Revival home is furnished like it would have been in about 1900. The museum also houses a century's worth of *The Diamond Drill*, the now defunct local newspaper, and other records. The place is more like the community attic than a true museum, but it does have a certain appeal. A children's toy room is a real charmer.

In Iron River
❧ **Iron County Historical Museum** (906-265-2617; www.ironcountymuseum .com), Brady at Museum Rd., off MI 189 or 2 miles off US 2 at Iron River. Open mid-May–Oct., Mon.–Sat. 9–5 and Sun. 1–5. Mining and logging operations are the theme of this small, but well-put-together museum near the site of the Caspian Mine. The museum also houses the Lee LeBlanc Wildlife Art Gallery. LeBlanc (1913–1988) was an Iron River native who went on to a career in Hollywood as an animator for Disney and later MGM, working on Looney Tunes and other cartoons. After his retirement in 1962 he switched from cartoon animals to real ones, becoming a well-known wildlife artist. In 1973 he won the federal duck stamp competition.

✻ Lodging

In Iron River
Lac O' Seasons Resort (906-265-4881 or 1-800-797-5226), 176 Stanley Lake Dr., Iron River. This classic resort offers 14 rental units with two to four bedrooms, either on Stanley Lake or tucked into the woods. Five are log homes, and all have TV sets. While the interiors are a bit dated, they are clean and serviceable and come with fully equipped kitchens. There is an indoor spa area. Outside there's a swimming dock in the lake and a sandy area for wading. Canoes and boats are available to guests. Innkeepers Randy and Nancy Schauweker have run the resort since 1973. Prices are $50–$75.

Chicaugon Lake Inn (906-265-9244; www.chicaugonlakeinn.com), 1700 CR 424, Iron River. This is a big, booming, modern motel with some whirlpool suites, microwaves, TV, and free Internet. The rooms are large. It's located near Chicaugon Lake, and there's a boat launch nearby for use by guests. The inn is linked to the Iron River Snowmobile Trails and has parking for plenty of machines. It's also attractive to downhill and cross-country skiers using Ski Brule, which is 10 miles away. Rates are $50–$80.

In Crystal Falls

The Listening Inn (906-822-7738; www.thelisteninginn.com), 339 Clark Rd., Crystal Falls. Innkeepers Carol and Leslie Kufahl offer a log guesthouse on 560 acres near the Paint River. This is a good place to get back to nature, as there are black bear, eagles, owls, beaver, otter, coyotes, wolves, and moose nearby. The Paint is a classic U.P. trout stream and is also fun for paddle sports. Rates are $80.

Lake Mary Resort (906-875-6151 or 906-774-3873), 461 Lake Mary Rd., Crystal Falls. Open May–Nov. Paul and Rose Scheibe are the owners of this classic set of U.P. cabins on a small inland lake. It's not fancy, but the small resort does offer a rustic setting for a week in the woods. The rooms are a bit cramped, but they suffice during summer months when you're mostly outdoors. There is a dock and a raft on the lake, and there are canoes, kayaks, and paddleboats for the use of guests. Weekly rates run $334–$518.

✳ Where to Eat

EATING OUT

In Crystal Falls

ᵞ **Bev's Supper Club** (906-875-3779; 2465 US 2, Crystal Falls, on the Michigan/Wisconsin border. There aren't many restaurants in the area, and this one is a welcome find. I arrived here with a group of anglers at closing time after a day on a river, and Bev herself kept the kitchen open so we could order. The service was great, even though we kept the cook and wait staff past their normal hours. We'd been trout fishing and paddling a nearby river all day, and we were a pretty rough and hungry looking lot of folks. The steaks were thick, and the broiled walleye was done to perfection, even at that late hour. Offerings include chicken, pasta, and chops. Prices are $10–$20.

In Iron River

ᵞ **Alice's** (906-265-4764), 402 W. Adams, Iron River. Open for dinner Tues.–Sun. This is a real find in the U.P. The pasta and gnocchi are made fresh daily, just the way Alice Tarsi, the owner, learned from her mother, Concetta. There is a picture of her mother outside on a sign that reads CUCINA DE MAMA (mother's cooking). The gnocchi, or potato dumplings, are topnotch. The full dinners were more than I could eat, even after a day of paddling the nearby Paint River, and half portions are available. No credit cards. Prices are $10–$20.

ᵞ **Depot Restaurant** (906-265-6341), 50 Fourth Ave./MI 189, Iron River. Open daily. The train dining car turned retro restaurant is aimed in the direction of lighter appetites, and it regularly delivers. The two cars are 1960s vintage Long Island commuter cars that were refurbished by owners Steve Shepich and Jo Werner to look like they were from the 1940s. Such an upscale place is difficult to find in the U.P. It's a fine place for breakfast, with waffles, omelets, pancakes, and homemade bagels. Prices are $8–$20.

ᵞ **Riverside Pizzeria** (906-265-9944), 98 E. Genesee St., Iron River.

Open daily. This is your basic main street pizza parlor where kids are welcome and the tables are big enough for large families. It's a cozy place where you can linger with locals, who make this their hangout. The Italian sausage on the pizza was the best choice. The pizzas are large enough for a big appetite. Prices are $8–$15.

Y **Kermit's Bar, Pizza Pub & Grill** (906-265-2790), 500 Washington, Stambaugh. While it's basic pub food at Kermit's, the kitchen is open until midnight, making it one of the few places to get something to eat that late in the area.

Scott's Subs, Pizza, Ice Cream Shop (906-265-5050), US 2 at MI 189, downtown Iron River. Open daily. This small sub shop is deceiving from the outside. At first it looks like a cross between a Dairy Queen and an old diner, but inside is the real find—about 100 different kinds of sandwiches. They also serve Jilbert's Ice Cream, which is made in the U.P. and is better than many of the upscale products on the market. No credit cards.

IRONWOOD

Ironwood is as far west as you can get and still be in Michigan. It's on the same latitude as St. Louis, Missouri. So, as some of the locals say, you may as well be in Wisconsin. And right across the border is Hurley, Wisconsin, which is the more bawdy of the twin towns.

Actually, Ironwood and Hurley were once the center of iron mining operations that stretched across the region in the Gegobic Range. The surrounding towns in Michigan and Wisconsin thrived from the mid-1880s until the late 1950s during the mining heyday. The area's population is about 6,000 today, but from the mid-1890s until the 1920s it ranged between 15,000 and 30,000. Many of the miners were Finns, Swedes, Italians, and English.

During the mining era, Hurley gained the reputation as the sin city of the region, and a railroad conductor supposedly coined the phrase "Hurley, Haywood and Hell." Starting at the border with Ironwood, Hurley's Silver Street once had 29 saloons, which also offered gambling and ladies of the night to miners. That tradition continues today. Silver Street is still filled with saloons, many of them offering topless dancing, making it the party destination for young males from the western Upper Peninsula.

The saloons weren't even closed during Prohibition during the 1920s, and Hurley became known as an open town for drinking, gambling, and prostitution. It drew Chicago gangsters, including Al Capone. In fact, Capone's brother, Ralph, eventually retired to Hurley and died in a nursing home there in the early 1970s.

One of the newest hot industries in the area is based on an old cap, not a nightcap. The Stormy Kromer is an unlikely looking affair, more akin to the headgear worn by Elmer Fudd than urban hats worn by gangsters. As legend has it, the hat was invented in 1903 by one George "Stormy" Kromer, a semipro baseball player and railroad engineer who got tired of having the wind blow his cap away while at the controls of a train engine. So he had his wife, of course, sew together a hat similar to his baseball cap, but with a band that pulled down over his ears for warmth and snugness. These days it's produced by the Jacuart Fabric Products plant in Ironwood.

GUIDANCE **Ironwood Area Chamber of Commerce** (906-932-1122; www .ironwoodmi.org), 150 N. Lowell, Ironwood. Located in the old train depot, which is also a museum. ATV permits can be obtained here, along with information. Open year-round, Mon.–Fri., 8–4.

✳ To See & Do

✎ **Old Depot Museum** (906-932-1122), 150 N. Lowell, Ironwood. Open late May–early Sept., 12–4. The Ironwood Area Historical Society runs this community-based museum, which looks like it was collected from old attics. It's more a collection of old things than a museum with a theme. The iron mine–related items give a glimpse of what it was like to be lowered into the ground and spend the day chipping away at the earth with a power drill. There are old miner's helmets, lanterns, and tools used in the numerous mines in the area.

✎ **Iron County Historical Museum** (715-932-5050), 303 Iron St., Hurley, Wis. Open Mon., Wed., Fri., and Sat. 9–2. Housed in the old Iron County Courthouse, the museum has three floors filled with exhibits on iron mining, logging, farming, and other activities engaged in by early settlers in the region. The photos show how quickly the region developed once iron ore was discovered in the mid-1880s. Railroads were quickly built, linking the area to Chicago. Admission is free.

✳ Lodging

Apart from area ski resorts, there isn't a great selection of lodging. There are some mom-and-pop motels along US 2 in Ironwood, but I found the best accommodations across the state line in Hurley.

IRONWOOD TRAIN DEPOT

MOTELS **Comfort Inn** (906-932-2224) 210 E. Cloverland Dr., Ironwood. As with most chains, the rooms are generic, but they're clean, roomy, and comfortable. The indoor pool is great for kids, especially in this region, where even in summer the weather can turn rainy and cool. It has free wireless, high-speed Internet, a plus in this region, which typically lacks such services. Rates are $50–$65.

Days Inn (715-561-3500; www.hurleydaysinn.com), 13355 North US 51, Hurley, Wis. This is a good place for business travelers and families with kids. The high-speed Internet access is a real plus in this area. The pool is a great place for the kids after a day on the road. The rooms are clean and larger. Rates are $50–$60.

Hurley Inn (715-561-3030) 1000 10th Ave., Hurley, Wis. This a full-service inn located near US 2, the major artery through the area, and it offers chain motel–style rooms that are clean, larger, and contemporary. It features an adequate but uninspired restaurant and bar. There is a pool, hot tub, and wireless Internet.

BED & BREAKFAST Black River Crossing (906-932-2604; www.blackriver crossing.com), N11485 Hedberg Rd., Bessemer. Stan and Sue Carr opened this contemporary log home as a B&B in 2002, and offer three bedrooms in a structure that's nearly an art gallery. Photos, woodcarvings, and paintings by local artists were used to furnish the B&B, and are for sale. There is a classic Finnish sauna cabin on the grounds. The Scandinavian modern furnishings blend well with the log cabin–style house. One room features a fireplace, while another has a hot tub. The B&B is located near the Ottawa National Forest and is popular with snowmobilers and other winter sports fans. Rates are $125–$159.

A STATUE OF HIAWATHA

✳ Where to Eat

EATING OUT There aren't a lot of options in Ironwood. Hurley, Wis., across the border has a good number of restaurants.

ɏ **Don & GG's** (906-932-2312), 1300 E. Cloverland Dr., US 2, Ironwood. Open daily for lunch and dinner. There is pub fare and dinners on tap, including whitefish, steak, chicken, and pasta. Lake trout is a specialty. Prices are $8–$12.

ɏ **Taconelli's Town House** (906-932-2101), 215 S. Suffolk, Ironwood. Open daily for lunch and dinner. The region's Italian heritage is alive and well here, with homemade gnocchi, lasagna, and other pastas. There are also ribs, steak, and seafood. Entrees are $8–$18.

The Pines Café (906-932-4207), 120 S. Suffolk, Ironwood. This is the place to go for breakfasts that include country gravy, omelets, and other hearty fare. I liked sitting at the counter with the locals. Prices are $5–$6.

Hurley Coffee Company (715-561-5500) Silver St., Hurley, Wis. Open daily. This place was a real find. While you can't go down a street in a major town without seeing a coffee shop every few blocks, you can go a hundred miles in the western U.P. without finding one.

✳ Selective Shopping

Masterpiece Boats and Up North Down South Potter (906-932-4375; www.masterpieceboats.com), 113 S. Suffolk St., Ironwood. Open Mon.–Sat., 10–5. The shop is an unlikely combination, fine pottery in the front and a boat-building operation in the back, but somehow Dennis and Terry Ann Swanson make it work. Dennis makes cedar-strip canoes, kayaks, and rowboats. The rowboats have proved popular in northern Wisconsin, where many small lakes have bans on motorized craft. Many of the cedar-strip canoes never touch water; they end up hanging from the ceilings of large resort homes in the upper Great Lakes region. Prices for the wooden rowboats start at about $1,200. The front of the shop is taken up by Terry Ann's pottery, which is made in the shop.

The Northwoods Niche (906-932-3316), 210 S. Suffolk St., Ironwood. Open Mon.–Sat., various hours. Deb Swartz is the owner/artist of this shop, which features the works of more than 70 local artists. There are also gift items.

Stormy Kromer Mercantile (1-888-455-2253; www.stormykromer.com), 1238 Wall St., Ironwood. Open Mon.–Fri., year-round. The Stormy Kromer has made a comeback in recent years in the Midwest, and the goofy cap with earflaps is seen on top of many heads. The hat was invented in 1903 by Stormy Kromer, a railroad engineer and baseball player, who kept losing his hat to the high winds while at work. He has his wife sew one with snug ear flaps that would make it stay put on cold winter nights in the Upper Midwest. Stormy eventually left his railroad job and started a factory to make the caps. The firm revived the design in recent years. They even make pink ones for children. They also make rugged, warm clothing at the factory in Ironwood. There are tours. Call ahead.

WATERSMEET, LAND O'LAKES & PORCUPINE MOUNTAINS WILDERNESS STATE PARK

While many Native Americans in the Upper Peninsula were pushed onto reservation lands, a small band of Chippewas escaped that fate. The Lac Vieux Desert Band was forced to move from their homelands near Watersmeet to the Chippewa reservation at L'Anse on Lake Superior. But as the story goes, members of the band quickly understood the workings of the white man's world of private property, and in the 1850s pooled the money they'd made from a winter of hunting and trapping and bought their native lands near Watersmeet at a public sale in Marquette. The band fought for formal recognition as a separate tribe, which finally came in 1988.

Watersmeet has a strong Native American presence—about 14 percent of the community of 1,400—and they have contributed greatly to the local economy with their tribe-owned gambling casino and hotel.

Don't neglect Land O'Lakes, Wisconsin, which lies on the border 8 miles south of Watersmeet right on the Michigan/Wisconsin border. Some resorts straddle the border, including a golf course where you can tee off in Wisconsin and drive your ball into Michigan. Some of the better lodging places and restaurants are located in Wisconsin.

GUIDANCE **Watersmeet Chamber of Commerce** (906-358-9961; www.watersmeet.org), P.O. Box 593, Watersmeet, MI 49969.

Land O'Lakes Chamber of Commerce (715-547-3432 or 1-800-263-3432; www.landolakes-wi.org), US 45 at CR B, Land O'Lakes, Wis.

✳ To See & Do

✿ **Paulding Light,** Old State Hwy. 45, 5 miles north of Watersmeet. A mysterious light shines at night, and has been a tourist attraction for years. Legend has it that it is the lantern of a railroad brakeman who died, and his ghost waves it at night as a warning. Some folks say they've seen the light, others are skeptical. True or not, there is a light, and you can see it. A U.S. Forest Service sign on Robbins Pond Road marks the spot.

✳ Outdoor Activities

The **Sylvania Wilderness Area** and the Cisco chain of 15 lakes attract kayakers and canoeists, anglers, and those just looking to get away. Most of the land in the area is part of the Ottawa National Forest, and plenty of camping is available.

GUIDES **Sylvania Outfitters** (906-358-4766; www.sylvaniaoutfitters.com), US 2, one mile west of Watersmeet. The outfitter supplies the gear and knows how to get into the 18,327-acre Sylvania Wilderness Area. Forest Service workers recommend that novice paddlers use the service. While the Sylvania Lakes area isn't that remote, it's not a trip to be taken lightly. Operated by Bob Zelinski for more than 30 years, the outfitter has helped folks explore the area in canoes and kayaks or on cross-country skies and snowshoes in winter. They hold a special-

KAYAKERS ENJOY THE SYLVANIA WILDERNESS AREA

use permit to provide paddle trips into the area. They also have good maps of the region. You could spend weeks exploring the 34 interconnected lakes, which require some portages.

✳ Lodging

Pineaire Resort Motel (906-544-2313), N2091 US 45, Watersmeet. These resort cabins are a nice break from standard motel rooms in the area and come at a reasonable price. There are two rooms to each unit, with some privacy. A play area is available for children and there's a walking trail behind the complex. Most of the nine cabins offer two beds, making this a decent choice for a snowmobiling group. The hot water is a bit sketchy. You have to let it run for a while before getting warm water for a shower. Rates are $50–$60.

Sunset Motel (906-358-4450; www.sunsetmotelinn.com), US 2 and US 45, Watersmeet. This side-of-the-road motel usually wouldn't rate a mention, but there aren't a lot of options

in Watersmeet. The rooms are clean and neat, but a little claustrophobic. It beats a night in a wet tent, though. Rates are $53–$143.

✳ Where to Eat

EATING OUT ☿ Lac Vieux Desert Resort Casino (906-358-4226), N5384 US 45, Watersmeet. The gambling casino and adjoining Dancing Eagles Hotel are owned and operated by the Lac Vieux Desert Band of Lake Superior Chippewa. The slot machines are whirling 24 hours a day, 365 days of the year. There are also card games. The full-service restaurant offers some of the better dining in the area, while the Thunderbird Sports Lounge offers pub food. The hotel is a modern 132-room facility with a pool and spa

HIKERS IN THE PORCUPINE MOUNTAINS WILDERNESS STATE PARK

PORCUPINE MOUNTAINS WILDERNESS STATE PARK

Porcupine Mountains Wilderness State Park (906-885-5275; www.michigan
.gov/dnr) is the largest state park in Michigan, with 60,000 acres, and it
offers a wide range of activities, from cross-country and downhill skiing to
backpacking and mountain biking. And with 24 miles of Lake Superior shoreline, it's a good destination for a canoe or kayak trip.

For years, many cross-country skiers have headed to the park in April
for spring skiing at its best. Temperatures hit the 40s and there's still snow
on the ground for trail skiing—and in your T-shirt, to boot.

The park has numerous trails for hiking and skiing, some of which are
open to mountain biking. The longest and most difficult is the 17.1-mile Lake
Superior Trail, which follows the lake from Presque Isle River to Lone Rock
on MI 107.

Mountain bikers have some good options, with nine trails dedicated to their sport: North Mirror Lake, River, Double, Triple, Nonesuch, East and West Vista, Log Camp, Deer Yard, and Superior Loop.

If you have limited time, there is one must-see: the Lake of the Clouds, which lies in the mountains and is undeveloped. Follow the signs from the eastern park entrance to the Lake of the Clouds Scenic Area and follow a short path to a viewing area.

There are some interesting alternatives to tent camping. The DNR rents yurts during winter and warmer months. The structures are 16 feet in diameter and are equipped with bunk beds, mattresses, a cook stove, axe, bow saw, and cooking and eating utensils. You have to get your own water, but it's still a nice step above backpacking. Reservations are suggested. Rates run $60.

There are also 17 rustic cabins scattered around the park. The most popular is the Lake of the Clouds cabin, which sleeps up to eight. Rates are $60. The DNR also rents **Kaug Wudjoo Lodge,** which was originally the park manager's residence. The interior is furnished with rustic cedar furniture and animal skins. A stone fireplace with a mounted fish dominates the living room. The lodge overlooks Lake Superior and sleeps up to 12. Rates are $1,225 per week. Reservations are required.

Camping ranges from backwoods sites with outhouses to group sites and car-camping areas. The cost for a backcountry camping permit is $14 a night.

Union Bay on the east side of the park offers 100 car campsites, but they fill up quickly. Michigan has a decent reservation system for sites: call 1-800-447-2757. There are indoor toilet facilities.

For a more rustic experience, head 25 miles west to the Presque Isle Campground, which has 50 sites. There is only a vault toilet. Campground fees are $16 per night.

The **Wilderness Visitor Center,** located in the park, is open daily May–mid-Oct., 10–6. Displays depict human history in the park, from Native American copper mining to lumber camps. There is a special program on black bear, of which there are many in the park. Other exhibits feature wildlife such as the gray wolf, peregrine falcon, and goshawk. There are nature hikes and special field trips for students.

The **State Park Concession Store** (906-885-5612) is in the Union Bay campground area on MI 107. The store sells food and beverages, firewood, ice, and gifts. It also rents mountain bikes, canoes, and kayaks, and provides shuttle service to all areas of the park.

rooms. Live entertainment is offered on weekends. Entrees are $18.

Ⴘ **The Vintage Inn Supper Club** (715-547-6761; www.gateway-lodge .com/dining), 4103 City Hwy. B, Land O'Lakes, Wis. Closed Tues.–Wed. Located just across the border in Wisconsin. The décor is classic North Woods, but the food and service were disappointing. Burgers, steak, and fish are on the menu. We'd recommend just having a drink here and heading someplace else to eat. Prices are $8–$20.

CAMPS Ⴘ **Brent's Camp** (715-547-3487; www.brents-camp.com), 6882 Helen Creek Rd., Land O'Lakes, Wis. Open late May–early Sept. The fishing camp, founded in 1896, is really a resort on Mamie Lake in the Cisco chain of lakes. It could be used as a setting for a beer commercial. The lodge restaurant dates from 1906 and now houses a tavern with a view of the lake and dining room with high-beamed ceilings, all done in knotty pine. There are 11 cabins for rent, one of which holds up to six people. All are vintage log buildings. While it looks like a guy-type place, you could take a family here. There is a sandy beach for kids and a playground. Rates are $700–$1,000 a week or $125–$175 daily.

INDEX